Horace Smith, Thomas Spooner Soden

A Manual of the Law of Landlord and Tenant

Horace Smith, Thomas Spooner Soden

A Manual of the Law of Landlord and Tenant

ISBN/EAN: 9783337315054

Printed in Europe, USA, Canada, Australia, Japan

Cover: Foto ©Suzi / pixelio.de

More available books at **www.hansebooks.com**

A MANUAL

OF THE

LAW OF LANDLORD AND TENANT

BY

HORACE SMITH, B.A.

OF TRINITY HALL, CAMBRIDGE, AND OF THE INNER TEMPLE AND MIDLAND CIRCUIT,
BARRISTER-AT-LAW;

AND

THOMAS SPOONER SODEN, M.A.

OF EXETER COLLEGE OXFORD, AND OF THE MIDDLE TEMPLE AND MIDLAND CIRCUIT,
BARRISTER-AT-LAW.

EDITED BY

LEWIS W. CAVE, B.A.

OF LINCOLN COLLEGE, OXFORD, AND OF THE INNER TEMPLE AND MIDLAND CIRCUIT,
BARRISTER-AT-LAW.

EDITOR OF

"ADDISON ON CONTRACTS," "BURNS' JUSTICE OF THE PEACE," ETC.

LONDON:

DAVIS & SON, 57 CAREY STREET, LINCOLN'S INN, W.C.

1871.

SAN FRANCISCO:

PREFACE BY THE AUTHORS.

SOME time ago Mr Cave conceived the idea of writing, for the use of the profession generally, a Manual of the Law of Landlord and Tenant, which should hold a middle place between the elaborate but expensive treatise of Woodfall, and the outlines contained in the Lectures of Mr J. W. Smith. He accordingly sketched out the ground-plan of the present work, and had written some portions of it, when he found himself unable, from the pressure of other business, to carry out his design.

Under these circumstances the authors, at his request, undertook to continue the work thus interrupted; and, in the course of their labours, have had the advantage of consulting with Mr Cave, and of submitting the proof-sheets to him for revision.

The authors have spared no pains in endeavouring to make the Treatise as accurate as possible, and hope it will prove to be a clear and concise statement of the law, as well as a useful book of reference.

HORACE SMITH.
THOMAS SPOONER SODEN.

TEMPLE, *May* 1871.

TABLE OF CONTENTS.

PART I.
CREATION OF TENANCY.

CHAPTER I.
WHO MAY BE LESSORS.

	PAGE		PAGE
1. TENANTS IN FEE-SIMPLE	2	6. MORTGAGOR AND MORTGAGEE	13
2. TENANTS IN TAIL—	2	7. LORDS OF MANORS AND	
at common law	2	COPYHOLDERS	14
enabling statutes	3	8. CORPORATIONS—	16
requisites of leases	4	*the crown*	16
fines and recoveries	5	*municipal corporations*	16
3. TENANTS FOR LIFE—	5	*ecclesiastical persons*	16
at common law	5	*enabling and disabling statutes*	17
by statute	6	9. PARISH OFFICERS	20
tenant pur autre vie—	8	10. GUARDIANS—	21
tenants after possibility of issue extinct	9	*guardians in socage*	21
tenants in dower or jointure	9	*testamentary guardians*	22
husband leasing wife's land	9	11. EXECUTORS AND ADMINISTRATORS	22
4. PERSONS HAVING LESS THAN A FREEHOLD INTEREST—	11	12. TRUSTEES OF BANKRUPTCY	23
tenant for years	11	13. PERSONS UNDER DISABILITY—	23
from year to year	12	*lunatics*	23
for less than years	12	*persons in a state of intoxication*	24
at will	12	*persons under duress*	25
5. JOINT-TENANTS AND TENANTS IN COMMON	12	*persons attainted*	25
		married women	26
		infants	27

CHAPTER II.
WHO MAY BE LESSEES.

	PAGE		PAGE
1. PERSONS UNDER DISABILITY—	29	2. CORPORATIONS—	32
lunatics	29	*corporations*	32
persons outlawed	29	*ecclesiastical persons*	32
aliens and denizens	30		
married women	31	3. PARISH OFFICERS, &c.	33
infants	31		

CHAPTER III.

WHAT MAY BE LEASED.

	PAGE		PAGE
1. THINGS IN GRANT—	36	*tolls*	39
advowsons	36	*offices*	39
tithes	36	*pensions*	40
commons and estovers	37	*rents and annuities*	40
ways	38	*other incorporeal hereditaments*	40
corrodies	38	2. THINGS IN LIVERY—	41
franchises	39	*lodgings*	41

CHAPTER IV.

HOW DEMISES ARE MADE.

	PAGE		PAGE
1. DISTINCTION BETWEEN LEASES—		(a) EXPRESS—	116
by deed, leases by writing not under seal, and leases without writing	42	*payment of rent*	117
		payment of taxes	118
statute of frauds	46	*repairs*	120
effect of non-compliance with	48	*husbandry*	124
presumed yearly tenancy	48	*insurance*	124
2. RECITALS	53	*not to underlet or assign*	125
3. WORDS OF DEMISE—	56	*not to carry on certain trades*	127
distinction between leases and agreements	56	*trading with particular persons, or within a particular radius*	128
distinction between leases and licenses	68	*quiet enjoyment*	130
stamp	68	*renewal of leases*	132
4. PARCELS DEMISED—	80	(b) IMPLIED—	135
exceptions and reservations	89	*payment of rent*	137
5. HABENDUM—	93	*repairs*	137
commencement of term	94	*husbandry*	138
duration of term	98	*for title*	139
tenancy at will	101	*quiet enjoyment*	139
option to determine	107	*other implied covenants*	140
6. REDDENDUM—	108	8. PROVISOS AND CONDITIONS—	141
from what rent issues	108	*not to assign license*	142
its nature and incidents	109	9. POWERS OF RE-ENTRY—	147
7. COVENANTS	114	*void and voidable leases*	150
		10. LEASES UNDER POWERS	151
		11. LEASES BY ESTOPPEL	156

PART II.
CONTINUATION OF THE TENANCY.

DIVISION I.—RIGHTS OF LANDLORD.

CHAPTER I.
PAYMENT OF RENT.

	PAGE		PAGE
1. TIME WHEN PAYABLE	159	sewers' rates	167
2. MODE OF PAYMENT	162	poor-rates	167
		other rates	168
3. DEDUCTIONS—	164	tithe rent-charge	169
land tax	166		
income-tax	166	4. APPORTIONMENT	170

CHAPTER II.
REMEDIES FOR NON-PAYMENT.

	PAGE		PAGE
1. ACTION—	180	(c) WHAT MAY NOT BE DISTRAINED—	196
use and occupation	181	things absolutely privileged	196
debt	182	things conditionally privileged	201
2. DISTRESS—	183	(d) WHERE THE DISTRESS MAY BE MADE	201
definition of	183	(e) WHEN THE DISTRESS MAY BE MADE	204
(a) WHO MAY DISTRAIN—	184	(f) HOW A DISTRESS SHOULD BE MADE	207
joint-tenants	185		
coparceners	186	(g) WHAT TO BE DONE WITH IT	211
tenants in common	186	(h) TENANT'S REMEDIES—	220
husband and wife	187	when no rent is due at the time	221
tenant pur autre vie	188		
tenant by elegit	188	distraining for more rent than is due	221
mortgagee	188		
agents, bailiffs, and receivers	189	twice for the same rent	221
executors and administrators	190	for excessive distress	222
sequestrators	192	things not the subject of distress	223
(b) WHAT MAY BE DISTRAINED—	381	for other illegal acts	224
general rule	192	rescue	225
growing crops, hay, straw, &c.	193	replevin	225

CHAPTER III.
REPAIRS AND CULTIVATION.

	PAGE		PAGE
1. WASTE—	228	2. FIRE	232
without impeachment of waste	231	3. CULTIVATION	233

CHAPTER IV.
REMEDIES FOR NON-REPAIR AND WASTE.

1. ACTION—	236	3. INJUNCTION—	239
action for non-repair	236	*at common law*	239
action for waste	237	*in Chancery*	239
2. ENTRY OR EJECTMENT	238		

DIVISION II.—RIGHTS OF TENANT.

CHAPTER I.
POSSESSION AND QUIET ENJOYMENT.

1. RIGHT TO POSSESSION AND QUIET ENJOYMENT	242	2. REMEDIES FOR DISTURBANCE	243
		3. RIGHT TO A LEASE	244

PART III.
DETERMINATION OF THE TENANCY.

CHAPTER I.

EFFLUXION OF TIME, ... 246

CHAPTER II.

SURRENDER.

	PAGE		PAGE
1. EXPRESS AT COMMON LAW, AND SINCE THE STATUTE OF FRAUDS—	. 248	2. BY OPERATION OF LAW— taking a new lease . . 250 other acts . . . 251	. 250
who may surrender	. 249	by merger . . .	. 252
to whom surrender may be made	. 249	3. EFFECT OF A SURRENDER ON UNDER-LEASES—	. 254
in what words	. 249	operation of merger	. 255

CHAPTER III.

FORFEITURE.

1. RE-ENTRY FOR—	. 256	2. WAIVER . . .	. 259
by whom	. 256	3. DISCLAIMER . . .	. 262
for non-payment of rent	. 257		

CHAPTER IV.

NOTICE TO QUIT.

1. FORM OF NOTICE	. 264	4. HOW SERVED .	. 272
2. WHEN TO BE GIVEN	. 268	5. WAIVER OF NOTICE .	. 272
3. BY AND TO WHOM GIVEN	. 270		

CHAPTER V.

HOLDING OVER.

1. SMALL TENEMENTS ACT	. 275	3. DOUBLE VALUE	. 284
2. DESERTION BY TENANT	. 281	4. DOUBLE RENT	. 287

CHAPTER VI.

EMBLEMENTS.

1. WHERE THERE IS NO CONTRACT— . . .	. 288	2. WHERE THERE IS A CONTRACT . . .	. 292
where they may be claimed	. 288		
out of what claimed	. 291		
entry to take them .	. 292		

CHAPTER VII.

FIXTURES.

	PAGE		PAGE
1. WHERE THERE IS NO AGREEMENT—	298	2. WHERE THERE IS AN AGREEMENT—	311
tenant's fixtures	300	*valuation*	315
trade fixtures	303		
agricultural fixtures	307		
when to be removed	309		

PART IV.
CHANGE OF PARTIES.

CHAPTER I.
BY ACT OF PARTIES.

1. BY LANDLORD—	317	4. COVENANTS RUNNING WITH LAND—	324
attornment	318	*word "assigns," use of*	326
2. BY TENANT	321		
3. CONSEQUENCES OF ASSIGNMENT—	321	5. ASSIGNMENT OF PART	328
at common law	321		
by 32 Hen. VIII., c. 34	322		

CHAPTER II.
BY ACT OF LAW.

1. DEATH—	330	3. MARRIAGE—	341
of lessor	330	*of female lessor*	342
of lessee	331	*of female lessee*	343
		Married Women's Property Act	345
2. BANKRUPTCY	334	4. WRITS OF EXECUTION	348

INDEX TO CASES CITED.

A.

	PAGE
Abadam v. Abadam	166
Abbey v. Petch	196
Abbott v. Parsons	505
—— v. Weekly	34
Accidental Death Insurance Co. v. Mackenzie	321
Ackland v. Lutley	96, 256
Ackroyd v. Smith	40
Acocks v. Phillips	161
Acton v. Pritcher	17
Adams v. Gibney	6, 139, 331
—— v. Grane	198, 201
Agard v. King	105
Aldenburgh v. Peaple	204
Alderman v. Neat	57, 59, 64
Alebury v. Walby	342
Alexander v. Dyer	183
Alford v. Vickery	272, 273
Allason v. Stark	21, 33
Allen v. England	50
—— v. Taylor	130
—— v. Flicker	216
—— v. Sharp	226
Althain's Case	94, 229
Amitt v. Breame	95
Anderson v. The Midland Railway Co.	67, 102
Andrew v. Hancock	166
Andrew's Case	330
Andrews v. Paradise	131, 132
—— v. Russell	216
Angell v. Randall	182
Angerstein v. Handsou	138, 233
Ankerstein v. Clark	187
Anon.	28, 30, 330
Anthony v. Breton Market Co.	139
Appleby v. Myers	115
Appleton v. Doily	191
Archer v. March	129

	PAGE
Arden v. Pullen	137
—— v. Sullivan	48
Ards v. Watkin	329
Armfield v. White	118
Arnold v. Bidgood	23
—— v. Ridge	351
Arnsby v. Woodward	149, 150, 257
Arthur v. Lamb	241
Arundel (Earl of) v. Lord Gray	251
Ashcroft v. Bourne	284
Ashfield v. Ashfield	27
Ashton v. Jones	33
Aspdin v. Austin	137, 141
Atkinson v. Baker	94
Attack v. Bramwell	207, 220
Att.-Gen. v. Cox	149, 255, 327
—— v. Glyn	33
—— v. Great Yarmouth	15
—— v. Lewin	21, 33
—— v. Shield	166
Aubrey v. Fisher	230
Auriol v. Mills	323, 348
Aveline v. Whisson	43
Avenell v. Croker	216

B.

Bacore v. Gyrling	92
Badeley v. Vigurs	250, 328
Badger v. Ford	14
—— v. Shaw	314
Bagge v. Mawby	206
Bagot v. Bagot	229
Bagshaw v. Gilliard	213
Bailey v. De Crespigny	115, 143
—— v. Hudgson	241
—— v. Cathrey	30
Baker v. Greenhill	119
—— v. Holtzapffell	182
Baldwin's Case	94

INDEX TO CASES CITED.

	PAGE
Ball v. Cullimore	101, 102, 104
Bally v. Wells	127
Bamford v. Creasy	239
Bankart v. Tennant	245
Banks v. Rebbech	102, 279
Bandy v. Cartwright	139
Bannister v. Hyde	206, 208
Barclay v. Raine	325
——, ex parte	315
Barden's Case	289
Bargent v. Thomson	239
Barker, in re	232
—— v. Hodgson	115
Barfoot v. Freswell	137
Barlow v. Rhodes	88
Barnard v. Godscall	324
Barry v. Nugent	58
Barry v. Stanton	144
Barton v. Brown	80
Barwick v. Foster	178
Basten v. Carew	283, 284
Bastow & Co., in re	341
Bassett v. Lewis	95
Batchelor v. Gage	323
Bateman v. Allen	10
Bates v. Dandy	344
Bathurst (Earl of) v. Burden	239
Baxter v. Brown	59, 64
Bayley v. Bradley	53, 181
—— v. Fitzmaurice	98
Baylis v. Dineley	27, 31
—— v. Foster	222
—— v. Le Gros	121, 148, 149, 150, 238, 257
Baynham v. Guy's Hospital	133
Baynes v. Smith	184
Beale v. Sanders	48, 51
Beaty v. Gibbons	296
Beardmore v. Wilson	11
Beaufort (Duke of) v. Bates	239
Beavan v. Delahay	204, 292, 293
—— v. Macdonell	24
Beckett v. Bradley	158
Beck v. Rebow	302
Bedford Union v. Bedford Improvement Commissioners	118
Becley v. Perry	317, 324
Beere v. Windebanke	38
Bees v. Williams	252
Begbie v. Hayne	189
Belaney v. Belaney	252
Belcher v. M'Intosh	123
Belfour v. Weston	182
Bell v. Nixon	39
Bellasis v. Burbrick	183

	PAGE
Bellingham v. Alsop	12, 13
Bennett v. Bayes	210
—— v. Herring	238
—— v. Ireland	233
—— v. Robins	190
—— v. Womack	118, 127
Benson v. Chester	87
Bentley, ex parte, re West	314
Bermondsey, Vestry of, v. Brown	34
Berrey v. Lindley	48, 51, 53, 105
Berry v. Taunton	144
Bertie v. Beaumont	50, 182
Berwick (Mayor of) v. Oswald	115
Bessell v. Landsberg	250
Bethell v. Blencowe	70, 268
Bettisworth's Case	87
Bevan v. Habgood	13
Beverley v. Lincolnshire Gas Coke Co.	181
Bevil's Case	225
Bickford v. Parson	138, 323
Bicknell v. Hood	65, 101
Bidder v. Trinidad Petroleum Co.	312
Biggins v. Goode	222
Bignell v. Clarke	211
Birch v. Wright	12, 105, 181
Bird v. Baker	93, 107
—— v. Elwes	120, 121
—— v. Higginson	37, 43, 112
—— v. Gt. Eastern Railway Co.	40, 68
Birmingham Gas Light Co. in re Adams	337
Bisco v. Holt	17
Bishop v. Bryant	216, 222
—— v. Elliott	303, 312
—— v. Howard	49, 106, 247
Blake v. Gold	83
Blatchford v. Cole	95, 285
—— v. Plymouth	90
Blight v. Page	115
Bliss v. Collins	170
Blount v. Pearman	69
Blyth v. Dennett	273
Boase v. Jackson	69
Bogg v. Midland Railway Co.	133
Bolton's Case, in re	76
Bond v. Rosling	66
—— v. Kennington	200
Bonsher v. Morgan	36, 37
Boodle v. Campbell	163, 171
Boone v. Eyer	141
Booth v. Macfarlane	287
Boraston v. Green	293, 294
Boulton v. Reynolds	210
Bowen v. Owen	211

INDEX TO CASES CITED.

	PAGE
Bower v. Hill	88
Bowes v. Croll	52, 116
Bowles v. Poore	187
Bowman v. Taylor	53, 55
Boyd v. Shorrock	314
Boydell v. M'Michael	313, 339
Bracebridge v. Cook	253
Bradbury v. Wright	108, 118
Braithwaite v. Cooksey	204
—— v. Hitchcock	48, 51, 185
Bramley v. Chesterton	274
Branscombe v. Bridges	224
Brashier v. Jackson	64, 140
Brason v. Dean	115
Brawley v. Wade	192
Brecknock Canal Co. v. Pritchard	122
Bredell v. Constable	190
Brereton v. Tuochey	133
Brett v. Cumberland	324, 342
Brewer v. Hill	37, 65, 125
—— v. Eaton	260
Brewster v. Kitchell	115, 167
—— v. Kitchen	118
Brennon v. Bolton	245
Bridges v. Hitchcock	133
—— v. Potts	176
—— v. Smyth	185
Bridgland v. Shapter	43
Briggs v. Sowry	340
Bristol (Dean of) v. Jones	124
Britton v. Cole	29
Broadwood, ex parte	313
Brocklington v. Saunders	52, 296
Broking v. Cham	131
Bromley v. Holder	203
Brook v. Biggs	320
Brooke v. Bulkeley	325
Brooks v. Foxroft	13
Broom v. Hore	329
Brown v. Arundell	198
—— v. Burtinshaw	107, 252
—— v. Blunden	121
—— v. Glen	207
—— v. Powell	210
—— v. Raymond	126
—— v. Shevill	198, 201
—— v. Storey	189, 319
—— v. Tighe	133
—— v. Warren	44
Browning v. Dann	208
—— v. Wright	132
Brudnell's Case	247
Brummel v. Macpherson	145
Brunswick (Duke of) v. Slowman	207

	PAGE
Brydges v. Kilbourne	240
Buck v. Nurton	87
Buckland v. Butterfield	303
—— v. Hall	125
—— v. Papillon	126
Buckley v. Kenyon	111
—— v. Nightingale	331
—— v. Pirk	325
—— v. Taylor	204
Bull v. Parker	211
—— v. Sibbs	182, 183
Bullen v. Denning	90
Bullock v. Dommit	122, 233
Bulwer v. Bulwer	291
Burdett v. Withers	123, 237
Burchell v. Hornsby	238
Burn v. Cambridge	13
—— v. Phelps	270
Burne v. Richardson	185, 192, 204
Burnett v. Lynch	139, 243, 323
Burrowes v. Gradin	48
Burt v. Haslett	316
Burton v. Barclay	183, 252, 254
—— v. Brown	80, 81
Butt's Case	185

C.

	PAGE
Cadogan v. Kenuet	41, 172
Caldecott v. Smithies	274, 293
Calvaleiro v. Puget	150
Calvin's Case	30, 31
Camden (Marquis of) v. Battenbury	49, 51, 113, 181, 182
Campbell v. Loader	279
—— v. Leach	111
—— v. Lewis	325
—— v. Wenlock	138
Carnarvon (Earl of) v. Villebois	251
Cannan v. Hartley	250, 252
Cannock v. Jones	121, 123
Cannon v. Smallwood	226
Capel v. Buszard	201
Capenhurst v. Capenhurst	116
Carden v. Tuck	82
Cardigan (Earl of) v. Armitage	89, 90
Carpenter v. Buller	54, 56
—— v. Collins	104
—— v. Parker	14
Carr v. Benson	41, 57, 68
Carter v. Carter	163, 221
Cartwright's Case	12
Carver v. Richards	151
Cary v. Matthews	189
Cattley v. Arnold	173, 176

INDEX TO CASES CITED.

	PAGE
Caton v. Coles	345
Catt v. Tourle	127, 128
Cattel v. Carrol	5
Caudell v. Shaw	343
Chadwick v. Clarke	70
Challoner v. Davis	248
Chamberlaine v. Turner	83
Chamberlayne's Case	213
Chamberlayne v. Dumorier	241
Chandler v. Doulton	222
Chantflower v. Priestly	131
Chaplin v. Southgate	131
Chapman v. Beecham	95
—— v. Bluck	59
—— v. Towner	51, 63, 269
Chard v. Tuck	82
Chauntler v. Robinson	237
Chatfield v. Parker	350
Chowne v. Baylis	26
Cheetham v. Hampson	237
Chetham v. Williamson	93
Chelsea Waterworks v. Bowley	165
Chesterfield, Earl of, v. Bolton	233
Chilcote v. Youlden	277
Child v. Chamberlain	189, 217
Cholmondely (Lord) v. Clinton	103
Christopher v. Sparke	102
Christ's Hospital (Governors of) v. Harrild	108, 118
Christy v. Tancred	182, 274
Church v. Brown	125, 126
Churchward v. Ford	181, 182
Claridge v. Mackenzie	158, 320
Clark v. Gaskarth	193
—— v. Crownshaw	312
Clarke v. Clarke	13
—— v. Cogge	37, 38, 41, 43
—— v. Fuller	98
—— v. Holford	161
—— v. Moore	48
—— v. Roystone	138, 293
—— v. Sydenham	95
—— v. Webb	183
—— v. Westrope	295
Clarkson v. Earl of Scarborough	173
Clayton v. Blakey	48, 101, 104
—— v. Burtenshaw	63, 69
—— v. Corby	88
Clerk v. Clerk	13
Clifford v. Watts	115
Climie v. Wood	315
Clinan v. Cooke	98
Clowes v. Hughes	188
Clulow, re	173
Clun's Case	161, 162, 172

	PAGE
Cobb v. Stokes	269
Cockerell v. Owerell	104
Cockson v. Cock	325
Coe v. Clay	140, 243
Coffin v. Coffin	241
Cole v. Sury	160
Colgrave v. Dias Santos	301, 302, 313, 315
Cole's Case	326
Collett v. Curling	160
Collier v. Nokes	161
Collins v. Crouch	332
—— v. Harding	41, 170, 172
—— v. Sillye	126, 144
Coomber v. Howard	160
Coombs v. Beaumont	313
Congleton (Mayor of) v. Pattison	127, 325, 327, 328
Congham v. King	328
Constable v. Nicholson	34
Connor v. Bentley	226
Cooch v. Goodman	43
Cooke v. Loxley	320
Cooper v. Woolfit	291
—— v. Robinson	96
—— ex parte, re North London Railway Company	153
Corder v. Drakeford	69
Cornish v. Searell	320
—— v. Cleife	121
—— v. Stubbs	247
Cosser v. Collinge	321
Coster v. Wilson	203
Cotesworth v. Spokes	259, 260
Cotsworth v. Bettison	225
Cother v. Merrick	113
Coupland v. Maynard	250
Cousins v. Philipps	134
Cowan v. Milbourne	150
Coward v. Gregory	124
Cowper v. Fletcher	13
Cox v. Bent	49, 185
Cramer v. Mott	207
Crane v. Taylor	18
Creak v. Brighton	281
Crockford v. Alexander	313
Croft v. Lumley	143, 148, 260, 273
Cromwell's Case	81, 141
Crosier v. Tomlinson	201
Cross v. Elgin	86
—— v. Jordan	259
Crossley v. Lightowler	88
Crouch v. Fastolfe	162
Crowley v. Vitty	48, 250, 273
Crowther v. Ramsbotham	209

INDEX TO CASES CITED.   xvii

	PAGE		PAGE
Crusoe v. Bugby	125, 144	Denn v. Rawlings	270
Cudlip v. Rundall	91, 110	—— v. Hopkinson	266
Culling v. Tuffnall	306, 312	—— d. Jacklin v. Cartwright	108, 109
Culwich v. Swindell	315	Dennis v. Laurie	126
Cumming v. Bedborough	167	Dent v. Dent	40
Cumming v. Ince	25	Derisley v. Custance	331
Curling v. Mills	86	Digby v. Atkinson	125
Curtis v. Spitty	328	Diusdale v. Isles	12, 97, 104
—— v. Wheeler	12, 185	Dobbyn v. Somers	41, 43
Cuthbertson v. Irving	14, 157, 158	Dodd v. Acklom	252, 255
Cutter v. Powell	141	—— v. Morgan	207, 213, 225
Cutting v. Derby	161, 266, 271	Dodson v. Sammell	334
		Doe d. Abdy v. Stevens	149
D.		—— d. Agar v. Brown	95
		—— d. Angell v. Angell	235
Dale's Case	8	—— d. Antrobus v. Jepson	150
Dalton v. Whittem	197, 223, 225	—— d. Armstrong v. Wilkinson	264
Dalby v. Hirst	233, 295, 297	—— d. Aslin v. Summerset	13, 271
Dancer v. Hastings	190	—— d. Bailey v. Foster	21, 266
Dangerfield v. Thomas	339	—— d. Baker v. Jones	125, 261
Daniel, re, ex parte Ashby	314	—— d. Barker v. Goldsmith	256
—— v. Gracie	109, 184	—— d. Barber v. Laurence	357
Daniels v. Davison	104	—— d. Bartlett v. Rendle	151
Dann v. Spurrier	108	—— d. Barney v. Adams	14, 256
Darlington v. Pritchard	157	—— d. Bastow v. Cox 49, 103, 104, 106
Darby v. Harris	197	—— d. Beach v. Lord Jersey	82
Darcy (Lord) v. Askwith	228, 230, 231	—— d. Beaden v. Pyke	254
—— v. Powell	200	—— d. Bennett v. Long	262
—— v. Sear	38	—— d. Bennett v. Turner	101, 104
—— v. Underwood	149, 150, 237	—— d. Biddulph v. Poole	251
—— v. Aston	223	—— d. Bodd v. Archer	266
Davis v. Gyde	163	—— d. Bord v. Burton	102
—— v. Burrell	275	—— d. Boscawen v. Bliss	145
—— v. Eyton	143, 291	—— d. Bowley v. Barnes	21
—— v. Connop	294	—— d. Bridger v. Whitehead	124, 257
—— v. Jones	67, 305, 306, 312, 316	—— d. Bridgman v. David	340
—— v. Mason	128	—— d. Brierly v. Palmer	273
Davison d. Brumley v. Stanley	250, 251	—— d. Bromfield v. Smith	53, 269
		—— d. Brown v. Brown	85
Davison v. Gent	252	—— d. Bryan v. Bancks	18, 149, 150
—— v. Wilson	275	—— d. Brune v. Prideaux	49
Dawson v. Cropp	206	—— d. Buross v. Lucas	272
—— re	314	—— d. Calvert v. Frowd	262, 263, 270
—— v. Dyer	243	—— d. Castleton v. Samuel	98
Day v. Duberley	344	—— d. Chadborn v. Green, 100, 106, 268
—— v. Fynn	86	—— d. Chawner v. Boulton	189
Dean v. Allalley	300, 305, 312	—— d. Cheney v. Batten	261, 286, 287
Decharms v. Horwood	13	—— d. Cheere v. Smith	127, 339
Deering v. Farrington	136	—— d. Chippendale v. Dyson	259
Dejoncourt v. Rogers	191	—— d. Clarke v. Smaridge	268
Delaney v. Fox	158	—— d. Clements v. Collins	82
De la Rue v. Fortescue	239	—— d. Collins v. Weller	6, 10
De Medina v. Norman	139	—— d. Coore v. Clare	61
De Nicols v. Saunders	319	—— d. Cox v. Day	96
Dendy v. Nicholl	259, 260, 273	—— d. Cox v. ——	264

INDEX TO CASES CITED.

Doe d. Da Costa v. Wharton 350, 351
—— d. Darke v. Bowditch 148, 256, 253
—— d. Darlington v. Ulph 93, 96, 125
—— d. Davenport v. Rhodes . 267
—— d. Davenish v. Moffatt 51, 269
—— d. David v. Williams 204, 263
—— d. Davis v. Elsam . . 148
—— d. Davis v. Evans . . 262
—— d. Davies v. Thomas . . 104
—— d. Digby v. Steel . . 267
—— d. Dillon v. Parker . . 262
—— d. Dixie v. Davies 49, 103, 106
—— d. Dixon v. Roe . . 258, 259
—— d. Douglas v. Lock, . 90, 111
—— d. Downe v. Thompson . 157
—— d. Duke of Bedford v. Kightley 264
—— d. Dunning v. Cranstown . 83
—— d. Earl of Egremont v. Courtenay . . . 251
—— d. Earl of Egremont v. Williams . . . 18, 153
—— d. Earl Manvers v. Mizem 271
—— d. Edney v. Benham 21, 109, 184
—— d. Edney v. Billett . . 109
—— d. Ellerbrock v. Flynn 256, 262
—— d. Evans v. Evans . 25, 144
—— d. Eyre v. Lambley . . 266
—— d. Fisher v. Giles . 103, 270
—— d. Fleming v. Somerton . 268
—— d. Flower v. Peck . . 125
—— d. Foley v. Wilson . 102, 231
—— d. Forster v. Wandlass . 258
—— d. Freeland v. Burt . . 85
—— d. Freeman v. Bateman . 257
—— d. Gardner v. Kennard . 142
—— d. Goodbehere v. Bevan 143,144,339
—— d. Goodsell v. Inglis 269, 273
—— d. Goody v. Carter . . 104
—— d. Gorst v. Timothy . . 267
—— d. Graves v. Wells . . 262
—— d. Gray v. Stanion . 102, 251
—— d. Green v. Baker . 149, 268
—— d. Grethon v. Roe . . 259
—— d. Griffith v. Lloyd . . 35
—— d. Griffith v. Pritchard 25, 259, 261
—— d. Groves v. Groves . . 101
—— d. Grubb v. Lord Burlington 228, 230
—— d. Grubb v. Grubb . . 262
—— d. Grubb v. Burlington . 230
—— d. Grundy v. Clarke . . 20
—— d. Hall v. Benson . 160, 266
—— d. Harris v. Masters . . 157
—— d. Haverson v. Franks . 259
—— d. Hayes v. Sturges . . 22

Doe d. Henniker v. Wall . 141, 142
—— d. Hiatt v. Miller . . 102
—— d. Higginbotham v. Barton 105
—— d. Higgs v. Terry . . 20
—— d. Hills v. Morris, . . 238
—— d. Hinde v. Vince . . 256
—— d. Hitchings v. Lewis . 258
—— d. Hobbs v. Cockle . . 20
—— d. Holcomb v. Johnson . 97
—— d. Holland v. Worsley 125, 126
—— d. Hollingworth v. Stennett 247
—— d. Huddlestone v. Johnson 252
—— d. Hughes v. Bucknell . 14
—— d. Hughes v. Corbett . . 269
—— d. Hughes v. Derry . . 102
—— d. Hughes v. Jones . . 348
—— d. Hall v. Wood 49, 51, 101, 107
—— d. Jackson v. Ashburner 57, 58, 62
—— d. Jackson v. Ramsbottom 158
—— d. Jacobs v. Phillips . . 270
—— d. Jeffreys v. Whittick . 263
—— d. Jones v. Jones 102, 104, 270
—— d. Kindersley v. Hughes . 271
—— d. King v. Grafton . 106, 107
—— d. Knight v. Quigley . . 270
—— d. Knight v. Rowe . . 125
—— d. Kirby v. Carter . . 18
—— d. Lansdell v. Gower 21, 106, 107, 262
—— d. Leeming v. Skinow . 158
—— d. Leeson v. Sayer . 269, 270
—— d. Lewis v. Lord Cawdor . 104
—— d. Lindsey v. Edwards . 320
—— d. Lloyd v. Ingleby . . 143
—— d. Lloyd v. Powell . 143, 339
—— d. Lockwood v. Clarke . 340
—— d. Lord Anglesea v. Rugeley 143
—— d. Lord v. Crago . . 49
—— d. Lord Huntingtower v. Culliford . . . 265, 266
—— d. Lord MacCartney v. Crick 264,273
—— d. Lord Suy and Sele v. Gay 23
—— d. Lyster v. Goldwin 265, 267, 271, 286
—— d. Maberley v. Maberley 23, 333
—— d. Mann v. Walters . . 271
—— d. Marlow v. Wiggins . 320
—— d. Marquis of Bute v. Guest 141
—— d. Marquis of Hertford v. Hunt . . . 273
—— d. Marriott v. Edwards . 257
—— d. Marsack v. Read . . 271
—— d. Martin v. Watts 6, 105, 106, 107
—— d. Matthews v. Jackson 265, 286
—— d. Matthewson v. Wrightman 267

INDEX TO CASES CITED.   xix

	PAGE		PAGE
Doe d. Mayor of Richmond v. Morphett	265, 267	Doe d. Rogers v. Cadwallader	103
—— d. Meyrick v. Meyer	80, 83	—— d. Rogers v. Pullen	102
—— d. Milburn v. Edgar	102	—— d. Rudd v. Golding	256
—— d. Miller v. Rogers	31	—— d. Rutren v. Lewis	260
—— d. Mitchinson v. Carter	125, 143	—— d. Savage v. Stapleton	98
—— d. Monck v. Geeckie	48, 100	—— d. Shaw v. Steward	339
—— d. Moore v. Lawder	104, 270	—— d. Sheppard v. Allen	145
—— d. Morecraft v. Moux	260	—— d. Shore v. Porter	105
—— d. Morgan v. Church	266	—— d. Shrewsbury v. Wilson	18
—— d. Murray v. Bridges	251, 258	—— d. Simpson v. Butcher	6
—— d. Murrell v. Milward	250, 252	—— d. Smelt v. Furchaw	259
—— d. Muston v. Gladwin	124, 125, 148	—— d. Smith v. Galloway	83, 84
—— d. Nash v. Birch	149, 150	—— d. Snell v. Tom	103, 270
—— d. Neville v. Dunbar	272	—— d. Southhouse v. Jenkins	3
—— d. Neville v. Rivers	342	—— d. Spencer v. Godwin	148
—— d. Newby v. Jackson	102, 151	—— d. Spicer v. Lea	96, 266
—— d. Nicholl v. M'Kaeg	102	—— v. Spiller	267
—— d. Norton v. Webster	20, 87	—— d. Stanway v. Rock	102
—— d. Oldershaw v. Breach	51	—— d. Sturgess v. Tatchell	23
—— d. Palk v. Marchetti	134, 149	—— d. Taylor v. Johnson	260
—— d. Parker v. Boulton	102	—— d. Tennyson v. Lord Yarborough	18, 19
—— d. Parkin v. Parkin	83	—— d. Thomas v. Roberts	38
—— d. Parry v. Hazell	106	—— d. Thompson v. Amey	48, 51, 247
—— d. Peacock v. Raffan	106	—— d. Tilt v. Stratton	51, 53, 269
—— d. Pearson v. Ries	61	—— d. Timmis v. Steele	93, 94
—— d. Pennington v. Taniere	6, 48, 52	—— d. Tomes v. Chamberlaine	102, 270
—— d. Philip v. Benjamin	255	—— d. Tressider v. Tressider	15
—— d. Phillips v. Rollings	3, 262	—— d. Tucker v. Morse	6, 105, 107
—— d. Pitcher d. Donavan	106, 107, 265	—— d. Vaughan v. Meyler	170
—— d. Pitman v. Sutton	125	—— d. Wadmore v. Selwyn	98
—— d. Pitt v. Hogg	143	—— d. Walker v. Groves	58
—— d. Pitt v. Laming	126, 143	—— d. Warthman v. Miles	269
—— d. Pitt v. Shewin	124, 125	—— d. Warner v. Brown	44, 268
—— d. Plevin v. Brown	320	—— d. Waters v. Houghton	70
—— d. Plumer v. Mainby	268	—— d. Webb v. Dixon	108
—— d. Poole v. Errington	13	—— d. Westmorland v. Smith	185
—— d. Potter v. Archer	6	—— d. Wheeldon v. Paul	258
—— d. Powell v. Rowe	259	—— d. Whayman v. Chaplin	266, 271
—— d. Price v. Price	102, 104	—— d. Whittaker v. Hales	102, 103
—— d. Prior v. Ongley	49, 158, 257, 271	—— d. Williams v. Humphrey	273
—— d. Pritchard v. Dodd	57	—— d. Williams v. Pasquali	262
—— d. Pritchett v. Mitchell	48	—— d. Williams v. Lloyd	33
—— d. Putland v. Hilder	270	—— d. Wilkinson v. Goodier	103
—— d. Rains v. Kneller	256	—— d. Williams v. Smith	265, 266, 267
—— d. Rawlings v. Walker	45, 252, 265	—— d. Wyatt v. Stagg	250
—— d. Richardson v. Thomas	17	—— d. Wilson v. Phillips	256
—— d. Rigge v. Bell	48, 51, 52	—— d. Wright v. Smith	320
—— d. Robertson v. Gardiner	206, 271	—— d. Wyndham v. Carew	143, 148
—— d. Robinson v. Bousfield	15	Doidge v. Bowers	49, 101
—— d. Robinson v. Dobell	268	Dolby v. Isles	158
—— d. Robinson v. Hinde	109	Dollen v. Batt	114
—— d. Roby v. Maisey	103, 270	Donellan v. Read	48, 113
—— d. Rodd v. Archer	266	Doran v. Carroll	240
		Dorrell v. Collins	91

INDEX TO CASES CITED.

	PAGE
Doughty v. Bowman	327
Downes v. Cooper	158
Downshire (Marquis of) v. Lady Sandys	241
Dowse v. Cale	121
Drake v. Mitchell	163
—— v. Monday	57
Drant v. Browne	70
Draper v. Crofts	182, 274
—— v. Thompson	207
Drue v. Baylie	192
Druce v. Baltz	192
—— v. Denison	11
Drury v. Macnamara	48, 140
—— v. Molins	239, 240
Duck v. Braddyll	69, 193, 198
Dudley v. Folliott	131
Dudley (Lord) v. Ward (Lord)	305, 308, 309
Duigan v. Walker	128
Dumpor's Case	144
—— v. Syms	144, 261
Duncomb v. Reeve	213
Dumergue v. Ramsay	312
Dunk v. Hunter	63, 113
Dunn v. Low	216
—— v. Sayles	141
—— v. Spurrier	6
Dunstan v. Burweld	342
Duppa v. Mayo	161, 178, 204, 257, 261
Durham and Sunderland Railway Co. v. Walker	89
Dyke v. Sweeting	330
Dykes v. Blake	86

E.

East v. Harding	15
East India Company v. Vincent	6
Easterby v. Sampson	326
Easton v. Pratt	15, 123, 152
Eaton v. Lyon	133
—— v. Southby	200
Ecclesiastical Commissioners v. Merrall	10, 106
—— of Ireland v. O'Connor	171
Edge v. Strafford	46, 48, 181
Edward v. Hodges	282
Edwards v. Countess of Warwick	172
—— v. Dick	18
—— v. Milbank	152
Egler v. Marsden	180
Eldridge v. Stacey	206, 208
Elliott v. Bishop	298, 301, 312, 316
—— v. Ince	24

	PAGE
Elliott v. Johnson	52, 236, 323
—— v. Turner	100
Elliot v. Rogers	180
Ellis v. Taylor	210
Elves v. Crofts	129
Elwes v. Maw	298, 299, 304, 305, 306, 308
Ely (Dean of) v. Cash	205
Emmens v. Elderton	141
Emery v. Barnett	279
Emott's Case	41, 172
Empson v. Soden	303
Enys v. Donnithorne	95, 97
Etherton v. Popplewell	209, 216, 220, 224
Evans v. Elliott	189, 319
—— v. Roberts	292
—— v. Wright	219
Evelyn v. Chichester	28
Ewer v. Moyle	170
Exhall Mining Co., in re	341
Eyre v. Countess of Shaftesbury	21

F.

Fabian's Case	161
Factor v. Samyne	344
Famtille d. Mytton v. Gilbert	39, 157
Fairburn v. Eastwood	312
Fairfax (Lord) v. Derby (Lord)	191
Falmouth (Earl of) v. Thomas	138, 233
Fancy v. Scott	90
Farewell v. Dickinson	112
Farmer v. Rogers	250
Farrall v. Davenport	244
—— v. Hilditch	137
Farrance v. Elkington	287
Farrant v. Lovel	239, 241
Faviel v. Gaskoin	138, 294, 296, 297
Fenn v. Grafton	82
Fearon v. Norvall	278
Fenn v. Smart	256, 257
Fenner v. Duplock	320
Fenny v. Child	101
Fenton v. Clegg	23
Fentou v. Logan	199, 201
Feret v. Hill	150
Festing v. Tayler	166
Few v. Parkins	121
Field v. Adames	200
—— v. Beaumont	83
Fielden v. Slater	127
Fieldin v. Tattershall	296
Filliter v. Phippard	232

Finch's Case	23
Finch v. Miller	211
—— v. Throckmorton	261
Findon v. M'Laren	198
Fisher v. Algar	216
—— v. Dixon	304, 305
—— v. Forbes	289
Fiske v. Campion	170
Fitzgerald v. Fitzgerald	11
Fitzherbert v. Shaw	300, 311
Fleming v. Snook	240
Flight v. Glossop	328
Foley v. Addenbroke,	306, 312
Folkingham v. Croft	125, 126
Foord v. Noll	211
Foote v. Berkeley	95
Foquet v. Moor	48, 250
Ford v. Tynte	241
Foster v. Mapes	131
Fowell v. Tranter	108
Fowle v. Welsh	131
Fox v. Pursell	244
—— v. Swann	144
Frame v. Dawson	245
Francis v. Wyatt	201
Franklin v. Carter	167
Franklinski v. Ball	14
Fraser v. Skey	139
Freshfield v. Reed	153
Frusher v. Lee	196
Fryer v. Coombs,	153
Fuller v. Abbott	166
Furley v. Bristol and Exeter Railway Company	48
—— v. Wood	266
Furneaux v. Fotherby	202
Furnival v. Crewe	133
Furnivall v. Grove	250, 252, 255

G.

Gage v. Smith	231
Gale v. Bates	296
Gambrell v. Earl Falmouth	206
Gardiner v. Williamson	35, 43, 112
Garth v. Cotton	241
Gas Light Company v. Turner	115, 151
Gaston v. Frankum	31
Gaters v. Madeley	343
Geeckie v. Monk	48
George v. Chambers	226
Gethin v. Wilks	340
Gibson v. Doeg	145
—— v. Kirk	180, 181, 183
—— v. Smith	241

Gibson v. Ireson	198
—— v. Wells	229, 238
Gie v. Rider	251
Gifford v. Young	330
Giles v. Hooper	137
—— v. Spencer	204
Gill v. Gawin	192
Gillingham v. Gwyes	201
Gilman v. Elton	198
Gisbourn v. Hurst	198
Gladman v. Plumer	319
Glover v. Cope	324
Godfrey v. Tucker	348
—— v. Little	86
Goff v. Harris	299
Golt v. Gaudy	138
Goode v. Harrison	27
—— v. Howells	37
Goodright d. Carter v. Strahan	26
—— d. Charter v. Cardwent	260, 273
—— v. Mark	107, 142
—— v. Vivian	90
—— v. Richardson	95, 108
—— v. Davids	256, 261
Goodtitle v. Badtitle	284
—— d. Clarges v. Funucan	18, 151, 152, 153
—— d. Dodwell v. Gibbs	93, 94
—— v. Herbert	104, 270
—— v. Morse	157
—— v. Way	58, 64
Goodwin v. Longhurst	15
Gordon v. Woodford	231
Gore v. Bowser	348
—— v. Gibson	24
—— v. Lloyd	160
Goreley, ex parte	232
Gorges v. Stanfield	231
Gorton v. Falkner	197, 201, 300
—— v. Gregory	326, 328
Gott v. Gandy	138
Gould v. Bradstock	208
Gouldsworth v. Knights	21
Gourlay v. Duke of Somerset	143
Governors Christ Hospital v. Harrild	108, 118
Grace, ex parte	27, 32
Graham v. Wade	166
—— v. Allsopp	163
Granger v. Collins	140, 243
Grant v. Oxford Local Board	57, 68
—— v. Ellis	205
Grantham v. Hawley	291
Gravenor v. Woodhouse	320
Graves v. Weld	292

c

INDEX TO CASES CITED.

	PAGE
Gray v. Bompas	274
Green v. Eales	123, 237
—— v. James	157, 324
Greene v. Cole	229
Greenaway v. Hart	114, 158, 327
Greenwood v. Tyber	10
Gregory v. Doidge	320
—— v. Wilson	239
Grey de Wilton (Lord) v. Saxon	239, 240
Griffin v. Scott	216
—— v. Stanhope	142
Griffinhoofe v. Dunbar	169
Griffith v. Harrison	151
Griffiths v. Puleston	204, 292, 293
—— v. Stephens	226
Grimman v. Legge	252, 255
Grosvenor v. Green	321
Grute v. Locroft	12
Grymes v. Boweren	301
Guardians Bedford Union v. Bedford Improvement Commissioners	118
Guardians Woodbridge Union v. Guardians of Colneis	
Gudgen v. Besset	180
Gulliver d. Tasker v. Burr	105
Gully v. Bishop of Exeter	82
Gutteridge v. Munyard	123
Gwynn, in re	337
Gybson v. Searle	36, 251

H.

	PAGE
Hadden v. Arrowsmith	15
Haines v. Welch	289
Hall v. Burgess	176, 181, 285
Hall v. Betty	139
Hall v. City of London Brewery Company	139
Hall v. Lund	80
Hull v. Seabright	57
Haldane v. Johnson	162
Hallen v. Runder	301, 310, 313
Hallifax v. Chambers	138
Hamerton v. Stead	101, 251
Hammond v. Dodd	131
Hancock v. Austin	40, 57, 68, 184, 207
—— v. Caffyn	61, 243
Hands v. Slaney	32
Harbin v. Barton	12
Harcourt v. Wyman	342
Harding v. Hall	219
—— v. Crethorn	274
—— v. Wilson	88

	PAGE
Hardy v. Robinson	343
Hare v. Cator	328
—— v. Burgess	133
Harley v. King	324
Harnett v. Maitland	137, 229, 238
Harrington v. Ramsay	278
—— v. Wise	58
Harris v. Goodwyn	323
—— v. Greathed	83
—— v. Jones	122
Harrison v. Barnby	186
—— v. Barry	216
—— v. Blackburn	45
Harrow School v. Alderton	229
Harper v. Taswell	215
Hart v. Leach	219
—— v. Windsor	137
Hartshorne v. Watson	149, 150, 151
Harvey v. Brydges	
—— v. Harvey	302
—— v. Pocock	223
Haslett v. Burt	312
Hatch v. Hale	210
Haths v. Ash	96
Havergill v. Hare	57
Hawkins v. Kemp	151
Hawks v. Orton	243
Hay v. Palmer	172
Hayes v. Bickerstaff	131, 140
Hayling v. Okey	292
Hayne v. Cummings	114, 149, 238
—— v. Maltby	116, 142
Hayward v. Haswell	64
Head v. Starkey	120
Heap v. Barton	304, 310, 311
Hearne v. Allen	87
—— v. Tomlin	51
Hegan v. Johnson	65, 113, 185
Hele v. Bexley	50
Hellawell v. Eastwood	198, 299, 303
Hellier v. Casbard	137, 333
—— v. Sillcox	181
Henderson v. Squire	273
—— v. Hay	126
Henistead v. Phœnix Gas Co.	343
Henstead's Case	10, 13, 104
Herne v. Benbow	229, 238
Hetherley d. Worthington v. Weston	13
Hew v. Greek	116
Hewitt v. Isham	92
Hewlins v. Shippam	43
Hicks v. Downing	11
Hide v. Skinner	133
Higham v. Baker	88

INDEX TO CASES CITED. xxiii

	PAGE
Higham v. Cooke	95
Hill v. Barclay	238, 239
—— v. Grange	160
—— v. Manchester and Salford Waterworks Company	53
—— v. Saunders	10, 320, 342
—— v. South Staffordshire Railway Company	48
—— v. Tupper	40, 68
Hills v. Laming	53
—— v. Street	217
Hinchcliffe v. Earl of Kinnoul	88
Hinde v. Gray	129
Hindley v. Emery	239
Hirst v. Horn	267, 286
Hitchcock v. Coker	129
Hitchman v. Walton	103
Hobson v. Middleton	132
Hoby v. Roebuck	185
Hodges v. Lawrence	201
Holcombe v. Hewson	128
Holding v. Piggott	138, 293
Holford v. Hatch	125, 328
Holgate v. Kay	171
Holland v. Palser	161
Hollis v. Carr	137
Holmes v. Blogg	28, 31
Holtzappfel v. Baker	233
Hool v. Bell	191
Hope v. Booth	51, 102
—— v. Mayor of Gloucester	133
Hopkins v. Helmore	161
—— v. Prescott	39
Hopwood v. Whaley	332
—— v. Barefoot	118
Horn v. Baker	298, 312
Horner v. Graves	129
Hornidge v. Wilson	332
Hooper v. Clark	68
Horsfall v. Hey	313
—— v. Testar	121
Horton v. Westminster Improvement Commissioners	53
Houghton v. Koenig	339
How v. Kennett	183
Howe v. Scarrutt	10, 342
—— v. Synge	166
Howell v. Maine	342
Howlett v. Strickland	138
Howton v. Fearson	38, 41, 43
Huddlestone v. Woodroffe	81
Hudson v. Hudson	22
Huffell v. Armitstead	106, 107, 269
Hughes v. Clarke	116
—— and Crowther's Case	247

	PAGE
Hughes v. Hughes	190
—— v. Palmer	150
—— v. Robotham	248, 253
Hungerford v. Clay	14
—— v. Beecher	53
Hunt v. Bishop	148, 323, 325
—— v. Colson	30
—— v. Remnant	323
—— v. Singleton	18, 85
Huntley v. Russell	228, 229, 299
Hurst v. Hurst	295
Hutchins v. Chambers	206, 222
—— v. Martin	259, 251
—— v. Scott	160, 207
Huton v. Huton	144
Hutton v. Warren	124, 138, 229, 233, 293, 295, 297
Hutt v. Morrell	194
Hyatt v. Griffiths	247, 273
Hyde v. Graham	40, 68
—— v. Hill	166
—— v. Moakes	252
—— v. Watts	125

I.

Ibbs v. Richardson	274
Ingulden v. May	133
Inman v. Stamp	46, 48
Isherwood v. Oldknow	15, 114, 152
Ive v. Sams	92, 251
Izon v. Gorton	282, 333

J.

Jack v. M'Intyre	84
Jackman v. Hoddesden	15
Jackson v. Cator	6, 239, 240, 241, 244
—— v. Cobbin	140
—— v. Hoddesden	15
—— v. Mordant	10
—— v. Neal	15
Jacob v. King	226
—— v. Seward	232
Jacques v. Withy	115
Jagon v. Vivian	151
Jalentine v. Denion	185
James v. Plant	38, 88, 89
—— re	22
Jay v. Richardson	127
Jenkins v. Gething	303
—— v. Green	19, 91
—— v. Church	6
—— v. Yates	6
Jenner v. Clegg	185, 273

INDEX TO CASES CITED.

	PAGE
Jenner v. Morgan	172
—— v. Yolland	223, 324
Jenney v. Brook	92
Jennings v. Major	211
Jephson v. Jackson	57
Jerman v. Orchard	82, 94
Jerritt v. Weare	131
Jervis v. Tomkinson	93, 97
Jevens v. Harridge	30
Jewel's Case	113
Jewell v. Stead	128
Jinks v. Edwards	48, 140, 243
Job v. Banister	133, 239
John v. Jenkins	63, 250
Johnson v. Faulkner	194, 199
—— v. Jones	163
—— v. Uplam	210
—— v. Warwick	23
Johnstone v. Huddlestone	252, 269, 287
Jolly v. Arbuthnot	50
—— v. Handcock	342
Jones v. Chapman	276
—— v. Carter	149, 161
—— v. Clark	
—— v. Davies	253, 254
—— v. Edney	128
—— v. Hill	229
—— v. Jones	126
—— v. Marsh	272
—— v. Mills	106, 269
—— v. Morris	164
—— v. Nixon	268
—— v. Owen	279
—— v. Phipps	267
—— v. Reynolds	63, 183
—— v. Shears	48, 274
—— v. Thompson	183
—— d. Trimleston v. Nunan	57
—— v. Verney	6
Joule v. Jackson	199
Jourdain v. Wilson	325
—— v. Steere	13
Juste v. Darby	251

K.

	PAGE
Kearsey v. Carstairs	337
Kearsley v. Oxley	331
Keech v. Hall	13, 103, 270
Keen v. Priest	201, 204, 223, 225
Kelly v. Clubbe	183
Kemp v. Cruwes	192
—— v. Derrett	97, 106, 107, 205
Kendall v. Baker	110
Kenney v. May	216

	PAGE
Kensey v. Langham	36
Kerby v. Harding	206, 209
Kerslake v. White	85
Kepp v. Wiggett	56
Ketsey's Case	31
Kettley v. Elliott	29
Key ex parte	337
Kidwelly v. Brand	258, 328
Kimpton v. Eve	239, 240
King v. England	217
—— v. Jones	331
Kingdon v. Nottle	331
Kingsbury v. Collins	289, 292
Kingston's (Duchess of,) Case	353
Kinlyside v. Thornton	236, 238
Kinnersley v. Orpe	125
Kintrea v. Perston	139
Kirtland v. Pounsett	51, 102
Knevett v. Poole	289, 291
Knight v. Bennett	48, 184
—— v. Egerton	222
—— and Norton's Case	25
—— v. May	
—— v. Mory	144
Knowles v. Blake	225
—— v. Powell	29
Kooystra v. Lucas	38, 88

L.

	PAGE
Lady Montague's Case	15
Laing v. Meandor	211
Ladd v. Thomas	224
Lainson v. Tremere	53, 54, 56
Lake v. Smith	286
Lamb v. Reaston	83
Lambert v. Austin	191
—— v. Norris	113
Laming v. Laming	132
Lampet's Case	3
Lancaster (Duchy of,) Case of	28
Lane v. Dixon	198
Lane's Case	43
Langley v. Hammond	38, 89
Lant v. Norris	121
Lanyon v. Crane	109
Lapiere v. M'Intosh	30
Latham v. Attwood	291
—— v. Spedding	279
Lawton v. Lawton	301, 304, 305, 308
—— v. Salmon	305, 308
Lay v. Mottram	137
Layton v. Harvey	213
Leach v. Thomas	137

INDEX TO CASES CITED.

	PAGE
Leader v. Homewood	311
Lear v. Caldecott	206, 222
Leather Cloth Co. v. Lorsout	129
Lee v. Cooke	216
—— v. Risdon	298, 303, 308, 313
—— v. Smith	52, 105
Leeds v. Cheetham	182
Leftley v. Mills	161
Legh v. Hewitt	138, 233
Lehmann v. M'Arthur	147
Leigh v. Heald	81, 92
—— v. Lillie	295
—— v. Shepherd	186
Le Keux v. Nash	324
Levi v. Lewis	158, 181, 182
Lewis v. Hilliard	97
Liford's Case	92, 300
Lilley v. Harvey	279
—— v. Whitney	94
Lindsay v. Lynch	245
Line v. Stephenson	136
Lingwood v. Stowmarket Co.	244
Linwood v. Squire	116
Litchfield v. Ready	45
Llewellyn v. Rous	176
—— v. Williams	96
Lloyd v. Cheetham	40
—— v. Crisp	144, 145
—— v. Davies	188, 319, 348, 351
—— v. Jones	279
—— v. Langford	250
—— v. Rosbee	286
—— v. Tomkies	131
Load v. Green	149
Locke v. Furze	243, 244
—— v. Matthews	104
Lockwood v. Wood	34
Loft v. Dennis	182, 233
Logan v. Hall	321
London & N.W. Railway Co. v. Garnett	128
—— & N.W. Railway Co. v. MacMichael	32
—— Cotton Co., in re	341
—— v. Sonthwell	92
—— & Westminster Loan & Discount Co. Limited v. Drake	254
—— (Mayor of) v. Hedger	239, 241
Lord Cholmondely v. Lord Clinton	103
—— Darcy v. Askwith	228, 230, 231
—— Dudley v. Lord Warde	305, 308, 309
—— Fairfax v. Lord Derby	191
—— Grey de Wilton v. Saxon	239, 240
—— Paget's Case	95

	PAGE
Lord Rockingham v. Penrice	172, 173
—— Stafford v. Buckley	82
—— Strafford v. Lady Wentworth	172, 173, 178
—— Vaux's Case	100
—— Ward v. Lumley	182
—— Windsor v. Bury	144
Lougher v. Williams	325, 330
Lowe v. Griffiths	32
—— v. Ross	181, 183
—— v. Peers	114
Lowndes v. Fountain	295
Lowthal v. Tomkins	350
Lucas v. Commerford	238
—— v. Tarleton	209, 215
Lucy v. Levington	131, 140
Ludford v. Barber	6
Lumley v. Hodgson	318
Luttrell v. Weston	15
Luxmore v. Robson	122, 237
Lyde v. Russell	309
Lyon v. Reed	157, 250, 252
—— v. Tomkins	209, 217, 219, 224
—— v. Weldon	216

M.

	PAGE
Mabie's Case	91
Macher v. Foundling Hospital	145
M'Garth v. Shannon	249
Mackay v. Mackreth	12
Mackintosh v. Trotter	310, 311
M'Loish v. Tate	161
Madden v. White	27
Magdalene College (Case of)	17
Maitland v. Mackinnon	80, 86
Makin v. Watkinson	121
Maldon's Case	58
Mallam v. Arden	160
Manby v. Long	189
—— v. Scott	26
Mann v. Lovejoy	185
Manning v. Fitzgerald	83, 85
—— v. Lunn	211
Mansfield v. Blackburn	304, 305
—— (Earl of) v. Blackburne	312
Mantle v. Wollington	13
Mantz v. Goring	123
Markby, in re	176
Marker v. Kenrick	236, 238
Markham v. Stanford	39
Marlborough (Duke of) v. Osborne	109
Marquis of Camden v. Battenbury	49, 51, 113, 181, 182

INDEX TO CASES CITED.

	PAGE
Marquis of Downshire v. Lady Sandys	241
Marsh v. Bruce	324
—— v. Curteys	126, 260
Marshall v. Pitman	226
—— v. Powell	70
Martin v. Gilham	138, 238
—— v. Roe	300, 303, 310
—— v. Pycroft	244
Martyn v. Clue	124, 138, 325
—— v. Williams	322, 323
Martyr v. Bradley	312
—— v. Laurence	84
Marwood v. Waters	279
Mary Portington's Case,	141
Mason v. Corder	145
—— v. Newland	213
Massay v. Goodall	295
Master, &c. of St Cross v. Lord Howard de Walden	110
Masters v. Farris	221
Mather v. Fraser	314
Mathew v. Blackmore	136
Matin v. Williams	322, 323
Matthews v. Whetton	15
Matthias v. Mesnard	198
Maund's Case,	161, 257
Mayhew v. Suttle	50
Mayor of Berwick v. Oswald	115
—— of Congleton v. Pattison	127
—— of London v. Hedger	239, 241
—— of Poole v. Whitt	348
Mechelen v. Wallace	45
Meggison v. Bowers	112
—— v. Lady Glamis	37
Melling v. Leake	104
Mellows v. May	251
Mennie v Blake	226
Merrill v. Frame	130, 136
Messenger v. Armstrong	269, 273, 286
Messent v. Reynolds	139, 243
Messing v. Kemble	220, 224
Metcalf v. Scholey	348
Metropolitan Assurance Co. v. Browu	103
Michell v. Hughes	339
Middlemore v. Goodale	325, 342
Middleton v. Greenwood	244
Midgley v. Lovelace	186
Miller v. Green	194
—— v. Mainwaring	95
—— v. Rogers	31
Milliner v. Robinson	13
Mills v. Goff	265
—— v. Trumper	173, 176

	PAGE
Milner v. Milnes	343
—— v. Horton	132
Minshall v. Lloyd	298, 309, 310, 311, 316
Minshull v. Oakes	326, 327
Mitcalfe v. Westaway	90
Mitchell v. Lee	183
Mollett v. Brayne	252
Molton v. Camroux	24
Monk v. Cooper	122
Monks v. Dykes	41, 106, 107
Montague's, Lady, Case	15
Moody v. Garnon	170
Moore v. Earl of Plymouth	90, 93, 257
—— v. Drinkwater	223
—— v. Musgrove	95
Morewood v. Wilks	26
Morgan v. Bissell	62, 64
—— v. Earl of Abergavenny	200
—— v. Hunt	132
—— v. Pike	116
—— v. Slaughton	126
Morland v. Cook	325
Morley v. Pincombe	197, 200
Morris v. Coleman	128
—— v. Dimes	84
—— v. Edgington	38
—— v. Moore	343
Morrison v. Chadwick	137, 171, 251
Mortimer v. Hartley	100
Morton v. Woods	103, 158, 188
Moss v. Gallimore	12, 49, 105, 188, 209, 319
Moule v. Garrett	324
Mountjoy's Case	110, 185
Mountnoy v. Collier	182
Mousley v. Ludlam	294
Moyle v. Moyle	229, 231
Muncay v. Dennis	138, 293, 294
Mumford v. Gething	129
Murley v. M'Dermott	88
Murray v. King	163
Muspratt v. Gregory	199, 201

N.

Nargett v. Nias	201
Nash v. Lucas	206, 207
—— v. Palmer	131
Naylor v. Collinge	311
Neale d'Leroux v. Parkin	86
—— v. Mackenzie	37, 57, 171
—— v. Ratcliffe	121, 124
Neave v. Moss	158
Nepean v. Doe	206

INDEX TO CASES CITED. xxvii

	PAGE
Neville v. Rivers	342
Newbury White, in re, v. Wakley	121
Newling v. Dobell	130
Newman v. Anderton	41, 112, 184
Newson v. Smythies	274
Newton v. Allin	171
—— v. Harland	275
—— v. Scott	340
Niblet v. Smith	193, 197, 225, 305
Nicholls, re	162
Nicholson v. Rose	244
Nickells v. Atherstone	252
Nixon v. Freeman	204, 208
Noke's Case	139
Norris v. Harrison	173
North v. Wyard	342
Northampton Gas Co. v. Parnell	116
Northcote v. Underhill	116
Norton, in re	337
—— v. Ackland	324
Norway v. Rowe	239
Nott v. Bound	218
Nunn v. Fabian	244
Nuttall v. Staunton	204

O.

Oakley v. Monck	6, 49, 52
Oates v. Frith	113
Obroyd v. Crampton	39
Odell v. Wake	324
Ognel's Case	187, 191
Oland's Case	289, 291
Oldershaw v. Holt	176
Onley v. Gardiner	88
Onsley v. Fisk	82
Onslow v. ——	239, 296
—— v. Corrie	324
Opperman v. Smith	202
Orme v. Broughton	331
Osborn v. Carden	21
Osborne v. Wickenden	187
—— v. Wise	38, 41, 43
Owen v. De Beauvoir	206
—— v. Legh	194, 215
Owens v. Wynne	206
Oxley v. James	12, 105

P.

Packer v. Gibbins	182, 233
Packington's Case	241
Page v. More	266, 284, 286
Paget's (Lord) Case	95
Paget v. Foley	205

	PAGE
Pain v. Coombs	244
Palmer v. Earith	118, 167
—— v. Edwards	185, 328
Pannell v. Mill	89, 90
Papillon v. Brunton	271, 272
Paradine v. Jane	230
Paramour v. Yardley	23
Pargeter v. Harris	53, 158
Parker v. Constable	268
—— v. Harris	109
—— v. Ibbetson	139
—— v. Plumber	81
—— v. Taswell	140, 244
—— v. Whyte	127, 241
Parmenter v. Webber	11, 143, 185, 250
Parrott v. Anderson	163
Parry, ex parte	341
—— v. Deere	69
—— v. Duncan	202
—— v. Harbert	144
—— v. Hindle	10, 187, 342
Parsons v. Gingell	199
Partington v. Woodcock	189
Partridge v. Foster	348
Patrick v. Balls	43
Patten v. Reid	332
Paul v. Nurse	127
Paxton v. Newton	238
Payler v. Homersham	83
Payne v. Burridge	118
—— v. Haine	123, 237
Peacock v. Purvis	194, 200
Pearce v. Cheslyn	60, 70
Pearse v. Morrice	39
Pearson v. Glazebrook	279
Pease v. Chaytor	226
Pellatt v. Boosey	259
Pemberton v. Vaughan	129
Penfold v. Abbott	136, 332
Pennant's Case	204, 261
Penniall v. Harborne	124
Pennington v. Cardale	149, 150
Penry v. Brown	121, 303, 312
Penton v. Robart	300, 304, 305, 308, 310
Peppercorn v. Hofman	210
Perham, in re	283
Perkins v. Bradley	26
Perring v. Brook	61
Perry v. Davis	148
—— v. Edwards	131
Peter v. Kendall	38, 251
Petrie v. Daniel	294
Petrie v. Dawson	313
Phillips v. Berryman	226
—— v. Pearce	20, 21

	PAGE		PAGE
Phillips v. Smith	228, 230, 231	Powell v. Rees	333
—— v. Whitsed	209	Powley v. Walker	124, 138
Philpott v. Hoare	325	Pratt v. Brett	239, 240
Phipps v. Sculthorpe	158, 252	Preece v. Corrie	11, 185, 192
Pierce v. Corrie	143	Prescott v. Boucher	191
Piggott v. Birtles	193, 201, 215, 222	Press v. Parker	85
Pigot v. Garnish	21, 22	Price v. Dyer	108
—— v. Stratton	244, 254	—— v. Salusbury	245
Pike v. Eyre	12	—— v. Williams	18
Pilbrow v. Atmospheric Railway Co.	53	—— v. Worwood	260
Pilkington v. Hastings	210	Prince's Case	23
—— v. Peach	30	Procter v. Sargent	129
—— v. Scott	129, 141	Progress Assurance Co., in re	341
Pilton, ex parte	282, 283	Propert v. Parker	127
Pincomb v. Thomas	92	Prosser v. Phillips	70
Pincro v. Judson	60	Proud v. Bates	90
Pinder v. Ainsley	182	Proudlove v. Twenlow	194
Pinhorn v. Sonster	49, 103, 104	Pugh v. Arton	306, 309, 310
Pistor v. Cater	51	—— v. Griffiths	208
Pitcairn v. Ogbourne	21	—— v. Leeds, Duke of	96
Pitcher v. Tovey	332	Pullen v. Palmer	186, 187
Pitman v. Woodbury	116	Pullin v. Pullin	83
Pitt v. Shew	197, 216	Pyer v. Carter	88
—— v. Smith	24	Pyne v. Dor	231
—— v. Snowden	190	Pyot v. St John	300
Place v. Fagg	300, 314		
Platt v. Sleap	253	R.	
Playfair v. Musgrove	348		
Pleasant v. Benson	254, 270	R. v. Aldborough	12
Pleazance v. Higham	64	—— v. Aylesbury, with Walton	118
Pluck v. Digges	192	—— v. Bardwell	50
Plummer v. Whitely	176	—— v. Chawton	100
Plymouth (Countess of) v. Throgmorton	172	—— v. Cheshunt	50
		—— v. Collett	101
Pointer v. Buckley	217	—— v. Earl of Pomfret	111
Polden v. Bastard	88	—— v. Eastbourne	30
Pollen v. Brewer	104	—— v. Filloughley	101, 102
Pollitt v. Forrest	184	—— d. Hall v. Bulkely	151
Pomery v. Partington	151	—— v. Herstmonceaux	106, 107
Poole v. Archer	233	—— v. Holland	30
—— v. Bentley	59	—— v. Hornchurch	14
—— v. Longueville	192	—— v. Hoseaston	226
—— Mayor of, v. Whitt	348	—— v. Hull Dock Company	168
—— v. Warren	284, 286	—— v. Jobbling	101
Poole's Case	197, 304, 305, 306, 309	—— v. Kelstern	49
Pope v. Biggs	189	—— v. Lakenheath	102
Pordage v. Cole	141	—— v. Lee	303
Porphrey v. Legingham	223	—— v. Leigh	230
Porris v. Allen	250	—— v. Lenthall	39
Porter v. Swetnam	137	—— v. Londonthorpe	302
Portman v. Harrell	203	—— v. Mitcham	165
Postlethwaite v. Lewthwaite	133	—— v. Morrish	57, 68
Potter v. North	87	—— v. Nicholson	38
Poultney v. Holmes	185	—— v. North Staffordshire Railway Company	303
Powell v. Thomas	244		

INDEX TO CASES CITED. xxix

	PAGE		PAGE
R. v. Oakley	21	Rickman v. Johns	190
— v. Old Alreaford	81	Ridgway v. Lord Stafford	196
— v. Otley	299	Right d. Bassett v. Thomas	57
— v. Saffron Walden	128	—— d. Fisher v. Cuthell	266
— v. Sewell	282	—— d. Flower v. Darby	105, 106, 268
— v. Sherrington	21	—— d. Green v. Proctor	57
— v. Shipdam	50	—— d. Lewis v. Beard	102
— v. Smyth	275	Ringer v. Cann	53, 83, 183
— v. Snape	50	Riseley v. Ryle	184
— v. Southampton Dock Company	303	Roach v. Garvan	22
— v. Spurrell	50	—— v. Wadham	328
— v. St Austell	111	Roads v. Trumpington	68
— v. St Dunstan's	301, 302	Roberts v. Barker	138, 295
— v. Stamper	53	—— v. Davey	149, 150, 257
— v. Stock	49	—— v. Karr	83
— v. Sutton	21	Robertson v. Norris	342
— v. Thorp	22	Robinson v. Button	83
— v. Topping	143, 312	—— v. Hoffman	186
— v. Watt	37	—— v. Learoyd	285
— v. Welby	14	—— v. Tongue	36
— v. Westbrook	109, 111	—— v. Waddington	209, 215
— v. Weste	49, 184	—— v. Walter	201
Rainsford v. Smith	56	Robson v. Flight	153
Ramsbottom v. Buckhurst	351	Rockingham (Lord) v. Peurice	172, 173
Rand v. Vaughan	203	Rodgers v. Parker	194, 216, 219
Randal v. Dean	189	Roe d. Bainford v. Hayley	107, 325
Rankin v. Lay	244	—— d. Bendale v. Sumerset	22
Rannie v. Irving	129	—— d. Blair v. Street	272
Rashleigh v. Williams	131	—— d. Dingley v. Sales	126, 144
Rawlings v. Morgan	122, 323	—— d. Earl Berkley v. Archbishop of York	250
Rawson v. Eicke	64	—— d. Gregson v. Harrison	125, 127, 145, 261
Raymond v. Fitch	331	—— d. Hunter v. Galliers	125, 143, 340
Read v. Bailey	192	—— d. Goatley v. Paine	260
Rede v. Burley	199	—— d. Jordon v. Ward	6, 265
—— v. Farr	149, 150	—— d. Jordon v. Prideaux	6
Reed v. Deere	70	—— d. Parry v. Hodgson	22
Rees v. Philipps	3	—— d. West v. Davis	258
—— v. Errington	256	—— v. Wiggs	271
—— v. King	259	Roffey v. Henderson	311
Reeve v. Bird	252	Rogers v. Dock Company at Kingston-upon-Hull	268
Regnart v. Porter	49, 184	—— v. Birkmire	201
Reid v. Parsons	149	—— v. Humphreys	188, 189, 318
Reynall, ex parte	314, 339	—— v. Pitcher	320, 350
Reynel's Case	89	Rollason v. Leon	60
Reynolds v. Oakley	192	Rolph v. Crouch	244
Richards v. Easto	232	Rouch v. Great Western Railway Company	143
—— v. Richards	343	Rowdon v. Malster	3
—— v. Sely	57	Rowe v. Young	162
Richardson v. Evans	145	Rowls v. Gells	168
—— v. Gifford	48, 51, 52, 101	Rubery v. Jervoise	133
—— v. Hall	183, 345		
—— v. Langridge	51, 100, 101		
—— v. Lovejoy			
Ricketts v. Weaver	331		

XXX   INDEX TO CASES CITED.

	PAGE
Rubery v. Stephens	332, 333
Rumball v. Munt	21
Rushden's Case	170
Rushworth's Case	86
Russell v. Rider	206
—— v. Shenton	237
—— v. Stokes	327
Ryan v. Clark	45
—— v. Shilcock	207, 208

S.

Sabbarton v. Sabbarton	152
Sacheverell v. Froggatt	113
Salisbury's (Bishop of) Case	16
Salmon v. Matthews	112, 113, 172
—— v. Swan	252
Salop's, Countess of, Case	232
Salter v. Bunsden	221
—— v. Grosvenor	32
—— v. Kidgley	53, 56
Saltoun v. Houston	137
Sampson v. Easterby	137
Sanders v. Karnell	52
Sapsford v. Fletcher	163
Saunders v. Merryweather	14
—— v. Musgrave	102
—— v. Watson	26
Saward v. Leggatt	123
Say v. Smith	100
Scarpellini v. Atcheson	343
Scholis v. Hargreaves	87
Schroder v. Ward	123
Scot v. Scot	258
Scott v. Scholey	348
Sedden v. Senate	132
Selby v. Browne	149
—— v. Greaves	40, 41
Sells v. Hoare	222
Semayne's Case	207
Semor v. Armytage	294, 297
Severn v. Clark	137
Sharp v. Waterhouse	137, 141
—— v. Key	351
—— v. Sharp	44
Sharpe v. Poole	187
Sharp's Case	44
Shaw v. Bran	26
—— v. Coffin	142
—— v. Kay	93, 97
—— v. Stenton	131, 132
Sheecomb v. Hawkins	152
Sheen v. Rickie	298
Shelburn, Earl of, v. Biddulph	132
Shepherd v. Hodsman	39

	PAGE
Sherrington v. Yates	343
Shirley v. Newman	268
Shopland v. Radlen	190
—— v. Ryoler	21
Simmons v. Norton	229, 931
Simpson v. Clayton	325, 328
—— v. Gutteridge	22
—— v. Hartopp	197, 200
—— v. Margitson	100
Six Carpenters' Case	210, 211, 220, 224
Skidmore v. Booth	208
Skinner, in re,	337
Skull v. Glenister	41, 43
Slack v. Sharp	172, 255
Slater v. Brady	27
—— v. Stone	123
—— v. Trimble	27
Sleap v. Newman	332
Sleddon v. Cruikshank	313
Slipper v. Tottenham Junction Railway Co.	143
Smith v. Ashforth	222, 223
—— v. Adkins	21, 33
—— v. Barrett	16
—— v. Bole	92
—— and Bustard's Case	258
—— v. Carter	239, 240
—— v. Chance	295
—— v. Clark	272
—— v. Compton	132
—— v. Day	95
—— v. Eldridge	181
—— v. Goodwin	206, 210, 224
—— v. Humble	166, 167
—— v. Doe d. Jersey, Earl of	153, 259
—— v. Malings	170, 171
—— v. Mapleback	112, 138, 185, 250
—— v. Marable	137
—— v. Martin	82, 87
—— v. Mayor of Harwich	141
—— v. Peat	122, 237
—— v. Scott	183
—— v. Smith	334
—— v. Twoart	181
—— v. Walton	266
—— v. White	151
—— v. Wright	213, 225
Smyth v. Carter	239, 240
—— v. Nangle	133
Smythe, ex parte	173
Snelgar v. Henston	187
Somerset, Duke of, v. Fagwell	39, 43
Southampton v. Brown	113
Soulsby v. Neving	285
Souter v. Drake	189

INDEX TO CASES CITED.

	PAGE
South-Eastern Railway Co. v. Wharton	53, 54
Southgate v. Chaplan	131
Sparke's Case	12
Sparrow v. Hawkes	268
Spargo v. Brown	222
Spencer's Case	41, 116, 327
Spyve v. Toplam	94
Stafford (Lord) v. Buckley	82, 185
St Albans (Duke of) v. Ellis	116
St Aubyn v. St Aubyn	173, 176
St Cross (Master of) v. Lord Howard de Walden	110
St Nicholas Deptford v. Scetchley	21
Staines v. Morris	323
Stainforth v. Fox	57
Standen v. Christmas	136, 323
Stanley v. Hayes	131
—— v. Twogood	123, 237
—— v. Wharton	203
Stansfeld v. Mayor of Portsmouth	310
Staple v. Heydon	41, 43
Stedman v. Page	186
Steele v. Mart	96
—— v. Midland Railway Co.	82
Stephens v. Bridges	253
Stevens v. Copp	142
Stevenson v. Lambard	171, 179, 328, 329
Stiles v. Cowper	6
Stockly v. Stockly	244
Stockport Waterworks Co. v. Potter	40, 68
Stokes v. Russell	135, 327
Stone v. Rogers	69
—— v. Whiting	252
Storer v. Hunter	312
Storey v. Johnson	28
Stowe v. Jackson	343
Stott v. Clegg	39
Strafford (Lord) v. Buckley	82
—— (Lord) v. Lady Wentworth	172, 173, 178
Stranks v. St John	139
Stratton v. Pettitt	66
Strickland v. Maxwell	269, 272, 294
Strongfield v. Buck	56
Stroud, in re	49
—— v. Rogers	180
Strowd v. Willis	56
Strutt v. Finch	84
Styles v. Wardle	96
Suffield v. Brown	88
Sullivan v. Bishop	286, 287
Sumner v. Brownilow	310, 311

	PAGE
Surcombe v. Pinniger	244
Sureper v. Randall	12
Surplice v. Farnsworth	138, 182
Sury v. Brown	37, 38
Sutherland v. Briggs	244
Sutton's Case	39
—— v. Temple	137, 138
Swaine v. Holman	31
Swan v. Stransham	136
Swann v. Earl of Falmouth	201, 210, 222
Swatman v. Ambler	116
Sweet v. Seager	118
Swift v. Eyres	83
Swinfen v. Bacon	285
Swire v. Leech	198
Sym's Case	344
Symons v. Symons	172

T.

	PAGE
Tabian and Windsor's Case	
Tancred v. Christy	274
—— v. Leyland	209
Taswell v. Parker	67
Tate v. Gleed	192
Tatem v. Chaplin	325
Tayleur v. Wildin	273
Taylor v. Caldwell	57, 68
—— v. Chapman	252
—— v. Cole	275, 350, 351
—— v. Fitzgerald	95
—— v. Henniker	209, 221
—— v. Lamira	173
—— v. Martindale	82
—— v. Shum	324, 332
Taylorson v. Peters	204, 283
Tennant v. Field	210
Tew v. Jones	102, 182
Theobald v. Duffey	30
Thomas v. Cook	252
—— v. Hayward	127
—— v. Fredericks	37, 40
—— v. Parker	51, 52
—— v. Harries	210, 213
—— v. Thomas	88
—— v. Cadwallader	124
Thompson v. Gayon	134
—— v. Hakewill	328
—— v. Lapworth	120
—— v. Mashiter	198
—— v. Thompson	163
—— v. Waterlow	38
—— v. Wilson	252

	PAGE
Thompson v. Pettitt	223
Thorn v. Woolcombe	11, 143, 255
Thornton v. Adams	203
—— v. Finch	348
—— v. Sherratt	128
Thorpe v. Eyre	293
Threr v. Bastou	254
Thresher v. East London Waterworks Co.	121, 305, 311, 312, 315
Thrustout d. Levick v. Coppin	23
Thunder d. Weaver v. Belcher	12, 13, 103
Thursby v. Plant	324
Tidey v. Mollett	66, 67, 141
Tidswell v. Whitworth	120
Tilney v. Norris	831
Timmins v. Rowlinson	105, 264, 285, 287
Tinckler v. Prentice	161, 166, 257
Tipping v. Eckersley	241, 244
Tisdale v. Essex	57, 131
Todhunter, ex parte	337
Toler v. Slater	10
Tomlinson v. Day	171
Toleman v. Portbury	124, 127, 257
—————— (second case). See Add.	
Toms v. Wilson	258
Tooker v. Smith	52, 254
Torriano v. Young	254
Towne v. Campbell	106, 107
—— v. D'Heinrich	181
Townsend v. Stangroom	86
Trapp's Case	83
Trappes v. Harter	198, 299, 312
Tremeere v. Morison	332
Trent v. Hunt	14, 50, 209
Tress v. Savage	269
Trevillian v. Pine	189
Trevivan v. Lawrence	157
Trevor v. Roberts	57
Tritton v. Foote	133
Turnam v. Cooper	94
Turner's Case	344
Turner v. Allday	160
—— v. Barnes	204
—— v. Cameron	299
—— v. Cameron's Coalbrook Co.	182
—— v. Doe d. Bennett	101
—— v. Hodges	15, 101
—— v. Lamb	122, 237
—— v. Power	70
—— v. Turner	185
Tutton v. Darke	204
Twynam v. Pickard	328, 329

	PAGE
Tynte v. Hodge	116
Tyringham's Case	87

U.

Upwell Caroon's Case	30
Uthwatt v. Elkins	21, 33

V.

Vandenanker v. Desborough	339
Vane v. Lord Barnard	232
Vaspor v. Edwards	213
Vaughan, ex parte	277
—— v. Hancock	47
—— v. Manlove	232
—— v. Taff-Vale Railway Co.	232
Vaux's (Lord) Case	100
Veale v. Priour	39
—— v. Warner	53
Veness, ex parte	337
Vere v. Sweden	126
Vernon v. Smith	326
Vigers v. Dean and Chapter of St Paul's	319
Vivian v. Blomberg	18
Vyvyan v. Arthur	136, 326

W.

Wade v. Baker	21
—— v. Marsh	190
Wakefield v. Brown	325
Wakeman v. Lindsey	208, 209
—— v. Walker	37
Walker v. Gode	49
—— v. Richardson	33, 252
—— v. Wakeman	37
Walker's Case	170, 171
Wallace v. King	216, 220
—— v. M'Laren	187
Waller v. Andrews	118, 167
Wallis v. Delmar	104
—— v. Harrison	342, 344
Walls v. Atcheson	252
Walmsley v. Milne	50, 103, 198, 298, 306, 339
Walsall v. Heath	10
Walter v. Rumball	209, 217, 222
Walton v. Waterhouse	122
Wankford v. Waukford	22
Wansborough v. Maton	299, 312
Ward v. Const	165, 166
—— v. Day	68, 205, 259
—— v. Shew	190

INDEX TO CASES CITED

	PAGE
Ward (Lord) v. Lumley	182
Wardell v. Usher	308
Wardroper v. Cutfield	176
Waring v. King	182, 274
Warman v. Faithfull	59
Warner's Case	20
Washbourn v. Black	214
Waterfall v. Peuistone	198, 314
Watkins v. Milton	57, 68
Watkinson v. Mann	17
Watson v. Main	202
—— v. Holme	166
—— v. Waud	184
Watts v. Kelson. See *Add.*	
Webb v. Plummer	124, 138
—— v. Russell	
135, 253, 254, 255, 257, 323, 327	
Weddall v. Capes	250
Weekley v. Wildman	34
Weeton v. Woodcock	310
Weigal v. Waters	122, 233
Welby v. Welby	83
Wells v. Foster	40
—— v. Moody	222
West v. Blakeway	303, 312
—— v. Dobb	147, 149, 325, 327
—— v. Fritchie	49, 103
Westwood v. Cowne	216
Wetherall v. Geering	126
Wetherell v. Howells	
229, 231, 308, 312, 316	
Whalley v. Thompson	88
Wharton v. Maylor	200
Wheatley v. Boyd	116
Wheeler v. Copeland	285
—— v. Heydon	18
—— v. Stevenson	259
—— v. Tootel	176
Whistler v. Paslow	92
Whitaker v. Wisbey	26
White v. Bayley	49, 101, 104
—— v. Hunt	337
—— v. Nicholson	137, 138
—— v. Willis	226
Whiteacre d. Boult v. Symonds	273
Whitehead v. Bennett	306
—— v. Taylor	189, 191
Whitfield v. Brandwood	166
—— v. Pindar	173
—— v. Weedon	237
Whitley v. Roberts	186
Whitlock v. Horton	12, 57
Whitmore v. Empson	314
Whittaker v. Barker	296
Whittle v. Frankland	141

	PAGE
Whittome v. Lamb	114
Wickham v. Hawker	90
—— v. Lee	285
—— v. Marquis of Bath	33
Wigglesworth v. Dallison	291, 292, 293
Wight v. Dicksons	128
Wigstow's Case	300
Wilbraham v. Livsay	127
Wilder v. Speer	211, 213
Wildman v. Wildman	11
Wiles v. Woodward	53
Wilkins v. Wingate	180
—— v. Wood	138
Wilkinson v. Colley	271, 284
—— v. Hall	57, 106, 107, 286
—— v. Rogers	127
Williams v. Bosanquet	45, 183, 337
—— v. Burrell	
136, 139, 140, 323, 325, 331	
—— v. Cheney	126
—— v. Cooper	262
—— v. Day	241
—— v. Evans	315
—— v. Earle	325, 326, 328
—— v. Hayward	111, 172
—— v. Holmes	198
—— v. M'Namara	241
—— v. Sawyer	250
—— v. Stiven	204
Willis v. Whitewood	21
Willoughby v. Foster	83
Wills v. Stradling	244
Wilmot v. Rose	234
Wilson, *ex parte*	50, 102
—— v. Abbott	106, 107
—— v. Anderson	82
—— v. Chisholm	60
—— v. Ducket	199
—— v. Hart	127, 128, 327
—— v. Nightingale	209
—— v. Sewell	250, 252
—— v. Whatley	312
—— v. Weller	226
—— v. Wilson	124
—— v. Wigg	332
Wilton v. Dunn	164, 189
Wiltshear v. Cottrell 197, 293, 298, 312	
Winch v. Winchester	86
Winchester (Bishop of) v. Wright	183
Windham v. Windham	83
Windsor, Dean and Chapter of, v.	
Gover	37, 112, 325
Windsor (Lord) v. Bury	144
Windsor's (Dean of) Case	325
Winn v. Ingleby	193, 197, 301

INDEX TO CASES CITED.

	PAGE
Winnard v. Foster	226
Winter v. Loveday	152
Winterbottom v. Ingham	102
Winterbourne v. Morgan	216, 220, 224
Wiscot's Case	10
Wise v. Bellent	187
Witty v. Williams	162
Wolveridge v. Steward	323
Womersley v. Dally	297
Wood and Chivers' Case	161, 258
—— v. Clarke	199
—— v. Copper Miners' Company	116
—— v. Day	158
—— v. Hewett	198
—— v. Leadbetter	40, 68
—— v. Nunn	207
—— v. Tait	106
Woodbridge Union v. Colneis	49, 180
Woodcock v. Gibson	21
—— v. Nuth	252
Woods v. Durrant	214
—— v. Pope	237
Woodward v. Aston	251
Woolaston v. Hakewill	11, 143, 328, 331, 332, 333
—— v. Stafford	206
Worcester School Trustees v. Rowlands	237
Worledge v. Benbury	15
Worthington v. Gimson	88
—— v. Warrington	69

	PAGE
Worthington v. Wigley	163
Wotley v. Gregory	135, 209
Wotton v. Harvey	226
—— v. Steffendord	30
Wright v. Burroughes	328, 329
—— v. Dewas	194, 195, 200
—— v. Stavert	41, 47
—— v. Smith	285
—— v. Trerezant	58
Wyburd v. Tuck	93, 97
Wyndham v. Way	92, 303, 308
Wynne v. Wynne	343

Y.

Yates v. Cole	328
—— v. Edwards	
—— v. Eastwood	219
Yellowley v. Gower	137, 229
Yeo v. Leman	166
Young v. Badfoot	253
—— v. Holmes	23
—— v. Mantz	123
—— v. Manton	123
—— v. Raincock	53, 56

Z.

Zouch d. Abbot v. Parsons	27, 28, 250
—— v. More	39

INDEX OF STATUTES.

	PAGE
20 Hen. III. c. 2 (repealed)	289
51 ,, c. 4	213
52 ,, c. 4	213, 222, 224
52 ,, c. 13	229
52 ,, c. 15	201
6 Edw. I. c. 5	229
13 c. 5, s. 1.	2
18 c. 5, s. 1.	2
21 Hen. VIII. c. 15 (repealed)	45
,, c. 15, s. 2	46
28 ,, c. 11	288
32 ,, c. 16, s. 13	30
32 ,, c. 28	3, 10
32 ,, c. 28, s. 1	17
32 ,, c. 34	257, 232, 238
32 ,, c. 34, s. 2	322
32 ,, c. 37, s. 1, 4	191
32 ,, c. 37, s. 3	187
5 & 6 Edw. VI. c. 16.	39
1 & 2 Philip & Mary, c. 12	213, 217
,, s. 1	224
1 Eliz. c. 19	17
13 ,, c. 10	17, 18
14 ,, c. 11	17, 18
18 ,, c. 6	109
,, c. 11	17, 109
39 ,, c. 5, s. 2	17
43 ,, c. 9, s. 8	17
1 Jac. 1. c. 3	17
12 Car. II. c. 24, s. 8, 11	22
17 ,, c. 7, s. 2	227
,, s. 4	206
19 ,, c. 6	8
,, s. 2, 3	9
22 & 23 Car. II. c. 12	110
2 Will. & Mary, sess. 1, c. 5, s. 2	214, 215, 219
,, c. 5,	221, 224
,, s. 3	193, 199
,, s. 4	225
1 Anne, c. 7, s. 5	16
4 ,, c. 16, s. 10	14
4 & 5 Anne, c. 16	318

	PAGE
6 Anne, c. 18	9
,, s. 1, 7	346
,, s. 8, 11, 12	347
,, s. 35	345
,, c. 31	230, 232
8 ,, c. 14, s. 6	204
,, s. 7	205
4 Geo. II. c. 28, s. 1	284
,, s. 2	259, 260
,, s. 5	194
,, s. 6	134, 254
,, s. 13	283
9 ,, c. 36	33
11 ,, c. 19	194, 176
,, s. 1	202
,, s. 2	174
,, s. 3	175
,, s. 4–7	203
,, s. 8	193, 203, 215, 225
,, s. 9	209, 215
,, s. 10	213, 224
,, s. 14	180
,, s. 15	172
,, s. 16	281
,, s. 17	282
,, s. 18	287
,, s. 19	219, 220
5 Geo. III. c. 17	36
13 ,, c. 81, s. 15	14, 37
14 ,, c. 78, s. 83	326
,, s. 86	232
38 ,, c. 5, s. 4	172
,, s. 17, 18, 35	165
,, c. 87, s. 6	23
39 & 40 ,, c. 41	18, 19
49 ,, c. 126	39
56 ,, c. 50, s. 1	195, 199, 233
,, s. 2	234
,, s. 3–6	195, 199
57 ,, c. 52	281
,, s. 17	282
,, c. 93	216

INDEX TO STATUTES.

			PAGE
57 Geo. III. c. 93, s. 2			218
59 ,, c. 12, s. 12			33
,, s. 17		20,	33
,, s. 24, 25			277
3 Geo. IV. c. 126			39
,, s. 57			39
4 ,, c. 95, s. 51			39
9 ,, c. 85			33
1 Will. IV. c. 65			134
,, s. 12		22, 31,	32
,, s. 15		31,	32
,, s. 16, 17			28
2 & 3 Will. IV. c. 42, s. 5, 11			277
3 & 4 ,, c. 27, s. 2			205
,, s. 7			103
,, s. 42			205
,, c. 42, s. 2		238,	333
,, s. 3			183
,, s. 37, 38			
		191,	192
,, c. 74,			342
,, s. 41, 54			5
,, s. 77, 79			26
4 & 5 ,, c. 22			176
,, s. 1			173
,, c. 76, s. 23			33
5 & 6 ,, c. 76, s. 94, 96			16
6 & 7 ,, c. 20			18
,, c. 64			18
,, c. 71, s. 56			110
,, s. 67, 80, 81			169
,, c. 72			176
1 & 2 Vict. c. 74, s. 1			275
,, c. 106, s. 28			32
,, c. 110, s. 11			348
3 & 4 ,, c. 84, s. 13		281,	283
5 & 6 ,, c. 27		18,	19
,, c. 35, s. 60		120,	166
,, s. 73			167
,, s. 103		114,	120
,, c. 97, s. 2			225
,, c. 108			19
6 & 7 ,, c. 30			225
7 & 8 ,, c. 66, s. 4			30
,, s. 7, 14, 15, 16			31
8 & 9 ,, c. 18			82
,, c. 106, s. 1			48
,, s. 2			35
,, s. 3		47, 100,	248
,, s. 4			140
,, s. 9		543,	125
8 & 9 ,, c. 124			130
9 & 10 ,, c. 74			34
,, c. 95, s. 122			278
12 & 13 Vict. c. 26, s. 2			154

			PAGE
12 & 13 Vict. c. 67 s. 3-7			155
,,			192
,, c. 92, s. 5			211
,, s. 6			212
,, c. 106			334
,, c. 106, s. 144			234
13 ,, c. 17			154
,, s. 2			153
,, s. 2, 3			156
13 & 14 ,, c. 60			339
,, c. 97			168
14 & 15 ,, c. 25			176
,, s. 1	6, 8, 107,		289
,, s. 2	194, 200,		289
,, s. 3			308
,, c. 104			20
15 & 16 ,, c. 48			24
,, c. 76, s. 41			226
,, s. 40			303
,, s. 141			344
,, s. 210			258
,, c. 79, s. 13			277
16 & 17 ,, c. 70, s. 127, 129, 130,			
131, 133, 134			24
17 & 18 ,, c. 10			129
,, c. 36			314
,, c. 60, s. 1			212
,, c. 116			20
,, c. 125, s. 61			183
,, c. 125, s. 79-82			239
18 & 19 ,, c. 63			34
,, c. 70, s. 18			34
19 & 20 ,, c. 74			20
,, c. 108			227
,, c. 108, s. 2			258
,, s. 25, 51, 52			279
,, s. 50			278
19 & 20 ,, c. 108			226
,, s. 63, 65, 66, 67,			
71,			227
,, c. 120	9, 22, 28		342,
,, c. 120, s. 4			17
,, s. 32			10
,, s. 32			3
,, s. 32			15
,, s. 32			4
,, s. 33, 34, 41, 43,			7
,, s. 35			4
,, s. 36			24
,, s. 44			8
21 & 22 ,, c. 57, s. 1, 4	19,		20
,, c. 75, s. 3			34
,, c. 77			22
,, c. 77, s. 3			15
,, s. 8			10

INDEX TO STATUTES. xxxvii

		PAGE			PAGE
21 & 22 Vict.	c. 77, s. 8	7	26 & 27 Vict.	c. 106	33
,,	c. 12, s. 5	277	29 & 30.	c. 57	33
22 and 23	c. 21, s. 25	25	30 & 31	c. 102, s. 6	168
,,	c. 35, s. 1	145	,,	c. 106, s. 13	33
,,	s. 2	146	,,	c. 143	20
,,	s. 3	329	31 & 32	c. 44	33
,,	s. 7	326	,,	c. 104	335
,,	s. 12	153	,,	c. 111	20
,,	s. 27	232, 333	,,	c. 114, s. 9	20
,,	s. 28	334	32 & 33	c. 71	334, 335
,,	c. 46	20	,,	c. 71, s. 14	23, 335
23 ,,	c. 15	69	,,	s. 15	339
23 & 24	c. 30	34	,,	s. 20, 22, 23	335
,,	c. 38	145	,,	s. 24	336
,,	c. 38, s. 6	261	,,	s. 25	337
,,	c. 41	34	,,	s. 26, 27	339
,,	c. 124	20	,,	s. 34, 35	340
,,	c. 126	227	,,	s. 117	339
,,	c. 136, s. 13	277	33 & 34	c. 23	25
,,	c. 154	176	,,	c. 23, s. 1, 10	30
24 & 25	c. 105, 131	20	,,	c. 35	176
,,	c. 105	19	,,	c. 44, s. 1	75
,,	c. 125	34	,,	c. 93	9, 11, 27, 341, 345, 348
,,	c. 134	334			
25 & 26	c. 17	33	,,	c. 97	69, 70, 80, 163, 316
,,	c. 52	19			
,,	c. 99	334			

ADDENDA.

Page 88, note (*w*), *add*—"See Watts *v.* Kelson, L. R. 6 Ch. App. 166."

Page 257, note (*j*), *add*—"See also Toleman *v.* Portbury, L. R. 6 Q. B. 245."

Page 260, line 4, *add*—"A statement in particulars, delivered in an action of ejectment, alleging a second breach of covenant in not paying rent, will not operate as a waiver of a prior forfeiture in permitting a sale by auction on the premises without the landlord's consent."—Toleman *v.* Portbury, *supra.*

ERRATA.

Page 168, note (*n*)—This Act seems to be wholly repealed by the 32 & 33 Vict. c. 41, s. 6.

Page 168, note (*o*)—So much of any local statute as relates to the rating of owners instead of occupiers is repealed by the 32 & 33 Vict. c. 41, s. 6, so far as the same applies to any poor-rate made after the 29th September 1869.

Page 168, line 3 from bottom of page—By the 32 & 33 Vict. c. 41, s. 1, occupiers of tenements let for not more than three months may deduct the poor-rate from their rents; and by sect. 8, where an owner having undertaken to pay the rates omits to do so, the occupier may pay and deduct the amount from his rent; and see sect. 12, where a distress is levied on the occupier.

A MANUAL

OF THE

LAW OF LANDLORD AND TENANT.

PART I.

CREATION OF THE TENANCY.

CHAPTER I.

WHO MAY BE LESSORS.

	PAGE		PAGE
1. TENANTS IN FEE SIMPLE	2	7. LORDS OF THE MANOR AND COPYHOLDERS	14
2. TENANTS IN TAIL—		8. CORPORATIONS—	
at common law	2	the crown	16
enabling statutes	3	municipal corporations	16
requisites of leases	4	ecclesiastical corporations	16
fines and recoveries	5	enabling and disabling statutes	17
3. TENANTS FOR LIFE—			
at common law	5	9. PARISH OFFICERS	20
by statute	6	10. GUARDIANS—	
tenant pur autre vie	8	in socage	21
tenants after possibility of issue extinct	9	testamentary guardians	22
tenants in dower or jointure	9	11. EXECUTORS AND ADMINISTRATORS	22
husband leasing wife's lands	9		
4. PERSONS HAVING LESS THAN A FREEHOLD INTEREST—		12. TRUSTEES OF BANKRUPTS	23
tenants for years	11	13. PERSONS UNDER DISABILITY—	
from year to year	12	lunatics	24
for less than years	12	persons in a state of intoxication	25
at will	12	persons under duress	25
5. JOINT-TENANTS AND TENANTS IN COMMON	12	persons attainted	25
6. MORTGAGOR AND MORTGAGEE	13	married women	26
		infants	27

By law all land is ultimately held of the sovereign. No subject, therefore, can possess a greater estate in

A

law than a tenancy, a word which implies the holding from some superior; but the more ordinary use of the word tenancy is where it is intended to mean a holding for a certain definite term, subject to some rent or fine, accompanied by certain obligations of the lessor and lessee respectively. Upon such a holding arises the ordinary relation of landlord and tenant; and it is to the nature and incidents of such a holding, and the obligations arising from it, that the present volume is intended to be confined. In the present chapter it is proposed to show who may be lessors.

1. TENANTS IN FEE-SIMPLE.

The tenant in fee-simple has the entire uncontrolled disposition of the property, and may demise for any term whatever (*a*). By the common law, any person seised of an estate in fee-simple in lands could convey the lands to be held of himself in fee-simple, and thus create a tenancy in fee-simple between himself and his grantee; but by the statute of *quia emptores* (*b*), there can no longer be held of a subject any tenancy in fee-simple which has been created since the passing of that Act (*c*).

2. TENANTS IN TAIL.

At common law.

At common law a tenant in tail might make a lease for his own life (*d*). If a tenant in tail after the statute *De donis* (*e*) made a lease for years and died, the lease was not absolutely determined by his

(*a*) Com. Dig. tit. Estate (G) 2.
(*b*) 18 Ed. I. c. 1.
(*c*) Stephen's Blackstone, i. 240.

(*d*) Com. Dig. tit. Estate (G) 2.
(*e*) 13 Ed. I. c. 1.

death, but the issue in tail might affirm or avoid it (*f*). Acceptance of the rent or fealty, or bringing an action for recovery thereof, or an action of waste, were such acts as would amount to a confirmation, because these plainly manifested an intent to keep the lessee in possession upon the terms of his lease (*g*). But if the tenant made an under-lease, and the issue in tail accepted rent from the under-lessee, this would have been no confirmation of the lease. If the tenant *assigned* part of the land for the residue of the term, and the issue accepted rent from the assignee, this would have confirmed the lease (*h*). If the tenant in tail died whilst the right of the lessee was but an *interesse termini* (*i*), and the issue entered and aliened, the alienee might elect to confirm or avoid the lease (*j*). But if the tenant in tail granted an immediate lease, and the issue aliened without entry, the alienee was bound by the lease, by reason that the issue had only a right of entry, which is not alienable (*k*). Neither persons in remainder nor in reversion were bound by the leases of the tenant in tail; against them such leases were void, and they could not confirm them on the death of the tenant in tail.

By the 32 Hen. VIII., c. 28, a tenant in tail was enabled to make leases for twenty-one years or three lives, if such leases were made in conformity with the provisions of the statute (*l*). Such leases were bind-

Enabling statutes.

(*f*) Bac. Abr. Leases (D) 1; Co. Litt. 45.
(*g*) Bac. Abr. Leases (D) 1.
(*h*) Bac. Abr. Leases (D) 1.
(*i*) See *infra*, c. 4, s. 1 n.
(*j*) Bac. Abr. Leases (D) 1; Co. Litt. 349.
(*k*) Bac. Abr. tit. Leases, 311, 315, 324.
(*l*) See Rowdon *v.* Maltster,

Cro. Car. 42; Doe *v.* Jenkins, 5 Bing. 469; Rees *v.* Phillips, Wight. 69; Doe *d.* Phillips *v.* Rollings, 4 C. B. 180; Bac. Abr. tit. Leases (D); Co. Litt. 44 a; 8 Co. 34; Lampet's case, 3 Co. 64 b. The above statute is repealed by the 19 & 20 Vict. c. 120, s. 32. See *post*, p. 4.

ing on the issue in tail, but not on the remainder-man or reversioner.

Requisites of leases under. To make a good lease under the above statute, the following requisites were necessary:—1st, That the lease should be by indenture, not by deed poll, which was required in order that the tenant might be liable to actions of covenant in case of his committing breaches of its stipulations; 2dly, That it should begin from the day on which it was made, which was intended to prevent its termination from being postponed to a very distant period, since otherwise a tenant in tail might have granted a lease to begin twenty years hence, and then, if he had himself died about that period, it would have taken effect almost entirely out of the estate of the issue (*m*); 3dly, That any other lease in being of the same land should be surrendered or expired within a year of making the new one, since otherwise the reversion immediately expectant on the interest of the person in possession would have been out of the issue in tail so long as the two leases continued concurrent; 4thly, The lease must not have exceeded three lives or twenty-one years since it was thought unjust to keep the issue longer out of possession; 5thly, The lease must have been of lands which had been usually let for twenty years before the lease made; 6thly, The rent accustomably paid during that period, or a greater rent, must have been reserved upon it; and, lastly, It must not have been without impeachment of waste (*n*).

The statute of Hen. VIII. is repealed by the 19 & 20 Vict., c. 120, ss. 32, 35, by which a tenant in tail of settled estates has the same power to make leases as

(*m*) See s. 2, Bac. Abr. tit. Leases (E).

(*n*) See s. 1, *post*, p. 17, and Bac. Abr. tit. Leases (E); Co. Litt. 44 a b.

a tenant for life has (*o*). Leases made by persons having an estate in right of their churches are, however, excepted in the repealing section, and therefore as to them the statute of Hen. VIII. still applies (*p*).

By the 3 & 4 Will. IV., c. 74, called the Act for the Abolition of Fines and Recoveries, after the 31st day of December 1833, every actual tenant in tail (*q*), whether in possession, remainder, contingency, or otherwise, has full power to dispose of for an estate in fee-simple absolute, *or for any less estate*, the lands entailed as against issue in tail (*r*), and if there be a protector of the settlement, with his consent as against all persons whose estates are to take effect after the determination, or in defeasance of such estate tail (*s*). By sect. 41 every assurance by a tenant in tail, except a lease not exceeding twenty-one years, commencing from the date of such lease, or from any time not exceeding twelve months from the date of such lease, at a rack-rent, or not less than five-sixths of a rack-rent, is inoperative, unless such assurance is enrolled in Chancery within six months after its execution (*t*).

Fines and recoveries.

3. TENANTS FOR LIFE.

At common law a tenant for life cannot make a lease to continue longer than his own life. It determines

At common law.

(*o*) See *infra*, Tenant for Life, p. 6.
(*p*) See *infra*, p. 17.
(*q*) See *infra*, pp. 26, 24, and 27, as to infants, lunatics, or married women, who are tenants in tail. See 19 & 20 Vict. c. 120.
(*r*) Sect. 15.
(*s*) Sect. 34.
(*t*) The deed may be enrolled by either vendor or purchaser, and the enrolment should be made as soon as possible after execution. Cattell *v.* Carroll, 4 Y. & C. 228. If the lands lie in a register county, the deed must, it is conceived, be enrolled in compliance with the local Acts, as well as under this Act. Enrolment is not necessary for a lease of copyhold land, but there must be an entry on the court rolls. 3 & 4 Will. IV. c. 74, s. 54.

mines absolutely on his death (*u*), or at the end of the then current year of the tenancy (*v*), and cannot be confirmed by any acts of the remainder-man or reversioner (*w*); but such acts will be evidence of a new tenancy from year to year on the terms of the original lease (*x*). If the remainder-man, however, lies by, and with notice of what the tenant is about to do permits him to lay out money in rebuilding, equity will interfere and prevent him from insisting on the determination of the lease (*y*).

By statute.

By the 19 & 20 Vict., c. 120, s. 32, " It shall be lawful for any person entitled to the possession or to the receipt of the rents and profits of any settled estates for an estate for life (*z*), or for a term of years determinable with his life, or for any greater estate, either in his own right or in right of his wife, unless the settlement shall contain an express declaration that it shall not be lawful for such person to make such demise; and also for any person entitled to the possession or to the receipt of the rents and profits of any unsettled estates as tenant by the curtesy or in dower, or in right of a wife who is seised in fee, without any application to the Court (*a*), to demise the same, or any part thereof, except the principal mansion-house and the demesnes thereof and other

(*u*) Bac. Abr. Leases (I); Adams *v.* Gibney, 6 Bing. 656.
(*v*) 14 & 15 Vict. c. 25, s. 1.
(*w*) Doe d. Simpson *v.* Butcher, Doug. 50; Jenkins d. Yates, *v.* Church, Cowp. 482; Roe d. Jordan *v.* Ward, 1 Hen. Bl. 97; Doe d. Potter *v.* Archer, 1 Bos. & Pul. 531; Ludford *v.* Barber, 1 T. R. 86; Jones *v.* Verney, Willes. 196.
(*x*) Doe d. Martin *v.* Watts, 7 T. R. 83; Doe d. Collins *v.* Weller, ib. 478; Roe d. Jordan *v.*

Prideaux, 10 Exch. 157; Doe d. Tucker *v.* Moore, 1 B. & Ad. 365; Doe d. Pennington *v.* Taniere, 12 Q. B. 998; Oakley *v.* Monck, L. R. 1 Excb. 159.
(*y*) Stiles *v.* Cowper, 3 Atk. 692; East India Co. *v.* Vincent, 2 Atk. 83; Jackson *v.* Cator, 5 Ves. 688; Dunn *v.* Spurrier, 7 Ves. 231, 235, 236.
(*z*) This will include a tenant in tail after possibility of issue extinct. See sect. 2.
(*a*) Of Chancery.

lands usually occupied therewith, from time to time, for any term not exceeding twenty-one years, to take effect in possession: provided that every such demise be made by deed, and the best rent that can reasonably be obtained be thereby reserved, without any fine, or other benefit in the nature of a fine, which rent shall be incident to the immediate reversion; and provided that such demise be not made without impeachment of waste, and do contain a covenant for payment of the rent, and such other usual and proper covenants as the lessor shall think fit; and also a condition of re-entry on non-payment, for a period of not less than twenty-eight days, of the rent thereby reserved, and on non-observance of any of the covenants or conditions therein contained; and provided a counterpart of every deed of lease be executed by the lessee."

By sect. 33, " Every demise authorised by the last preceding section shall be valid against the person granting the same, and all other persons entitled to estates subsequent to the estate of such person under or by virtue of the same settlement, if the estates be settled; and, in the case of unsettled estates, against all persons claiming through or under the wife (or husband), as the case may be, of the person granting the same;" and by the 21 & 22 Vict., c. 77, s. 8, against the wife of a husband entitled in her right.

By the 19 & 20 Vict., c. 120, s. 34, " The execution of any lease by the lessor or lessors shall be deemed sufficient evidence that a counterpart of such lease has been duly executed by the lessee, as required by this Act."

By sect. 41, " For the purposes of this act a person shall be deemed to be entitled to the possession, or to the receipt of the rents and profits of estates, although his estate may be charged or incumbered either by himself or by the settlor, or otherwise howsoever, to any extent; but the estates or interests of the parties entitled to any such charge or encumbrance shall not be affected by the acts of the person entitled to the possession, or to the receipt of the rents and profits as aforesaid, unless they shall concur therein."

By sect. 43, " Nothing in this Act shall authorise the granting of a lease of any copyhold or customary hereditaments not warranted by the custom of the manor, without the consent of the lord, nor otherwise prejudice or affect the rights of any lord of a manor."

By sect. 44, " The provisions of this Act shall extend to all settlements, whether made before or after it shall come in force, except those as to demises to be made without application to the Court, which shall extend only to settlements made after this Act shall come in force."

Tenant *pur autre vie.*

A tenant *pur autre vie* is in the same position as an ordinary tenant for life, except that his leases will determine, not on his own death, but on that of the *cestui que vie*, or rather at the expiration of the then current year of the tenancy (*b*); and he may therefore make a lease to commence after his own death (*c*). By the 19 Car. II., c. 6, after reciting that whereas divers lords of manors and others have use to grant states by copy of court-roll, for one, two, or more lives, according to the custom of their several manors, and have also granted estates by lease for one or more life or lives, or else for years determinable upon one or

(*b*) 14 & 15 Vict. c. 25, s. 1.   (*c*) Dale's case, Cro. Eliz. 182.

more life or lives, it is enacted by sect. 2, that "if the person or persons for whose life or lives such estates have been or shall be granted, as aforesaid, shall remain beyond the seas, or elsewhere absent themselves in this realm, by the space of seven years together, and no sufficient and evident proof be made of the lives of such person or persons respectively in any action commenced for recovery of such tenements by the lessors or reversioners, in every such case the person or persons upon whose life or lives such estate depended shall be accounted as naturally dead; and in every action for the recovery of the said tenement by the lessors or reversioners, their heirs or assignees, the judges before whom such action shall be brought shall direct the jury to give their verdict as if the person so remaining beyond the seas, or otherwise absenting himself, were dead." Sect. 3 contains a proviso respecting persons evicted under the Act, when the *cestuis que vie* turn out not to be dead. The 6 Anne, c. 18, contains provisions enabling the Court of Chancery, in certain cases, to cause the *cestuis que vie* to be produced.

The estates of tenants after possibility of issue extinct, by the curtesy, or in dower or jointure, though growing out of the original estate of inheritance, afford them no more than a life-interest; such tenants, therefore, stand precisely on the same footing as tenants for life, and are restricted to the like limits in the disposal of their respective lands (*d*). Tenants after possibility of issue extinct, by the curtesy, tenants in dower or jointure.

First, As to wife's freehold (*e*); at common law, a lease by deed made by the husband and wife, or by Husband leasing wife's land.

(*d*) See *ante*, p. 6, Tenants for Life, and 19 & 20 Vict. c. 120.
(*e*) See *post*, p. 26, Married Women; and Part 4, c. 2, s. 3, Married Women's Property Act, 1870.

the husband alone, of the wife's freehold is good during the coverture (*f*). Upon the death of the husband in the wife's lifetime, it is voidable by her, but may be confirmed by her; as, for instance, by the acceptance of rent due after the husband's death (*g*). But where a lease is made by husband and wife without deed, it is void as against the surviving wife, for it cannot be said to be her lease (*h*). If the husband survives his wife, and becomes tenant by the curtesy, the lease as against him will be good during his life, or until the end of the term, if that should first happen; but if the husband survives the wife, and does not become tenant by the curtesy, the lease, upon the wife's death, will be void as against her heir-at-law, and those claiming through her (*i*).

By the Enabling Act, 32 Hen. VIII., c. 28, husbands seised in right of their wives, or jointly with their wives, for any estate in fee or in tail, were empowered to grant leases for any term not exceeding twenty-one years or three lives, subject to certain restrictions; (*j*) but this Act was repealed by the 35th sect. of the 19 & 20 Vict., c. 120.

By the 19 & 20 Vict., c. 120 (*k*), ss. 32, 33, amended by the 21 & 22 Vict., c. 77, s. 8, a hus-

---

(*f*) Wiscot's case, 2 Co. R. 61 b; Bateman v. Allen, Cro. Eliz. 438; Bac. Abr. tit. Leases (C) 1; 2 Wms. Saund. 180 n (q).

(*g*) Henstead's case, 5 Co. R. 10; Co. Litt. 55 b; Anon. Dyer, 159 pl. 36. 1 Roll Abr. 349; Greenwood v. Tyber, Cro. Jac. 563; Jackson v. Mordaunt, Cro. Eliz. 112; Doe d. Collins v. Weller 7 T. R. 478; Parry v. Hindle, 2 Taunt. 180; 2 Wms. Saund. 180 n (q); and see Toler v. Slater, L. R. 3 Q. B. 42; 37 L. J. Q. B. 93.

(*h*) Walsall v. Heath, Cro. Eliz. 656; Greenwood v. Tyber, Cro. Jac. 564; 2 Wms. Saund. 180 a (n).

(*i*) Howe v. Scarrott, 4 H. & N. 723, 28 L. J. Ex. 325; Hill v. Saunders, 2 Bing. 112 (on appeal), 4 B & C. 529.

(*j*) See *ante*, Tenants in Tail, p. 4, and Ecclesiastical Corporations, p. 16; also Bac. Abr. tit. Leases (C) 1; and 2 Wms. Saund. 180 n (q).

(*k*) This Act (s. 35) repealed the Enabling Act of 32 Hen. VIII. c. 28.

band seised in right of his wife of any settled estates for an estate for life, or for a term of years determinable with her life, or for any greater estate (unless the settlement contains an express declaration to the contrary); and also a husband entitled to the possession, or to the receipt of the rents and profits of any *unsettled estates*, as tenant by the curtesy, or in right of a wife who is seised in fee, can, without any application to the Court of Chancery, make leases for any term not exceeding twenty-one years, if made in accordance with the provisions of these statutes (*l*).

Secondly, as to the wife's chattel interests (not being choses in action), the husband, at common law, has the absolute disposal of them during his life (*m*), and may not only make leases of them to commence *in presenti*, but even to commence after his death (*n*).

4. Persons having less than a Freehold Interest.

A tenant for years may part with any portion of his term by way of lease, and the grantee thereof will become his tenant; but if he make a lease for the whole of his term, it will operate as an assignment, and no tenancy will be created between him and the grantee, who will hold of the lessor of whom the tenant for years himself held, and will, in fact, occupy his place (*o*).

<small>Tenants for years.</small>

(*l*) See *ante*, Tenants in Tail, pp. 3 and 4.
(*m*) But he cannot devise them, for his devise does not take effect until his death, when his interest ceases. Bac. Abr. tit. Baron and Feme, c. 2.
(*n*) Co. Litt. 46 b, 300, 351 a. See Druce *v*. Denison, 6 Ves. 385; Wildman *v*. Wildman, 9 Ves. 177; Fitzgerald *v*. Fitzgerald, 8 C. B. 592; Bac. Abr. tit. Baron and

Feme, c. 2; but see *infra*, "Married Women's Property Act, 1870," Part 4, c. 2, s. 3.
(*o*) Hicks *v*. Downing, 1 Ld. Raym. 99; Wollaston *v*. Hakewill, 3 M. &. G. 297; Thorn *v*. Woolcombe, 3 B. & Ad. 586; Preece *v*. Corrie, 5 Bing. 24. Parmenter *v*. Webber, 8 Taunt. 593; Beardmore *v*. Wilson, L. R. 4 C. P. 57; 38 L. J. C. P. 91.

CREATION OF TENANCY. [PART I.

Tenant from year to year. A tenant from year to year is considered to have such an interest in the land demised that he may lease it for years, and the term will continue in force so long as his own tenancy lasts (*p*). So also he may under-let from year to year, and the lease will operate as a demise from year to year during the continuance of the original demise (*q*), and, in either case, he will have a reversion (*r*).

Tenants for less than years. Under a tenancy for one year, or for less than one year, provided it is for a term fixed and certain, the tenant has the same power of assigning or leasing as a tenant for years (*s*).

Tenants at will. Tenants at will, or on sufferance, cannot demise (*t*).

5. JOINT-TENANTS, TENANTS IN COMMON, AND COPARCENERS.

Joint-tenants should join in making a lease, for if one of two joint-tenants make a lease of the whole, his moiety only will pass (*u*); and if a lease purporting to be made by both is executed by one only, it will pass nothing more than the moiety of him who has executed it (*v*). A lease of his moiety by a joint-tenant, who subsequently dies, will bind the survivor, and this even if the lease be made to commence after the lessor's death (*w*). Where joint-

---

(*p*) Mackray *v.* Mackreth, 4 Doug. 213.
(*q*) Oxley *v.* James, 13 M. & W. 209.
(*r*) Pike *v.* Eyre, 9 B. &. C. 909; Curtis *v.* Wheeler, Moo. & M. 495.
(*s*) Rex *v.* Aldborough, 1 East. 598; Shep. Touch, 268.
(*t*) Sureper *v.* Randal, Cro. Eliz. 156; Sparke's case, Cro. Eliz. 156; Moss *v.* Gallimore, 1 Doug. 279;
Thunder *d.* Weaver *v.* Belcher, 3 East. 449; Jones *v.* Clerk, Hard. 47; Dinsdale *v.* Iles, 2 Lev. 88, S.C., Sir T. Ray. 224, 1 Ventr. 247; Birch *v.* Wright, 1 T. R. 382.
(*u*) Bellingham *v.* Alsop, Cro. Jac. 53; Co. Litt. 186 a.
(*v*) Cartwright's case, 1 Vent. 136.
(*w*) Grute *v.* Locroft, Cro. Eliz. 287; Harbin *v.* Barton, Moor. 395; Whitlock *v.* Horton, Cro.

tenants make a lease, and one dies, the survivors are entitled to the whole rent, and the interest of the lessee continues (x). Tenants in common cannot make a joint-lease of the whole of their estate (y); and if the lease purport to do so, it is merely the lease of each for their respective parts, and the confirmation of each for the part of the other; neither is there any estoppel, because an actual interest passes from each (z). If one joint-tenant or tenant in common makes a lease for years of his part to his companion, this is good, and such a lease extinguishes the jointure for the time, and gives a right of distress (a). So also a joint-lease by coparceners operates as a several demise by each of her own share (b). One coparcener cannot sue separately for her portion of the rent accruing to her and her fellows upon a lease made by the ancestor (c), although it would probably be different if the lease had been made by the coparceners.

6. Mortgagor and Mortgagee.

All leases made by a mortgagor subsequent to the mortgage and before the foreclosure, except under an express power (d), are void as against the mortgagee (e); but such leases are by estoppel good as between

Jac. 91; Bellingham v. Alsop, Cro. Jac. 52; Clerk v. Clerk, 2 Vern. 323, Litt. s. 289.

(x) Henstead's case, 5 Co. Rep. 10 b; Doe d. Aslin v. Summersett, 1 B. & Ad. 135, 140.

(y) Com. Dig. Estates, (K.) 8; Burne v. Cambridge, 1 Moo. & R. 539; Heatherley d. Worthington v. Weston, 2 Wils. 232; Doe v. Errington, 1 A. & E. 750.

(z) Mantle v. Wollington, Cro. Jac. 166; Brooks v. Foxcroft, Clayt. 137; Jurdain v. Steere, Cro. Jac. 83; Com. Dig. tit. Estates (G.) 6, (K.) 8; Bac. Abr.,

Joint-Tenants and Tenants in Common, 1 Roll. Ab. 877, (L.) 48, 52.

(a) Bac. Abr. tit. Leases, 401; Co. Litt. 186 a; Cowper v. Fletcher, 34 L. J. Q. B. 187.

(b) Milliner v. Robinson, Moore, pl. 939.

(c) Decharms v. Horwood, 10 Bing. 526.

(d) Bevan v. Habgood, 30 L. J. Ch. 107.

(e) Powell on Mortgages, 157; Keech v. Hall, 1 Doug. 21; Thunder d. Weaver v. Belcher, 3 East. 449–451.

the parties (*f*). The mortgagee in possession cannot make a lease so as to bind the mortgagor if he should afterwards redeem (*g*), unless to avoid an apparent loss, and merely of necessity. In practice, when it is necessary to make a lease of the mortgaged premises, both mortgagor and mortgagee should join in the lease (*h*). With respect to a lease of lands mortgaged after the making of the lease, the tenants may safely continue to pay their rents to the mortgagor until they receive notice from the mortgagee (*i*).

7. LORDS OF THE MANOR AND COPYHOLDERS.

Lords of manors may make voluntary grants of copyholds as well as admittances, according to the custom of the manor (*j*). Where there is no custom for that purpose, the lord of the manor cannot make a new grant of copyhold (*k*).

By 13 Geo. III., c. 81, s. 15, lords of manors, with the consent of three fourths of the commoners, may demise for not more than four years any part of the wastes and commons, not exceeding one-twelfth part, for the best rent that can be obtained by auction, the same to be applied in draining, fencing, and improving the residue. A copyholder cannot make a lease for more than one year without a license or by special custom, without thereby incurring a forfeiture of his

---

(*f*) Cuthbertson *v.* Irving, 28 L. J. Ex. 306.

(*g*) Hungerford *v.* Clay, 9 Mod.; 1 Powell on Mortg. 188; Franklinski *v.* Ball, 34 L. J. Ch. 153.

(*h*) Doe *d.* Barney *v.* Adams, 2 C. & J. 232; Doe *d.* Hughes *v.* Bucknell, 8 C. & P. 566; Carpenter *v.* Parker, 3 C. B. N.S. 206; Franklinski *v.* Ball, *supra*;

Saunders *v.* Merryweather, 3 H. & C. 902.

(*i*) See *post*, Part 4, c. 1, s. 1, Attornment; 4 Anne, c. 16 s. 10; Trent *v.* Hunt, 9 Exch. 14–23.

(*j*) Badger *v.* Ford, 3 B. & A. 153; Rex *v.* Welby, 2 M. & S. 504.

(*k*) Rex *v.* Hornchurch, 2 B. & Ald. 189.

estate (*l*); but he may for a less term by custom of the manor (*m*).

By special custom a copyholder may make a lease for years, or for life, without license from the lord (*n*). A custom for copyholders in fee to lease for any number of years, without license, on condition of the term ceasing on the lessor's death, is a good custom (*o*). The powers of leasing given by sect. 32 of 19 and 20 Vict., c. 120 (*p*), are extended by 21 and 22 Vict. c. 77, s. 3, to the lords of settled manors to give licenses to their copyhold and customary tenants to grant leases. The copyholder, however, having license to demise, ought not to exceed the license (*q*), but he may lease for a shorter term than that permitted by the license (*r*). A tenant at will of a manor cannot grant a copyholder license to alien for years; and if a tenant for life of a manor grants a license to alien for years, it determines at his death (*s*). A lease by a copyholder, without license of the lord, and contrary to the custom of the manor, is good against all but the lord (*t*). If a copyholder make a lease with license, the lessee may assign without license, or make an under-lease (*u*).

(*l*) Anon. Moor. 184; East. *v.* Harding, Cro. Eliz. 489; Jackman *v.* Hoddesden, Id. 351.
(*m*) 1 Scriven on Copyholds, 457. As to what is a lease by a copyholder for more than one year, see Lady Montague's case, Cro. Jac. 301; Luttrell *v.* Weston, Id. 308; Matthews *v.* Whetton, Cro. Car. 233.
(*n*) 1 Scriven on Copyholds, 457.
(*o*) Turner *v.* Hodges, Hutt. 101.
(*p*) See *ante*, s. 2, Tenants for Life, p. 5.
(*q*) Hadden *v.* Arrowsmith, Owen 73; Cro. Eliz. 461; Jackson *v.* Neal; Cro. Eliz. 394; Com. Dig. tit. Copyhold (K) 3 Doe d. Robinson *v.* Bousfield, 6 Q. B. 492.
(*r*) Goodwin *v.* Longhurst. Cro. Eliz. 535; Worledge *v.* Benbury, Cro. Jac. 437; Isherwood *v.* Oldknow, 3 M. & S. 382; Easton *v.* Pratt, 2 H. & C. 676.
(*s*) Com. Dig. tit. Copyhold (C.) 3.
(*t*) Doe d. Tressider *v.* Tressider, 1 Q. B. 416; Doe d. Robinson *v.* Bousfield, 6 Q. B. 492.
(*u*) Com. Dig. Copyhold (K) 3.

8. CORPORATIONS.

Corporations. At common law a corporation may make a lease by deed under their seal for any term of years or for lives, consistently with their estate, which lease will be binding upon their successors, except in cases where their power so to demise has been taken away by Act of Parliament, or is affected by their bye-laws and private statutes (*v*).

The Crown. By the 1 Anne, c. 7, s. 5, the Crown is restrained from granting leases for a longer term than twenty-one years or three lives, and subject to certain conditions; and with respect to building or repairing leases, to fifty years or three lives.

Municipal corporations. The power of municipal corporations to lease their lands is restrained by the 5 & 6 Will. IV., c. 76, ss. 94–96, by which they are prohibited from granting leases for a longer term than thirty-one years without the consent of the Lords Commissioners of the Treasury, except in the case of renewed leases (*w*), and building leases for terms not exceeding seventy-five years.

Ecclesiastical and eleemosynary corporations. At the common law, ecclesiastical corporations aggregate and eleemosynary corporations, could make any lease they thought fit to make consistent with their estate, and so could ecclesiastical corporations sole, with the consent of certain other persons. Thus, for example, archbishops and bishops could make leases with the consent of their dean and chapter (*x*).

(*v*) Smith *v.* Barrett, 1 Sid. 161. But a tenancy from year to year may arise under a demise by a corporation not under seal. See Ecclesiastical Commissioners *v.* Merrall, L. R. 4 Ex. 162; 38 L. J. Ex. 93.

(*w*) Att.-Gen. *v.* Gt. Yarmouth, 21 Beav. 625.

(*x*) Bishop of Salisbury's case, 10 Rep. 60; Anon. Dyer, 58 b, pl. 7; Co. Litt. 301 a; Bac. Abr. Leases (G) 2. As to the persons by whom confirmation is to be made, see Woodfall, Landlord and Tenant, p. 21, 9th ed.

By the 32 Hen. VIII., c. 28, s. 1 (called the Enabling Statute) (*y*), all persons seised of lands in fee-simple in right of their churches (*z*), (except parsons and vicars) (*a*), could make leases for twenty-one years, or three lives, without the confirmation of any person, provided they conformed to the conditions imposed by the statute (*b*). These large powers were found inconvenient in practice, and have been restrained by several statutes (*c*), the result of which is as follows:—

Enabling statute.

1. Where archbishops and bishops do not follow the provisions of the statute 32 Hen. VIII., c. 28, they may make leases for twenty-one years, or three lives (but for no longer period), with the confirmation of their deans and chapters, so that they pursue the provisions of the 1 Eliz., c. 19 (*d*).

Disabling statutes.

2. All other ecclesiastical corporations *sole*, including parsons and vicars *with confirmation*, and all ecclesiastical and eleemosynary corporations *aggregate* (*e*) *without confirmation*, may make leases for the like period, following the provisions of the 1 Eliz., c. 19, 13 Eliz., c. 10, and 18 Eliz., c. 11; but all ecclesiastical and eleemosynary corporations (except archbishops and bishops) may lease their houses in

(*y*) This Act has been repealed by 19 & 20 Vict. c. 120, except so far as relates to leases made by persons having an estate in right of their churches.

(*z*) This extends to prebendaries, chancellors, archdeacons, precentors. Acton *v.* Pritcher, 4 Leon. 51; Watkinson *v.* Mann, Cro. Eliz. 349; Bisco *v.* Holt, Lev. 112, Sid. 158. It has been doubted whether a perpetual curate is within this Act. Doe *d.* Richardson *v.* Thomas, 9 A. & E. 556.

(*a*) See sect. 4.

(*b*) The conditions are stated *ante*, p. 3.

(*c*) The following are the *Disabling Statutes*:—1 Eliz. c. 19; 13 Eliz. c. 10; 14 Eliz. c. 11; 18 Eliz. c. 11; 39 Eliz. c. 5, s. 2; 1 Jac. I. c. 3. By the 43 Eliz. c. 9, s. 8, all judgments had for the intent to have and enjoy any lease contrary to the above statutes, are declared void.

(*d*) See Bac. Abr. tit. Leases, p. 330.

(*e*) Case of Magdalen College, 11 Rep. 76.

cities and towns, corporate boroughs, or market-towns, with not more than ten acres of land appurtenant, for forty years, subject to the provisions of the 14 Eliz., c. 11, ss. 17, 19 (*f*).

These statutes were further amended by the 39 & 40 Geo. III., c. 41, which permitted ecclesiastical corporations, sole or aggregate, to apportion the rents of lands formerly demised by one lease among the several parts in which it might be demised (*g*). The 6 & 7 Will. IV., c. 20, explained by the 6 & 7 Will. IV., c. 64, imposed certain restrictions on the renewal of leases by ecclesiastical persons.

Enabling statutes. By the 5 Vict., c. 27 (*h*), incumbents of ecclesias-

(*f*) Bac. Abr. tit. Leases, p. 331; Crane *v.* Taylor, Hob. 269; Hunt *v.* Singleton, Cro. Eliz. 564. The three statutes (13 Eliz. c. 10, 14 Eliz. c. 11, 18 Eliz. c. 11) are to be read together as forming one law on the same subject-matter, and where leases of houses, &c., which were exempted out of the 13 Eliz. by the 14 Eliz., do not observe the provisions of the latter statute, they fall within the general enactments of the first statute, and are made void thereby. In other words, a lease not warranted by 14 Eliz. remains restrained by the 13 Eliz., which makes leases against that act void. *Per* Tindal, C.J., in Vivian *v.* Blomberg, 3 Bing. N.C. 324, 325. It is apparent from the statutes 32 Hen. VIII. c. 28, and 13 Eliz. c. 10, that the Legislature meant to confine the authority to let to lands formerly let, and capable of producing profit. Goodtitle *d.* Clarges *v.* Hunucar, 2 Doug. 565. As to construction of these statutes, see Doe *d.* Tennyson *v.* Lord Yarborough, 7 Moore, 258, S.C. 1 Bing. 24; Bac. Abr. tit. Leases; 1 Platt on Leases, p. 240; and Chitty's Statutes, "Leases." A lease declared void by the 13 Eliz. has been held good during the life of the lessor, *per* Bayley, J., in Doe *d.* Bryan *v.* Banks, 4 B. & A. 407; and even after the lessor's death such a lease is not void, but voidable, and may be confirmed by his successor, *per* Holroyd, J., in Edwards *v.* Dick, 4 B. & A. 217.

(*g*) See Doe *d.* Shrewsbury *v.* Wilson, 5 B. & A. 386; Doe *d.* Egremont *v.* Williams, 11, Q. B. 688.

(*h*) Previous to this statute all colleges, cathedrals, and other ecclesiastical or eleemosynary corporations, and all parsons and vicars, were restrained from making any leases of their lands unless under the following regulations:—1st, The leases not to exceed twenty-one years, or three lives from the making; 2d, The accustomed rent or more was to be yearly reserved thereon, respecting which the 39 & 40 Geo. III. c. 41, is particularly explanatory; 3d, Houses in corporation or market towns might be let for forty years, provided they were

tical benefices were enabled, with the consent of the bishop and patron, to lease lands (*i*) belonging to their benefices on farming leases for fourteen years, subject to certain restrictions. And by the 24 & 25 Vict., c. 105, no grant by copy of court-roll, or any lease by any future prebendary (*j*), rector, vicar-perpetual, curate, or incumbent of their lands is to be valid, unless made in conformity with the provisions of the 5 Vict., c. 27 (*k*).

By "The Ecclesiastical Leasing Act (1842)" (*l*), as amended by "The Ecclesiastical Leasing Act (1858)" (*m*), all ecclesiastical corporations, sole and aggregate, are enabled, *with the consent of the Ecclesiastical Commissioners for England*, and with such further consents as are therein mentioned, to grant building and repairing leases for any term not exceeding ninety-nine years (*n*); leases of running water, way-leaves, and other rights and easements, for any term not exceeding sixty years (*o*); also mining leases

not the mansion-house of the lessors, nor had above ten acres of ground belonging to them, provided the lessees were bound to keep them in repair; 4th, Where there was an old lease no concurrent lease could be made, unless where the old one would expire within three years; 5th, Leases might not be renewed before their expiration, unless according to the provisions of 39 & 40 Geo. III. c. 41, s. 10, and 6 & 7 Will. IV. c. 20, and c. 64; 6th, No lease could be made without impeachment of waste; 7th, All bonds and covenants tending to frustrate the provisions of the statutes 13 & 18 Eliz. were void. Woodfall, "Landlord and Tenant," 6th edit., p. 17.

(*i*) Glebe lands which have been usually let on lease by incumbents are not within the Act. Jenkins *v.* Green, 28 L. J. Ch. 822, S.C. 28 Beav. 87.

(*j*) See further 25 & 26 Vict. c. 52.

(*k*) Green *v.* Jenkins, 29 L. J. Ch. 505, S.C. 28 Beav. 87. At common law, a lease by the incumbent of a benefice, in whatever terms it was framed, operated as a demise so long only as he continued incumbent, for he could not pass a greater interest. Wheeler *v.* Heydon, Cro. Jac. 328; Price *v.* Williams, 1 M. & W. 6; Doe *d.* Kirby *v.* Carter, Ry. & Moo. 237; Doe *d.* Tennyson *v.* Yarborough, 1 Bing. 24.

(*l*) 5 & 6 Vict. c. 108. This Act is not to restrain existing powers of leasing. Sect. 8.

(*m*) 21 & 22 Vict. c. 57.

(*n*) Sect. 1.

(*o*) Sect. 4.

for any term not exceeding sixty years (*p*). All of which leases are subject to certain restrictions and conditions for the benefit of their successors; and it must be made to appear to the satisfaction of the Ecclesiastical Commissioners that such leases are for the permanent advantage of the estate before their consent is given (*q*).

By the 14 & 15 Vict., c. 104, entitled "An Act to facilitate the Management and Improvement of Episcopal and Capitular Estates for England"(*r*), ecclesiastical corporations are enabled, with the approval of the Church Estate Commissioners, from time to time to grant mining or building leases as therein mentioned (*s*).

9. PARISH OFFICERS.

Churchwardens and overseers.

The 59 Geo. III., c. 12, s. 17, vests in the churchwardens and overseers of the poor, in the nature of a body corporate, all buildings, lands, and hereditaments belonging to the parish (*t*). And this Act, its

(*p*) Sect. 6.
(*q*) 21 & 22 Vict. c. 57, s. 1.
(*r*) Amended by 17 & 18 Vict. c. 16; 17 & 18 Vict. c. 116; 19 & 20 Vict. c. 74; 20 & 21 Vict. c. 74; 22 & 23 Vict. c. 46; 23 & 24 Vict. c. 124; 24 & 25 Vict. cc. 105, 131; 30 & 31 Vict. c. 143; 31 & 32 Vict. c. 111; 31 & 32 Vict. c. 114, s. 9.
(*s*) Sect. 9.
(*t*) Previously to the passing of this act, great difficulty was experienced on the subject of leases of parish property; for although, by special custom of London, the parson and churchwardens of a parish were a corporation to purchase and demise lands (Warner's Case, Cro. Jac. 532), yet, in

general, neither churchwardens nor overseers, separately or conjointly, in respect of their official capacity, had any legal interest in parish property to demise. Co. Litt. 3 a; Doe *d*. Grundy *v*. Clarke, 14 East. 488; Phillips *v*. Pearce, 5 B. & C. 433; Doe *d*. Higgs *v*. Terry, 4 A. & E. 274; Doe *d*. Hobbs *v*. Cockell, 4 A. & E. 478; Doe *d*. Norton *v*. Webster, 12 A. & E. 444, note (*a*). But before the statute, a person holding under a lease granted by parish officers, of lands belonging to the parish, was a tenant from year to year. Doe *d*. Higgs *v*. Terry, see *supra*; Doe *d*. Hobbs *v*. Cockell, see *supra*.

object being the proper management of parochial property, applies to those cases only where the rents are applicable solely to parochial purposes, which are under the control of parish officers (*u*); and the terms of the statute must be strictly followed in the execution and drawing of the leases (*v*). Copyholds do not appear to be within the Act (*w*).

10. GUARDIANS.

A guardian in socage (*x*) may make leases of the infant's land in his own name, for he has not merely a bare authority, but an interest in the land descended (*y*); and a guardianship by election involves a similar power of leasing the estate of the infant (*z*). Such leases, if they extend beyond the time of the guardianship, may be confirmed by the infant on attaining full age (*a*).

Guardians in socage.

A guardian by nature cannot make any leases either in his own name or in the name of the infant (*b*). It is said that he may make a lease at will (*c*).

(*u*) Per Parke, B., Uthwatt *v.* Elkins, 13 M. & W. 777; Allason *v.* Stark, 9 Ad. & E. 255; Att.-Gen. *v.* Lewin. 8 Sim. 366. See also Gouldsworth *v.* Knight, 11 M. & W. 337; Smith *v.* Adkins, 8 M. & W. 362; St Nicholas, Deptford, *v.* Sketchley, 8 Q. B. 394; Rumball *v.* Munt, 8 Q. B. 382; Doe *d.* Edney *v.* Benham, 7 Q. B. 976; Doe *d.* Bowley *v.* Barnes, 8 Q. B. 1037.

(*v*) Phillips *v.* Pearce, 5 B. & C. 433; Doe *d.* Landsell *v.* Gower, 21 L. J. Q. B. 57; 17 Q. B. 589; Woodcock *v.* Gibson, 4 B. & C.462.

(*w*) Doe *d.* Bailey *v.* Foster, 3 C. B. 215.

(*x*) Bac. Abr. tit. Leases (I) 9. See Crabb's Digest of the Statutes, vol. i. p. 39.

(*y*) Shopland *v.* Ryoler, Cro. Jac. 55-59, 1 Blac. Com. 461, Co. Litt. 87 b; R. *v.* Oakley, 10 East. 494; Eyre *v.* Countess of Shaftesbury, 2 P. Wms. 108; R. *v.* Sherrington, 3 B. & A. 714; R. v. Sutton, 3 A. & E. 597. See also Wade *v.* Baker, 1 Ld. Raymond, 131; Osborn *v.* Carden, Plowd. 293; Willis *v.* Whitewood, 1 Leon. 322, Keilw. 46 b.

(*z*) 1 Blac. Com. 462; Co. Litt. 87 b; Pitcairn *v.* Ogbourne, 2 Ves. 375.

(*a*) Bac. Abr. tit. Leases (I) 9.

(*b*) Bac. Abr. tit. Leases (I) 9.

(*c*) Willis *v.* Whitewood, Owen, 45, 1 Leon. 322; Pigot *v.* Garnish, Cro. Eliz. 678; Bac. Abr. tit. Leases (I) 9.

Testamentary guardians.

A testamentary guardian, or one appointed pursuant to the 12 Car. II., c. 24, ss. 8–11, is the same in interest and office as a guardian in socage (*d*). But it has been doubted whether a lease for years, made by the testamentary guardian of an infant, is not absolutely void (*e*).

A guardian appointed by the Lord Chancellor must obtain the sanction of the Court of Chancery before he can make a lease (*f*).

11. Executors and Administrators.

Executors and administrators.

Executors and administrators, after they have obtained letters of administration, may, by virtue of their office, dispose absolutely of terms of years, which are vested in them in right of their testators or intestates (*g*). A lease by one of several executors is as valid as if made by all, and the same rule applies to administrators (*h*). Where a testator specifically bequeathed by will a term of years, and the executor or administrator with the will annexed assents to the bequest, and afterwards leases the same, such lease would be void, as the legal interest in the term is vested in the legatee upon such assent; but until

---

(*d*) Ibid. See 1 Blac. Com. 462; R. *v*. Thorp, Carth. 384; Pigot *v.* Garnish, Cro. Eliz. 678, 734; Roach *v.* Garvan, 1 Ves. 158.

(*c*) Roe *d.* Parry *v.* Hodgson, 2 Wils. 129, 135. A devise to a person as guardian, that he may "receive set and let" for his ward, gives him an authority only, and not an interest. Pigot *v.* Garnish, Cro. Eliz. 678.

(*f*) See 11 Geo. IV. & 1 Will. IV. c. 65, s. 12 ; 19 & 20 Vict. c. 120, amended by 21 & 22 Vict.

c. 77 ; Rex *v.* Sutton, 3 A. & E. 608 ; *Re* James, deceased, L. R. 5 Eq. 334. See *ante*, p. 5, Tenant for Life.

(*g*) 2 Wms. Executors, 878, 6th edition ; Bac. Abr. tit. Leases (I) 7 ; Roe *d.* Bendall *v.* Summerset, 2 Wm. Blac. 692 ; Wankford *v.* Wankford, 1 Salk. 301 ; Hudson *v.* Hudson, 1 Atk. 461.

(*h*) Doe *d.* Hayes *v.* Sturges, 7 Taunt. 217 ; Simpson *v.* Gutteridge, 1 Mad. 609, 616.

CH. I.] WHO MAY BE LESSORS. 23

then, the term remains in the executor, who can dispose of the same (*i*).

An infant may be appointed executor, but *if sole executor*, by the 38 Geo. III., c. 87, s. 6, he is altogether disqualified from executing his office during his minority, and administration, with the will annexed, is usually granted to the guardian of such infant, or to such other person as the Court shall think fit, until such infant attains twenty-one (*j*).

A married woman may be appointed executrix, but her husband has a joint-interest with her in the effects of the testator. She can, therefore, do no act as executrix or administratrix without her husband's consent. The husband is enabled by law to assume the whole administration, and to act in it to all purposes without her consent (*k*).

12. TRUSTEES OF BANKRUPTS.

Leases could formerly be made by assignees of bankrupts, and may now be made by the trustees under the new Act (*l*). *Trustees of bankrupts.*

13. PERSONS UNDER DISABILITY.

A lease executed by a person of unsound mind, in the ordinary course of affairs, is binding on him and *Lunatics and idiots.*

(*i*) Paramour *v.* Yardley, Plowd. 539; Young *v.* Holmes, 1 Stra. 70; Doe *d.* Lord Say and Sele *v.* Guy, 3 East. 120, 4 Esp. 154; Johnson *v.* Warwick, 17 C. B. 516; Fenton *v.* Clegg, 9 Exch. 680; Doe *d.* Sturgess *v.* Tatchell, 3 B. & Ad. 675; Doe *d.* Maberley *v.* Maberley, 6 C. & P. 126; 2 Wms. on Exors. 1275, 6th edition.

(*j*) 1 Wms. on Exors. 222, 6th edition; Finch's case, 6 Co. Rep. 63; Prince's case, 5 Co. Rep. 29; Cro. Eliz. 718.

(*k*) See *post*, Married Women, p. 26; Arnold *v.* Bidgwood, Cro. Jac. 318; Thrustout *d.* Levick *v.* Coppin, 2 Wm. Blac. 801.

(*l*) See the 32 & 33 Vict. c. 71, s. 14, pl. 4, *post*, Part 4, c. 2, s. 4.

those who represent him, unless it can be shown that the lessee had notice of the lessor's state of mind. If it can be proved that the lessee knew, or ought to have known, of the lessor's incapacity, and took advantage of it, a lease executed under such circumstances is void (*m*).

By the 16 & 17 Vict., c. 70, s. 129, the committee of a lunatic may make building and other leases; by sects. 130 and 131, he may make mining leases; by sect. 133, he may execute leasing powers of a lunatic having a limited estate; by sect. 134, he may renew leases (*n*).

And by the 15 & 16 Vict., c. 48, committees of lunatics can direct repairs and improvements upon the land of lunatics, or make allowances to tenants executing the same.

By the 36 sect. of the 19 & 20 Vict., c. 120, all powers (*o*) given by that Act, and all applications to the Court of Chancery, and consents to such applications, may be given by the committees on behalf of lunatics; but in case of a lunatic tenant in tail, no application to the Court, or consent to such application, is to be made or given by committees without the special direction of the Court.

Persons in a state of intoxication.

A lease made by a person when deprived of his reason by drink is void, if the lessee had notice of the lessor's incapacity (*p*).

(*m*) Molton *v.* Camrour, 2 Ex. 487, in error, 4 Ex. 17; Elliot *v.* Ince, 7 De G. M. & G. 475, 487, 26 L. J. Ch. 821; Beavan *v.* M'Donnell, 10 Ex. 184, 23 L. J. Ex. 327.
(*n*) As to disposing of undesirable leases, see sect. 127.
(*o*) See *ante*, Tenants for Life p. 5.
(*p*) Gore *v.* Gibson, 13 M. & W. 623. See *Per* Alderson, B., in Molton *v.* Camrour, 2 Ex. 491; Pitt *v.* Smith, 3 Camp. 33.

A lease made by a person under duress is voidable at the election of the party intimidated. Duress is defined to be where one is manifestly imprisoned or restrained of his liberty contrary to law, until he executes a deed or bond to another (*q*).

Persons under duress.

Real estate was not forfeited on conviction for treason or felony without attainder; and persons attainted of treason or felony might, before office found, lease their lands, except as against the Crown, or the lord of whom the land is held (*r*). And now, by the 33 & 34 Vict., c. 23, forfeitures for treason or felony are abolished, except forfeiture consequent upon outlawry.

Persons attainted or outlawed.

A convict (*s*), against whom judgment of death or penal servitude has been pronounced or recorded upon any charge of treason or felony, is, while subject to the Act, incapable of alienating or charging any property, or making any contract, except as thereinafter provided (*t*).

By sects. 9 to 12, an administrator under the Act has absolute power to let, mortgage, &c., any part of the property of the convict which he shall think fit.

By sect. 18, the property reverts to the convict, except so far as is necessary for the care of the property, upon completion of his sentence or pardon, or to his representatives upon his death.

By 22 & 23 Vict., c. 21, s. 25, "When a right of entry upon lands or other hereditaments shall have accrued to Her Majesty or her successors, such right

(*q*) Knight and Norton's case, 3 Leon. 239, 2 Inst. 482; Cumming *v.* Ince, 11 Q. B. 112.
(*r*) Doe *d.* Evans *v.* Evans, 5 B. & C. 584; Doe *d.* Griffith *v.* Pritchard, 5 B. & Ad. 765.
(*s*) See sect. 6.
(*t*) Sect. 8. See sect. 30, where the convict is lawfully at large.

may be exercised or enforced without any inquisition being taken or office being found, or any actual reentry being made on the premises." It would seem that "such right must be exercised or enforced" before an attainted felon would become incapable of leasing his lands. A lease or assignment of the personal estate of a felon before a conviction, if *bona fide* and for good consideration, is valid even as against the Crown (*u*).

<small>Married women.</small>

A lease by a *feme covert* is void at common law, and no subsequent act of confirmation, after the removal of the disability, can render such a lease valid (*v*). For by marriage the free agency of the wife is suspended, and the husband acquires an immediate right to the rents and profits of her freehold estates (*w*). Without his consenting to and joining in the disposal of her lands, all conveyances by her are void at common law, and over her chattel interests (not being choses in action) the husband has the sole dominion during his life (*x*).

By the Act for the abolition of fines and recoveries (*y*), married women, being tenants in fee, in tail, or for life, or for years, may make leases by deed for any term consistent with their estates, provided the husband concurs in the deed, and the wife acknowledges it before a judge, or before two perpetual commissioners, as directed by the Act (*z*), or before a county court judge (*a*).

(*u*) Morewood *v.* Wilks, 6 C. & P. 144; Shaw *v.* Bran, 1 Stark R. 319; *In re* Saunders *v.* Watson, 4 Giff. 179, 32 L. J. Ch. 224; Perkins *v.* Bradley, 1 Hare 219; Whitaker *v.* Wisbey, 12 C. B. 44; Chowne *v.* Baylis, 31 Beav. 351.

(*v*) Goodright *d.* Carter *v.* Strahan, Cowp. 201, Lofft. 763.

(*w*) See *ante*, p. 10, Husband Leasing Wife's Land.

(*x*) Manby *v.* Scott, Smith's L. C. 2; Blac. Com. 293; Co. Litt. 46 b. But see *post*, "Married Women's Property Act, 1870," Part 4, c. 2, s. 3.

(*y*) 3 & 4 Will. IV. c. 74, ss. 77–79.

(*z*) Sect. 79.

(*a*) 19 & 20 Vict. c. 108, s. 73. The lease requires enrolment in Chancery if the married woman

A married woman, who has property settled to her separate use without any restraint on alienation, is deemed in equity to be a *feme sole*, and she may dispose of it accordingly (*b*). And property acquired by a married woman under the "Married Women's Property Act, 1870" (*c*), is deemed to be property held and settled to her separate use.

A lease made by an infant (*d*) or person under the age of twenty-one years (*e*) is voidable (*f*). On his attaining full age, he, or his heir upon his death, can elect to ratify or avoid such a lease (*g*). To avoid a lease made by an infant, under which the lessee is in possession, some act of notoriety is necessary on the part of the infant upon attaining twenty-one; for instance, ejectment, entry, or demand of possession. The mere execution of a new lease to another lessee is not sufficient to divest the estate created by the first lease (*h*). The chief point to be attended to in considering what amounts to a confirmation is, whether the lease was for the benefit of the infant(*i*). Thus where a lease made by an infant manifestly imports a benefit to himself, he cannot upon attaining full age avoid the lease on the ground of infancy if he still retains the benefit, and, within a reasonable time after he comes of age, does not dis-

Infants.

is a tenant in tail. See *ante*, Tenants in Tail, p. 2.
(*b*) Sugden on Powers, c. 4, s. 1.
(*c*) See *infra*, Part 4, c. 2, s. 3.
(*d*) See *post*, c. 2, s. 1.
(*e*) By custom in some places an infant is of full age at fifteen to make leases that shall bind him. Co. Litt. 45 b.
(*f*) Bac. Abr. Leases; Zouch *d.* Abbot *v.* Parsons, 3 Burr. 1806;
4 Cruise, 74, s. 67; *per* Best, J., in Goode *v.* Harrison, 5 B. & Ald. 159; and *per* Buller, J., in Maddon *v.* White, 2 T. R. 161.
(*g*) Baylis *v.* Dineley, 3 M. & S. 477; Litt. s. 547.
(*h*) Slater *v.* Trimble, 14 Ir. Com. L. R. 342 Q. B.; Slater *v.* Brady, ib. 66.
(*i*) Zouch *d.* Abbot *v.* Parsons, 3 Burr. 1798; *Ex parte* Grace, 1 B. & P. 377.

affirm the lease (*j*). And slight acts have been held to amount to a confirmation of such leases. Thus where an infant made a lease for years, and at full age said to the lessee, " God give you joy of it," this was held to be a confirmation of the lease (*k*). So where an infant makes a lease, and accepts rent after coming of age, he thereby affirms the lease (*l*). So where an infant made a lease of land, and after attaining full age mortgaged the land by a deed which recited the lease, this was held to be a confirmation of the lease (*m*). An infant can make a lease without rent, to try his title (*n*).

The lease of an infant, to be good, must be his own personal act, for he cannot appoint an agent. Therefore a lease made by his next friend or agent cannot bind him, nor can he ratify it after he is of full age (*o*). But an infant is bound by a lease made in his corporate capacity (*p*). Thus a lease by the king or queen regnant, whether of lands held in right of the Crown or of the Duchy of Lancaster, cannot be avoided on the ground of infancy (*q*).

By the 11 Geo. IV. & 1 Will. IV., c. 65, ss. 16, 17, infants are empowered to grant renewals of leases under the direction of the Court of Chancery, and the Court can direct leases of land belonging to infants when it is for the benefit of the estate (*r*).

(*j*) Ashfield *v.* Ashfield, Sir W. Jones, 157 ; Ketsey's case, Cro. Jac. 320 ; Holmes v. Blogg, 8 Taunt. 35 ; Evelyn *v.* Chichester, 3 Burr. 1717.

(*k*) Anon. 4 Leon. 4 ; Bac. Abr. tit. Estate (B).

(*l*) Ashfield *v.* Ashfield, Sir W. Jones, 157.

(*m*) Story *v.* Johnson, 2 J. & C. Exch. 586.

(*n*) Zouch *d.* Abbot *v.* Parsons, 3 Burr. 1798.

(*o*) Doe *d.* Thomas *v.* Roberts, 16 M. & W. 778.

(*p*) Bro. Abr. tit. Age, pl. 80.

(*q*) Case of Duchy of Lancaster, Dyer, 209 b, Plowd. 212 b.

(*r*) See *ante*, Tenants for Life, p. 5 ; 19 & 20 Vict. c. 120 ; and Guardians, *ante*, p. 21.

CHAPTER II.

WHO MAY BE LESSEES.

	PAGE		PAGE
1. PERSONS UNDER DISABILITY—		2. CORPORATIONS—	... 32
lunatics	... 29	corporations	... 32
persons outlawed	... 29	ecclesiastical persons	... 32
aliens and denizens	... 30		
married women	... 31	3. PARISH OFFICERS, &c.	... 33
infants	... 31		

ALL persons are capable of being lessees of demisable property; in some cases demises, however, may be avoided in respect of the persons to whom they are made (*a*).

1. PERSONS UNDER DISABILITY.

Idiots and lunatics may take leases for their own benefit (*b*). The committee of a lunatic may surrender leases and accept renewals for the benefit of the lunatic, upon certain conditions, under the 16 & 17 Vict., c. 70, ss. 113–115; and the committee, or an attorney appointed by the lord of the manor, may, by sect. 108, be admitted tenant of copyhold land on behalf of the lunatic. *Lunatics.*

Outlaws may be lessees, but leases taken by them for chattel interests are forfeited to the Crown (*c*). Persons attainted may be lessees, but their leases were *Persons outlawed or attainted.*

(*a*) 2 Cruise Dig. 79, s. 85; Kettley *v.* Elliot, Cro. Jac. 320; Brownl. 120, 2 Bulst. 69.
(*b*) Co. Litt. 2 b.
(*c*) Knowles *v.* Powell, Owen, 16; Brittain *v.* Cole, 1 Salk. 395; Bac. Abr. tit. Outlawry (D) 2.

forfeited to the Crown (*d*). But by the 33 & 34 Vict., c. 33, ss. 1, 10, forfeiture for treason or felony, except that consequent upon outlawry, is abolished, and the property of the convict vests in the administrator under the Act (*e*).

Aliens and denizens.

At common law an alien friend might take a lease of a house or of lands; but the estate thereby granted upon office found would forthwith devolve to the Crown (*f*). But an alien friend who is a *merchant* might take a lease of a house for carrying on his trade, and the Crown could not seize such lease, unless he abandoned the realm (*g*). An alien husband will not be entitled to a term vested in the wife (*h*).

By the 7 & 8 Vict., c. 66, s. 4, alien subjects of a friendly state may take and hold personal property, except chattels real; and by sect. 5 (*i*), alien friends may take and hold land for twenty-one years, for the purpose of residence, or of occupation by them or their servants, or for the purpose of any trade, business, or manufacture, as fully as if they were natural-born subjects. By sect. 6, aliens, when naturalised

(*d*) Co.Litt.2b;Shep.Touch.235.
(*e*) See *ante*, p. 25.
(*f*) Co. Litt. 2 b ; Shep. Touch. 235 ; Calvin's case, 7 Rep. 49. As to purchases by an alien in the name of a trustee, see R. *v.* Holland, Styles, 20, S. C. 1 Roll. Abr. 194, 1, 13.
(*g*) Co. Litt. 2 b ; see R. *v.* Eastbourne, 4 East. 107. But on the death of the lessee the lease shall go to the Crown, and not to his executors or administrators. Co. Litt. 2 b ; but see Anon. 1 And. 25, and Sir Upwell Caroon's case, Cro. Car. 8.
(*h*) Theobald *v.* Duffy, 9 Mod. 102 ; 2 Vin. Abr. 260.

(*i*) Sect. 5 in effect repealed the 32 Hen. VIII. c. 16, s. 13, by which all leases of dwelling-houses or shops to an alien artificer or handicraftsman were made void. This Act was strictly construed in favour of aliens. See Jevens *v.* Harridge, 1 Wms. Saund. 5th ed. 6, and notes ; Co. Litt. 2 b ; and Hargrave and Butler's notes, n 7. See Pilkington *v.* Peach, 2 Show. 134. For decisions on this section, see Lapierre *v* M'Intosh, 9 Ad. & E. 157 ; Wootton *v.* Steffenoni, 12 M. & W. 129; Bailey *v.* Cathery, 1 Dowl. N.S. 456.

pursuant to the provisions of this Act (*j*), are to enjoy the same rights as natural-born subjects.

Alien enemies cannot hold leases for any purpose whatever.

A denizen (*k*) may take lands by purchase or devise, but not by inheritance. He may therefore be a lessor or lessee (*l*).

A *feme covert* (*m*) can take a lease, her husband's express assent not being necessary, as the estate vests till dissent. But she may avoid it after his death (*n*). If a lease be made to a husband and wife, and she agree to it, she must pay the rent, and she will be chargeable with the arrearages incurred during the coverture and for waste (*o*). {Married Women.}

By the 1 Will. IV., c. 65, ss. 12, 15, leases to married women, under the direction of the Court of Chancery, may be surrendered and renewed as therein stated.

Infants may accept leases, and upon attaining full age they may affirm or avoid them (*p*). The election to avoid a lease must be made by the infant within a reasonable time after he comes of age (*q*). But it seems that an infant who has taken possession {Infants.}

(*j*) Sects. 7-14, 16. See s. 15, which reserves to aliens rights enjoyed before the Act passed. Doe *d*. Miller *v*. Rogers, 1 C. & K. 390.

(*k*) Co. Litt. 129 a; Calvin's case, 9 Rep. 25 b.

(*l*) 1 Blac. Com. 374. See 12 & 13 Will. III. c. 2.

(*m*) See *post*, Part 4, c. 2, s. 3.

(*n*) Swaine *v*. Holman, Hobart, 204; Co. Litt. 3 a. See Gaston *v*. Frankum, 2 De G. & S. 561, as to a married woman's separate estate being bound for payment of the rent.

(*o*) Com. Dig. tit. Baron and Feme, s. 2; 2 Inst. 303; 2 Roll. 287; 1 Roll. Abr. 349, pl. 2; Brownl. 31; Dyer, 13 b.

(*p*) Ketsey's case, Cro. Jac. 320; Baylis *v*. Dyncley, 3 M. & S. 477.

(*q*) Holmes *v*. Blogg, 8 Taunt. 35. If an infant pay money as a premium for a lease, which he avoids upon coming of age, and never derives benefit from the occupation, he cannot recover such money in an action for money had and received. Holmes *v*. Blogg, *supra*.

under a lease which is disadvantageous to him, is bound, after coming of age, until he disclaims (r). Even during infancy he may be liable for the use and occupation of *necessary* lodgings suitable to his degree (s). If a person jointly interested with an infant in a lease obtain a renewal to himself only, and the lease prove beneficial, he shall be held to have acted as trustee, and the infant may claim the share of the benefit; but if it do not prove beneficial, he must take it on himself (t).

By the 1 Will. IV., c. 65, ss. 12, 15, leases to infants may, under the direction of the Court of Chancery, be surrendered or renewed in the mode therein stated.

2. CORPORATIONS.

Corporations. Corporations (u) aggregate may be lessees (v). A lease however to a corporation sole (for instance, a lease to a bishop and his successors), on the death of the bishop will go to his executors (w); but by custom it may go to his successors, as in the case of the Chamberlain of London (x).

One member of a corporation cannot make a lease to another member, nor can he take a lease from the corporation (y).

Ecclesiastical persons. By the 1 & 2 Vict., c. 106, s. 28, spiritual persons performing the duties of any ecclesiastical office cannot take leases for occupation by themselves of more than eighty acres of land without the written permission of the bishop of the diocese.

(r) The London and North-Western Railway Co. v. M'Michael, 5 Exch. 114, 20 L. J. Ex. 97.
(s) Hands v. Slaney, 8 T. R. 578; Lowe v. Griffiths, 1 Scot. 458.
(t) *Ex parte* Grace, 1 B. & P. 376.
(u) See *ante*, c. 1.
(v) Bac. Abr. tit. Corporations (E) 4.
(w) Co. Litt. 46 b.
(x) 2 Bac. Abr. 14.
(y) Salter v. Grosvenor, 8 Mod. 303.

Trustees for charitable uses may take leases of land in England or Wales, if made according to the Mortmain Acts (z).

Leases made in pursuance of the 31 & 32 Vict., c. 44, entitled "An Act for facilitating the acquisition and enjoyment of Sites for Buildings for Religious, Educational, Library, Scientific, and other charitable purposes," are exempt from the provisions of the Mortmain Act.

By the 59 Geo. III., c. 12, ss. 12, 17, churchwardens and overseers are made a corporation of a peculiar kind, and can take land on lease for the purposes of the Act (a).

Parish officers, &c.

Guardians of unions may, by order of the Poor-law Commissioners, and with the consent of the ratepayers, hire buildings for union workhouses, pursuant to the 4 & 5 Will. IV., c. 76, s. 23.

By the 30 & 31 Vict., c. 106, s. 13, the guardians may, with the approval of the Poor-law Board, hire or take on lease temporarily, or for a term of years not exceeding five, any land or buildings for the purpose of the relief or employment of the poor, and the use of the guardians or their officers, without any order of the said Board under seal.

(z) 9 Geo. II. c. 36; 9 Geo. IV. c. 85; 24 & 25 Vict. c. 9; 25 & 26 Vict. c. 17; 26 & 27 Vict. c. 106; 27 Vict. c. 113; 29 & 30 Vict. c. 57; Wickham v. Marquis of Bath, 35 L. J. Ch. 5; Doe d. Williams v. Lloyd, 5 Bing. N. C. 741; Walker v. Richardson, 2 M. & W. 882; Att.-Gen. v. Glyn, 12 Sim. 84; Ashton v. Jones, 28 Beav. 460.

(a) See ante, p. 20, c. 1, s. 3; Smith v. Adkins, 8 M. & W. 362; Uthwatt v. Elkins, 13 M. & W. 777; Allason v. Stark, 9 A. & E. 255; Att.-Gen. v. Lewin, 8 Sim. 366.

CREATION OF TENANCY. [PART I.

By the 24 & 25 Vict., c. 125, overseers of parishes in England, whose population does not exceed 4000 persons, may, subject to the conditions, and for the purposes therein mentioned, take land on lease (*b*).

(*b*) As to leases to trustees of friendly societies, see 18 & 19 Vict. c. 63; leases to trustees of public baths, 9 & 10 Vict. c. 74. As to canal and railway companies, see 21 & 22 Vict. c. 75, s. 3; 23 & 24 Vict. c. 41. As to leases of land for free public libraries, museums, see 18 & 19 Vict. c. 70, s. 18. Leases to ratepayers for public improvements may be made pursuant to 23 & 24 Vict. c. 30. A lease cannot generally be granted to the inhabitants of a parish, see Weekly *v.* Wildman, 1 Lord Raymond, 405, 407; Abbot *v.* Weekly, 1 Lev. 176; Lockwood *v.* Wood (in error), 6 Q. B. 62; Constable *v.* Nicholson, 14 C. B. N.S. 230, 32 L. J. C. P. 240. But see The Vestry of Bermondsey *v.* Brown, 14 W. R. 213 M. R.

CHAPTER III.

WHAT MAY BE LEASED.

	PAGE		PAGE
1. THINGS IN GRANT,	36	*offices*	39
advowsons,	36	*pensions*,	40
tithes,	36	*rents and annuities*,	40
commons and estovers,	37	*other incorporeal heredi-*	
ways,	38	*taments*,	40
corrodies,	38	2. THINGS IN LIVERY,	41
franchises,	39	*lodgings*,	41
tolls,	39		

As a general rule, leases for life or lives, for years or at will, may be created of anything corporeal or incorporeal that lieth in livery (*a*) or in grant (*b*). But where there is a demise of premises, and an entire rent is reserved, if any part of the premises could not be legally demised, the demise is void (*c*).

Goods and chattels may also be leased for years. Thus cattle and other live or dead stock may be demised, and the lessee will have the use and profit of them during the term. The interest, however, of the lessee therein differs from the interest which he has in lands. For the lessor can have no certain reversion in live animals, and though the lessee has no right to sell or destroy them or give them away, yet, if they

---

(*a*) Now by the 8 & 9 Vict. c. 106, s. 2, all *corporeal* tenements and hereditaments are deemed to lie in grant, so far as regards the conveyance of the immediate freehold.

(*b*) Shep. Touch. 268; Bac. Abr. tit. Leases (A); 2 Cruise, ss. 22-24.

(*c*) Doe d. Griffith *v.* Lloyd, 3 Esp. 78; Gardiner *v.* Williamson, 2 B. & Ad. 336.

die during the term, they become the absolute property of the lessee (*d*). So, whether they live or die, the young ones coming from them belong absolutely to the lessee as profits arising from the animals demised. In a lease of dead goods and chattels, however, if anything be added for repairing, mending, and improving thereof, the lessor shall have the improvements and additions with the things demised after the term is ended (*e*).

1. Things in Grant.

Incorporeal hereditaments are rights issuing out of a thing corporate (whether real or personal), or concerning or annexed to or exercisable within the same (*f*). They lie in grant, and are usually capable of being the subjects of a demise.

Advowsons. Advowsons may be demised (*g*). Thus, if an advowson, or tithes, or any incorporeal hereditament, is leased for years, an action of debt may be maintained for the rent agreed on (*h*). So if a vacancy occur while an advowson is leased, the lessee shall present, and if the lessee himself accepts a presentation from the lessor, it will be a surrender of his term (*i*).

Tithes. Tithes are an ecclesiastical inheritance collateral to the land, and properly due to an ecclesiastical person (*j*).

(*d*) Bac. Abr. Leases (A) ; Litt. s. 71 ; Collins *v.* Harding, Cro. Eliz. 606.

(*e*) Bac. Abr. Leases (A).

(*f*) Co. Litt. 19, 20.

(*g*) Kensey *v.* Langham, Cas. temp. Talbot, 144 ; Robinson *v.* Tongue, 3 P. Wms. 461. See *infra*, Tithes, 5 Geo. III. c. 17.

(*h*) 2 Woodd. 69 ; Rog. Ecc. L. 17 ; Co. Litt. 119 b.

(*i*) Bac. Abr. tit. Leases (A) ; 2 Cruise, 22, 24 ; Bousher *v.* Morgan, 2 Anst. 404 ; Gybson *v.* Searle, Cro. Jac. 84.

(*j*) Comyn's Digest, Dismes (A). Although, in common parlance, tithes were often said to be *let* to the farmer, and although such arrangements were common throughout England, and were constantly carried into effect without deed,

By the 5 Geo. III., c. 17 (*k*), it is enacted, that leases already made, or that shall be made, of tithes, tolls, and other incorporeal hereditaments, for one, two, or three life or lives, or for any term not exceeding twenty-one years, by ecclesiastical persons, or any other person who is enabled by statute to make leases for one, two, or three life or lives, or for any term not exceeding twenty-one years, of any lands, tenements, or corporeal hereditaments, shall be valid as against such lessors and their successors.

Common, or right of common (a profit which a man hath in the land of another, as to feed his beasts, to catch fish, to dig turf, or to cut wood), can be demised (*l*).

Commons and estovers.

The 13 Geo. III., c. 87, s. 75, empowers the lord of any manor, with the consent of three-fourths of the persons having the right of common upon the wastes

---

yet in point of fact these species of arrangements, made without deed, by which the tenant retained the tithes, and paid the clergyman or other tithe-owner a yearly sum, were not *leases* in the eye of the law, but mere *sales* by the tithe-owner to the terre-tenant; and the proof of this was, that if the tithe-owner found it necessary to bring an action for the stipulated sum, he declared not for rent, but for tithes sold and delivered, just in the same form in which the vendor of any other sort of goods declared. In common parlance, however, it was very usual to denominate such an arrangement a *letting of the tithes*, and indeed it did so far resemble a yearly tenancy, that, in the absence of express stipulation to the contrary, it required half a year's notice to put an end to it. Smith's Landlord and Tenant, p. 77. See Goode *v.* Howells, 4 M. & W. 198; Neale *v.* Mackenzie, 2 C. M. & R. 84, S. C. (in error); 1 M. & W. 747; Bird *v.* Higginson, 2 A. & E. 696; Thomas *v.* Fredericks, 10 Q. B. 775; Meggison *v.* Lady Glamis, 7 Ex. 685.

(*k*) As to leases of tithes made before this statute, see Shep. Touch, 241; Brewer *v.* Hill, 2 Anst. 413; Bousher *v.* Morgan, ib. 404; Walker *v.* Wakeman, 1 Vent. 294; 2 Lev. 150 S. C. nom.; Wakeman *v.* Walker, 1 Keb. 597; The Dean and Chapter of Windsor *v.* Gover, 2 Saund. 302, 304, c (12). See *infra*, Part 2, Div. 1, c. 2, ss. 1, 2, and Part 3, c. 2.

(*l*) Sury *v.* Brown, Latch. 99; Benson *v.* Chester, 8 T. R. 396, 401; Clark *v.* Cogge, Cro. Jac. 170, 190; 1 Stephen's Blackstone, 648.

and commons within the manor, at any time to demise or lease, for any term or number of years not exceeding four, any part of such wastes and commons, not exceeding a twelfth part thereof, for the best and most improved yearly rent that can be obtained by public auction. The clear net rents are to be applied to fence, drain, and otherwise improve the residue of the wastes and commons.

Estovers (*m*) (a reasonable allowance of wood, fuel, and repairs that every tenant for life may take of common right upon the land demised to him) can be leased. The grantee of house-bote or hay-bote may let it to another (*n*).

Ways.

A right of way is demisable with the land to which it is legally appurtenant, and will pass without being mentioned, as will also other easements (*o*).

Corrodies.

A corrody is a right of sustenance, or to receive certain allotments of victual and provision for one's maintenance. In lieu of which, especially when due from ecclesiastical persons, a pension or sum of money was sometimes substituted. A corrody was chargeable on the person of the owner of the inheritance in respect thereof (*p*). If one had a corrody for life, he might let it to another, or to the grantor himself (*q*).

(*m*) A different thing from common of estovers, which is a right to cut wood upon the soil of a stranger.
(*n*) Shep. Touch. 222; Bac. Abr. tit. Leases (A); Clark *v.* Cogge, Cro. Jac. 170, 190.
(*o*) Osborne *v.* Wise, 7 C. & P. 761; Clark *v.* Cogge, Cro. Jac. 170; Howton *v.* Fearson, 8 T. R. 50; Sury *v.* Pigot, Popham, 166; James *v.* Plant, 4 A. & E. 749; Kooystra *v.* Lucas, 4 B. &

A. 830; Morris *v.* Edgington, 3 Taunt. 24; Davies *v.* Sear, L. R. 7 Eq. 427. See however Thompson *v.* Waterlow, 37 L. J. Ch. 495, L. R. 6 Eq. 36; Langley *v.* Hammond, 37 L. J. Ex. 118, L. R. 3 Ex. 161.
(*p*) 2 Blac. Com. 40.
(*q*) Bac. Abr. tit. Leases (A); R. *v.* Nicholson, 12 East. 330; Peter *v.* Keudal, 6 B. & C. 703; Beere *v.* Windebanke, Sid. 80.

Franchises (*r*) can be demised. Thus, a fair, or a market, or a ferry, with the right of taking toll, can be demised; so also can a franchise of forest, chase, park, warren, or fishery. Where, however, the franchise is a personal immunity, no lease can be granted (*s*).

Franchises.

So tolls can be leased (*t*).

Tolls.

Leases of offices which touch the administration or execution of justice, or the receipt of revenue, are prohibited by the 5 & 6 Edw. VI., c. 16, and the 49 Geo. III., c. 126 (*u*). But such offices as merely require common diligence, and may be executed by deputy without ill consequence to the public, may be leased for years (*v*). Also such offices as are merely ministerial in courts of justice (*w*). Dignities or honours cannot be leased (*x*).

Offices.

(*r*) Franchise and liberty are synonymous terms, and their definition is a royal privilege, or branch of the crown's prerogative in the hands of a subject. Finch, L. 164.

(*s*) Duke of Somerset *v.* Fogwell, 5 B. & C. 875, 2 Blac. Com. 40; Bac. Abr. tit. Leases (A). See *infra*, Offices.

(*t*) Fairtitle *d.* Mytton *v.* Gilbert, 2 T. R. 169, 3 Geo. IV. c. 126, 4 Geo. IV. c. 95, s. 51; Bell *v.* Nixon, 9 Bing. 393; Pearse *v.* Morrice, 5 B. & Ad. 396; Olroyd *v.* Crampton, 4 Bing. N. C. 24; Shepherd *v.* Hodman, 18 Q.B.316; Markham *v.* Stamford, 14 C.B.N. S. 376; Gunning on Tolls, 140. By the 3 Geo. IV. c. 126, s. 57, all contracts or agreements for the letting of turnpike tolls, signed by the trustees, or their clerk, and the lessee or farmer, are declared to be valid. See Markham *v.* Stamford, *supra*; Stott *v.* Clegg, 13 C. B. N. S. 619, 32 L. J. C. P. 102.

(*u*) Reynel's case, 9 Co. 95 a; Sutton's case, 6 Mod. 57.

(*v*) Hopkins *v.* Prescott, 4 C. B. 578. See notes, Chitty's Statutes, tit. Offices, pp. 465–467; Rex *v.* Lenthal, 3 Mod. 145 : Bac. Abr. tit. Leases (A); *e.g.*, the offices of postmaster general, king's printer, wardens of ports and havens, gun-founder, parkkeeper, gauger, aulnager, garbler of spices, and registrar of policies of assurance in London. See Veale *v.* Priour, Hard. 352; Zouch *v.* Moore, 2 Roll. R. 274, Hard. 354; Bac. Abr. tit. Offices (H); Com. Dig. Offices (B) 7.

(*w*) For instance, surveyor of the green wax, sealer of writs and subpœnas. Bro. Abr. tit. Leases, 40.

(*x*) Bac. Abr. tit. Leases (A).

Pensions.

So pensions granted by the crown, wholly or in part, in respect of future services which the recipient may be called upon to render, cannot be leased (*y*).

Rents and annuities.

Rents and annuities (*z*) can be granted by way of lease (*a*).

Other incorporeal hereditaments.

Whatever may be granted and parted with for ever may be leased (*b*). Thus rights of hunting, shooting, fishing, which are interests in the realty, may be leased. Mere easements in gross, however, it would seem, are not the subjects of demise (*c*). Thus in Hill *v.* Tupper (*d*), an incorporated canal company by deed granted to the plaintiff the sole and exclusive right or liberty of putting or using pleasure-boats for hire on their canal. It was held that the grant did not create such an interest or estate in the plaintiff as to enable him to maintain an action in his own name against a person who disturbed his right of putting and using pleasure-boats for hire on the canal. So in Handcock *v.* Austen (*e*), A, the owner of certain lace-machines, paid 12s. a week to B for permission to place the machines in a room in B's factory, and for free ingress and egress to the room for himself and workmen for the purpose of working and inspecting the machines. B supplied the necessary steam power for working the machines, payment for

---

(*y*) Wells *v.* Forster, 8 M. & W. 149; Lloyd *v.* Cheetham, 30 L. J. Ch. 640; Dent *v.* Dent, 36 L. J. P. & M. 61.

(*z*) An annuity which is descendible to a man's heirs is an incorporeal hereditament. Co. Litt. 20 a.

(*a*) Bac. Abr. tit. Leases; Thomas *v.* Fredericks, 10 Q.B.775; Co. Litt. 144 b; Com. Dig. tit. Annuity (A) 1, (E).

(*b*) Bac. Abr. tit. Leases.

(*c*) Hill *v.* Tupper, 32 L. J. Ex. 217; Wood *v.* Leadbetter, 13 M. & W. 838; Ackroyd *v.* Smith, 19 L. J. C. P. 315; Stockport Waterworks Company *v.* Potter, 3 H. & C. 300; Bird *v.* Great Eastern Railway Company, 19 C. B. N.S. 268; Hyde *v.* Graham, 1 H. & C. 593; Selby *v.* Greaves, 37 L. J. C. P. 251.

(*d*) 32 L. J. Ex. 217.

(*e*) 14 C. B. N.S. 429; 32 L. J. C. P. 252.

which was included in the above sum. It was held that as there was no demise to A of any part of the room, the relation of landlord and tenant was not created between him and B (*f*).

Corporeal hereditaments in expectancy lie in grant, and are capable of being demised.

2. THINGS IN LIVERY.

Corporeal hereditaments which consist wholly of substantial and permanent objects, such as lands and houses, &c., were, if in possession before the 8 & 9 Vict., c. 106 (*g*), said to lie in livery. They are the subjects of demise; and incorporeal rights appurtenant thereto—for instance, rights of way or other easements —will pass by a demise of the land (*h*).

Parts of any dwelling-house or other tenement may be demised. Where parts of a dwelling-house are let, they are called lodgings or apartments (*i*); and if let furnished, the rent is deemed to issue out of the realty, and not partly out of the furniture (*j*).

Lodgings.

(*f*) See Selby *v.* Greaves, 37 L. J. C. P. 257; Wright *v.* Stavert, 2 E. & E. 721, 29 L. J. Q. B. 161; Carr *v.* Benson, L. R. 3 Ch. Ap. 524.
(*g*) See *supra*, p. 35, n. (*a*).
(*h*) Skull *v.* Glenister, 16 C. B. N.S. 81; Dobbyn *v.* Somers, 13 Ir. Com. L. Rep. N.S. 293, Q. B.; Osborne *v.* Wise, 7 C. & P. 761; Clark *v.* Cogge, Cro. Jac. 170, 190, Staple *v.* Heydon, 6 Mod. 1, 3; Howton *v.* Fearson, 8 T.

R. 50, 56; Bac. Abr. tit. Offices (H).
(*i*) Monks *v.* Dykes, 4 M. & W. 567.
(*j*) Newman *v.* Anderton, 2 B. & P. New. R. 224; Spencer's case, 5 Co. R. 16, 1 Smith L. C. 36; Cadogan *v.* Kennet, Cowp. 432; Collins *v.* Harding, Cro. Eliz. 606, 13 Co. R. 57; Emott's case, Dyer, 212 b; Selby *v.* Greaves, 37 L. J. C. P. 257. See *infra*, c. 4, s. 6.

CHAPTER IV.

HOW DEMISES ARE MADE.

	PAGE
1. DISTINCTION BETWEEN LEASES BY DEED, LEASES BY WRITING NOT UNDER SEAL, AND LEASES WITHOUT WRITING—	42
statute of frauds	46
effect of non-compliance with presumed yearly tenancy ...	48
2. RECITALS	53
3. WORDS OF DEMISE— *distinction between leases and agreements*	56
distinction between leases and licenses	68
stamp	68
4. PARCELS DEMISED—	80
exceptions and reservations	89
5. HABENDUM—	93
commencement of term ...	94
duration of term	98
tenancy at will	101
option to determine ...	107
6. REDDENDUM—	108
from what rent issues ...	108
its nature and incidents ...	109
7. COVENANTS—	114
(*a*) EXPRESS—	116

	PAGE
payment of rent ...	117
payment of taxes ...	117
repairs	120
husbandry	124
insurance	124
not to under-let or assign	125
certain trades	127
trading with particular persons, or within a particular radius ...	128
quiet enjoyment	130
renewal of leases ...	132
(*b*) IMPLIED—	135
payment of rent ...	137
repairs	137
husbandry	138
for title	139
quiet enjoyment ...	139
other implied covenants	141
8. PROVISOS AND CONDITIONS—	141
not to assign	142
license	144
9. POWERS OF RE-ENTRY—	147
void and voidable leases	150
10. LEASES UNDER POWERS	151
11. LEASES BY ESTOPPEL ...	156

1. DISTINCTION BETWEEN LEASES BY DEED, LEASES BY WRITING NOT UNDER SEAL, AND WITHOUT WRITING.

WE have seen that, as a general rule, a lease of any corporeal or incorporeal hereditament, can be created for life or lives, for years, or at will (*a*). But the distinction which existed between things lying in livery

(*a*) See *supra*, c. 3, p. 35.

and things lying in grant, rendered a different mode of conveyance necessary in their alienation.

The conveyance of things lying in grant (*b*), as remainders, reversions, and other incorporeal hereditaments, which were incapable of actual possession or transfer, was effected by grant under seal (*c*). Thus a lease in writing, not under seal, of a several fishery in a public river has been held to be void (*d*). So a lease of tithes (*e*), or of a right of way, or of a right of passage for water (*f*), or of a right to shoot over a manor, or fish in certain ponds (*g*), or the like, if not under seal, is invalid. Where, however, there is a demise of a corporeal hereditament to which an incorporeal right is appurtenant, the incorporeal right passes with the conveyance of the corporeal thing demised (*h*). Thus a right of way appurtenant to the land will pass by a parol demise of the land (*i*); or a right to dig turf (*j*), or a market with a right to take tolls made appurtenant to the land by act of Parliament, may be demised without deed (*k*).

Leases by deed.

Leases made by the sovereign, or by corporations, or by husband and wife, must be by deed (*l*).

At common law leases of things lying in livery

(*b*) See *supra*, c. 3, s. 1.
(*c*) Bird *v.* Higginson, 2 A. & E. 696. Quære, a lease under seal should, since the passing of the Statute of Frauds, be signed? Cooch *v.* Goodman, 2 Q. B. 596; Shep. Touch. 56, n. 24; Aveline *v.* Wbisson, 4 M. & Gr. 801.
(*d*) Duke of Somerset *v.* Frogwell, 5 B. & C. 875.
(*e*) Gardiner *v.* Williamson, 2 B. & Ad. 336.
(*f*) Hewlins *v.* Shippam, 5 B. & C. 221.
(*g*) Bird *v.* Higginson, 2 A. & E. 696.

(*h*) Howton *v.* Fearson, 8 T. R. 50, 56; Skull *v.* Glenister, 16 C. B. N.S. 81, 32 L. J. C. P. 185.
(*i*) Ibid. Osborne *v.* Wise, 7 C. & P. 761; Clark *v.* Cogge, Cro. Jac. 170-190; Staple *v.* Heydon, 6 Mod. 1, 3, but see *ante*, p. 38, n. (*o*).
(*j*) Dobbyn *v.* Somers, 13 Ir. Com. L. Rep. N.S. 293, Q. B.
(*k*) Bridgland *v.* Shapter, 5 M. & W. 375.
(*l*) Lane's case, 2 Rep. 17; Patrick *v.* Balls, Carth. 390, S. C. Lord Raymond, 136. See *ante*, p. 39, n. (*t*), as to lease of turnpike tolls.

Leases by writing not under seal.

might have been made by writing not under seal, as well as by deed, and may still be made by writing without seal.

Leases without writing.

Things lying in livery (*m*), that is, things capable of actual possession or transfer, might have been granted or transferred at common law, either for lives or years by parol, without any instrument either in writing or under seal. A feoffment (*n*), or lease with livery of seisin, was formerly the usual mode of conveying freehold interests in land in possession. The livery formed the essential part of the conveyance, and a deed or charter of feoffment, or lease, although under seal, was only deemed evidence of the grant, and was not essential to its validity (*o*). Neither a feoffment nor freehold lease was effectual at common law to pass an estate unless the grantor was in possession, so as to enable him to complete the grant or demise by livery, or, if a tenant for years was in possession (*p*), unless he consented to the livery.

Leases for years, however, are chattels real. They were originally for short terms, and conferred only a right to receive the profits of the land; but the legal seisin of the freeholder was not transferred nor disturbed, as the lessee was considered only to hold possession for the benefit of the reversioner. So, if a tenant for years was deprived of the possession, no means were provided by which he could be restored to the occupation of the soil; his only remedy was founded on the contract which constituted the lease; and the

(*m*) See c. 3, p. 41.
(*n*) See now 8 & 9 Vict. c. 106.
(*o*) Co. Litt. 9 a, 49 a, 169 a; Sharp's case, 6 Rep. 261, S. C.; Sharp *v.* Sharp, Cro. Eliz. 482.

It would appear from Doe. *d.* Warner *v.* Brown, 8 East. 167, and Brown *v.* Warner, 14 Ves. 158, that leases for life must have been created by deed.
(*p*) 3 Dyer, 363 a, pl. 22.

words of demise were construed as a covenant entitling the tenant to recover damages as a recompense for the loss of possession. But in the reign of Henry VIII. (*q*) a tenant for years was enabled to falsify a common recovery, from which time leases for long terms of years were granted, and were considered permanent interests; but the distinction between chattels real and freehold estates still continues a marked feature in the laws relating to real property (*r*).

A lease for years, therefore, was considered simply as a contract or agreement between the lessor and the lessee for the possession (*s*) and profits of the lands for a determinate period, on the one side, and a recompense by rent or other consideration, on the other (*t*).

It follows that leases for years of things lying in livery, being mere chattel interests arising from the contracts between the parties, may commence *in presenti* or *in futuro;* but until entry the lessee has no estate, though upon the making of the lease he immediately acquires an *interesse termini*, which may be granted away as a right, or extinguished by a release, but cannot be conveyed as an estate (*u*).

(*q*) 21 Hen. VIII. c. 15.
(*r*) Bac. Abr. tit. Leases (A); Co. Litt. 384 n (332), by Butler.
(*s*) By the 21 Henry VIII. c. 15, a tenant can recover possession. Bac. Abr. tit. Leases (A).
(*t*) Bac. Abr. tit. Leases (A K).
(*u*) Com. Dig. Estates by Grant (G) 14; 1 W. Saund. 250 f (1); Williams *v.* Bosanquet, 1 B. & B. 238; Ryan *v.* Clarke, 14 Q. B. 65; Harrison *v.* Blackburn, 17 C. B. N.S. 678, 34 L. J. C. P. 109; Doe d. Rawlings *v.* Walker, 5 B. & C. 118; Co. Litt. 46 b, 270 a; Litchfield *v.* Ready, 5 Ex. 939. An *interesse termini* is that interest which the lessee has in the term, whether commencing *in presenti* or *in futuro*, before he makes an actual entry into the lands. Where indeed the term is created under the Statute of Uses, there the statute transfers the possession to the use, and no entry is necessary; consequently in such a case an *interesse termini* cannot properly speaking exist. Shep. Touch. 267 e

Statute of Frauds.

To remedy the evils arising from verbal demises, the Statute of Frauds was passed (*v*). The object of the statute was to do away with the old method of transferring interests in land.

By sect. 1 of this statute it was enacted, that "all leases, estates, interests of freehold, or terms of years, or any uncertain interests, of, in, to, or out of, any messuages, manors, lands, tenements, or hereditaments, made or created by livery of seisin only, or by parol, and not put in writing, and signed by the parties so making or creating the same, or their agents thereunto lawfully authorised by writing, shall have the force and effect of leases or estates at will only, and shall not either in law or equity be deemed or taken to have any other or greater force or effect, any consideration for making any such parol leases or estates to the contrary notwithstanding."

"Except (*w*), nevertheless, all leases not exceeding the term of three years from the making thereof, whereupon the rent reserved to the landlord during such term shall amount unto two third parts at the least of the full improved value of the thing demised."

And the 4th section enacts, "That no action shall be brought whereby to charge the defendant upon any *contract* or sale of lands, tenements, and hereditaments, or any interest in or concerning them, unless the agreement (*x*) upon which such action

---

(*v*) 29 Car. II. c. 3.
(*w*) Sect. 2.
(*x*) A mere agreement to let lodgings (see *ante*, p. 41), not amounting to an actual demise, is a contract for an interest in land within this section, and must therefore be in writing. Edge *v.* Strafford, 1 C. & J. 391; Inman *v.* Stamp, 1 Stark. R. 12. And the furniture agreed to be let therewith forms an inseparable part

shall be brought, or some note or memorandum thereof, shall be in writing, signed by the party to be charged therewith, or some other person thereunto lawfully authorised."

The 8 & 9 Vict., c. 106, s. 3, enacts, that "a lease required by law to be in writing of any tenements or hereditaments, shall be *void at law* (y), unless made by deed."

Therefore, by the conjoint operation of the Statute of Frauds and the 8 & 9 Vict., c. 106, s. 3, all leases of any estate in any corporeal hereditament must be put in writing, and signed by the parties, or their agents authorised in writing; and such leases are *void at law*, unless they are made by deed. But there must be excepted leases of any estate in any corporeal hereditament for three years, or for any less term, which can still be made by word of mouth; provided such leases comply with the conditions mentioned in the 2nd section of the Statute of Frauds.

It must be borne in mind that leases, or agreements for leases, for three years, or for any less term, satisfying the conditions named in the 2nd section, fall within the provisions of the 4th section of the Statute of Frauds. Therefore whatever remedies may attach to them in their *character* as leases, no action can be brought upon such contracts unless there is some note in writing, signed by the party charged, or his agent, who need not be authorised in writing.

of the contract. Mechlen *v.* Wallace, 7 A. & E. 49; Vaughan *v.* Hancock, 3 C. B. 766. See also Wright *v.* Stavert, 2 E. & E. 721, 29 L. J. Q. B. 161.

(y) See *infra*, s. 2, Difference between Leases and Agreements.

Thus no action will lie on a verbal lease against the lessee for not taking possession (*z*), nor against the lessor for not giving up possession on the day agreed upon for the commencement of the term (*a*).

Effect of non-compliance with the Statute of Frauds.
By the terms of the Statute of Frauds, a lease (not complying with the conditions therein named) of any estate in any corporeal hereditament, for any term, is declared to have the force and effect of *an estate at will only* (*b*).

Presumed yearly tenancy.
This estate at will (*c*) may, like any other estate at will, be changed into a tenancy from year to year, by payment of rent after entry, or other circumstances indicative of an intention to create such yearly tenancy (*d*). Thus in Knight *v.* Bennett (*e*), which was an action of replevin, plaintiff entered a farm under an *oral* agreement for a lease for ten years, the rent (the amount not being mentioned) was to be paid half yearly; no lease was ever executed, but plaintiff occupied and paid a certain rent for two years; it was held that the lessor might distrain. Gaselee, J., said,

(*z*) Inman *v.* Stamp, 1 Stark. 12; Edge *v.* Strafford, 1 C. & J. 391.
(*a*) Drury *v.* Macnamara, 5 E. & B. 612; Jinks *v.* Edwards, 11 Ex. 775.
(*b*) Sect. 1.
(*c*) See *infra*, s. 4, Duration of Term as to Estate at Will.
(*d*) Doe d. Rigge *v.* Bell, 5 T. R. 471; Clayton *v.* Blakey, 8 T. R. 3; Berry *v.* Lindley, 3 M. & Gr. 498; Regnart *v.* Porter, 7 Bing. 453; Braithwaite *v.* Hitchcock, 10 M. & W. 494; Doe d. Thomson *v.* Amey, 12 A. & E. 476; Arden *v.* Sullivan, 14 Q. B. 832; Doe d. Pritchett *v.* Mitchell, 1 B. & B. 11; Doe d. Pennington *v.* Taniere, 12 Q. B. 998; Hill *v.* South Staffordshire Ry. Co. 11 Jurist, N.S. 192 L. J.; Crowley *v.* Vitty, 7 Ex. 319; 21 L. J. Ex. 136; Geeckie *v.* Monk, 1 C. & K. 307; Doe d. Monk *v.* Geeckie, ib. 307, 5 Q. B. 841; Clarke *v.* Moore, 1 Jon. & Lat. 723; Burrows *v.* Gradin, 1 D. &. L. 213; Donellan *v.* Read, 3 B. & Ad. 889; Foquet *v.* Moor, 1 Ex. 370; Furley *v.* Bristol and Exeter Ry. Co. 7 Ex. 415; Jones *v.* Shears, 4 A. & E. 832; Richardson *v.* Gifford, 1 A. & E. 52; Beale *v.* Sanders, 3 Bing. N. C. 850. See cases cited in notes 2 Smith L. C. 98.
(*e*) 3 Bing. 361.

"The agreement for a lease for ten years not having been reduced into writing, was invalid; but the plaintiff having entered and occupied for more than a year under the terms of that agreement, it is clear, according to the cases, that he was tenant from year to year."

Payment of rent is only one of the things which afford evidence of a yearly tenancy. For if a party enter and promise to pay a rent certain, or if he settle it in account, a tenancy from year to year may be presumed (*f*). Thus in Cox *v.* Bent (*g*), which was an action of replevin, plaintiff, who had, under an agreement for a lease, admitted a charge of half a year's rent in an account between himself and his landlord, was thereby held to have become tenant from year to year.

But where payment of rent, unexplained, would ordinarily imply a tenancy from year to year, the circumstances under which such payment was made may be proved for the purpose of repelling such an implication (*h*).

In order, however, that a tenancy at will should inure as a tenancy from year to year, it must be proved that the parties agreed to vary it by a new contract for a tenancy from year to year (*i*).

(*f*) Regnart *v.* Porter, 7 Bing. 451.
(*g*) 5 Bing. 185.
(*h*) Walker *v.* Gode, 30 L. J. Ex. 172; Doe *d.* Lord *v.* Crago, 6 C. B. 90; Oakley *v.* Monck, 3 H. & C. 706, 34 L. J. Ex. 137; The Marquis of Camden *v.* Battenbury, 5 C. B. N.S. 808; Doe *d.* Burne *v.* Prideaux, 10 East. 158.
(*i*) Doidge *v.* Bowers, 2 M. & W. 365; Doe *d.* Hall *v.* Wood, 14 M. & W. 687; Doe *d.* Lord *v.* Crago, 6 C. B. 98; Bishop *v.* Howard, 2 B. & C. 100; Doe *d.* Basto *v.* Cox, 11 Q. B. 122, 17 L. J. Q. B. 3; Doe *d.* Dixie *v.* Davies, 7 Ex. 89; Pinhorn *v.* Souter, 8 Ex. 763; *In re* Stroud, 8 C. B. 502; Doe *d.* Prior *v.* Ongley, 10 C. B. 25; The Guardians of the Woodbridge Union *v.* The Guardians of Colneis, 13 Q. B. 269; West *v.* Fritche, 3 Ex. 218; Oakley *v.* Monck, 3 H. & C. 706, 34 L. J. Ex. 137.

The occupation must have been as tenant. Therefore an agent or servant, if he is allowed to occupy premises belonging to his principal or master, for the more convenient performance of his duties, acquires no *estate* therein, even though he is also allowed to use the premises for the carrying on of his own business (*j*). Nor does the fact that the servant receives less wages by reason of his occupation of premises for the mere performance of his duties make any difference (*k*). The question in such cases is, whether the occupation is that of a tenant, or merely one necessarily connected with the service of the master.

Nor is the occupation of a mortgagor, in actual possession, or in receipt of the rents and profits, sufficient as between himself and the mortagee to create a tenancy, although, for some purposes, his occupation may resemble a tenancy at will (*l*).

Nor will an occupation under an agreement for the purchase of land create an implied tenancy from

(*j*) White *v.* Bayley, 10 C. B. N.S. 227, 30 L. J. C. P. 253.
(*k*) Bertie *v.* Beaumont, 16 East. 33 ; Rex *v.* Stock, 2 Taunt. 339 ; Mayhew *v.* Suttle, 4 E. & B. 347, 357, 23 L. J. Q. B. 372, 24 ib. 54 ; R. *v.* Shipdam, 3 D. & R. 384 ; R. *v.* Bardwell, 2 B. & C. 161 ; R. *v.* Kelstern, 5 M. & S. 136 ; R. *v.* Cheshunt, 1 B. & A. 473 ; R. *v.* Snape, 6 A. & E. 278 ; Allan *v.* England, 3 F. & F. 49 ; Hunt *v.* Colson, 3 Moo. & St. 790. Where a servant, as part remuneration for his services, occupies premises of his master without paying rent, in order to ascertain whether the servant is a substantial "householder" within the 43 Eliz. c. 2, s. 1, so as to be eligible for the office of overseer of the poor, the question is whether the occupation is subservient and necessary to the service? If it is, the occupation is that of the master; if it is not, the occupation is that of a tenant, and the servant is a householder. Reg. *v.* Spurrell, L. R. 1 Q. B. 72, 35 L. J. M. C. 74.

(*l*) Birch *v.* Wright, 1 T. R. 382. See the judgment of Buller, J., *ex parte* Wilson, 2 V. & B. 252 ; Moss *v.* Gallimore, 1 Smith's L. C. 470 (4th ed.) ; Trent *v.* Hunt, 9 Ex. 14 ; Hele *v.* Lord Bexley, 20 Beav. 127 ; Jolly *v.* Arbuthnot, 28 L. J. Ch. 547, 550 ; Walmsley *v.* Milne, 7 C. B. N.S. 115, 29 L. J. C. P. 97. See *infra*, Duration of Term, p. 98.

year to year, though it may create a tenancy at will (*m*).

Moreover, the payment of rent by the occupier must have reference to a year, or some aliquot portion of a year (*n*).

In Braithwaite *v.* Hitchcock (*o*) Parke, B., says, "Although the law is clearly settled, that where there has been an agreement for a lease, and an occupation without payment of rent, the occupier is a mere tenant at will, yet it has been held that if he subsequently pay rent under that agreement, he thereby becomes tenant from year to year. Payment of rent, indeed, must be understood to mean *payment with reference to a yearly holding*, for in Richardson *v.* Langridge, a party who had paid rent under an agreement of this description, but had not paid it with reference to a year, or any aliquot part of a year, was held nevertheless to be a tenant at will only."

If a person under a lease void by the Statute of Frauds becomes tenant from year to year, by occupation and payment of a yearly rent, he will be considered as holding upon all the terms of his lease, so far as they are applicable to or are not inconsistent with a tenancy from year to year (*p*). Thus in Doe *d.*

(*m*) Doe *d.* Newby *v.* Jackson, 1 B. & C. 448 ; Kirtland *v.* Poussett, 2 Taunt. 145; Hearne *v.* Tomlind, Peake, 192 ; Hope *v.* Booth, 1 B. & Ad. 498. See *infra*, Duration of Term, p. 98.
(*n*) Richardson *v.* Langridge, 4 Taunt. 128; Braithwaite *v.* Hitchcock, 10 M. & W. 497 ; Doe *d.* Hall *v.* Wood, 14 M. & W. 682. See the judgment of Williams, J., in The Marquis of Camden *v.* Battenbury, 5 C. B. N.S. 812.

(*o*) 10 M. & W. 497.
(*p*) Doe *d.* Rigge *v.* Bell, 5 T. R. 471 ; Beale *v.* Sanders, 3 Bing. N. C. 850 ; Richardson *v.* Gifford, 1 A. & E. 52 ; Doe *d.* Thompson *v.* Amey, 12 A. & E. 476 ; Doe *d.* Oldershaw *v.* Breach, 6 Esp. 106 ; Thomas *v.* Packer, 1 H. & N. 669 ; Pistor *v.* Cater, 9 M. & W. 315; Chapman *v.* Towner, 6 M. & W. 100 ; Doe *d.* Tilt *v.* Stratton, 4 Bing. 446 ; Berry *v.* Lindley, 3 M. & Gr. 511; Doe *d.* Davenish

Rigge v. Bell (*q*), where the defendant entered on a farm, and paid rent under a lease for seven years, not in writing, and one of the terms of the lease was that he was to quit at Candlemas, it was held that if the lessor chose to determine the tenancy before the expiration of the seven years, he could only put an end to it at Candlemas.

So again in Richardson *v.* Gifford (*r*), where the defendant occupied a house, &c., under an agreement void by the Statute of Frauds, and by his agreement promised to keep the premises in repair during his tenancy, he was held bound by his promise to repair. So a stipulation "to keep open the shop, and use best endeavours to promote the trade of it during the tenancy," is consistent with a tenancy from year to year (*s*). So is a stipulation that the tenant shall be paid for tillages on the expiration of his tenancy (*t*). A proviso for re-entry, for non-payment of rent, or for non-performance of covenants, has been held consistent with an implied yearly tenancy (*u*). But a stipulation for two years' notice to quit is inconsistent with a tenancy from year to year (*v*). So it would seem is a covenant to build or a stipulation to do more than tenantable repairs (*w*).

Where a person has entered under a lease void by

v. Moffat, 15 Q. B. 257 ; Lee *v.* Smith, 9 Ex. 662. See also Doe *d.* Pennington *v.* Taniere, 12 Q. B. 998; Oakley v. Monck, L. R. 1 Ex. Ch. 159. But a mere assignment by a lessee will not render the assignee liable to the stipulations in the lease without some act, such as payment of rent, to raise the presumption of a new tenancy. Elliott *v.* Johnson, L. R. 2 Q. B. 120.

(*q*) 5 T. R. 471.
(*r*) 1 A. & E. 52.
(*s*) Sanders *v.* Karnell, 1 F. & F. 356.
(*t*) Brocklington *v.* Saunders, 13 W. R. 46, Q. B.
(*u*) Thomas *v.* Parker, 1 H. & N. 669.
(*v*) Tooker *v.* Smith, 1 H. & N. 732.
(*w*) Bowes *v.* Croll, 6 E. & B. 264.

the Statute of Frauds, and has become, by implication, tenant from year to year, such tenancy may be determined by the usual notice to quit at the end of the first or any subsequent year thereof; and the tenancy will cease on the expiration of the term mentioned in the instrument, and the premises may then be recovered without any notice or demand (*x*). Thus where a tenant entered under an agreement for a lease for seven years, which was never executed, it was held that he was not entitled to notice to quit at the end of the seven years (*y*).

2. RECITALS.

Recitals of former instruments, or of some ante- Recitals. cedent circumstances which have led to the lease in question, are convenient for the sake of clearness and elucidation. They also explain the intention and meaning of the parties (*z*). As a lease by deed operates like any other deed as an estoppel, parties are generally prevented from afterwards disputing the facts therein recited (*a*). The question how far parties are bound by recitals in deeds has been much discussed. The doctrine of Lord Coke, that "a recital

(*x*) Doe *d*. Tilt *v*. Stratton, 4 Bing. 446; Doe *d*. Bromfield *v*. Smith, 6 East. 530.
(*y*) Doe *d*. Tilt *v*. Stratton, *supra*. See Berry *v*. Lindley, 3 M. & G. 498.
(*z*) See Cruise's Digest, title xxxii. Deed, c. xxi. s. 22; see Ringer *v*. Cann, 3 M. & W. 343.
(*a*) As to estoppel by recital, see Salter *v*. Kidgley, 1 Show. 58; Com. Dig. Estoppel (A) 2; Veale *v*. Warner, 1 Saund. Wills, 325 a, n. (c); the notes to the Duchess of Kingston's case, 2 Smith, L. C. 656 (5th edition); Lainson *v*. Tremere, 1 A. & E. 762; Bow-

man *v*. Taylor, 2 A. & E. 278; Hills *v*. Laming, 9 Exch. 256; R. *v*. Stamper, 1 Q. B. 123; Hill *v*. Manchester and Salford Waterworks Co. 2 B. & Ad. 544; Pargeter *v*. Harris, 7 Q. B. 708; Bayley *v*. Bradley, 5 C. B. 396; Young *v*. Raincock, 7 C. B. 310; Horton *v*. Westminster Improvement Commissioners, 7 Ex. 780; Hungerford *v*. Beecher, 5 Ir. Eq. R. N.S. 417; Pilbrow *v*. Atmospheric Railway Co. 5 C. B. 440; Wiles *v*. Woodward, 5 Ex. 557; South-Eastern Railway Co. *v*. Wharton, 31 L. J. Ex. 515.

doth not conclude because it is no direct affirmation" (b), has been expressly overruled. The law on this subject has been thus stated by Parke, B., in Carpenter v. Buller (c) :—" If a distinct statement of a particular fact is made in the recital of the bond or other instrument under seal, and a contract is made with reference to that recital, it is unquestionably true that, as between the parties to that instrument and in an action upon it, it is not competent for the party bound to deny the recital, notwithstanding what Lord Coke says on the matter of recital in Coke Littleton, 352 b; and a recital in instruments not under seal may be such as to be conclusive to the same extent. A strong instance as to a recital in a deed is found in the case of Lainson v. Tremere (d), where, in a bond to secure the payment of rent under a lease, it was recited that the lease was at a rent of £170, and the defendant was estopped from pleading that it was £140 only, and that such amount had been paid. So where other *particular* facts are mentioned in a condition to a bond, as that the obligor and his wife should appear, the obligor cannot plead that he appeared himself, and deny that he is married, in an action on the bond (e). All the instances given in Com. Dig. *Estoppel* (A) 2, under the head of ' Estoppel by Matter of Writing ' (except one which relates to a release), are cases of estoppel in actions on the instrument in which the admissions are contained. By his contract in the instrument itself a party is assuredly bound, and must fulfil it. But there is no authority to show that a party to the instrument would be estopped in an action by the other party, not founded on the deed, and *wholly collateral* to it (f), to dispute the facts so

(b) Co. Litt. 352 b.
(c) 8 M. & W. 212.
(d) 1 A. & E. 792.
(e) 1 Roll. Abr. 873, c. 25.

(f) See the South-Eastern Railway Co. v. Wharton, 31 L. J. Ex. 515, 6 H. & N. 520.

"admitted, though the recitals would certainly be evidence. For instance, in another suit, though between the same parties, where a question should arise whether the plaintiff held at a rent of £170 in the one case, or was married in the other case, it could not be held that the recitals in the bond were conclusive evidence of these facts. Still less would matter alleged in the instrument wholly immaterial to the contract therein contained; as, for instance, suppose an indenture or bond to contain an unnecessary description of one of the parties as assignee of a bankrupt, overseer of the poor, or as filling any other character, it could not be contended that such statement would be conclusive on the other party in other proceedings between them." Thus in Bowman v. Taylor (g) a deed recited that the plaintiff had invented certain improvements for which he had obtained a patent, and the defendant, in consideration of a license to use it, entered into a covenant, for breach of which he sued; the defendant, by his plea, traversed the invention of the plaintiff, and such plea was held bad on demurrer; the passage from Coke Littleton above quoted (h) was cited. However, the Court was unanimous in giving effect to the estoppel. "The law of estoppel," said Taunton, J., "is not so unjust or absurd as it has been too much the custom to represent. The principle is, that where a man has entered into a solemn engagement by and under his hand and seal as to certain facts, he shall not be permitted to deny any matter to which he has so assented. The question here is whether this be a matter so assented to by the defendant under his hand and seal, that he shall not be permitted to deny it in pleading? It is said that the allegation in the deed is made by way of recital; but I do not see that a statement such

(g) 2 A. & E. 278.   (h) 352 b.

as this is the less positive because it is introduced by a ' whereas.' "

It would therefore appear that, in order to make a recital operate as an estoppel, there must be—(1.) A distinct statement (*i*) of some material (*j*) particular (*k*) fact; (2.) A contract made with reference to such statement. But if it is the recital by one party of a fact within his knowledge, on the faith of which the other party contracted, the latter may perhaps not be estopped. Thus in Stronghill *v.* Buck (*l*), Paterson, J., said, in delivering the judgment of the Court, "When a recital is intended to be a statement which all parties to the deed have mutually agreed to admit as true, it is an estoppel upon all. But when it is intended to be the statement of one party only, the estoppel is confined to that party, and the intention is to be gathered from construing the instrument. All the cases were brought forward and considered in Young *v.* Raincock (*m*), and we have no doubt that the result of them is as above stated."

As to when a recital in a deed amounts to a covenant, see tit. Covenant (*n*).

3. WORDS OF DEMISE.

Distinction between leases and agreements.

The usual words of demise are—"demise, lease, and to farm let." But any other words which are sufficient to explain the intent of the parties, that the

---

(*i*) See Kepp *v.* Wiggett, 10 C. B. 35.
(*j*) Carpenter *v.* Buller, *supra*.
(*k*) See Rolle's Abrg. Estoppel (P), pl. 1 & 7 ; Com. Dig. Estoppel (A) 2 ; Salter *v.* Kidley, 1 Show. 59 ; Rainsford *v.* Smith, Dyer, 196 a, note ; Stroud *v.* Willis,
Cro. Eliz. 762. See judgment of Lord Denman in Lainson *v.* Tremere, *supra;* Doe *d.* Jeffreys *v.* Bucknell, 2 B. & Ad. 278.
(*l*) 14 Q. B. 787.
(*m*) 7 C. B. 310.
(*n*) *Post*, s. 7.

CH. IV.] HOW DEMISES ARE MADE. 57

one shall divest himself of the exclusive (*o*) possession, and the other come into it for a determinate time—whether such words run in the form of a license (*p*), covenant (*q*), or agreement (*r*)—are of themselves sufficient, and will, in construction of law, amount to a lease for years, as effectually as if the most proper and pertinent words had been used for the purpose (*s*). Thus a license to enjoy or inhabit a house has been deemed a demise of it (*t*). So if A, by articles, covenant with B that he shall have, hold, or enjoy certain lands for a certain time, this amounts to a lease; but if A covenant with B that C shall have, hold, or enjoy them, it is otherwise (*u*). So where the owner of the fee agreed to convey the premises to B for a certain number of years, at a certain rent, and the instrument contained the usual covenants for payment of rent, &c., this was holden to be a lease (*v*). So where A *agreed to let*, &c., it was holden to be a present demise (*w*). So where B agreed " to pay the sum of £140 per annum, in quarterly payments, for the house and premises at, &c.,

(*o*) See R. *v.* Morrish, 32 L. J. M. C. 245; Taylor *v.* Caldwell, 32 L. J. Q. B. 164, 3 B. & S. 826; Handcock *v.* Austin, 32 L. J. C. P. 252, 14 C. B. N.S. 429.

(*p*) Hall *v.* Seabright, 1 Sid. 428, 2 Keb. 561; Jepson *v.* Jackson, 2 Lev. 194; Trevor *v.* Roberts, Hard. 366; R. *v.* Winter, 2 Salk. 388; Watkins *v.* Overseers of Milton, L. R. 3 Q. B. 350, 37 L. J. M. C. 73; Grant *v.* Oxford Local Board, L. R. 4 Q. B. 9; Carr *v.* Benson, L. R. 3 Ch. App. 524. For the distinction between leases and licenses, see *post*, p. 68.

(*q*) Drake *v.* Monday, W. Jones, 231, Cro. Car. 207; Right *d.* Green *v.* Proctor, 4 Burr. 2208; Right *d.* Bassett *v.* Thomas, 3 Burr. 1441; Whitlock *v.* Horton,

Cro Jac. 91; Jones *d.* Trimleston *v.* Inman, Irish T. R. 433; Doe *d.* Pritchard *v.* Dodd, 5 B. & Ad. 689; Richards *v.* Sely, 2 Mod. 79; Havergill *v.* Hare, 3 Bulst. 252.

(*r*) See *infra*.

(*s*) Bac. Abr. tit. Lease (K). See Wilkinson *v.* Hall, 3 Bing. N. C. 532; Neale *v.* Mackenzie, 1 M. & W. 759.

(*t*) Bac. Abr. tit. Lease (K); 1 Leon. 129.

(*u*) Bac. Abr. tit. Lease (K); Drake *v.* Monday, Cro. Car. 207; Tisdale *v.* Essex, Hob. 34; Doe *d.* Jackson *v.* Ashburner, 5 T. R. 163.

(*v*) Alderman *v.* Neat, 4 M. & W. 704.

(*w*) Staniforth *v.* Fox, 7 Bing. 590.

for the term of seven, fourteen, or twenty-one years, at his option, at the end of every seven years, the rent to commence on the 1st January 1827," this was held to be a lease (*x*). A stipulation that a lease shall be afterwards drawn up between the parties, does not of itself indicate an intention that the instrument should not operate as a present demise, but merely that a more formal instrument should thereafter be executed by them, to effectuate the same thing, as being more satisfactory than the present instrument. Therefore, where by articles between A and B, it was covenanted and agreed that A "*doth let*" certain lands to B, for five years from Michaelmas then next, at a certain rent; and it was also covenanted that a lease should be made and sealed, according to the effect of these articles, before the feast of All Saints; this was holden to amount to an immediate lease, by reason of the words "doth let," in the present tense, and that the covenant for a future lease was only for further assurance; and the rather, in this case, as the time at which the future lease was to be executed was after the commencement of the term (*y*). So where A and B entered into an agreement with C, whereby they agreed " with all convenient speed to grant to him a lease of, and they did thereby set and let to him," certain premises, for a certain term, at a certain rent, the lease to contain certain covenants, in stipulating for one of which the words "this demise" occurred, the Court held

---

(*x*) Wright *v.* Trevezant, M. & M. 231, 3 C. & P. 441.

(*y*) Harrington *v.* Wise. Cro. Eliz. 486, Noy. 57. See Barry *v.* Nugent, cited in Doe *v.* Ashburner, 5 T. R. 165; Doe *v.* Groves, 15 East. 244; Goodtitle *v.* Way, 1 T. R. 735. The earliest case upon this point arose before the Statute of Frauds, upon these words, " I will you *shall have* a lease for twenty-one years of my lands in D, paying ten shillings yearly rent : *make a lease in writing, and I will seal it.*" This was held to be a valid lease. Moor. pl. 31; 3 Edw. VI. S. C. cited as Maldon's case, Cro. Eliz. 33.

this to be a good lease *in præsenti*, with an agreement to execute a more formal and perfect lease *in futuro;* the operative words of demise, "set and let," being in the present tense, made it a demise; and the word "demise," in the stipulation as to the covenants, showed that the parties intended it to be so (*z*). So where, by an instrument in writing, A agreed to let, and B agreed to take, a certain piece of land, for a certain term, at a certain rent; and in consideration of a lease to be granted for the said term, B agreed to lay out £2000, within four years, in building certain houses upon it, and A agreed to grant a lease, or leases, as soon as the houses should be covered in, and B agreed to take such leases, and to execute counterparts, the agreement to be considered binding till one fully prepared could be produced; the Court held this to be a lease (*a*). Lord Ellenborough, C.J., in giving judgment, said—"The rule to be collected from all the cases is, that the intention of the parties, as declared by the words of the instrument, must govern the construction; and here their intention appears to have been, that the tenant, who was to expend so much capital upon the premises within the first four years of the term, should have a *present legal interest* in the term, which was to be binding upon both parties; though when a certain progress should be made in the buildings, a more formal lease, or leases, in which, perhaps, the premises might be more particularly described, for the convenience of underletting or assigning, might be executed." So where A agreed to grant, seal, and execute to B "a legal and effectual lease" of certain premises, for a certain term,

---

(*z*) Baxter *v.* Brown, 2 W. Bl. 973.
(*a*) Poole *v.* Bentley, 12 East. 168. See also Warman v. Faithful, 5 B. & Ad. 1042; Alderman *v.* Neat, 4 M. & W. 704; Chapman *v.* Bluck, 4 Bing. N. C. 187.

from a day then past, at a certain rent, and to contain certain covenants, and, in the meantime, until such lease should be executed, B was to pay rent and to hold the premises subject to the covenants above mentioned; this was holden to be an actual demise, and not merely an agreement. No doubt the parties intended that a more formal contract should be executed; but as the tenant was to hold, in the meantime, on certain terms there set out, this was deemed to be a demise of the premises on those terms (*b*). By a "memorandum of *agreement*," between A and B, after reciting that A and C had abandoned the annexed contract for taking and letting certain land (and which contract was in effect a lease), it was agreed that A should let and B should take the same lands upon the conditions contained in the annexed contract, " the said rent to be paid by quarterly payments, and to be in amount £220; and we further bind ourselves, each to the other, to execute a similar agreement to the one recited and referred to." This agreement was stamped as a lease, but the one annexed to it had no stamp. The Court held that the stamped agreement incorporated the unstamped one, and that the two together might be given in evidence as a lease (*c*). So where the instrument was as follows:—
" September 21, 1829.—K. agrees to let and P. to take a house in its unfinished state, for the term of sixty years, at the rent of £525, payable quarterly, the first payment for the half-quarter at Christmas next,—P. to insure the premises, and to have the benefit of an insurance lately paid,—a lease and counterpart to be prepared at the expense of P., and to contain all the clauses, covenants, and agreements which K. entered

(*b*) Pinero *v.* Judson, 6 Bing. 206; Wilson *v.* Chisholm, 4 C. & P. 474.

(*c*) Pearce *v.* Cheslyn, 4 A. & E. 225.

into in the lease granted to him;" this was held to be an actual lease, and not a mere agreement for a lease (*d*), for several reasons:—First, the stipulation for a future lease was not executory merely, because the terms of it were ascertained, for it was to contain all the clauses in the lease granted to K. Secondly, although no precise day was fixed for the commencement of the rent, yet the tenant was to do the repairs, and, at Christmas following, to pay half a quarter's rent. Thirdly, the express words were, "agrees to let, and agrees to take;" and upon these the party was put into immediate possession. Fourthly, the tenant was to put the premises into repair; and, lastly, he was to insure (*e*).

But it is also laid down in Bacon's Abridgment (*f*), that "if the most proper and authentic words or form of words, whereby to describe and pass a present lease for years, are made use of, yet if upon the whole deed there appears no such intent, but that they are only preparatory, and relate to a future lease to be made, the law will rather do violence to the words than break through the intent of the parties." Therefore, if the instrument contain an express stipulation that it shall not be deemed or taken to be a lease or actual demise, it is clear that it must be deemed an agreement merely, and not a lease (*g*). Thus where a party agreed that, in case he should become entitled to certain copyhold premises on the death of another, he would immediately demise them to J. S., this was held to be an agreement only, and not a lease (*h*). So where an instrument contained a stipulation, that out of the

(*d*) Doe *v.* Ries, 8 Bing. 178 S. P.; Hancock *v.* Caffyn, 8 Bing. 358.
(*e*) See the judgment of Tindal, C.J., p. 181.
(*f*) Tit. Leases (K).
(*g*) Perring *v.* Brook, 7 C. & P. 360, 1 Moo & R. 510.
(*h*) Doe *v.* Clare, 7 T. R. 739.

rent mentioned a proportionate abatement should be made in respect of certain excepted premises, it was held that the parties intended to execute an agreement only; for until the rent should be apportioned, the lessor could not distrain for it (*i*). Thus in Doe *d.* Jackson *v.* Ashburner (*j*), where the words were, " Articles of agreement between S. and J., entered into in regard to his fulling-mills, &c. . . . that the said mills, &c., . . . he *shall enjoy*, and I engage to give him a lease in, for the term of thirty-one years, from Whitsuntide 1784, at the clear yearly rent of £110;" the instrument was held to be only an agreement for a lease. Lord Kenyon in his judgment said, " Here the words are, ' he shall enjoy and I engage to give him a lease,' &c. And the single question is, what was the intention of the parties using those expressions? Was it that this agreement should confer the legal interest? or, was it not in their contemplation that there should be another instrument to give that legal interest? The latter words clearly show that it was the intention of the parties that there should be some further assurance. It was *in fieri* at that time. . . . All the cases cited may be answered by the observation that there were either express words of present demise, or equivocal words, accompanied with others, to show the intention of the parties that there should not be a future lease; but in this case, where the context, in which I find the words ' shall enjoy,' imports that the parties do not mean that they should operate as a present demise, I think we should decide contrary to the intention of the parties if we were to determine that they should have that effect." So where there were words of present demise, but the amount of rent, the periods of payment, and other

(*i*) Morgan *v.* Bissell, 3 Taunt. 65.   (*j*) 5 T. R. 163.

terms of the holding were not mentioned, except as they were to be contained in a lease, which was to be prepared; this was held to be an agreement only, and not a lease (*k*). So an agreement "to let," with a purchasing clause, the tenant to enter any time on or before February 11, 1820, was held to be an agreement, and not a lease (*l*). Bayley, J., in giving judgment, said (*m*)—"In the case of Morgan *v.* Bissell (*n*), the rule is laid down thus, that although there are words of present demise, yet if we can collect on the face of the instrument the intent of the parties to give a future lease, it shall be considered an agreement only." So where by the instrument the rent was to be fixed by valuation, and the tenant was to find sureties for the payment of it, the Court held that it was not a lease, but an agreement only (*o*). So where a person proposed by letter to take a lease of a mine at a certain royalty and rent, the term to be about forty years from the 24th June then next, to which the other party by letter answered that he agreed to the terms, and should be happy to grant a lease conformable thereto; these letters were held to constitute an agreement only, and not a lease, because the matter was altogether *in futuro*, and much remained to be done (*p*). So where A by an instrument in writing agreed to grant at the time thereinafter mentioned, a lease of certain premises to B for fifty-nine years from the 28th March then last past, at a certain rent, payable quarterly, and B agreed to accept and take the lease and execute a counterpart, and in a subsequent part of the instrument it was stipulated

(*k*) Chapman *v.* Towner, 6 M. & W. 100; Clayton *v.* Burtenshaw, 5 B. & C. 41.
(*l*) Dunk *v.* Hunter, 5 B. & A. 322.
(*m*) Ibid. 326.

(*n*) 3 Taunt. p. 71, per Mansfield, C.J.
(*o*) John *v.* Jenkins, 1 C. & M. 227.
(*p*) Jones *v.* Reynolds, 1 Q. B. 506, 1 Gale & D. 62.

that the lease thereby agreed to be granted should be granted immediately after A should obtain a lease of the premises from C, to which he was entitled under a certain agreement; the Court held that this could not be deemed a lease, as the parties knew that there was no power to grant one (*q*). So where the instrument stated that the party was " contented to demise," &c., it was held that the word " contented " imported merely approbation of something to be done thereafter, and that the instrument therefore was not to be deemed a lease, but an agreement only (*r*). In Brashier *v.* Jackson (*s*), where a party agreed to grant a lease of premises for a certain term, at a certain rent, to be entered upon immediately, such lease to contain certain covenants, and all other usual and reasonable covenants; this was held to be an agreement, and not a lease; for what were reasonable covenants might be matter of dispute between the parties (*t*). So where by a written instrument A agreed to grant to B a lease of certain premises for seven years, at a certain rent, the lease to contain certain covenants, but at the end of the instrument there was a memorandum that B should have the option of having the lease for fourteen years; this was held to be an agreement, and not a lease (*u*). So where A agreed to grant B a lease of certain premises, for a certain term from the 25th of December then next, at a certain rent, the covenants to be the same as in a former lease of the same premises, and it was stipulated that until such lease should be granted, it should be lawful for A to distrain for the rent; this was held to be an agreement only,

(*q*) Hayward *v.* Haswell, 6 Ad. & E. 265.
(*r*) Pleazance *v.* Higham, 2 Mod. 81.
(*s*) 6 M. & W. 549.
(*t*) See Morgan *v.* Bissell, 3 Taunt. 65; Goodtitle *v.* Way, 1 T. R. 735. See also Alderman *v.* Neat, 4 M. &. W. 704; Baxter *v.* Brown, 2 W. Bl. 973.
(*u*) Rawson *v.* Eike, 7 A. & E. 451.

for if the parties intended that it should operate as a lease, the latter stipulation as to the power of distress would have been unnecessary (v). So where A agreed that he would grant B a lease of certain premises for fourteen years from the 25th December then last past, at £40 a year; but if B should pay him £40 before the end of the first quarter, then the rent should be reduced to £35; this was held not to be a lease (w).

The result, therefore, to be collected from the preceding decisions is, that an instrument containing words of present demise shall operate as a lease for years; a demise is thereby created, and a mere additional stipulation for the future execution of a formal lease is considered only in the nature of an agreement for further assurance. The intention of the parties is to be collected from the words of the instrument in the first place; but if the terms of the instrument be ambiguous, the nature of the estate and the acts of the parties may be resorted to as a guide.

The interpretation of instruments of this nature has, however, been affected by the 8 & 9 Vict., c. 106, s. 3, which enacts that a lease *required by law* (x), to be in writing, of any tenements and hereditaments made after 1st October 1845, is "void at law" unless it be by deed. But although it is void as a *lease*, yet it may operate as an agreement for a lease. In construing written instruments, purporting to demise corporeal hereditaments for a term required by law to be in writing under seal, the Courts have usually considered that such instruments (although in

(v) Bicknell v. Hood, 5 M. & W. 104.
(w) Hegan v. Johnson, 2 Taunt. 148. An agreement for a composition in lieu of tithes cannot be deemed a lease, for nothing is thereby demised. Brewer v. Hill, 2 Anst. 413.
(x) See *supra*, p. 47.

E

terms leases, and therefore void at law) may operate as agreements (*y*) for leases (*z*). At any rate, if a person is let into possession under an instrument void as a lease, and pays rent, that instrument may be used as evidence of the terms of the holding and the amount of the rent (*a*).

So in Rollason *v.* Leon (*b*), Bramwell, B., said, " I am of opinion that the plaintiff is entitled to the judgment of the Court. I confess I have always thought that the case of Stratton *v.* Pettit (*c*) was not rightly decided, and I should like to see it reviewed in a Court of Error. I think that case was wrong, on the ground that the judgment was based on reasoning inapplicable to the case of instruments made since the statute 8 & 9 Vict., c. 106. Before that statute parties might equally as well be supposed to contemplate a present actual demise as a prospective demise; but since the statute, when they cannot let for a period exceeding three years, except by deed, they may very reasonably be supposed, when they do not agree by

---

(*y*) It must be an agreement in conformity with the 4th section of the Statute of Frauds.

(*z*) Bond *v.* Rosling, 30 L. J. Q. B. 227, 1 B. & S. 371; Rollason *v.* Leon, 31 L. J. Ex. 96; 7 H. & N. 73; Tidey *v.* Mollett, 33 L. J. C. P. 235; 16 C. B. N.S. 298, overruling Stratton *v.* Pettit, 24 L. J. C. P. 182; 16 C. B. 420.

(*a*) Tress *v.* Savage, 4 E. & Bl. 36; Arden *v.* Sullivan, 14 Q. B. 832; see *supra*, s. 1. Thus in Lee *v.* Smith, 9 Ex. 663, it was held that the agreement, not being under seal, was void as a lease; but Martin, B., stated it to be his impression that it might be referred to for the purpose of seeing what the terms of the tenancy were; and Parke, B., stated that he did not dissent from that proposition.

(*b*) 31 L. J. Ex. 96; 7 H. & N. 73.

(*c*) 24 L. J. C. P. 182; 16 C. B. 420. In that case, by articles of agreement in writing, dated the 3d April 1854, plaintiff agreed to let, and defendant agreed to take, certain premises for the term of five years, and the defendant to purchase the same at the end of five years, yielding to the plaintiff, as well for the rent for the five years, as for the purchase, £70. The Court held that the intention of the parties, as declared by the words of the instrument, was to create a lease, but as it was not by deed, it was void.

deed, in using the words, '*agree to let*,' to mean what they actually say, and not an absolute lease."

So in Tidey *v.* Mollett (*d*), Erle, C.J., said, "I think the writing upon which this case turns is an agreement. The judges of this country were at one time not disposed to look upon writings such as this as agreements, but wishing to escape from the Statute of Frauds, they held them to be leases. Now, however, since the statute of 8 & 9 Vict., c. 106, making leases not under seal void, it has been the practice, for a very similar reason to that which existed before, to hold them to be agreements."

Again, such instruments being void as leases, may, it seems, be considered as agreements, so that a Court of Equity would enforce specific performance. Thus, in Taswell *v.* Parker (*e*), where an instrument void at law as a lease was sought to be enforced in equity, the Lord Chancellor (Lord Chelmsford), on appeal, in affirming the decree for specific performance made by Vice-Chancellor Stuart, says, "The legislature appears to have been very guarded in language, for it uses the expression *shall be void at law*—that is, as a lease. If the Legislature had intended to deprive the document of all efficacy, it would have said that the instrument shall be void *to all intents and purposes*. There are no such words in the Act. I think it would be too strong to say, that because it is void as a lease, it cannot be used as an agreement enforceable in equity, the intention of the parties having been that there should be a lease, and the aid of equity being only invoked to carry that intention into effect" (*f*).

(*d*) 33 L. J. C. P. 235 ; 16 C. B. N.S. 298 ; see also Anderson *v.* The Midland Railway Co. 30 L. J. Q. B. 94.

(*e*) 2 De G. & Jon. 559.
(*f*) See Davis *v.* Jones, 17 C. B. 625.

68 CREATION OF TENANCY. [PART I.

Distinction between leases and licenses.

Where the intention of the parties, as expressed in the instrument, is that the one shall divest himself of the exclusive possession of the subject-matter, and the other come into it for a determinate period, that is a lease (*g*). But if the intention of the parties is that the instrument should operate as a mere license, and that exclusive possession should not be given, then it is not a lease, although it may contain the usual words of demise (*h*).

A license, determined by a month's notice, to fasten boats to moorings, on payment towards the expenses of maintaining the moorings of the annual sum of £30, does not amount to a demise (*i*).

A liberty to take ore in a particular tract of country, and pay £25 a year rent for it, does not amount to a lease (*j*); and so also of a license to shoot (*k*), or to exercise a right of way (*l*). But where the words used in the agreement show an intention to give exclusive possession, there a tenancy will be created (*m*).

Stamp.

The distinction between a lease and a mere agreement or license was formerly of considerable importance, in consequence of the different stamp which the instrument required according as it fell within the one

(*g*) Reg. *v.* Morrish, 32 L. J. M. C. 245.
(*h*) Taylor *v.* Caldwell, 3 B. & S. 826; 32 L. J. Q. B. 164; Hancock *v.* Austin, 14 C. B. N. S. 634; 32 L. J. C. P. 252.
(*i*) Watkins *v.* Overseers of Milton, L. R. 3 Q. B. 350; 37 L. J. M. C. 73; Grant *v.* Oxford Local Board, L. R. 4 Q. B. 9. See Hill *v.* Tupper, 2 H. & C. 121; 32 L. J. Ex. 217; Stockport Waterworks Co. *v.* Potter, 3 H. & C. 300.

(*j*) Ward *v.* Day, 4 B. & S. 337; 5 Id. 359; 33 L. J. Q. B. 3; ib. 254; Carr *v.* Benson, L. R. 3 Ch. Ap. 524.
(*k*) Bird *v.* Great Eastern Railway Co. 19 C. B. N.S. 268. See Hooper *v.* Clark, 8 B. & S. 150; L. R. 2 Q. B. 200.
(*l*) Wood *v.* Leadbitter, 13 M. & W. 838; Hyde *v.* Graham, 1 H. & C. 593.
(*m*) Roads *v.* Churchwardens of Trumpington, L. R. 6 Q. B. 56; 40 L. J. M. C. 35.

class or the other. By the 23 Vict., c. 15, however, the stamp upon an agreement for a lease, for any term not exceeding seven years, was the same as for a lease; and now, by the 33 & 34 Vict., c. 97, s. 96, the term is extended to thirty-five years. In future, therefore, leases, and not mere agreements, will be made.

The *ad valorem* stamp duty on a lease is to be regulated by the consideration appearing on the face of it, although it may not be that which is actually paid (*n*). A lease containing several demises at distinct rents must be stamped according to the aggregate of the stamps required for the several demises (*o*).

It was held that if a lease contained a contract for the purchase of goods, it could not be given in evidence to prove the sale of the goods unless it had a lease stamp, although it might have had an agreement stamp (*p*). Now, by the 33 & 34 Vict., c. 97, s. 97, pl. 1, where part of the consideration consists of goods, &c., the value of the goods is to be deemed a consideration in respect of which the lease is chargeable with *ad valorem* duty (*q*).

A lease containing a right of purchasing the premises for a certain sum, only requires a single lease stamp (*r*).

If a stamped lease be altered by a new document,

(*n*) Duck *v.* Braddyll, M'Clel. 217; 13 Price 455; and see 33 & 34 Vict. c. 97, s. 97, pl. 2, *post* p. 75.
(*o*) Boase *v.* Jackson, 3 B. & B. 185; Blount *v.* Pearman, 1 Bing. N. C. 408; Parry *v.* Deere, 5 A. & E. 551.

(*p*) Corder *v.* Drakeford, 3 Taunt. 382; Clayton *v.* Burtenshaw, 5 B. & C. 41; Stone *v.* Rogers, 2 M. & W. 443.
(*q*) See the sect. *post*, p. 74.
(*r*) Worthington *v.* Warrington, 5 C. B. 636.

that will require a stamp (*s*), unless the alterations are merely an expression of what was before intended (*t*).

Where a document is a mere proposal for a lease which is subsequently agreed to by parol, it does not require a stamp (*u*); but where it is itself a concluded agreement, although unexecuted, it is otherwise (*v*).

Where the terms are agreed upon by parol, and only recognised by a subsequent instrument, it need not be stamped (*w*).

Where an unstamped agreement was incorporated in a subsequent stamped agreement, it was held the two constituted a perfect lease, and might be both given in evidence (*x*).

Though an oral lease for three years may be good, yet if it is reduced into writing it must be stamped (*y*).

It is proposed, in dealing with the present subject, only to refer to those general provisions of the latest Stamp Act which seem most material to the present work, and also to those special provisions which relate to stamps on leases and other matters bearing on the relations between landlord and tenant.

" The Stamp Act, 1870," which came into operation on 1st January 1871, enacts, by sect. 3, that

(*s*) Reed *v*. Deere, 7 B. & C. 261.
(*t*) Doe *d*. Waters *v*. Houghton, 1 Man. & R. 208.
(*u*) Drant *v*. Browne, 3 B & C. 665.
(*v*) Chadwick *v*. Clarke, 1 C. B. 700; Turner *v*. Power, 7 B. & C. 625.
(*w*) Bethell *v*. Blencowe, 3 M. & G. 119. See Marshall v. Powell, 9 Q. B. 779.
(*x*) Pearce *v*. Cheslyn, 4 A. & E. 225.
(*y*) Prosser *v*. Phillips, Bull. N. P. 269.

CH. IV.] HOW DEMISES ARE MADE. 71

" from and after the commencement of this Act, and subject to the exemptions contained in the schedule to this Act, and in any other Acts for the time being in force, there shall be charged for the use of Her Majesty, her heirs and successors, upon the several instruments specified in the schedule to this Act, the several duties in the said schedule specified, and no other duties." This in effect repeals all progressive duty, which is not mentioned in the Act or in the schedule thereto.

The Stamp Act, 1870, 33 & 34 Vict. c. 97— 99.

Sect. 7 provides that instruments written upon stamped paper, or subsequently stamped, are to be so stamped as to make the stamp appear upon the face of the instrument, and so as it cannot be used for any other instrument. Where there are more than one instrument on one paper, each must be stamped.

Sect. 8 provides that, except where it is provided to the contrary, an instrument containing separate matters is to be separately charged, and where it is made for considerations for which it is chargeable with *ad valorem* duty, and also for a further consideration, it is to be charged for such further consideration separately (*z*).

By sect. 9, instruments are to be stamped with the stamps which are appropriated to them by words on the face of the stamp.

By sect. 10, the facts affecting the amount of the stamp, &c., are to be set forth in the instrument, under certain penalties.

By sect. 15—(1.) " Except where express provision

(*z*) See, however, sect. 98, pl. 2, *post*, p. 75.

to the contrary is made by this or any other act, any unstamped or insufficiently stamped instrument may be stamped after the execution thereof, on payment of the unpaid duty, and a penalty of £10; and also by way of further penalty, where the unpaid duty exceeds £10 of interest on such duty, at the rate of £5 per centum per annum, from the day upon which the instrument was first executed, up to the time when such interest is equal in amount to the unpaid duty. And the payment of any penalty or penalties is to be denoted on the instrument by a particular stamp. (2.) Provided as follows :—(*a*) Any unstamped or insufficiently stamped instrument, which has been first executed at any place out of the United Kingdom, may be stamped at any time within two months after it has been first received in the United Kingdom, on payment of the unpaid duty only. (*b*) The Commissioners may, if they think fit, at any time within twelve months after the first execution of any instrument, remit the penalty or penalties of any part thereof."

By sect. 16—(1.) " Upon the production of an instrument chargeable with any duty as evidence in any Court of civil judicature, in any part of the United Kingdom, the officer whose duty it is to read the instrument shall call the attention of the judge to any omission or insufficiency of the stamp thereon ; and if the instrument is one which may legally be stamped after the execution thereof, it may, on payment to the officer of the amount of the unpaid duty, and the penalty payable by law on stamping the same as aforesaid, and of a further sum of £1, be received in evidence, saving all just exceptions on other grounds. (2.) The officer receiving the said duty and penalty shall give a receipt for the same, and make an entry in a book kept for that purpose of the payment of the amount thereof, and shall communicate to the Commissioners the name or title of the cause or proceeding in which, and of the party from whom, he received the said duty and penalty, and the date and description of the instrument, and shall pay over to the Receiver-General of inland revenue, or to such other person as the Commissioners may appoint, the money received by him for the said duty and penalty. (3.) Upon production to the Commissioners of any instrument in respect of which any duty or penalty has been paid as aforesaid, together with the receipt of the said officer, the payment of such duty and penalty shall be denoted on such instrument accordingly."

By sect. 17, " Save and except as aforesaid, no instrument executed in any part of the United Kingdom, or relating, wheresoever executed, to any property situate, or to any matter or thing done, or to be done, in any part of the United Kingdom, shall, except in criminal proceedings, be pleaded or given in evidence, or admitted to be good, useful, or available in law or equity, unless it is duly stamped in accordance with the law in force at the time when it was first executed."

Sects. 18–20 relate to proceedings for getting instruments stamped by Commissioners, after which they become admissible in evidence, notwithstanding any objection relating to duty.

By sect. 23, " Except where express provision is made to the contrary, all duties are to be denoted by impressed stamps only."

Sect. 24 relates to the proper mode of cancelling an adhesive stamp by writing the name and date across it, without which it will not be deemed duly stamped, unless it is otherwise proved that the stamp was affixed at the proper time.

The most material of the special regulations of the statute are as follows:—

AS TO DUPLICATES AND COUNTERPARTS.

By sect. 93, the duplicate or counterpart of an instrument chargeable with duty (except the counterpart of an instrument chargeable as a lease, such counterpart not being executed by or on behalf of any lessor or grantor), is not to be deemed duly stamped, unless it is stamped as an original instrument, or unless it appears by some stamp impressed thereon that the full and proper duty has been paid upon the original instrument, of which it is the duplicate or counterpart.

AS TO LEASES, &C.

By sect. 96—(1.) An agreement for a lease or tack, or with respect to the letting of any lands, tenements, or heritable subjects, for any term not exceeding thirty-five years, is to be charged with the same duty as if it were an actual lease or tack made for the term and consideration mentioned in the agreement. (2.) A lease or tack made subsequently to, and in conformity with, such an agreement, duly stamped, is to be charged with the duty of sixpence only.

By sect. 97—(1.) Where the consideration, or any part of the consideration, for which any lease or tack is granted or agreed to be granted, does not consist of money, but consists of any produce or other goods, the value of such produce or goods is to be deemed a consideration in respect of which the lease, or tack, or agreement is chargeable with *ad valorem* duty, and where it is stipulated that the value of such produce or goods is to amount at least to, or is not to exceed, a given sum; or where the lessee is specially charged with, or has the option of paying after, any permanent rate of conversion, the value of such produce or goods is for the purpose of assessing the *ad valorem* duty, to be estimated at such given sum, or according to such permanent rate. (2.) A lease or tack or agreement, made either entirely or partially for any such consideration, if it contains a statement of the value of such consideration, and is stamped in accordance with such statement, is, so far as regards the subject-matter of such statement, to be deemed duly stamped, unless or until it is otherwise shown that such statement is incorrect, and that it is in fact not duly stamped.

By sect. 98—(1.) A lease or tack or agreement for a lease or tack, or with respect to any letting, is not to be charged with any duty in respect of any penal rent, or increased rent, in the nature of a penal rent, thereby reserved or agreed to be reserved or made payable, or by reason of being made in consideration of the surrender or abandonment of any existing lease, tack, or agreement of, or relating to, the same subject-matter. (2.) No lease made for any consideration or considerations in respect whereof it is chargeable with *ad valorem* duty, and in further consideration either of a covenant by the lessee to make, or of his having previously made, any substantial improvement of or addition to the property demised to him, or of any covenant relating to the matter of the lease, is to be charged with any (*a*) duty in respect of such further

(*a*) This is a re-enactment of the 33 & 34 Vict. c. 44, s. 1,

consideration. (3.) No lease for a life or lives not exceeding three, or for a term of years determinable with a life or lives not exceeding three, and no lease for a term absolute, not exceeding twenty-one years, granted by an ecclesiastical corporation, aggregate or sole, is to be charged with any higher duty than 35s. (4.) No lease for a definite term exceeding thirty-five years, granted under the "Trinity College (Dublin) Leasing and Perpetuity Act, 1851," is to be charged with any higher duty than would have been chargeable thereon, if it had been a lease for a definite term, not exceeding thirty-five years. (5.) No lease or tack, or agreement for a lease or tack in Scotland, of any dwelling-house or tenement, or part of a dwelling-house or tenement, for any definite term not exceeding a year, at a rent not exceeding the rate of £10 per annum, is to be charged with any higher duty than one penny.

By sect. 99, the duty upon an instrument chargeable with duty as a lease or tack for any definite term less than a year of—(1.) any dwelling-house or tenement, or part of a dwelling-house or tenement, at a rent not exceeding the rate of £10 per annum; (2.) any furnished dwelling-house or apartments; or upon the duplicate or counterpart of any such instrument, may be denoted by an adhesive stamp, which is to be cancelled by the person by whom the instrument is first executed.

By sect. 100—(1.) Every person who executes or prepares, or is employed in preparing, any instrument upon which the duty may, under the provisions of the last preceding section, be denoted by an adhesive

which was passed in consequence of the decision *In re* Bolton's Lease, L. R. 5 Ex. 82; 39 L. J. Ex. 51.

CH. IV.] HOW DEMISES ARE MADE.

stamp, and which is not, at or before the execution thereof, duly stamped, shall forfeit the sum of £5. (2.) Provided that nothing in this section contained shall render any person liable to the said penalty of £5 in respect of any letters or correspondence.

By the schedule to the above Act, the following (amongst other) stamp duties are imposed, viz.:— *Schedule of stamp duties.*

Agreement for a lease, or tack, or for any letting. See Lease.

Agreement, or any memorandum, of an agreement, made in England or Ireland under hand only, or made in Scotland without any clause of registration, and not otherwise specifically charged with any duty, whether the same be only evidence of a contract, or obligatory upon the parties from its being a written instrument, ... £0 0 6

Exemptions.

(1.) Agreement or memorandum the matter whereof is not of the value of £5.

(2.) Agreement or memorandum for the hire of any labourer, artificer, manufacturer, or menial servant.

(3.) Agreement, letter, or memorandum made for or relating to the sale of any goods, wares, or merchandise.

(4.) [Not copied.] And see sect. 36.

Covenant. Any separate deed of covenant (not being an instrument chargeable with *ad valorem* duty, as a conveyance on sale or mortgage) made on the sale or mortgage of any property, and relating solely to the conveyance or enjoyment of, or the title to, the property sold or mortgaged, or to the production of the muniments of title relating thereto, or to all or any of the matters aforesaid—

Where the *ad valorem* duty in respect of the consideration or mortgage money does not exceed 10s., { A duty equal to the amount of such *ad valorem* duty.

In any other case, . . . £0 10 0

CREATION OF TENANCY. [PART I.

Deed of any kind whatsover, not described in this
schedule, ... £0 10 0
And see sect. 4.

Duplicate or counterpart of any instrument chargeable with any duty—

Where such duty does not amount to 5s., { The same duty as the original instrument.

In any other case, . . . 0 5 0
And see sect. 93.

Lease or tack—

(1.) For any definite term less than a year—

(a) Of any dwelling-house or tenement, or part of a dwelling-house or tenement, at a rent not exceeding £10 per annum, . 0 0 1

(b) Of any furnished dwelling-house or apartments where the rent for such term exceeds £25, . . . 0 2 6

(c) Of any lands, tenements, or heritable subjects, except or otherwise than as aforesaid, { The same duty as a lease for a year at the rent reserved for the definite term.

(2.) For any other definite term, or for any indefinite term;

Of any lands, tenements, or heritable subjects—

Where the consideration, or any part of the consideration, moving either to the lessor, or to any other person, consists of any money, stock, or security—

In respect of such consideration, { The same duty as a conveyance on a sale for the same consideration.

Where the consideration, or any part of the consideration, is any rent—

In respect of such consideration;

If the rent, whether reserved as a yearly rent or otherwise, is at a rate or average rate :—

CH. IV.] HOW DEMISES ARE MADE. 79

	If the term is definite, and does not exceed 35 years, or is indefinite.			If the term, being definite, exceeds 35 years, but does not exceed 100 yrs.			If the term, being definite, exceeds 100 years.		
	£	s.	d.	£	s.	d.	£	s.	d.
Not exceeding £5 per annum,	0	0	6	0	3	0	0	6	0
Exceeding £5, and not exceeding £10,	0	1	0	0	6	0	0	12	0
„ 10, „ „ „ 15,	0	1	6	0	9	0	0	18	0
„ 15, „ „ „ 20,	0	2	0	0	12	0	1	4	0
„ 20, „ „ „ 25,	0	2	6	0	15	0	1	10	0
„ 25, „ „ „ 50,	0	5	0	1	10	0	3	0	0
„ 50, „ „ „ 75,	0	7	6	2	5	0	4	10	0
„ 75, „ „ „ 100,	0	10	0	3	0	0	6	0	0
„ 100,									
For every full sum of £50, and also for any fractional part of £50 thereof,	0	5	0	1	10	0	3	0	0
Of any other kind whatsoever not hereinbefore described,	...			...			0	10	0

And see sects. 96–100.

Schedule, inventory, or document of any kind whatsoever referred to, in, or by, and intended to be used, or given in evidence as part of, or as material to, any other instrument charged with any duty, but which is separate and distinct from, and not indorsed on or annexed to, such other instrument—

Where such other instrument is chargeable with any duty not exceeding 10s., { The same duty as such other instrument.

In any other case, . . . £0 10 0

Exemptions.

(1.) [Not copied.]

(2.) Any public map, plan, survey, apportionment, allotment, award, and other parochial or public document and writing, made under or in pursuance of any act of Parliament, and deposited or kept for reference in any registry, or in any public office, or with the public books, papers, or writings of any parish.

Surrender—
Of copyholds. See Copyhold.
Of any other kind whatsover, not chargeable with
duty as conveyance on sale or mortgage,   £0 10 0

4. PARCELS DEMISED.

The parcels demised.

The tenements or parcels intended to be demised are next specified. They should be described with a reasonable degree of accuracy. Farming leases, after setting out the names or denominations and boundaries of the subject of the demise, usually refer to the occupation of the preceding tenant, and state the name by which the farm is known. The extent of land which general words inserted in a lease embrace depends on the object and intention of the parties, to be collected from the instrument (*b*).

The rule is, that whatever constitutes the essence of the thing granted, or is parcel of it, will pass with it, although it be accidentally severed at the time of the lease. Therefore, by the lease of a mill, the millstone passes, though severed at the time; and by the lease of a house the door-keys, &c., pass, although by accident they may not be in their places when the lease is made (*c*).

The word "land" will, unless a contrary intention is shown, be sufficient to pass, not only the soil, but all that grows or is built upon its surface, together with all that lies below it; but in general the particular subjects of demise are specified (*d*). A "farm" includes the farmhouse and buildings, and the lands

(*b*) See Doe *d*. Meyrick *v.* Meyer, 2 Cr. & J. 223; Maitland *v.* Mackinnon, 32 L. J. Ex. 49, 1 H. & C. 607; Hall *v.* Lund, 32 L. J. Ex. 113.

(*c*) See Shep. Touch. 89, 90, 246.

(*d*) Co. Litt. 4 a; Burton *v.* Brown, Cro. Jac. 648.

usually occupied therewith. A *grange* includes not only barns, but stables and outhouses used for the purpose of husbandry (e).

In some cases a grant of the *produce* of the soil will pass the soil itself; thus *pasture* will be taken not only as the *feeding on the land*, but as the land itself; and so the grant of a *wood* will pass the soil as well as the timber (*f*). And it would appear that a lease of the "issues and profits" of land would pass the land itself; for to have the issues and profits is the same thing as to have the land itself (*g*). If a grant be made of a "boilery of salt," the land passes, for that is the whole profit (*h*). By the grant of a forest, park, chase, or warren, in the soil of the grantor, the soil as well as the privilege passes; but it is otherwise if the soil be another's (*i*). The grant of a sheep-walk or a fold-course may include the soil by custom of the country (*j*). The lease of a fishery of a pond, with the spear-sedge, and the flags and the rushes growing in and about the same, has been held to pass the soil (*k*). If garden ground be let for years, and the lessee demise part of the term to an under-tenant, who builds upon it, by a grant of the garden ground the buildings thereon will pass (*l*). Where an annual sum was payable as tenant's damages, besides a way-leave rent for a coal railway passing through a farm, it was left to the jury to say whether the land covered by the railway passed by the agreement of letting to the tenant; because, if it did, the tenant, and not the landlord, was

(e) See the various tenements accurately described, Co. Litt. 4, 5.
(f) Co. Litt. 4 b. See Leigh v. Heald, 1 B. & Ad. 622.
(g) Parker v. Plumber, Cro. Eliz. 190.
(h) Co. Litt. 4 b.
(i) Cromwell's case, Dyer, 169 b.
(j) Huddlestone v. Woodroffe, 2 Roll. R. 61.
(k) Rex v. Old Alresford, 1 T. R. 358.
(l) Burton v. Brown, Cro. Jac. 648.

F

entitled to the sum payable as tenant's damages (*m*). A "messuage" is synonymous with dwelling-house, though more comprehensive (*n*), and will include adjacent buildings, orchard, and curtilage (*o*). The word "house," it seems, would comprise all that would pass by a grant of a messuage (*p*). The word "tenement" extends to everything that may be holden, and includes not merely land, but every inheritable right issuing out of, annexed to, or exercisable in land, such as advowsons, tithes, rents, &c. (*q*); but in leases it is commonly used in a restricted sense, as applicable only to houses and buildings. The word "hereditaments" extends not only to lands and tenements, but to some of the subjects of inheritable personal property, such as heirlooms (*r*). The word "premises" is very often introduced into leases, both as a term of reference and as a term of description; when used as a term of reference, it includes not only the parcels demised, but also the term granted (*s*).

It is a general rule in the construction of deeds that where lands are described (*t*) with sufficient certainty, as by giving a particular name to a close, the addition of an allegation mistaken or false respecting it, as,

(*m*) Wilson *v.* Anderson, 1 C. & K. 544.
(*n*) Doe *d.* Clements *v.* Collins, 2 T. R. 502, *per* Ashurst, J.
(*o*) Fenn *v.* Grafton, 2 Bing. N. C. 617 ; Shep. Touch. 94.
(*p*) See the cases cited in "Hodges on Railways," 174–174, as to the interpretation put by the Courts on the words "house or manufactory" in the 92d sect. of the Lands Clauses Consolidation Act, 8 & 9 Vict. c. 18. Consult also Hargr. note 21 to Co. Litt. 5 b; Chard *v.* Tuck, 3 Leon. 214;

Carden *v.* Tuck, Cro. Eliz. 89 S. C.; Smith *v.* Martin, 2 Saund. 400, note 2; Steele *v.* Midland Railway Co., L. R. 1 Ch. Ap. 275.
(*q*) Co. Litt. 6 a, 20 a ; Gully *v.* Bishop of Exeter, 4 Bing. 295.
(*r*) Lord Stafford *v.* Buckley, 2 Ves. Sen. 170 ; Taylor *v.* Martindale, 12 Sim. 158.
(*s*) Onsley *v.* Fisk, 1 Anders. 236 ; Jerman *v.* Orchard, Skin. 528.
(*t*) Doe *d.* Beach *v.* Lord Jersey, 1 B. & Ald. 550, 3 B. & C. 870.

for instance, in the name of the late occupier (*u*), or in the number of acres (*v*), or in the abuttals (*w*), or parish (*x*), or describing the premises as freehold instead of leasehold (*y*), or other mere misdescription (*z*), will not avoid the instrument (*a*). But where lands are described in general terms, the addition of a particular circumstance or description will operate by way of restriction or modification (*b*). Thus where an estate consisted of thirteen closes, and eight of the closes were *specifically* granted by name, it was ruled that the previous specific enumeration restrained the operation of the subsequent general words, and excluded the otherwise general effect of the deed, so that only the eight specified closes passed by the grant (*c*). So where one having customary tenements, *compounded* and *uncompounded*, surrendered to the use of his will "all and singular the lands, tenements, &c., whatsoever in the manor which he held of the lord by copy of court-roll, in whose tenure or occupation soever the same were, being of the yearly rent to the lord in the whole of £4, 10s. 8½d., *and compounded for*," it was held that the words "and compounded for" restrained the operation of the surrender

(*u*) Field *v.* Beaumont, 1 B. & Ald. 247; Welby *v.* Welby, 2 Ves. & B. 191; Pullin *v.* Pullin, 3 Bing. 47; Swift *v.* Eyres, Cro. Car. 546, W. Jones, 435, Roll Abr. 52 Graunts, pl. 26, 27 S. C.; Trapp's case, 3 Leon. 235; Windham *v.* Windham, 3 Dyer, 376; Chamberlaine *v.* Turner, Cro. Car. 129; Blake *v.* Gold. W. Jones, 379, Cro. Car. 447.
(*v*) Lord Willoughby *v.* Foster, 1 Dyer, 80 b.; Com. Dig. tit. Fait (E.), 4.
(*w*) Roberts *v.* Karr, 5 Taunt. 501.
(*x*) Lambe *v.* Reaston, 5 Taunt. 207; Robinson *v.* Button, 2 Roll Abr. 52, Graunts P. pl. 21.

(*y*) Doe d. Dunning *v.* Cranstoun, 7 M. & W. 1.
(*z*) See Manning *v.* Fitzgerald, *post*, p. 85.
(*a*) Doe d. Smith *v.* Galloway, 5 B. & Ad. 45, Com. Dig. tit. Fait (F.), 3 Preston Abstr. 206.
(*b*) Doe d. Smith *v.* Galloway, 5 B. & Ad. 45; Doe d. Parkin *v.* Parkin, 5 Taunt. 321; Harris *v.* Greathed, 8 East. 91; Bro. Abr. Graunts, pl. 92.
(*c*) Doe d. Meyrick *v.* Meyrick, 2 Cr. & J. 225; Payler *v.* Homersham, 4 M. & S. 423. But see Ringer *v.* Cann, 3 M. & W. 343.

to that description of copyholds then belonging to the surrenderer, and that the words " being of the yearly rent, &c., of £4, 10s. 8½d.," which were not referable to any actual amount of the rents, either compounded or uncompounded, though much nearer to the whole than to the compounded only, could not qualify or impugn that restriction (*d*).

If a grant be made of a certain farm called Lismote, now in the possession of J. S., the farm will pass to the grantee, although not in the possession of J. S., but of a different person, because the error in the name of the occupier will not vitiate the grant; but if the lands of Lismote extend into several parishes, and a grant is made of the lands of Lismote *situate in the parish of A*, then only so much of the lands as lie within the specified parish will pass, because the words " in the parish of A " are restrictive (*e*). Under a lease of all that part of the park called B, situate and being in the county of O, and now in the occupation of S, lying within certain specified abuttals, with all houses, &c., belonging thereto, and which now are in the occupation of S, a house on a part which was within the abuttals, but not in the occupation of S, was held to pass (*f*). By a lease of all that townland of B, containing 509 acres arable meadow and pasture, bounded by certain boundaries, it was held that 400 acres of bog and land reclaimed from bog within the boundaries passed (*g*). Where a lease of land was described by admeasurement, " with the

(*d*) R. *d*. Conolly *v.* Vernon, 5 East. 51. The cases are well distinguished in the judgment of the Court, delivered by Lord Ellenborough, C.J.; but see Strut *v.* Finch, 2 Sim. & St. 229.

(*e*) 3 Prest. Abstr. 206, *Falsa demonstratio non nocet;* Shep. Touch. 246.

(*f*) Doe *d*. Smith *v.* Galloway, 5 B. & Ad. 43. See Morris *v.* Dimes, 1 Ad. & E. 663; and Martyr *v.* Lawrence, 2 De G. J. & S. 261.

(*g*) Jack *v.* M'Intyre, 12 Cl. & Fin. 151.

houses now erected or to be erected thereon" (it being found as a fact by the jury, that at the time the lease was executed the foundations of the houses had been laid), it was held to be in effect the same as the lease of a specific house, and the actual measurements not corresponding with those stated in the lease, were held to be merely *falsa demonstratio* (*h*).

Where the demise is in its terms definite and certain, no evidence is admissible in contradiction of the instrument (*i*). But whether a particular thing be parcel of the demised premises, is matter of evidence to be collected from the nature of the subject, and from its state and condition at the time of making the demise (*j*). Thus a demise of a piece of ground, late in the occupation of J. S., will not pass a vault built under the ground demised, and which at the time of making the lease was in the tenancy of a third person (*k*). Nor will the demise of a messuage, with all the rooms thereto belonging, comprise a room which had been separated by a brickwork partition from the rest of the house, and which had not been used with it for many years prior to the making of the lease, although the room was situated within the external walls (*l*). Where there was in a lease a precise description by metes and bounds of a house and premises, but an adjoining stable occupied with the house for many years previously was not included in the metes and bounds; it was held that it did not pass under the words "together with all stables, &c.,

(*h*) Manning *v.* Fitzgerald, 29 L. J. Ex. 24.
(*i*) Doe *d.* Brown *v.* Brown, 11 East. 441; Doe *d.* Freeland *v.* Burt. 1 T. R. 701. See Hunt *v.* Singleton, Cro. Eliz. 473.
(*j*) Field *v.* Beaumont, 1 B & Ald. 247; Skipworth *v.* Green, 1 Stra. 610; Hall v. Lund, 32 L. J. Ex. 117.
(*k*) Doe *d.* Freeland *v.* Burt, 1 T. R. 701; Press *v.* Parker, 2 Bing. 456.
(*l*) Kerslake *v.* White, Appendix to Manning's 2 P. Digest, 368, 2d edit.; 2 Stark, 2 P. C. 508.

to the said premises hereby demised belonging or appertaining" (*m*).

Where the premises described by metes and bounds included a portion of a walk common to a row of houses, and also granted a right of way over the whole walk to the lessee; it was held that the premises as described by metes and bounds passed to the lessee notwithstanding the grant of the right of way (*n.*)

When the number of acres or estimated extent of the farm is specified, the words "more or less," or some equivalent expression, should be added, in order to show that the contents were mentioned as matter of general description in the lease, and not to regulate the quantity of land or amount of rent. The effect of the words "more or less," added to the statement of quantity, has not been absolutely fixed by decision, being sometimes considered as intending only to cover a small difference one way or the other, and sometimes as leaving the quantity altogether uncertain (*o*).

The word "appurtenances," is introduced into leases for the purpose of including any easements or

(*m*) Maitland *v.* Mackinnon, 32 L. J. Ex. 49.
(*n*) Curling *v.* Mills, 6 M. &. E. 173; for plan of the premises, see Dykes *v.* Blake, 4 Bing. N. C. 463.
(*o*) Marquis Townshend *v.* Stangroom, 6 Vesey, 341; Godfrey *v.* Little, 2 R. & My. 630-635; Winch *v.* Winchester, 1 Ves. & B. 375; Neale *d.* Leroux *v.* Parkin, 1 Esp. 229; Day *v.* Finn, Owen, 133; Cross *v.* Elgiu, 2 B. & Ad. 110; Rushworth's case, Clayton's Rep. 46. Questions on this subject often arise on contracts of sale, and serve to illustrate the construction of similar clauses in agreements for leases. Though the land is neither bought nor sold professedly by the acre in agreements for purchase, the presumption is that, in fixing the price, regard was had on both sides to the quantity which each party supposed the estate to contain. See Sugden's "Vendors and Purchasers," 324, 14th edit.

servitudes used or enjoyed with the demised premises (*p*).

In order to constitute an appurtenance, there must exist a propriety of relation between the principal or dominant subject, and the accessory or adjunct; which is to be ascertained by considering whether they so agree in nature and quality, as to be capable of union without incongruity (*q*). If a lease be made of a house and land, with a right of cutting turf on an adjacent bog, by such demise the right of turbary will be appurtenant to the house, and upon any assignment of the lessee's interest such right will pass as an appurtenance; but a right of cutting turf cannot be rendered appurtenant to land alone, as the fuel is only intended for consumption in a house (*r*). So common of pasture cannot be made appurtenant to a house without land attached to it on which cattle can be kept (*s*). Nor can land be made appurtenant to land, nor an incorporeal hereditament to things incorporeal.

The strict technical meaning of the word "appurtenances" is confined to the buildings, curtilage, and garden belonging to the house, and does not include land usually occupied with the house (*t*). If, however, it can be collected from the deed itself, that the parties did not intend to use the word in its strictly legal sense, the Court, in order to effectuate

(*p*) Potter *v.* North, 1 Saund. 350.
(*q*) See Gale on Easements, p. 11.
(*r*) Tyrringham's case, 4 Rep. 37; Co. Litt. 121 b.
(*s*) Scholes *v.* Hargreaves, 5 T. R. 46.

(*t*) Bro. Abr. Feoffments de Terres, pl. 53; Bettisworth's case, 2 Rep. 32 a; Hearne *v.* Allen, Cro. Car. 57; Buck *d.* Whalley *v.* Nurton, 1 B. &. P. 53; Doe *d.* Norton *v.* Webster, 12 A. & E. 442. See Smith *v.* Martin, 2 Saund. 401, note 2.

their object, will give to the word the meaning which the parties intended it to bear (*u*).

The length of time which will invest a hereditament with the quality of an appurtenance is not capable of accurate definition, but in order to pass as appurtenant by the assignment of a lease, it should acquire the *reputation* of being parcel of the premises comprised in the demise (*v*).

Easements and privileges legally appurtenant to property pass by a conveyance of the property simply without any additional words; but easements and privileges may be used or enjoyed with, or may be reputed to appertain to, property, and may be capable of being conveyed with it, without being legally appurtenant; and such easements will not pass by a conveyance of the property simply, or without being expressly mentioned (*w*).

If, however, any right of way or other easement is intended to be demised, the lease should extend to all ways or other easements appertaining to the demised premises, or *used and enjoyed* with any part thereof(*x*), because the operation of the word "appurtenances" will be restrained to a previously existing right, and will not include, for instance, a right of way over the

(*u*) See Barlow *v*. Rhodes, 1 Cr. & M. 439, *per* Lord Lyndhurst; Morris *v*. Edgington, 3 Taunt. 24.

(*v*) Higham *v*. Baker, Cro. Eliz. 16; Jennings *v*. Lake, Cro. Car. 168.

(*w*) See Davidson's Conveyancing, vol. i. 87; James *v*. Plant, 4 A. & E. 749, 5 B. & Ad. 791; Barlow *v*. Rhodes, 1 Cr. & M. 439; Bower *v*. Hill, 2 Bing. N. C. 339; Thomas *v*. Thomas, 2 Cr. M. & R. 34; Murley *v*. M'Dermott, 8 A. & E. 138; Hinchcliffe *v*. Earl of Kinnoul, 5 Bing. N. C. 1; Onley *v*. Gardiner, 4 M. & W. 496; Clayton *v*. Corby, 2 G. & D. 174; Worthington *v*. Gimson, 29 L. J. Q. B. 116; Suffield *v*. Brown, 33 L. J. Ch. 249; Crossley *v*. Lightowler, 36 L. J. Ch. 584; Pyer *v*. Carter, 1 H. & N. 916; Polden *v*. Bastard, L. R. 1, Q. B. 158.

(*x*) Whalley *v*. Thomson, 1 B. & P. 376; Harding *v*. Wilson, 2 B. & C. 100; Kooystra *v*. Lucas, 5 B. & Ald. 831; Barlow *v*. Rhodes, 1 Cr. M. & N. 439.

soil of the lessor which had been extinguished by unity of ownership; and such a privilege will not pass to the lessee unless it be a way of necessity, without the introduction of words showing the lessor's intention to create the right or servitude *de novo* (*y*).

Where there is no right of way, properly so called, but only a road used by the owner who leases the premises, and then accepts a surrender of part with all ways, &c., therewith now used and enjoyed, this does not give the owner a right of way. Such words will *revive* a right of way which once existed, but which remained in abeyance during the joinder of the dominant and servient tenements, but they will not *create* a right of way (*z*).

After the parcels are set out, exceptions and reservations are often inserted in favour of the lessor. An exception, being the act of the lessor, is construed strictly against him (*a*). An exception must consist of some component existing part of the *thing demised*, capable of being severed and distinguished from it; while a reservation (*b*) extends to some right or profit

Exceptions and reservations.

(*y*) James *v.* Plant, and other cases cited *supra*.
(*z*) Langley *v.* Hammond, L. R. 3 Ex. 161; 37 L. J. Ex. 118.
(*a*) Shep. Touch. 77; Earl of Cardigan *v.* Armitage, 2 B. & C. 197.
(*b*) Shep. Touch. p. 80. "A reservation is a clause of a deed whereby the lessor, &c., doth reserve some new thing to himself out of that which he granted before. . . . This doth differ from an exception, which is ever part of the thing granted, and of a thing *in esse* at the time . . . ." See also Co. Litt. 47 a; Brooke's Abr. tit. Reservations, pl. 46; Anon. Moor. 90, case 234; Anon.

3 Leon. 29, case 57, 54; case 79, 56; case 82. "A right of way cannot in strictness be made the subject either of exception or reservation, as it is neither parcel of, nor issuing out of, the thing granted. The former being essential to an exception, and the latter to a reservation. A right of way *reserved* (using that word in a popular sense) to a lessor is, in strictness of law, an easement newly created by way of grant from the lessee, in the same manner as a right of sporting or fishing." The Durham and Sunderland Railway Co. *v.* Walker, 2 Q. B. 967, *per* Tindal, C.J. See Pannell *v.* Mill, 3 C. B. 625.

which previously had no separate existence, but is to issue from or be derived out of the thing leased. The word "excepting" is often applied both to reservations and exceptions. But as they require remedies wholly different, they should be carefully distinguished (c).

The requisites to make a good exception are enumerated in "Sheppard's Touchstone" (d):—1. The exception must be in apt words, as "saving," "excepting," &c. 2. It must be part of the thing demised, as timber trees (e), mines, and quarries; and not of some other thing, as rent-heriot, suit of court, suit of mill, which are reservations (f); or liberty of hawking, hunting, fishing, and fowling, which are privileges or rights granted to the lessor, though words of reservation and exception be used (g). But where there was a lease of certain lands, together with all houses, water-courses, &c., excepting "a water-course flowing or descending from" a certain spot, through a meadow; it was held in this peculiar case to be an exception of the water itself, not of the channel through which it flowed (h). 3. It must be part only, and not the greater part. 4. It must be of such a thing as is severable from the thing granted, and not an inseparable incident. Thus if a lease be made of a

(c) Com. Dig. tit. Faits (E), 8; Pannell v. Mill, 3 C. B. 625; Fancy v. Scott, 2 M. & Ry. 335; Mitcalfe v. Westaway, 17 C. B. N.S. 658, 34 L. J. C. P. 114; Proud v. Bates, 11 Jur. N.S. 441, Wood, V.C.; Doe d. Douglas v. Lock, 2 A. & E. 743; Wickham v. Hawker, 7 M. & W. 76; Lord Cardigan v. Armitage, 2 B. & C. 197; Bullen v. Denning, 5 B. & C. 842; Goodright d. Peters v. Vivian, 8 East. 190; Moore v. Earl of Plymouth, 3 B. & Ald. 68.
(d) Page 77.

(e) As to the meaning of timber trees, see "Cragg on Trees and Woods."
(f) See Doe d. Douglas v. Lock, 2 A. & E. 743.
(g) Wickham v. Hawker, 7 M. & W. 76. See Fancy v. Scott, 2 M. & R. 335; Blatchford v. Plymouth, 3 Bing. N. C. 691; Co. Litt. 47 a, 143 a.
(h) Doe d. Egremont v. Williams, 17 L. J. Q. B. 154. See Blatchford v. Mayor of Plymouth, 3 Bing. N. C. 691.

rectory except the glebe, the exception is void, for no rectory can exist without a glebe; and so of a manor without the demesnes (*i*). 5. It must be of such a thing as he that doth except may have, and which properly belongs to him. Thus it must be of a particular thing out of a general, and not of a particular out of a particular, as of one acre out of twenty, or of a demise of house and shops, except the shops (*j*.) It must be certainly described and set down; as if a man grant all his lands in Essex, except his lands in Dale, or excepting one particular acre, such exception is good; but if the exception be of a chamber in a house, or of an acre, without saying which chamber or acre, the exception is void. But an *agreement to let* a farm, less a stated number of acres, will be supported in equity, though the lands *to be excepted* are not specified. Thus where a rector agreed to let a farm, except thirty-seven acres (not saying which), and the tenant took possession, but before the lease was executed, disputes arose respecting the lands to be taken by the rector, on a bill being filed against the tenant for non-performance of the agreement, it was held that the rector had a right to select the lands, as the lease had not been executed (*k*). A lease of lands excepted "all timber, timber trees, and other trees, &c., bushes and thorns, other than such bushes and thorns as should be necessary for the "repairs of the fences," the lessee covenanting to keep the fences in repair, and the lessor to find and provide, if growing on the premises, rough timber stakes and bushes; it was held that the provision as to bushes and thorns necessary for repairs was not an exception out of an exception, but that all trees, bushes,

(*i*) Mabie's case, Winch. 23.
(*j*) 2 Roll Abr. 453, 454; Dorrell *v.* Collins, Cro. Eliz. 6. See Cudlip *v.* Rundall, 3 Salk. 156.

(*k*) Jenkins *v.* Green, 28 L. J. Ch. 817.

and thorns were excepted out of the demise, whether part of a fence or not, or whether necessary for repairs or not (*l*).

The same rule as to what is included in the particular thing leased or granted applies to exceptions (*m*). Therefore an exception of all the wood will be an exception of the soil whereon the wood grows (*n*), unless it clearly appear that it was merely the intention of the parties to except only the wood itself (*o*). Thus in Leigh *v.* Heald (*p*), by the lease of a tenement described as containing nineteen acres, save and except all timber trees, wood, and underwoods, &c., six acres of the soil, which at the time of the lease were covered with growing wood, were not excepted. The question is, whether the expression extends to the place on which the trees grow, or merely to the trees, and must be governed by the intention, to be collected from the whole of the instrument.

A valid exception or reservation out of the demised premises cannot be made to a person who is a stranger to the estate. Thus upon a conveyance of lands in fee by a mortgagee, which was confirmed by the mortgagor, to the purchaser, it was covenanted that it should be lawful for the mortgagor, his heirs and assigns, to search for coal in the premises, and to take and carry away what should be found. It was held that this covenant could not operate as an exception or reservation in favour of the mortgagor, since he had no legal estate in him, and was in law no more than

(*l*) Jenney *v.* Brook, 6 Q. B. 323.
(*m*) Shep. Touch. 100. See Hewitt *v.* Isham, 7 Exch. 77; Liford's case, 11 Co. R. 51 b.
(*n*) Ive *v.* Sams, Cro. Eliz. 521; Bacon *v.* Gyrling, Cro. Jac. 296; Whistler *v.* Paslow, Cro. Jac. 487.

(*o*) Pincomb *v.* Thomas, Cro. Jac. 524. See Smith *v.* Bole, Cro. Jac. 458.
(*p*) 1 B. & Adol. 622. See also London *v.* Southwell, Hob. 304; Wyndham *v.* Way, 4 Taunt. 316.

a stranger to the estate, and could not except or reserve that which he had not before (*q*).

5. HABENDUM.

The object of the *habendum* is to fix with certainty the time for which the parcels demised are to be held, and to determine the quantity of the estate granted (*r*). The *habendum*, however, is not an essential part of a deed, for the premises are the operative part. But if no *estate* be mentioned in the premises, the grantee will take nothing under that part of the deed, except by implication and presumption of law. If a *habendum* follow, the intention of the parties as to the estate to be conveyed will be expressed in the *habendum*, consequently no implication or presumption of law can be made; and if the intention so expressed be contrary to the rules of law, the intention cannot take effect, and the deed will be void. Thus where freehold lands were conveyed to W., his heirs and assigns, to hold the same unto W., his heirs and assigns, *from and after the death of H.;* it was held that an immediate estate of freehold was given by the premises, and that the *habendum* had not the effect of rendering the conveyance void by limiting a freehold to commence *in futuro* (*s*). If land be granted to J. S. generally, without words of limitation, *habendum* for years, or at will, by the premises, J. S. would take an implied estate for life, but such implication is

Habendum.

(*q*) Chetham *v.* Williamson, 4 East. 469; Moore *v.* Lord Plymouth, 3 B. & Ald. 66.
(*r*) Shep. Touch. 75; Com. Dig. tit. Fait (E) 9.
(*s*) Goodtitle *d.* Dodwell *v.* Gibbs, 5 B. & C. 709, 717; judgment of Abbot, C.J., and cases there cited, as to the operation of the *habendum*. See also Doe *d.*
Timmis *v.* Steele, 4 Q. B. 667, Co. Litt. 299 a, Plowden, 153; Wyburd *v.* Tuck, 1 B. & P. 464; Shaw *v.* Kay, 1 Exch. 412; 2 Platt on Leases, pp. 47–81; Doe *d.* Darlington *v.* Ulph, 13 Q. B. 244; Bird *v.* Baker, 1 E. & E. 12; Jervis *v.* Tomkinson, 1 H. & N. 195.

controlled by the *express* estate mentioned in the *habendum* (*t*). Where an express estate is granted by the premises, and an estate is created by the *habendum* contrary to the rules of law, repugnant to or inconsistent with the estate in the premises, the premises will be effectual, and the *habendum* will be rejected; and this rule was established on the principle that deeds are to be construed in the manner most favourable to the grantee; the *habendum* was therefore allowed to enlarge, though not to abridge, the estate conferred by the premises (*u*). Thus if lands be granted to J. S. and his heirs, *habendum* to him for his own life, there the grantee takes an estate in fee-simple by the premises, and the *habendum* is void (*v*). But the premises of a deed may be qualified or explained by the *habendum*, where there is no inconsistency (*w*). Thus, if land be granted to A and his heirs, *habendum* to A and the heirs of his body, the premises will be qualified by the *habendum* (*x*).

Commencement of the term.

The time at which the term (*y*) is to commence must be stated with certainty. Thus where a lease for years was made on the 10th October, *habendum* from the 20th November, without saying in what year,

(*t*) Baldwin's case, 2 Rep. 24 a, Co. Litt. 183 a.
(*u*) Co. Litt. 299 a.
(*v*) Goodtitle *d.* Dodwell *v.* Gibbs, 5 B. & C. 739. See Lilley *v.* Whitney, 3 Dyer, 272 a; Jermon *v.* Orchard, 1 Salk. 346.
(*w*) Altham's case, 8 Rep. 154 b; Doe *d.* Timmis *v.* Steel, 4 Q. B. 227; Atkinson *v.* Baker, 4 T. R. 231. In Spyve *v.* Topham, 3 East. 114, where lands were granted by deeds of lease and release to J. T., his heirs and assigns, to hold the same unto G. B., his heirs and assigns, to the use of such persons and for such estate as J. T. should by any deed appoint, and in default thereof, to J. T. and G. B., and the heirs and assigns of J. T., the estate of G. B. being in trust for J. T., his heirs and assigns, it was held, in order to give effect to the deed, that the grant of the premises to J. T. might be rejected as surplusage, and the *habendum* prevail.
(*x*) Turnam *v.* Cooper, Cro. Jac. 476, Co. Litt. 21 a.
(*y*) Leases for lives may now commence *in futuro*. See *ante*, p. 35 n. (*a*).

or "next," or "last past," the lease was held to be void (z). But the commencement of the term may be fixed by reference to a contingency which must happen, although the time when it arises is uncertain (a). Thus a term may be created to commence on the death of lives in being (b), or on the determination of a subsisting term of years (c); and if the subsisting term be surrendered or forfeited, the second term will commence immediately (d). Neither is it necessary that the day of the commencement of the term should be expressly stated. Thus if a lease be made for so many years as J. S. shall name, then as soon as J. S. names the term, this ascertains as well the commencement as the duration (e).

In general, where the lease is by deed, and the time at which the term is to commence is not stated, the term commences from the delivery. So if no time of computation is mentioned, or the lease is to begin from the date, where there is no date, or from an impossible date (f), or from the end of a supposed former lease, where there is no such instrument, the commencement of the term will be reckoned from the delivery of the deed (g). The date of the deed is *prima facie* the date of its delivery, but it may be

(z) Anon. 1 Mod. 180; Bac. Abr. Lease (L).
(a) Shep. Touch. 100, 272.
(b) Bac. Abr. Lease (K); Goodright v. Richardson, 3 T. R. 463; Clarke v. Sydenham, Yelv. 85, Brownl. 136.
(c) Lord Paget's case, 1 Leon. 199; Smith v. Day, 2 M. & W. 684; Blatchford v. Cole, 5 C. B. N.S. 514; Doe d. Agar v. Brown, 2 E. & B. 331; Enys v. Donnithorne, 2 Burr. 1190; Moore v. Musgrove, Hob. 18.
(d) Co. Litt. 45 b; Plowd. 198.

(e) Co. Litt. 45 b; 6 Co. 35 a.
(f) In Chapman v. Beecham, 3 Q. B. 723, a deed having been made in the month of August in a leap-year, the words "29th February then next ensuing," were construed to mean the 29th February in the next leap-year.
(g) Higham v. Cooke, 4 Leon. 144, Co. Litt. 46 b; Amitt v. Breame, 1 Salk. 76; Taylor v. Fitzgerald, 2 Keb. 796; Bassett v. Lewis, 1 Lev. 77; Foote v. Berkley, 1 Lev. 235; Miller v. Mainwaring, W. Jones, 354.

shown that a lease was delivered on a day different from the day on which it bears the date; as where a lease was dated the 25th March 1783, and there being evidence to show that the lease was not executed till some time afterward, and the *habendum* was from the 25th March " now last past," the Court held that the term commenced from the 25th March 1783 (*h*). But although deeds take effect from the time at which they are delivered, and not from the day on which they are dated, yet if a reference is made *in the lease to the date of the lease, e.g.*, if the term is expressed to commence from the day of the date, its duration will be measured from that day, and not from the time at which the deed was actually delivered (*i*). Thus if a lease be dated the 1st of December, and be granted to commence " from henceforth," and be sealed and delivered on the 12th December, the lease in contemplation of law commences from the 1st of December (*j*).

If the holding is from a feast day, *e.g.*, from Michaelmas, parol evidence is not admissible to show that a holding from Old Michaelmas was intended (*k*). A term to commence from the date, or from the making, will be construed to include or exclude that day, according to the context and subject-matter, and in order to carry out the intention of the parties (*l*).

Leases for lives, as well as leases for terms of years, may now be made to commence from a day that is passed, or from a day to come, as well as from the

(*h*) Steele *v.* Mart, 4 B. & C. 272.
(*i*) Shep. Touch. 108; Haths *v.* Ash, 1 Ld. Raym. 84; Doe *d.* Cox *v.* Day, 10 East. 427; Styles *v.* Wardle, 4 B. & C. 908; Steele *v.* Mart, 4 B. & C. 272; Cooper *v.* Robinson, 10 M. & W. 694;

Doe *d.* Darlington *v.* Ulph, 13 Q. B. 204.
(*j*) Llewlyn *v.* Williams, Cro. Jac. 258.
(*k*) Doe *v.* Lea, 11 East. 312.
(*l*) Pugh *v.* Duke of Leeds, Cowp. 714; Ackland *v.* Letley, 9 A. & E. 879.

day of the making of the lease. The word term may signify either the time or the *estate*, limited by the demise, and it is a question of construction in what sense the word is used; and a lease may be so worded as to run from one date in point of computation, and from another in point of interest. Thus a lease for ten years from the 1st January last will begin *in interest* from the day of making, but in computation from last January; or a lease for ten years from the day of the date, but which is not to commence till the expiration of a subsisting lease for five years, will begin in computation from the date, but in interest from the expiration of the subsisting lease (*m*). So where a tenant entered before the execution of the lease, and had pulled down buildings, it was held that he was not liable for those acts in the covenant to repair contained in the subsequently executed lease, although the *habendum* referred to a period anterior to the acts complained of (*n*).

In general a letting by parol commences, where there is no evidence to the contrary, from the day of the tenant's entering (*o*). But where a tenant entered on the 21st November, which was the middle of the quarter, and at Christmas, the end of that quarter, paid his rent for that half quarter, and afterwards continued to pay rent half-yearly at Midsummer and Christmas, the tenancy was held to commence at Christmas (*p*). Where a tenant entered in the middle of a quarter, upon an agreement to pay rent " quarterly, and for the half quarter," the jury, under

(*m*) Enys *v.* Donnithorne, 2 Burr. 1190; Jervis *v.* Tomkinson, 1 H. & N. 195; Lewis *v.* Hilliard, 1 Sid. 374; Wyburd *v.* Tuck, 1 B. & P. 464; Dinsdale *v.* Isles, 1 Keb. 207.

(*n*) Shaw *v.* Kay, 1 Exch. 412.
(*o*) Kemp *v.* Derret, 3 Camp. 509.
(*p*) Doe *d.* Holcomb *v.* Johnson, 6 Esp. 10.

the judge's direction, found that the tenancy commenced from the quarter-day preceding the entry (*q*). In Doe *d.* Savage *v.* Stapleton (*r*), the tenant entered on the 1st August (the half quarter); at Michaelmas he paid the half quarter's rent. He afterwards paid rent on the usual feast days, and became tenant from year to year. The landlord gave a notice to quit, expiring with the half quarter. It was held not to be a necessary inference that the tenancy from year to year commenced at the half quarter, the landlord afterwards giving a notice to quit at Michaelmas. Where a lease is determined, and the tenant or his assignee holds over with the lessor's consent, he holds over as tenant from year to year on the terms reserved in the lease. The tenancy from year to year commences from the commencement of the lease (*s*).

Duration of the term. The extent and duration of the term in a lease, or in any agreement for a lease (*t*), should be ascertained with certainty, either by the express limitation of the parties, or as in the case of the commencement, by reference to some collateral or extrinsic circumstance which may with equal certainty fix its duration (*u*). As if a lease be made for so many years as A shall live, no certain number of years being named, the lease, as for a term, will be void. So if the parson of Dale make a lease for so many years as he shall be parson there, this is void, because it cannot be rendered certain. So if the lease be for years till A be promoted to a benefice (*v*). But although in these cases the de-

---

(*q*) Doe *d.* Wadmore *v.* Selwyn, Hil. T. 1807; Adam's Ejec. 107, 4th edition.
(*r*) 3 C. & P. 275.
(*s*) Doe *d.* Castleton *v.* Samuel, 5 Esp. 173.
(*t*) 29 Car. II. c. 3, s. 4; Bayley

v. Fitzmaurice (in error), 8 E. & B. 664, 27 L. J. Q. B. 143; Clinan *v.* Cooke, 1 Sch. & Lef. 22; Clarke *v.* Fuller, 16 C. B. N.S. 24.
(*u*) Bac. Abr. Leases (L), 3.
(*v*) Ibid. Shep. Touch. 275.

mises, as leases for years, may be void (*w*), yet they may operate as leases at will, or from year to year, and may be given in evidence as proof of the rent and other terms on which the lands are held. If a man make a lease for twenty years, if A so long live, or if A be parson of Dale for so long, here, as the term is defined, the lease is good, although liable to be determined upon the death of A, in the one case, or his ceasing to be parson, in the other (*x*). So if A have a piece of land of the value of £20 per annum, and make a lease of it to B, until he shall levy out of the profits thereof £100, this is void as a lease for years. But if A have a rent-charge of £20 per annum, and let it to B, until he shall have levied £100, this is a good lease for five years (*y*). And if a lease be made to A for so many years as A hath in the manor of Dale, and A have then a lease for ten years in that manor, this circumstance ascertains the term intended to be granted, and the lease will be good for ten years (*z*). So if a lease be made during the minority of J. S., or until J. S. shall come to the age of twenty-one, this is a good lease; for a reference to the age of J. S. will reduce the term to a certainty. But if a lease be made to A, till a child in *ventre sa mere* shall come to the age of twenty-one years, this is void (*a*).

The duration of the term may be either for a life or lives in being, or for years, or for any less period of time, either absolutely, or it may be determinable upon some contingency, such, for instance, as the expiration of a life or lives in being (*b*). But sometimes a lease is made without any limitation in respect of time.

(*w*) 6 Co. 36.
(*x*) Shep. Touch. 274, 275.
(*y*) Ibid.
(*z*) Ibid.
(*a*) Ibid.
(*b*) Shep. Touch. 274, 275. A

Where a lease is made by deed, and there are no express words limiting the duration of the term, the lessee takes an estate for his own life where the lessor is competent to grant such an interest (*c*). If the lease is by parol, and no term is specified, the lessee will be tenant at will (*d*), and he may, by payment of rent, or other circumstances, become tenant from year to year (*e*).

A lease for years, without any number being stated, is a lease for two years certain (*f*). A lease for one year certain, and so on from year to year, will create a tenancy for two years at the least (*g*). So a lease for the term of six months, and so on for six months to six months until six calendar months' notice is given, the first payment of rent to be on the 1st of July, is a tenancy for a year (*h*). Where a lease of lands was granted to another for ten years certain, and if at the end of every ten years the lessee should pay a certain quantity of tiles, he should have a perpetual demise of the land from ten years to ten years continually following, this was held a good lease for ten years only, but bad as to the rest for uncertainty (*i*). A lease for such a term as both parties please, is but a lease at will (*j*).

lease for ninety-nine years, if A and B so long live, is determinable by the death of A or B. A lease for ninety-nine years, if A or B so long live, lasts till the death of the survivor. Lord Vaux's case, Cro. Eliz. 269. See the judgment in Elliot *v.* Turner, 2 C. B. 461 ; Mortimer *v.* Hartley, 6 Ex. 60.

(*c*) Co. Litt. 42 a ; 8 & 9 Vict. c. 106, s. 3.

(*d*) See *infra*, Tenancy at Will, p. 101.

(*e*) See *supra*, p. 48, and *infra*, Tenancy at Will, p. 101.

(*f*) Bac. Abr. Leases (L), 3.

(*g*) Doe *d.* Chadborn *v.* Green, 9 A. & E. 658 ; Doe *d.* Monck *v.* Geeckie, 5 Q. B. 845.

(*h*) Reg. *v.* Chawton, 1 Q. B. 247 ; Simpson *v.* Margitson, 11 Q. B. 23.

(*i*) Say *v.* Smith, Plowd. 271.

(*j*) Bac. Abr. Leases (L), 3 ; Richardson *v.* Langridge, 7 Taunt. 128. As to the effect of provisions with respect to notices to quit, see *infra*, Part 3, c. 4, Notice to Quit.

A tenancy at will is a holding (*k*) by the express or implied consent of the owner, without raising any obligation on the part of either landlord or tenant to continue the tenancy for any *certain* term (*l*). A tenancy at will may be created by express agreement (*m*). Thus, in Doe *d.* Bastow *v.* Cox (*n*), A agreed to become tenant to C and D of certain premises *at their will and pleasure*, at certain rent payable quarterly. A remained in possession under this agreement two years and a half, and paid a year's rent; it was held that A was tenant at will. A tenancy at will is implied where a constructive tenancy from year to year would be inconsistent with the nature of the transaction, or would defeat the object of the parties. A demise for years, with a proviso that the lessor may enter at his will, is only a lease at will (*o*).

Tenancy at will.

A person put into possession of lands in which he has no freehold estate or tenancy for any certain term, under an executory agreement or accepted proposal for a future lease at a yearly rent, is only tenant at will prior to the payment of rent, or prior to any other act done from which a tenancy from year to year can be inferred (*p*); because the agreement for a future lease

(*k*) Co. Litt. 55 a. See the judgment of Byles, J., in White *v.* Bailey, 30 L. J. C. P. 256.
(*l*) Doe *d.* Bennett *v.* Turner, 7 M. & W. 226 ; Turner *v.* Doe *d.* Bennett, 9 M. & W. 643 ; Com. Dig. tit. Estate (H), 1 ; Richardson *v.* Langridge, 4 Taunt. 128.
(*m*) Ball *v.* Cullimore, 5 Tyrwh. 753 ; Richardson *v.* Langridge, 4 Taunt. 128 ; Cudlip *v.* Rundle, 4 Mod. 9 ; R. *v.* Fillongley, Cald. 569. See Marquis of Camden *v.* Batterbury, 5 C. B. N.S. 508.
(*n*) 11 Q. B. 122.

(*o*) Skarburg *v.* Pevenet, 21 Hen. VI. fol. 37 b, Year Book ; Turner *v.* Hodges, Litt. 235, by Yelverton.
(*p*) Fenny *d.* Eastham *v.* Child, 2 M. & S. 555; Hamerton *v.* Stead, 3 B. & C. 483, *per* Littledale, J. ; Richardson *v.* Gifford, 1 A. & E. 52 ; Doidge *v.* Bowers, 2 M. & W. 365 ; Bicknell *v.* Hood, 5 M. & W. 108 ; Rex *v.* Collett, R. & M. 498 ; Rex *v.* Jobling, Id. 525 ; Doe *d.* Groves *v.* Groves, 10 Q. B. 498 ; Doe *d.* Hull *v.* Wood, 14 M. & W. 682. See the notes to Clayton *v.* Blakey, 2 Smith's

does not confer any legal *estate*, and the tenancy at will created by putting the party in possession has no relation to the reserved rent; but after payment of any portion of the stipulated rent or other recognition of holding under such contract, a constructive tenancy from year to year is implied, subject to the terms of the agreement. If a person enter into possession of lands with the owner's consent or privity, pending a treaty for purchase or for a lease, a tenancy at will arises (*q*). If a person enter into or continue in possession of land, with the consent or privity of the owner, or if the owner recognise a person as having lawful occupation, or if the occupier be exempted from the consequences of a trespass by an implied license, he is tenant at will to the owner (*r*). A mortgagor in possession has often been called tenant at will to the mortgagee, but this relationship is perfectly anomalous and *sui generis;* there is no actual tenancy, for the mortgagor has not even the rights of a tenant at will, since he may be turned out of possession without notice to quit or demand of possession, and is not entitled to emblements (*s*). But a tenancy at will may, by express

L. C. 97; Doe *d.* Jones *v.* Jones, 10 B. & C. 178; Doe *d.* Nicholls *v.* M'Kaeg, 10 B. & C. 721; Rex *v.* Lakenheath, 1 B. & C. 531; Rex *v.* Fillongley, 1 T. R. 458; Doe *d.* Hughes *v.* Derry, 7 C. & P. 494; Doe *d.* Price *v.* Price, 5 Bing. 356.

(*q*) Right *d.* Lewis *v.* Beard, 13 East. 210; Doe *d.* Newby *v.* Jackson, 1 B. & C. 448; Ball *v.* Cullimore, 2 Cr. M. & R. 120; Doe *d.* Gray *v.* Stanion, 1 & M. W. 695; Kirtland *v.* Pounsett, 2 Taunt. 145; Hope *v.* Booth, 1 B. & Ad. 498; Doe *d.* Milburn *v.* Edgar, 2 Bing. N. C. 498; Winterbottom *v.* Ingham, 7 Q. B. 611; Doe *d.* Stanway *v.* Rock, 4 M. & Gr. 30; Doe *d.* Tomes *v.* Chamberlaine, 5 M. & W. 14;

Doe *d.* Bord *v.* Burton, 16 Q. B. 807; Doe *d.* Hiatt *v.* Miller, 5 C. & P. 595; *In re* Banks *v.* Rebbeck, 2 Low. M. & P. 452; Saunders *v.* Musgrave, 6 B. & C. 524; Anderson *v.* Midland Railway Co. 30 L. J. Q. B. 94. But see Doe *d.* Rogers *v.* Pullen, 2 Bing. N. C. 749; Doe *d.* Parker *v.* Boulton, 6 M. & S. 148; Tew *v.* Jones, 13 M. & W. 12.

(*r*) Doe *d.* Price *v.* Price, 9 Bing. 356; Doe *d.* Whitaker *v.* Hales, 7 Bing. 322, 323, 326; Doe *d.* Foley *v.* Wilson, 11 East. 57. See *post* 8, License.

(*s*) Christopher *v.* Sparke, 2 Jac. & W. 234, by Sir Thomas Plumer; Wilson *ex parte*, 2 Ves. & B. 252; Lord Cholmondeley *v.*

agreement, be created between a mortgagee and mortgagor (t). The notion of a mortgagor being in some cases tenant at will seems to be recognised by 3 & 4 Will. IV., c. 27, s. 7, which provides that no mortgagor shall be deemed to be a tenant at will to the mortgagee within the meaning of that clause. On the whole, it seems more correct to say that a mortgagor in possession is a tenant at sufferance only (u), or at most a *quasi* tenant at will, and he may be treated either as a tenant or trespasser at the election of the mortgagee. Therefore, where the mortgagor remains in possession, and the money is not repaid on the day stipulated, the mortgagee may eject the mortgagor without notice to quit or demand of possession; thereupon the mortgagee will be entitled to recover, together with the land, all the growing crops, fixtures, &c., in respect whereof the mortgagor will not be entitled to any compensation (v).

The peculiarity of this holding (tenancy at will) is that any act committed by either landlord or tenant inconsistent with its nature determines it, since the

Lord Clinton, 2 Jac. & W. 182; Hitchman v. Walton, 4 M. & W. 413; Doe d. Higginbotham v. Barton, 11 A. & E. 307; Doe d. Roby v. Maisey, 8 B. & C. 767; Doe d. Fisher v. Giles, 5 Bing. 421. See also the judgment of Buller, J., in Birch v. Wright, 1 T. R. 382, 383; Moss v. Gallimore, 1 Smith's L. C. 542, judgment of Ashurst, J.; see Coote on Mortgages, 319-24.
(t) Doe d. Basto v. Cox, 11 Q. B. 112; Doe d. Dixie v. Davies, 7 Ex. 89; Pinhorn v. Souster, 8 Ex. 763. See also Metropolitan Assurance Co. v. Brown, 4 H. & N. 428; Doe d. Rogers v. Cadwaller, 2 B. & Ad. 473; Doe d.

Whitaker v. Hales, 7 Bing. 322; Doe d. Wilkinson v. Goodier, 10 Q. B. 957; Doe d. Snell v. Tom, 4 Q. B. 615; West v. Fritchie, 3 Ex. 216; Morton v. Woods, 37 L. J. Q. B. 242.
(u) As to Tenancy at Sufferance, see *post*, 8 License.
(v) Woodfall, "Landlord and Tenant," p. 189, 10th ed.; Thunder d. Weaver v. Belcher, 3 East. 499; Doe d. Roby v. Maisey, 8 B. & C. 767; Doe d. Fisher v. Giles, 5 Bing. 421; Walmesley v. Milne, 7 C. B. N.S. 115, 133; Keach v. Hall, 1 Dougl. 21; Metropolitan Assurance Co. v. Brown, 4 H. & N. 428.

tenancy exists during the joint will of both parties (w). Thus in Doe d. Bennett v. Turner (x), the landlord had entered on the premises and cut some stone without the permission of his tenant at will. This act was held to operate as a determination of the tenancy. So, too, the death of either party determines the tenancy (y); but on the death of one of several lessors, the demise being joint, the interest survives (z). Thus acts of ownership inconsistent with the tenancy, exercised by either landlord or tenant on the land (a), or off the land, if the other party have notice thereof—as, for instance, alienation of the reversion with notice to the tenant, or assignment or underlease with notice to the landlord (b)—will determine the tenancy. The tenancy at will may also be determined by a demand of possession or express declaration of either of the parties (c).

Strict tenancies at will having been found inconvenient, leases for one year, and so from year to year,

(w) Co. Litt. 55 a, 68; Com. Dig. tit. Estate (H G).
(x) 7 M. & W. 226, 643. See also Doe d. Price v. Price, 9 Bing. 356.
(y) Crockerell v. Owerell, Holt, 417; Doe d. Lewis v. Lord Cawdor, 1 Cr. M. & R. 398; Co. Litt. 62 b.
(z) Henstead's case, 5 Rep. 10.
(a) See the judgment of Lord Denman in Doe d. Bennett v. Turner, 9 M. & W. 646; Doe d. Moore v. Lawdor, 1 Starkie R. 308; Pinhorn v. Souster, 8 Ex. 763; Carpenter v. Collins, Yelv. 73.
(b) Disdale v. Isles, 2 Lev. 88; Ball v. Cullimore, 2 Cr. M. & R. 120; Doe d. Goody v. Carter, 9 Q. B. 863. In Doe d. Davies v. Thomas, 6 Ex. 854, it was held that where a lessor became an insolvent debtor after the creation of the tenancy at will, the vesting order, with knowledge thereof to the tenant, determined the tenancy. Doe d. Jones v. Jones, 10 B. & C. 718; Goodtitle v. Herbert, 4 T. R. 680; Wallis v. Delmar, 29 L. J. Ex. 276; Daniels v. Davison, 16 Ves. 249; Pollen v. Brewer, 7 C. B. N. S. 371; notes to Clayton v. Blakey, 2 Smith's L. C. 97, 5th edition; Melling v. Leake, 16 C. B. 652. See the judgment of Byles, J., in White v. Bailey, 10 C. B. N.S. 227; Co. Litt. 55 b, note 15.
(c) Doe d. Bastow v. Cox, 11 Q. B. 122; Doe d. Price v. Price, 9 Bing. 356; Locke v. Matthews, 13 C. B. N.S. 753.

as long as both parties pleased, were introduced in the reign of Henry VIII., and such a lease was binding for two years certain; but prior to the reign of Geo. III. such tenancies could only have been constituted by express contract. Lord Mansfield, however, soon after he became Chief-Justice, established the present system of tenancies from year to year, determinable at the end of any year on giving six months' previous notice, and extended the principles applicable to such holdings to every tenancy which could afford reasonable ground for the inference (*d*).

The chief fact from which the inference is generally made that the parties intended to create a tenancy from year to year, is the payment of a yearly rent. So it is now settled that if a party enter into, or continue in possession of lands, under circumstances which would constitute him tenant at will, the payment of a yearly rent, or settlement of it in account with his landlord, renders him tenant from year to year (*e*). A tendency from year to year is a lease for a year certain, with a growing interest during every year thereafter, springing out of the original contract and parcel of it (*f*). If a party enter into possession under an executory agreement, or accepted proposal for a lease at a yearly rent, after receipt of rent, a tenancy from year to year will be inferred upon the terms of the intended lease, so far as they are applicable to such a tenancy (*g*).

(*d*) Agard *v.* King, Cro. Eliz. 775; Dean *d.* Jocklin *v.* Cartwright, 4 East. 31; Timmins *v.* Rowlinson, 3 Burr. 1603; Gulliver *d.* Tasker *v.* Burr, 1 W. Bla. 1171; Right *d.* Flower *v.* Darby, 1 T. R. 159; Doe *d.* Shore *v.* Porter, 3 T. R. 13.

(*e*) Doe *d.* Martin *v.* Watts, 7 T. R. 85; Doe *d.* Shore *v.* Porter, 3 T. R. 13; Doe *d.* Tucker *v.* Morse, 1 B. & Ad. 365; Berrey *v.* Lindley, 3 M. & G. 498; Lee *v.* Smith, 9 Ex. 662. See *ante*, p. 48, 101, Effect of Non-compliance with Statute of Frauds.

(*f*) Oxley *v.* James, 13 M. & W. 214.

(*g*) See *ante*, p. 51, 102, Effect of Non-compliance with Statute of Frauds.

Thus if a person enters upon, occupies, and pays rent for premises under a *parol* demise, made by a corporation, that person becomes tenant from year to year of the corporation, on such terms of the demise as are applicable to a yearly tenancy (*h*). So if a person enter into possession under a general letting, at a yearly rent, without any limit as to time, after any portion of the yearly rent is proved to have been received by the owner from the person in occupation of the premises, a tenancy from year to year is implied (*i*). But this rule is not applicable to the letting of lodgings (*j*). Thus where A let apartments in his house to B, at a rent payable half-yearly, B took possession at Michaelmas, and at Ladyday paid half a year's rent; in June B left without notice, and at the following Michaelmas paid half a year's rent; the Court held that a taking from year to year could not be implied from these facts (*k*). There may be a letting for a year, determinable as may be agreed upon between the parties; so in the same manner the periods at which rent is reserved have no *necessary* relation to the duration of the holding, or to the length of notice required (*l*). Acceptance of rent under a lease, void on the death of the tenant for life, or at the end of the then current year of his

---

(*h*) The Ecclesiastical Commissioners *v.* Merral, L. R. 4 Ex. 162, 38 L. J. Ex. 91; Wood *v.* Tate, 2 B. & P. N. R. 247.

(*i*) Doe d. Martin *v.* Watts, 7 T. R. 83; Bishop *v.* Howard, 2 B. & C. 100.

(*j*) See *per* Lord Mansfield in Right *v.* Darby, 1 T. R. 159, 162; Kemp *v.* Derret, 3 Camp. 510; Doe d. Landsell *v.* Gower, 17 Q. B. 589; Wilkinson *v.* Hall, 3 Bing. N. C. 508; Monks *v.* Dykes, 4 M. & W. 507.

(*k*) Wilson *v.* Abbott, 3 B. & C. 88. See also Rex *v.* Herstmonceaux, 7 B. & C. 551; Huffell *v.* Armistead, 7 C. & P. 56.

(*l*) Doe d. Parry *v.* Hazell, 1 Esp. 94; Doe d. Peacock *v.* Raffan, 6 Esp. 4; Doe d. Pitcher *v.* Donovan, 1 Taunt. 555; Doe d. Chadborn *v.* Green, 9 A. & E. 658; Towne *v.* Campbell, 3 C. B. 921; Jones *v.* Mills, 10 C. B. N. S. 788; Doe d. Kiog *v.* Grafton, 18 Q. B. 496; Doe d. Bastow *v.* Cox, 11 Q. B. 122; Doe d. Dixie *v.* Davies, 7 Ex. 89.

tenancy (*m*), by a remainderman, does not confirm the lease, but creates an implied tenancy from year to year, upon the terms of the old lease, so far as they are consistent with such a holding (*n*).

A general letting at a yearly rent, though payable quarterly, or an acceptance of a yearly rent, or rent measured by any aliquot part of a year, is evidence of a taking from year to year (*o*). Thus where premises were let at a yearly rent, payable weekly, with power to determine the tenancy at three months' notice from any quarter-day, it was held that a yearly tenancy was created determinable as agreed (*p*). But where houses or lodgings are let for an uncertain period, at a quarterly, monthly, or weekly rent, a quarterly, monthly, or weekly tenancy is usually presumed (*q*).

Sometimes the lease is for a certain number of years, determinable sooner at the election of the parties or one of them. Where the option is given expressly to each party, no difficulty can arise, and the term may be determined by either (*r*). A lease for twenty-one years, expressed "to be determinable, nevertheless, in seven or fourteen years, if the parties shall think fit," is determinable only by consent of *both* the

Option to determine.

(*m*) 14 & 15 Vict. c. 25, s. 1.
(*n*) Doe *d.* Martin *v.* Watts, 7 T. R. 85 ; Doe *d.* Tucker *v.* Morse, 1 B. & Ad. 365.
(*o*) Richardson *v.* Langridge, 4 Taunt. 128 ; Doe *d.* Hall *v.* Wood, 14 M. & W. 682 ; Rex *v* Herstmonceaux, 7 B. & C. 551.
(*p*) Rex *v.* Herstmonceaux, 7 B. & C. 551. See Doe *d.* Pitcher *v.* Donovan, 1 Taunt. 555; Brown *v.* Burtindshaw, 7 D. & R. 603.
(*q*) Wilkinson *v.* Hall, 3 Bing. N.

C. 508 ; Kemp *v.* Derrett, 3 Camp. 510 ; Huffel *v.* Armistead, 7 C. & P. 56 ; Doe *d.* Landsell *v.* Gower, 17 Q. B. 589 ; Towne *v.* Campbell, 3 C. B. 921 ; Doe *d.* King *v.* Grafton, 18 Q. B. 496 ; Wilson *v.* Abbott, 3 B. & C. 88 ; Monks *v.* Dykes, 4 M. & W. 567.
(*r*) Goodright *v.* Mark, 4 M. & S. 30 ; Bird *v.* Baker, 1 E. & E. 12 ; Roe *d.* Bainford *v.* Hayley, 12 East. 464.

parties (s). Where the instrument is silent as to the party who is to exercise the right to determine, the lessee only has the option of determining the lease at the specified time, on the principle that where the words of a grant are doubtful, they must be construed most strongly in favour of the grantee (t).

6. REDDENDUM.

The reddendum is that part of the lease by which the rent is reserved. No particular form of words is necessary, but the words "reserving," "rendering," "yielding," "paying," &c., are the words usually employed. The office of the reddendum is to define what rent shall be paid, to whom it shall be paid, at what time it shall be paid, how it shall be paid, and where it shall be paid.

From what rent may issue.

The distinctions which existed at common law between rent-services, rent-seck, and rent-charges, are now usually of little practical importance (u). Rent may be defined to be a certain return made by the tenant, either in labour, money, or provisions, for the estate demised to him; and, as a general rule, the rent must issue out of lands and corporeal tenements, as part of their actual or possible profits, and be payable

(s) Fowell v. Tranter, 34 L. J. Ex. 6.
(t) Dann v. Spurrier, 3 B. & P. 399; Price v. Dyer, 17 Ves. 356; Doe v. Dixon, 9 East. 15. See Goodright v. Richardson, 3 T. R. 462.
(u) See *infra*, Part 2, c. 2, s. 2, Distress; Bac. Abr. tit. Rent (A), 1-3; Co. Litt. 87 b, 143 b; Bradbury v. Wright, 2 Dougl. 624; Judgment of Buller, J., The

Governors of Christ's Hospital v. Harrild, 2 M. & Gr. 713. Rent-service is a rent reserved upon a grant or lease of lands as incidental to their tenure. Rent-charge is a rent granted out of lands by the owner to some other person with a clause of distress. Rent-seck is a rent-charge without clause of distress. Bac. Abr. Rent (A).

at fixed intervals during the tenancy (v). It is not necessary that the return should be in money, for the reservation may be the delivery of horses, capons, roses, spurs, wheat, or the like (w); or it may consist of the personal services of the lessee, in labouring or journeying for the lessor at certain stipulated times (x); as, for instance, to plough so many acres of land, to clean the parish church, or to ring the church bell at stated times (y).

The rent reserved, however, must be certain, the Nature of quantum or amount being either expressly stated with rent. certainty, or becoming so by reference to something else that can be certainly ascertained (z). Where, therefore, a man demised at will, reddendum *after the rate of* 18 *per annum, as long as the demise shall continue*, the reservation was held bad for uncertainty, for it might be in corn, or any other thing of value, and as no time was limited for the payment of it, an action might be brought every day for it (a). Where a marl-pit and brick-mine were demised (b), the tenant agreeing to pay so much a quarter for every yard of marl that he might get out, and 1s. 8d. per thousand for all the bricks that he might make; it was held that this reservation was sufficiently certain. If the reservation be of so many quarters of corn (c), it will be understood to mean

(v) Burton's Real Property, pp. 330, 331; Gilbert on Rents, p. 9; Co. Litt. 47 a, 141 b, 142 a.
(w) Co. Litt. 142 a.
(x) Lanyon v. Carne, 2 Saund. 165.
(y) Doe d. Edney v. Benham, 7 Q. B. 907; Doe d. Edney v. Billett, 7 Q. B. 967. See also Doe d. Robinson v. Hinde, 2 M. & Rob. 441, and the Duke of Marlborough v. Osborn, 5 B. & S. 67.
(z) Co. Litt. 96 a. See Dean

d. Jacklin v. Cartwright, 4 East. 31.
(a) Parker v. Harris, 1 Salk. 262.
(b) Daniel v. Garcie, 6 Q. B. 145. See judgment of Lord Denman in R. v. Westbrook, 10 Q. B. 205; Co. Litt. 96 a.
(c) A restriction occurs with regard to college leases created by statute, 18 Eliz. c. 6, by which it is directed that one third of the old rent then paid should for the

legal quarters, reckoning the bushel at eight gallons, although leases of the same lands prior to the 22 & 23 Car. II., c. 12, contained the same reservation, and the lessees had been accustomed to pay by composition, reckoning the bushel as nine gallons (*d*). A reservation of eight bushels of grain in lieu of one quarter is good, because it is all one in quality, value, and nature (*e*). In a lease of land for twenty-one years, from the 25th March 1848, it was covenanted that the lessee should pay a stipulated sum for the first year, with a proviso that the rent for each subsequent year of the term should be reduced or increased according to the "average price of wheat in any one year of the said term," such average "to be taken and ascertained from the then current year's averages, which were taken in the mouth of January in every year, under and by virtue of the Tithe Commutation Act, 6 & 7 Will. IV., c. 71, s. 56," which was the result of the sales "during the seven years ending on the Thursday next before Christmas-day then next preceding;" it was held that the rent might be computed according to such septennial average so published in each year (*f*).

future be reserved in wheat or malt, reserving a quarter of wheat for each 6s. 8d., or a quarter of malt for every 5s.; or that the lessees should pay the same according to the price that wheat or malt should be sold for in the market next adjoining to the respective colleges on the market-day before the rent became due. This sagacious plan is said to have been the invention of Lord-Treasurer Burleigh and Sir Thomas Smith, then principal Secretary of State, who, observing how greatly the value of money had sunk, and the price of all provisions risen, by the quantity of bullion imported from the newly-found America, devised this method for upholding the revenue of colleges. Their foresight and penetration have in this respect been very apparent. The corn rent has made the old rent approach in some degree nearer to its present value; otherwise it would seem that the principal advantage of a corn rent is to secure the lessor from the effect of a sudden scarcity of corn. 2 Blac. Com. 322.

(*d*) The Master, &c. of St Cross *v.* Lord Howard de Walden, 6 T. R. 338.

(*e*) Mountjoy's case, 5 Co. R. 3 b.

(*f*) Kendall *v.* Baker, 11 C. B. 482.

The rent must consist in something issuing out of the thing demised, though differing from it in nature; for if it be part of the thing itself, that would not be a reservation, but an exception (*g*). Thus, it is said—"If one grant land yielding for rent, money, corn, horse, spurs, or a rose, or any such like thing, this is a good reservation; but if the reservation be of the grass, or of the vesture of the land, or of a common, or other profit, to be taken out of the land, these reservations are void (*h*). A royalty payable by the tenant upon the bricks which are made out of the land demised is a rent (*i*). In the case of a demise of mines, the rent reserved may, it seems, consist of a portion of the ore, which is the substance of the land itself (*j*). The rent, as a general rule, must issue out of lands and such things as are capable of livery, and may be distrained upon (*k*). Thus a rent cannot issue out of a demise of an incorporeal hereditament, nor of goods; but a reservation in such a case may be binding on the parties as a contract. A rent reserved upon a lease of a future interest in land is good, for although the lessor cannot distrain during the continuance of the particular estate, yet there is a possibility of his doing so on its determination. A lease of the vesture or herbage of land reserving rent is good, as the lessor may come on the land and distrain the lessee's beast (*l*). The Crown, too, may reserve rent on a demise of an incorporeal hereditament, because by its prerogative a distress may be

(*g*) See *ante*, Exceptions from Demise, p. 89; 1 Inst. 47 a.
(*h*) Shephard's Touch. p. 80. See also Doe *d*. Douglas *v*. Lock, 2 A. & E. 744; Brooke's Abr. tit. Reservations, pl. 46; Co. Litt. 47 a.
(*i*) Reg. *v*. Westbrook, 10 Q. B. 178.
(*j*) Campbell *v*. Leach, Anst.

740; Buckley *v*. Kenyon, 10 East. 139; R. *v*. Earl of Pomfret, 5 M. & S. 139; but see R. *v*. The Inhabitants of St Anstoll, 5 B. & A. 693.
(*k*) Co. Litt. 47 a, 142 a; Bac. Abr. tit. Rent (B); Williams *v*. Hayward, 28 L. J. Q. B. 374.
(*l*) Co. Litt. 47, 142 a.

levied on all the lands of the lessee (*m*). It is a general rule that where rent is nominally reserved out of two things, one of which is capable of supporting a rent and the other not, it will be taken to issue wholly out of the former (*n*). Thus in Spencer's case (*o*), where a house and land, with a stock or sum of money, was demised, rendering rent, it was held that the rent issued out of the land only. But although the rent issues in these cases only out of the corporeal hereditament in point of remedy, it is considered to issue out of both in point of render (*p*). Thus in Gardiner *v.* Williamson (*q*), A, by instrument not under seal, agreed to let to B the rectory of L, and the tithes arising from the lands in the parish of L, and also a messuage used as a homestead for collecting the tithes, at the yearly rent of £200; it was held that as the agreement, not being under seal, did not operate as a demise of the tithes, the rent could not be distrained for, as there was no distinct rent reserved for the homestead.

Where a lessee simply covenants or promises to pay a certain sum yearly, without stating it as a consideration for the demise of the premises, it will not be a rent, but a sum in gross, to the payment of which he will be liable by reason only of his contract (*r*). Thus in Hoby *v.* Roebuck (*s*), where a lessee agreed to pay his lessor annually during the residue of the lessee's term, ten per cent. on the cost of new buildings if the lessor would erect them; it was held that

(*m*) Bac. Abr. tit. Rent (B).
(*n*) Newman *v.* Anderton, 2 N. R. 224; Salmon *v.* Matthews, 8 M. & W. 827; Farewell *v.* Dickenson, 6 B. & C. 251.
(*o*) 5 Rep. 16.
(*p*) Dean of Windsor *v.* Gover, 2 Wm. Saunds. 303; Gardiner *v.* Williamson, 2 B. & Ad. 336; Bird *v.* Higginson, 2 A. & E. 696, 6 A. & E. 824; Meggison *v.* Bowers, 21 L. J. Ex. 284.
(*q*) 2 B. & Ad. 336.
(*r*) Smith *v.* Mapelbach, 1 T. R. 441.
(*s*) 7 Taunt. 157.

this sum could not be distrained for as rent. So in Donellan v. Read (t), where a lessor demised premises for a term of years at £50 a year, and agreed with his tenant to lay out £50 in making certain improvements upon them, the tenant undertaking to pay him an increased *rent* of £5 a year during the term; it was held that this sum of £5 was not a rent in a legal sense of the word. If a person enters on and occupies the premises of another, but there is no demise, express or implied, he will be liable, not for rent, but for such sum as may be deemed a reasonable satisfaction to the owner of the premises for the use and occupation thereof (u). Rent, being incident to the reversion, will follow that reversion. Rent therefore should be reserved to the lessor, and not to a third party (v). Thus where a man seised in fee leases for life or years reserving rent, the whole rent which becomes due after his death goes with the reversion (as an incident thereof) to the heir, and not to the executor; for since, during the continuance of the particular estate, the reversioner loses the profits of the land, the rent ought to be paid to him as a compensation for the loss (w). Where there is any doubt as to the person to whom the reservation should be made, the clearest and safest way is to reserve the rent generally during the term, without saying to whom, and leave it to be distributed by the law in the mode pointed out in Whitlock's case (x); for if the re-

(t) 3 B. & Ad. 899. See also Lambert v. Norris, 2 M. & W. 333; Marquis of Camden v. Batterbury, 7 C. B. N.S. 804.

(u) Salmon v. Matthews, 8 M. & W. 833; Dunk v. Hunter, 5 B. & A. 325; Hegan v. Johnson, 2 Taunt. 148.

(v) Co. Litt. 47 b, 143 b; Com. Dig. tit. Rent (B), 5.

(w) Co. Litt. 47 a; Cother v. Merrick, Hard. 95; Bac. Abr. Executors (H), 3; Oates v. Frith, Hob. 130; Sacheverell v. Froggat, 2 Saund.; Southampton v. Brown, 6 B. & C. 718. But a reservation of rent to a third party is binding as a contract. Jewel's case, 5 Rep. 3.

(x) 8 Co. Rep. 70, 141.

servation of rent be general during the term, the law directs it to be paid according to the intent and nature of the thing demised (*y*). Thus if a person seised in fee settles his estate on himself for life, with remainders to other persons, reserving a leasing power, which he afterwards exercises, reserving rent to himself, his heirs, and assigns, those in remainder shall have the rent. So also where a person seised in fee settles his estate on A for life with remainders, and gives him a leasing power, which he exercises, reserving rent during the term, the remainder-men shall take, although neither heirs nor assigns of A (*z*).

7. COVENANTS.

A covenant is an engagement entered into under seal (*a*), whereby one person binds himself to do something beneficial to another, or to abstain from an act which, if done, would be prejudicial to another (*b*). The general principle is clear, that the landlord, having the *jus disponendi*, may annex whatever conditions he pleases to his lease, provided they are not illegal or impossible. A covenant therefore to do a thing which, upon the face of it, appears to be prejudicial to the public interest, or otherwise contrary to law, is *ipso facto* void (*c*). Thus if a lease is made for the express purpose of the premises being used to boil oil and tar,

(*y*) Whittome *v.* Lamb, 12 M. & W. 813; Dollen *v.* Batt, 27 L. J. C. P. 281.

(*z*) Greenway *v.* Hart, 23 L. J. C. P. 115; Isherwood *v.* Oldknow, 3 M. & S. 382.

(*a*) The word "covenant" used in an agreement not under seal may, in order to effectuate the intention of the parties, be construed to mean "contract," or "stipulation." Hayne *v.* Cummings, 16 C. B. N.S. 421.

(*b*) Bac. Abr. tit. Covenants.
(*c*) Shep. Touch. 163; Lowe *v.* Peers, 4 Burr. 2225. By 5 & 6 Vict. c. 35, s. 103 (Property-Tax Act), a covenant for the payment of rent in full without allowing a deduction for the property-tax, is void. See *infra*, Part 2, Div. 1, c. 1, s. 3, Deductions; and see *post*, Certain Trades, &c., p. 127.

contrary to the provisions of an Act of Parliament, the covenant for payment of rent is void (*d*). If a man covenant to do a thing which to-day is lawful, but to-morrow is by statute made unlawful, the covenant will be thereby extinguished; or if he covenant not to do a thing, and then a statute is made which compels him to do it, the covenant becomes void; but if he covenant to do that which is afterwards made unlawful in part only, it must be performed so far as it continues lawful. If a man covenant not to do a thing which is unlawful, and then a statute makes it lawful, the covenant is not thereby repealed; but if he covenant to do a thing unlawful by statute, the performance of the covenant is not rendered lawful by a repeal of the statute, for the covenant was void *in initio* (*e*). But there is nothing to prevent persons, if they so please, from binding themselves by a contract as to any future state of the law, although in general they are to be considered as contracting with reference to the law as it then exists (*f*). A covenant to do a thing which is impossible, if the impossibility exists at the time the covenant is made, is void; but if it be then possible, and afterwards become impossible, the covenantor will still be liable in the express words of his covenant (*g*.) Where a covenant seems to relate to something which is impossible, the Court will incline to the view that a man did not really warrant to be possible that which was impossible, if a reasonable construction suggests itself (*h*). Where a

(*d*) The Gas Light Co. *v.* Turner, 5 Bing. N. C. 666.

(*e*) Brewster *v.* Kitchell, 1 Salk. 198; Brason *v.* Dean, 3 Mod. 39; Jaques *v.* Withy, 1 H. Bl. 65. See the judgment in Baily *v.* Crespigny, L. R. 4 Q. B. 185.

(*f*) See judgment of Maule, J., in Mayor of Berwick *v.* Oswald, 3 E. & B. 665, 23 L. J. Q. B. 324.

(*g*) Shep. Touch. 663; Blight *v.* Page, 3 B. & P. 295, n. (*a*); Barker *v.* Hodgson, 3 M. & S. 267; 1 Rol. Abr. 420, C. 4, 8; Appleby *v.* Myers, L. R. 2 C. P. 651; Clifford *v.* Watts, L. R. 5 C. P. 577; 40 L. J. C. P. 36.

(*h*) *Per* Willes, J., Clifford *v.* Watts, *supra*.

covenant is dependent upon a conveyance of an estate which proves to be void, and no estate passes, the covenant is void (*i*). Thus a covenant in a lease to repair *during the term* is void, where the lessor does not execute the lease (*j*). But independent covenants in a lease may be enforced, although no estate passes (*k*). Covenants are such as either run with the land, or are merely personal. A covenant running with the land is one which affects the nature, quality, or value of the land demised, or the mode of enjoying it independently of collateral circumstances (*l*).

(a.) EXPRESS COVENANTS.

Express covenants. Express covenants are such as are created by the express words of the parties in a deed declaratory of their intentions; and in order to constitute such a covenant, the law does not require any precise or technical language. Thus words in the form of an exception or restriction may amount to a covenant (*m*). The lease in general contains express covenants by the lessee for the payment of the rent (*n*), for the payment of taxes, &c. (except the sewers' rate, land and property taxes), for the repair of the premises during the term, for leaving them at the end of the term in a proper state of repair, and for the insurance and rebuild-

(*i*) Capenhurst *v.* Capenhurst, Sir T. Raym. 27; Hayne *v.* Maltby, 3 T. R. 438.
(*j*) Pitman *v.* Woodbury, 3 Exch. 4; Linwood *v.* Squire, 5 Exch. 234; Wheatley *v.* Boyd, 7 Exch. 20; Swatman *v.* Ambler, 8 Exch. 72. Compare these cases with Hughes *v.* Clarke, 10 C. B. 905; Morgan *v.* Pike, 14 C. B. 473; Wood *v.* Copper Miners Co. 14 C. B. 594; Northampton Gas Co. *v.* Parnell, 15 C. B. 630; Bowes *v.* Croll, 6 E. & B. 255; Hew *v.* Greek, 3 H. & C. 391.

(*k*) Northcote *v.* Underhill, 1 Salk. 199.
(*l*) Spencer's case, 5 Rep. 16, 1st and 2d Resolutions. See *infra*, Part 4, c. 1, s. 4.
(*m*) The Duke of St Albans *v.* Ellis, 16 East. 352.
(*n*) A covenant may be inserted to pay interest on arrears of rent. Tynte *v.* Hodge, 2 H. & M. 287. See note by Mr Cole in Woodfall's "Landlord and Tenant," 1013, 9th edit.

ing of the premises in case of their destruction by fire. The lessee also usually covenants not to assign or underlet without the consent of the lessor, and sometimes not to carry on offensive trades. There is a covenant by the lessor, on the other hand, for quiet enjoyment; and he not unfrequently covenants to pay some of the rates or assessments, or a portion of them.

An express covenant for the payment of rent is inserted in every indenture of lease, and usually binds the lessee, his heirs, executors, administrators, and assigns to its performance. The lessee, and after his death, his personal representatives, having assets, are answerable for the rent during the continuance of the lease. If the covenant expressly include the heirs of the lessee, his real representatives having inherited assets from the ancestor will be chargeable for breach of the covenant, either in the lifetime of the lessee, or after his death. If the lease be assigned, the original lessee continues liable for the rent during the lease, in respect of privity of contract, and his heirs, if named, and his personal representatives, though not named, remain liable, so far as assets have come to their hands. The assignee is also liable for the rent in respect of the privity of estate (*o*) during his ownership.

Payment of rent.

The liability to pay taxes is usually provided for in the lease. The usual covenant by the tenant is "to pay all rates, taxes, duties, and assessments whatsoever, whether parochial, parliamentary, or otherwise, now charged, or hereafter to be charged, upon the demised premises, or any part thereof, or upon the rent, or any part thereof, except sewers' rates, land-tax, and

Payment of taxes.

(*o*) See *infra*, Part 4, c. 1, s. 4, Covenants Running with the Land.

property-tax." Sometimes there is an express covenant by the landlord to pay the land-tax (*p*).

If the lessee covenants to pay "all rates, taxes, and assessments," these include the land-tax; for when taxes are generally mentioned, they must be understood to signify parliamentary taxes, if the subject-matter will suffer it, and the lessee would consequently be charged with the payment of all land-taxes, even those imposed by act of Parliament, long after the commencement of the lease, notwithstanding the word "parliament" was not expressed in the covenant (*q*). In Bradbury *v.* Wright (*r*), the tenant covenanted to pay the rent "without any deduction, defalcation, or abatement, for or in any respect whatsoever." Upon this covenant he was held liable to pay the land-tax. A sewer's rate not being directly imposed, *i.e.*, fixed and assessed by act of Parliament, is not a parliamentary tax (*s*). So an improvement rate made by commissioners under a local act is not parochial or parliamentary (*t*). But it would seem that a county rate is a *parochial* tax (*u*). No doubt in Waller *v.* Andrews (*v*), where the tenant, by the agreement, was to pay "all outgoings whatsoever, rates, taxes, scots, &c., parliamentary and parochial," it was held that an extraordinary assessment, made by the commissioners upon the lands, was within the agreement;

(*p*) As to the land-tax, see *infra*, Part 2, Div. 1, c. 1, s. 3, Deductions.
(*q*) See Hopwood *v.* Barefoot, 11 Mod. 238; Brewster *v.* Kitchin, 1 Ld. Raym. 317; Armfield *v.* White, 1 Ry. & M. 246; Bradbury *v.* Wright, 2 Dougl. 624; Payne *v.* Burridge, 12 M. & W. 727; Governors of Christ's Hospital *v.* Harrild, 2 M. & Gr. 707; Bennett *v.* Wormack, 7 B. & C. 627. See also *infra*, Part 2, Div. 1, c. 1, s. 3, Deductions; Sweet *v.* Seager, 2 C. B. N.S. 189.
(*r*) 2 Dougl. 624.
(*s*) Palmer *v.* Earth, 14 M. & W. 428.
(*t*) Guardians of Bedford Union *v.* Bedford Improvement Commissioners, 7 Exch. 777.
(*u*) Reg. *v.* Inhabitants of Aylesbury, 9 Q. B. 261.
(*v*) 3 M. & W. 312.

but that was upon the ground of its being a *scot*, and not a parliamentary tax. In Baker *v.* Greenhill (*w*), a landlord was, with other landowners, liable to repair a bridge, *ratione tenuræ*. The tenant of the land had covenanted to pay the rent, "free and clear of and from any land-tax, and all other taxes and deductions whatsoever, either parliamentary or parochial, now already taxed or imposed upon the demised premises, or upon the tenant, his heirs, executors, administrators, or assigns in respect thereof, the landlord's property-tax or duty only excepted." Some local acts of Parliament, reciting the liability of the landlord *ratione tenuræ*, had enacted that he and the other landowners who were liable should keep the bridge in repair, and had enabled them to raise the requisite moneys by rates among themselves, according to the value of the lands chargeable, and had given them a power to levy the amount, if necessary, by distress. It was held that the liability to contribute to these repairs did not, by the operation of the local acts, become a parliamentary tax or deduction within the meaning of the covenant of the tenant. Lord Denman in giving the judgment of the Court, said:—" We are of opinion that the acts of Parliament for enabling persons interested to raise the necessary funds for the repairs of the bridge by contribution among themselves, do not impose any tax within the meaning of the covenant. The charge was already created, and the acts merely supply a more convenient mode for raising the necessary funds to meet it." Where a local act imposed duties of paving upon a landlord, and in default gave power to commissioners to execute the works, and recover expenses from the owner, it was held that the duty, in the first

(*w*) 3 Q. B. 148.

instance, was to *pave*, and not to *pay money*, and the tenant was therefore not liable to his landlord (x); but it is otherwise where a sum of money is levied upon premises (y). A covenant to pay taxes on the land does not extend to church and poor rates, for these are *personal* charges (z).

Sometimes the lessor covenants to pay the rates and taxes; sometimes the burden of them is thrown partly on the lessee and partly on the lessor. Such covenants are seldom interfered with by the Legislature. But the property-tax, which the landlord is bound to pay, forms an exception to this rule. (a).

Repairs.

The lessee's responsibility for repairs is generally limited by an express covenant (b), which will run with the land (c). Usually there are three covenants by the lessee relating to repairs in a lease of buildings:— First, During the term to repair and keep in repair, &c., the demised premises; secondly, To repair according to notice, with a provision for the lessor to enter and view the premises; thirdly, At the determination of the term to leave the premises in repair.

The covenant to repair generally, and the covenant to repair after notice, have been held to be distinct

---

(x) Tidswell *v.* Whitworth, L. R. 2 C. P. 326, 36 L. J. C. P. 103.

(y) Thompson *v.* Lapworth, L. R. 3 C. P. 149; 37 L. J. C. P. 74; and see Bird *v.* Elwes, L. R. 3 Ex. 255, 37 L. J. Ex. 91.

(z) Head *v.* Starkey, 8 Mod. 314. See Tidswell *v.* Whitworth, L. R. 2 C. P. 326.

(a) 5 & 6 Vict. c. 35, ss. 60, 103, extended and altered by 17 Vict. c. 10, and other acts. See *infra*, Part 2, Div. 1, c. 1, s. 3, Deductions.

(b) As to obligation to repair arising from the mere relation of landlord and tenant. See Implied Covenants, *post*, sub.-sect. (b), p. 135.

(c) See Part 4, c. 1, s. 4, Covenants Running with the Land.

and independent covenants (d); but they may be so joined as to make one entire covenant (e).

The lessor sometimes enters into a covenant to repair; but without an express covenant he cannot be compelled to repair (f).

Where the lessor covenanted to keep the "main walls, main timbers, and roofs" in repair, it was held that as to the main timbers and roofs, the lessor could have no knowledge of their state of repair without notice, and that therefore notice must be given by the lessee before he could bring an action upon the covenant (g).

On a demise of buildings a general covenant to repair has been usually construed to comprehend as well the buildings erected by the lessee as the buildings originally demised (h). So where a lessee erected fixtures for the purpose of trade, and afterwards took a new lease, to commence at the expiration of his former one, and the new lease contained a covenant to repair, it was held that he was bound to repair the fixtures (i).

Under a general covenant to repair, the lessee's liability is not confined to cases of ordinary and

(d) Baylis v. Le Gros, 4 C. B. N.S. 537; Few v. Perkins, L. R. 2 Ex. 92, 36 L. J. Ex. 54.
(e) Horsefall v. Testar, 7 Taunt. 385.
(f) Neale v. Ratcliffe, 15 Q. B. 916, 20 L. J. Q. B. 130; Cannock v. Jones, 3 Exch. 233; Bird v. Elwes, L. R. 3 Ex. 225, 37 L. J. Ex. 91.
(g) Makin v. Watkinson, L. R. 6 Ex. 25.

(h) Dowse v. Cale, 2 Vent. 126; Penry v. Brown, 2 Stark, 408; Brown v. Blunden, Skin. 121; In re Newbery, White v. Wakley, 28 L. J. Ch. 77, 26 Beav. 17; 17 Penry v. Brown, 2 Stark R. 403; but see Lant v. Norris, 1 Burr. 287; Cornish v. Cleife, 34 L. J. Ex. 19.
(i) Thresher v. East London Waterworks Co. 2 B. & C. 608.

gradual decay; but in a demise of buildings it extends to injuries done to them by fire, whether accidental or wilful, or by lightning, tempest, flood, or enemies, &c. (*j*). In consequence of this obligation, it is customary to introduce an exception against such accidents into the covenant (*k*). But a covenant to keep in the same state the woods, lands, and natural productions will not render the lessee liable for any injury which may arise to these from the act of God (*l*).

Under a covenant to repair and *keep* in repair the buildings demised during the term, the lessee is bound to keep them in repair at all times during the term (*m*); and the lessor, upon breach, can, during the term, recover damages commensurate with the injury done to his reversion (*n*).

Where the lessor brought an action for non-repair upon the determination of the lease, and had previously agreed by parol with a new tenant to pull down the buildings, and otherwise to improve the value of the property, it was held that the jury were not bound to give mere nominal damages (*o*).

A general covenant to repair is satisfied by the lessee keeping the premises in substantial repair (*p*).

(*j*) Brooke's Abr. Covenant, pl. 4; Walton *v.* Waterhouse, 2 Saund. 420; Bullock *v.* Dommitt, 6 T. R. 650; Brecknock Canal Company *v.* Pritchard, 6 T. R. 750. See *post*, Insurance, p. 124.
(*k*) But this exception will not bind the landlord to repair. Weigall *v.* Waters, 6 T. R. 488; Monck *v.* Cooper, 2 Ld. Raym. 1477.
(*l*) Shep. Touch. 173.

(*m*) Luxmore *v.* Robson, 1 B. & A. 584.
(*n*) Smith *v.* Peat, 9 Exch. 161; Turner *v.* Lamb, 14 M. & W. 412.
(*o*) Rawlings *v.* Morgan, 18 C. B. N.S. 776, 34 L. J. C. P. 185. It seems it might have been the same even if the agreement with the new tenant had been binding.
(*p*) Harris *v.* Jones, 1 Moo. & R. 173.

HOW DEMISES ARE MADE.

If it is a general covenant to keep old premises in repair, the lessee is not liable for dilapidations which are the result of time and the elements (*q*). But a covenant to keep old premises, and deliver them up, in good repair, means to put them into such repair as is suitable to their age and class; and the lessee is not justified in keeping them in bad repair because they were in that condition at the time when the covenant began to operate (*r*). The sufficiency of the repairs is a question of fact for the jury, who may consider *generally* the state of repair of the premises at the time of the making of the lease (*s*).

Where a lessee agrees to put the premises in "habitable repair," he is to put them in a state fit for the occupation of the class of persons likely to inhabit them (*t*). A lessee under a general covenant to repair is not liable for the extra expense of laying a new floor on an improved plan (*u*). A covenant to repair "all the external parts of the demised premises," includes the partition wall between the premises and an adjoining house, the external parts of premises being those which form the inclosure of them (*v*).

Sometimes the covenant is of a conditional nature, and it is part of the agreement that the landlord should in the first place put the premises into good repair (*w*); and until that is done, the lessee is not

(*q*) Gutteridge *v.* Munyard, 1 Moo. & R. 334.
(*r*) Payne *v.* Haine, 16 M. & W. 541, Easton *v.* Pratt, 33 L. & J. Ex. 233. See Schroder *v.* Ward, 13 C. B., N.S. 410.
(*s*) Stanley *v.* Towgood, 3 Bing. N. C. 4; Burdett *v.* Withers, 7 A. & E. 136; Mantz *v.* Goring, 4 Bing. N. C. 451; Young *v.* Manton, 6 Scott, 277.

(*t*) Belcher *v.* Mackintosh, 8 C. & P. 720, 2 Moo. & Ry. 186.
(*u*) Saward *v.* Leggatt, 6 C. & P. 613.
(*v*) Green *v.* Eales, 2 Q. B. 225.
(*w*) See Slater *v.* Stone, Cro. Jac. 645; Cannock *v.* Jones, 3 Exch. 233, 5 Id. 713.

liable for repairs (x). But a covenant to repair, "having or taking" sufficient wood, &c., from the premises "for the doing thereof," is an absolute covenant to repair, and not conditional to there being a sufficient supply of timber (y).

Husbandry.

In farming leases (z) it is usual for the lessee to covenant that he will manage his farm in a husband-like manner. The mere relation, however, of landlord and tenant creates an implied obligation to farm according to the custom of the country (a). Sometimes, however, the custom of the country may be excluded by the express provisions of the lease (b).

Insurance.

The lease should contain a covenant by the lessee, his executors, administrators, and assigns, to insure and keep insured during the term the buildings demised for a certain amount in some insurance office (c), in the joint names of the lessor and lessee, or either of them, according to the terms of the covenant (d). The covenant should also contain a clause for the production of the policy, and of the receipt for the premium during the year (e), and a provision that the money recoverable from the insurance office shall be applied in repairing or rebuilding the premises destroyed by fire. But where there is a covenant to

(x) Neale v. Ratcliff, 15 Q. B. 916, 20 L. J. Q. B. 120; Coward v. Gregory, L. R. 2 C. P. 153, 36 L. J. C. P. 1. See also Thomas v. Cadwaller, Willes, 496; Martyn v. Clue, 18 Q. B. 661.

(y) Dean of Bristol v. Jones, 1 E. & E. 484, 28 L. J. Q. B, 201.

(z) See Implied Covenants, *post*, sub.-sect. (b).

(a) Powley v. Walker, 5 T. R. 357. See Implied Covenants, *post*, sub.-sect. (b), and Repairs and Cultivation, *post*, Part 2, Divis. 1, c. 3.

(b) Webb v. Plummer, 2 B. & Ald. 750 : Hutton v. Warren, 1 M. & W. 466, 477.

(c) Doe d. Pitt v. Shewin, 3 Camp. 134.

(d) Doe d. Muston v. Gladwin, 6 Q. B. 953; Penniall v. Harborne, 11 Q. B. 368.

(e) Doe d. Bridger v. Whitehead, 8 A. & E. 571. See Toleman v. Portbury, L. R. 5 Q. B. Ex. Ch. 288, 39 L. J. Q. B. 136.

repair, the lessee's liability is not limited to the amount of the sum insured (*f*). A further provision may be made, that if the tenant omit to insure, the landlord may do it, and recover the money paid by distress or otherwise, as for rent in arrear. The ordinary covenant to insure is broken if the lessee fail to keep the premises insured for any time, however short (*g*). The breach of this covenant is a continuing breach, and the receipt of rent by the lessor after breach waives only that portion of the breach which has then actually occurred (*h*). If, however, the lessor, by his conduct, leads the lessee to believe that the covenant has been performed, he cannot recover in ejectment for a forfeiture, though there was no dispensation or release from the covenant (*i*).

In general the lessee also covenants not to underlet nor assign the premises, nor any part thereof, without the written consent or license of the lessor (*j*). If the covenant only restrains the lessee from assigning, he may underlet without his lessor's consent; but although an under-lease is no breach of a covenant not to assign, yet the converse of the proposition cannot be maintained (*k*). Covenants denying the privilege

Not to underlet nor assign.

(*f*) Digby *v.* Atkinson, 4 Camp. 275.
(*g*) Doe *d.* Pitt *v.* Shewin, 3 Camp. 134; Doe *d.* Darlington *v.* Ulph, 13 Q. B. 204; Wilson *v.* Wilson, 14 C. B. 616; Doe *d.* Flower *v.* Peck, 1 B. & A. 428; Hyde *v.* Watts, 12 M. & W. 254; Doe *d.* Baker *v.* Jones, 5 Exch. 498; but see Doe *d.* Pitt *v.* Laming, 4 Camp. 73.
(*h*) Doe *d.* Muston *v.* Gladwin, 6 Q. B. 953.
(*i*) Doe *d.* Knight *v.* Rowe, Ry. & Moo. 343; Doe *d.* Pitman *v.* Sutton, 9 C. & P. 706.
(*j*) It seems that a covenant of this kind, if inserted in very long leases, might be open to the objection of creating a perpetuity. See Platt on Covenants, 404; Roe *d.* Hunter *v.* Galliers, 2 T. R. 140; Buckland *v.* Hall, 8 Ves. 94; Church *v.* Brown, 15 Ves. 269; Folkingham *v.* Croft, 3 Anst. 701.
(*k*) Church *v.* Brown, 15 Ves. 265; Doe *d.* Mitchinson *v.* Carter, 8 T. R. 61; Crusoe *d.* Blencowe *v.* Bugby, 2 W. Bl. 766, 3 Wils. 234; Kynnersley *v.* Orpe, 1 Dougl. 57; Holford *v.* Hatch, ib. 183; Brewer *v.* Hill, 2 Anst. 413; Roe *d.* Gregson *v.* Harrison, 2 T. R. 425; Doe *d.* Holland *v.* Worsley, 1 Camp. 20.

of underletting can only extend to such underletting as would require a license. The exclusive enjoyment, therefore, of a room in the premises by a lodger will not occasion a breach of such a covenant (*l*). Where the lessor is desirous that the possession, as well as the property, should be confined to his lessee, express words prohibiting the privilege of taking in lodgers, or parting with the possession of the premises, or any part thereof, must be contained in the deed (*m*).

Although it is the practice to insert a covenant against underletting and assigning without the lessor's consent, and although such a covenant may be fair and reasonable, yet the better opinion seems to be, that an agreement for a lease, containing a stipulation that the lease to be granted shall contain all common and usual covenants, will not include this covenant, as common and usual covenants mean such covenants as are incidental to the lease (*n*).

A lease made to the lessee and his assigns, provided he shall not assign, is void; but it would have been good if the proviso had been that he shall not assign without consent (*o*). The former part of this proposition, however, has been denied (*p*). A covenant that the lessee, "his executors or administrators," will

(*l*) Doe *d*. Pitt *v*. Laming, 4 Camp. 73.
(*m*) Roe *d*. Dingley *v*. Sales, 1 M. & S. 297; Marsh *v*. Curtis, 2 And. 42, 90; Doe *d*. Holland *v*. Worsley, 1 Camp. 20; Church *v*. Brown, 15 Ves. 265. See Williams *v*. Cheney, 3 Ves. 61; Collins *v*. Silley, Sty. 265.
(*n*) Henderson *v*. Hay, 3 Bro. C. C. 632; Church *v*. Brown, 15 Ves. 258, 271; Morgan *v*. Slaughter, 1 Esp. 8; Folkingham *v*. Croft, 3 Anst. 700; Judgment of Sir W. Grant, M.R., in Jones *v*. Jones, 12 Ves. 186; Vere *v*. Loveden, 12 Ves. 179; Brown *v*. Raymond, 15 Ves. 528; Buckland *v*. Papillon, L. R. 1. Eq. 477.
(*o*) Shep. Touch. 123 n.
(*p*) Denis *v*. Laurie, Hardr. 427; Wetherall *v*. Gearing, 12 Ves. 511.

not assign, does not bind his assigns (*q*); but it will bind his executors or administrators (*r*).

Leeases very generally contain a covenant restraining the exercise of certain specified trades on the premises, and sometimes they go further and totally prohibit the carrying on of all trades and businesses whatsoever; also to prevent any sale by auction in the house (*s*). Covenants of this kind, when they affect the mode of occupation or enjoyment of the land demised, run with the land (*t*). Covenants in restraint of trade in a trading locality, and restrictions against particular trades, are not common and usual covenants (*u*). But where a public-house was described as held at a certain net rent, under common and usual covenants, and the lease contained a proviso for re-entry by the lessor, if any business but that of a victualler should be carried on in the house, it was held, upon proof that such a proviso was inserted in at least six out of ten leases of public-houses, that the proviso was common and usual (*v*). A covenant not to sell spirituous liquors, will not include wine (*w*). A cove-

Not to carry on certain trades.

(*q*) Doe *d*. Cheere *v*. Smith, 5 Taunt. 795; Bally *v*. Wells, 3 Wils. 33; Paul *v*. Nurse, 8 B. & C. 486.
(*r*) Roe *d*. Gregson v. Harrison, 2 T. R. 425.
(*s*) Parker *v*. White, 32 L. J. Ch. 520, 1 H. & M. 167. As to the person upon whom the burden of proof lies, see Toleman *v*. Portbury, L. R. 5 Q. B. Ex. Ch. 288, 39 L. J. Q. B. 136.
(*t*) Mayor of Congleton *v*. Pattison, 10 East. 136; Wilkinson *v*. Rogers, 2 De Gex J. & S. 62. When they are collateral, and relate to something to be done elsewhere than on the land demised, they do not run with the land; Thomas *v*.

Hayward, L. R. 4 Ex. 311. Such covenants bind assigns in equity, who have actual or constructive notice of them. See Jay *v*. Richardson, 30 Beav. 563; Wilson *v*. Hart, L. R. 1 Ch. Ap. 463; Catt *v*. Tourle, L. R. 4 Ch. Ap. 654, 38 L. J. Ch. 665; Fielden *v*. Slater, L. R. 7 Eq. 523. See *infra*, Part 4, c. 1, s. 4. Covenants Running with the Land.
(*u*) Wilbraham *v*. Livsey, 18 Beav. 206; Probert *v*. Parker, 3 Myl. & Cr. 280. See *ante*, Covenants not to Underlet, p. 125.
(*v*) Bennett *v*. Womach, 7 B. & C. 627.
(*w*) Fielden *v*. Slater, *supra*.

nant not to use a house as a beer-house, is not broken by the sale, under a license, of beer by retail to be consumed on the premises (*x*). As to the effect of a license granted and waiver in case of forfeiture, see *infra*, 8 and 9, and Part 3, c. 3, s. 1.

Trading with particular persons, or within a particular radius.
Sometimes the lessee covenants that he will deal with the lessor alone, as in the case where a public-house-keeper agrees to buy all his beer of his landlord. Such contracts are not favoured by the Courts, and it must be shown that the lessor faithfully performed his part of the contract, by supplying good beer (*y*). Such covenants are binding on an assignee with notice (*z*).

Where, upon a lease of limeworks, it was stipulated that the lessor should furnish, and the lessee take, coals from certain collieries, the collieries not furnishing sufficient, it was held that the lessee could not go elsewhere for the whole of his coals, but could only supply the deficiency (*a*).

A covenant is sometimes inserted in a lease to prevent one or other of the parties from exercising his trade within a certain radius (*b*). The covenant will not be good, if it be to the prejudice of the public generally; and therefore it must only affect a limited area, and must be made for a *bonâ fide* consideration (*c*). But

(*x*) London and North-Western Railway Co. *v.* Garnett, L. R. 9 Eq. 26.
(*y*) Thornton *v.* Sherratt, 8 Taunt. 529; Holcombe *v.* Hewson, 2 Camp. 391; Jones *v.* Edney, 3 Camp. 285.
(*z*) Wilson *v.* Hart, L. R. 1. Ch. Ap. 463; Catt *v.* Tourle, L. R. 4 Ch. Ap. 654, and see *ante*, p. 127, n. (t).

(*a*) Wight *v.* Dicksons, 1 Dow. 141.
(*b*) The distance is to be measured as the crow flies. See Duigan *v.* Walker, 1 Johns. 446, 28 L. J. Ch. 867; Reg. *v.* Saffron Walden, 9 Q. B. 76; Jewel *v.* Stead, 6 E. & B. 350.
(*c*) Davis *v.* Mason, 5 T. R. 118; Morris *v.* Coleman, 18 Ves. 438;

CH. IV.]   HOW DEMISES ARE MADE.   129

if there be no limit as to space, the contract is void, whether with or without consideration (*d*). In the case of Horner *v.* Graves (*e*), which turned on the question of space, it was stated that whatever restraint is larger than is necessary for the protection of the party, is oppressive, and therefore unreasonable. This proposition was supported by the Court of Exchequer Chamber (*f*), but they held, in the case before them, that there being no limit as to time did not make the contract unreasonable. But in the subsequent case of Archer *v.* Marsh, in which there was no limit as to time, the Court of Queen's Bench stated that the principle of the decision of the Court of Exchequer Chamber was, that the restraint of trade in that case could not really be injurious to the public, and that the parties must act on their view of what restraint may be adequate to the protection of the one, and what advantage a fair compensation for the sacrifice made by the other. They also stated that Horner *v.* Graves was overruled by the decision in Error (*g*).

The Court will not consider whether the consideration is adequate to the restraint, though there must be some consideration (*h*).

It seems that an injunction will issue to restrain a man who, as foreman or workman for another person,

Hitchcock *v.* Coker, 6 A. & E. 438; Archer *v.* Marsh, 6 A. & E. 959; Pilkington *v.* Scott, 15 M. & W. 657; Procter *v.* Sargent, 2 M. & E. 20; Rannie *v.* Irving, 7 M. & E. 969; Pemberton *v.* Vaughan, 10 Q. B. 87; Elves *v.* Crofts, 10 C. B. 241; Mumford *v.* Gething, 7 C. B. N.S. 305, 29 L. J. C. P. 105.
(*d*) Hinde *v.* Gray, 1 M. & G. 195. But see the Leather-cloth Company *v.* Lorsont, L. R. 9. Eq. 345, 39 L. J. Ch. 86.
(*e*) 7 Bing. 735.
(*f*) See Hitchcock *v.* Coker, *supra*.
(*g*) It does not appear that the case of Horner *v.* Graves was overruled, but it was distinguished from Hitchcock *v.* Coker.
(*h*) See the above cases, and Pilkington *v.* Scott, *supra*.

I

engages in a trade contrary to his covenant (*i*); but where the covenant was not to carry on a business "in his own name, or that of any other person," it was no breach to act as manager for another at a weekly salary (*j*).

Quiet enjoyment. Although an implied covenant for quiet enjoyment in a lease arises on the words demise, let, &c. (*k*), the lease in general contains an express covenant by the lessor, which may be either qualified or unqualified. A form of qualified covenant is given by the second schedule of the 8 & 9 Vict., c. 124, and is as follows:—" And the lessor doth hereby, for himself, his heirs, executors, administrators, and assigns, covenant with the said lessee, his executors, administrators, and assigns, that he and they, paying the rent hereby reserved, and performing the covenants hereinbefore on his and their part contained, shall and may peaceably possess and enjoy the said demised premises for the term hereby granted, without any interruption or disturbance from the said lessor, his executors, administrators, or assigns, or any other person or persons lawfully claiming by, from, or under him, them, or any of them."

Under a covenant of this description, any subsequent ejectment, or other interruption or disturbance, by any person who does not claim "by, from, or under" the lessor, would be no breach (*l*). So under such a covenant, a distress for previous arrears of land-tax, due from the lessor, would be no breach,

(*i*) Newling *v.* Dobell, 19 L. T. N.S. 408.
(*j*) Allan *v.* Taylor, 39 L. J. Ch. 627.
(*k*) See Implied Covenants, *post*, p. 139.

(*l*) Year Book, 26 Hen. VIII. 3 b; Merrill *v.* Frame, 4 Taunt. 329.

the words implying a claim by title from the lessor, and not a claim against him (*m*).

A general or unqualified covenant extends to the acts of all persons having lawful title, and is not confined to the acts of persons claiming through the lessor. Such covenants generally purport to assure against disturbance by " any person or persons whomsoever; " but these words will not include persons having no title, for " the law shall never judge that a man covenants against the wrongful acts of strangers, unless the covenant be full and express to that purpose " (*n*).

A covenant against the acts of a particular person by name will, however, include the acts of that person, whether he has title or not (*o*). And if there be express words in the covenant showing a clear intent to protect the lessee from unlawful as well as from lawful interruption—as, for instance, that the lessee shall enjoy against all " claiming, or pretending to claim," any right, &c.—the lessor will be bound by the express words (*p*). So when the lessor is a party named in the covenant, it will extend to all interruptions by him, whether rightful or wrongful (*q*). In Smith *v.* Compton, it was said that a covenant for title, unqualified in itself, and unconnected by words

(*m*) Stanley *v.* Hayes, 3 Q. B. 105.
(*n*) Year Book, 22 Hen. VI. 52 b; 32 Hen. VI. 32 b; Hayes *v.* Bickerstaff, Vaugh. 118; Tisdale *v.* Essex, Hob. 34; Chantflower *v.* Priestley, Cro. Eliz. 914; Broking *v.* Cham, Cro. Jac. 425; Hammond *v.* Dod, Cro. Car. 5; Nokes' case, 4 Rep. 80 b; Jerritt *v.* Weare, 3 Price, 595. See Dudley *v.* Folliott, 3 T. R. 584.
(*o*) Foster *v.* Mapes, Cro. Eliz. 212; Fowle *v.* Welsh, 1 B. & C.
29; Nash *v.* Palmer, 5 M. & S. 374; Shep. Touch. 166; Perry *v.* Edwards, 1 Stra. 400. See also Rashleigh *v.* Williams, 2 Vent. 62.
(*p*) Southgate *v.* Chaplan, in C. P. Com. 230 S.C.; Chaplan *v.* Southgate, in K. B. 10 Mod. 383; Lucy *v.* Levington, 1 Vent. 175; Hunt *v.* Allen, Wynch. 25.
(*q*) Lloyd *v.* Tomkies, 1 T. R. 671; Andrews *v.* Paradise, 8 Mod. 319; Shaw *v.* Stenton, 2 H. & N. 858.

with a qualifying covenant in the lease, must in a court of law be regarded as an absolute covenant for title (r).

Where the lessor covenanted that he had not done, nor permitted, nor suffered to be done, any act, &c., it was held that consenting to an act, which he could not prevent, was not a breach (s).

A breach of this covenant may be made, either by proceedings in law or by other acts. Where the covenant was, that the lessee should enjoy the estate discharged of tithes, it was held that the covenant was broken by a suit for the tithes, although the term was at an end (t); but a suit for waste is not a breach of the covenant for quiet enjoyment (u).

An act done in the assertion of title (v), and which disturbs the lessee in the full enjoyment of his property, amounts to a breach, as, for instance, the erection of a gate so as to interfere with the use of a close (w), or digging a quarry so as to interfere with the working of a mine (x).

Renewal of leases.

A covenant for the renewal of a lease runs with the land (y). But a covenant for a perpetual renewal,

---

(r) Smith v. Compton, 3 B. & Ad. 189, overruling Milner v. Horton, M'Clel. 647; and see Browning v. Wright, 2 B. & P. 13, where the qualifying covenants were connected with the unqualified covenant.

(s) Hobson v. Middleton, 6 B. & C. 295.

(t) Laming v. Laming, Cro. Eliz. 316.

(u) Morgan v. Hunt, 2 Ventr, 215.

(v) Sedden v. Senate, 13 East. 72.

(w) Andrews v. Paradise, 8 Mod. 318.

(x) Shaw v. Stenton, 2 H. & W. 858. As to remedies for a breach, see Part 3, Div. 2, c. 1.

(y) Earl of Shelburn v. Biddulph, 6 Bro. P. C. 363.

entered into by a lessor having a limited interest, does not bind the estate (*z*). A covenant for renewal which would create a perpetuity in the heirs of the body of a particular person is invalid (*a*). And in general the Courts will not construe a covenant for renewal to be perpetual (*b*), unless the intention of the parties is clearly expressed (*c*).

And where there is a proviso in general terms that the lease to be granted shall contain the same covenants and agreements as the lease containing the covenant, such a proviso has been held not to extend to the covenant for renewal (*d*).

With respect to what will create a forfeiture of the right of renewal, that will depend upon the terms of the covenant, and whether they have been sufficiently carried out or not (*e*).

The Court of Chancery will not generally relieve a lessee from the consequences of his laches (*f*); and where there is a covenant to renew, provided the covenants are kept by the lessee (*g*), or to renew at the end of the term, if it should not sooner determine through

---

(*z*) Brereton *v.* Tuohey, 8 Ir. Ch. R. 190; Postlethwaite *v.* Lewthwaite, 2 J. & H. 237, 31 L. J. Ch. 584.
(*a*) Hope *v.* Mayor of Gloucester, 7 De G. M. & G. 647, 25 L. J. Ch. 145.
(*b*) Baynham *v.* Guy's Hospital, 3 Ves. 298; Smyth *v.* Nangle, 7 Cl. & Fin. 405; Brown v. Tighe, 2 Cl. & Fin. 396.
(*c*) Hare *v.* Burgess, 4 Kay & J. 45, 27 L. J. Ch. 86 ; Bridges, *v.* Hitchcock, 1 Bro. P. C. 522; Furnival *v.* Crewe, 3 Atk. 83.

(*d*) 4 Jarm. Prec. 393, 3d edit.; Tritton *v.* Foote, 2 Bro. C. C. 636, 2 Cox, 174; Iggulden *v.* May, 7 East. 237 ; Hide *v.* Skinner, 2 P. Wins. 197.
(*e*) See Baynham *v.* Guy's Hospital, *supra;* Eaton *v.* Lyon, 3 Ves. 690 ; Bogg *v.* Midland Railway Co., L. R. 4 Eq. 310, 313, 36 L. J. Ch. 440 ; Rubery *v.* Jervoise, 1 T. R. 229.
(*f*) 4 Jarm. Prec. 397, 3d edit.
(*g*) Job *v.* Banister, 2 Kay & J. 374, 26 L. J. Ch. 125.

the lessee's default (*h*), the Court will not decree a specific performance of the covenant to renew, the tenant not having performed his part of the agreement.

As to renewals by minors and lunatics, see the 11 Geo. IV. & 1 Will. IV., c. 65, *ante*, pp. 24, 28.

In order to prevent the inconvenience arising from the refusal of under-lessees to surrender their under-leases, and so to prevent the renewal of leases, it is enacted by the 4 Geo. II., c. 28, s. 6, that "in case any lease shall be duly surrendered, in order to be renewed, and a new lease made and executed by the chief landlord or landlords, the same new lease shall, without surrender of all or any the under-leases, be as good and valid, to all intents and purposes, as if all the under-leases derived thereout had been likewise surrendered at or before the taking of such new lease; and all and every person and persons in whom any estate for life or lives, or for years, shall from time to time be vested by virtue of such new lease, and his, her, and their executors and administrators, shall be entitled to the rents, covenants and duties, and have like remedy for recovery thereof; and the under-lessees shall hold and enjoy the messuages, lands, and tenements, in the respective under-leases comprised, as if the original leases out of which the respective under-leases are derived had been still kept on foot and continued; and the chief landlord and landlords shall have and be entitled to such and the same remedy, by distress or entry in and upon the messuages, lands, tenements, and hereditaments comprised in any such under-lease, for the rents and duties reserved by such

---

(*h*) Thompson *v.* Guyon, 5 Sim. 65, cited 2 K. & J. 381.

CH. IV.]   HOW DEMISES ARE MADE.   135

new lease, so far as the same exceed not the rents and duties reserved in the lease out of which such under-lease was derived, as they would have had in case such former lease had been still continued, or as they would have had in case the respective under-leases had been renewed under such new principal lease; any law, custom, or usage to the contrary hereof notwithstanding."

The effect of the above section is to leave untouched the sub-lease created before a surrender, but to give the lessee a right to surrender, notwithstanding the sub-lease (*i*).

By the 8 & 9 Vict., c. 106, s. 9, when the reversion expectant on a lease merges, the estate which confers the next vested right shall be deemed the reversion for some purposes (*j*). As at common law the obligations of the parties were incident to the immediate reversion, and were extinguished upon merger of the reversion, the above statute was passed substituting the next vested right for the reversion (*k*).

(b.) IMPLIED COVENANTS.

Implied covenants, and covenants *in law*, are such

Implied covenants and covenants in law.

(*i*) See Cousins *v.* Phillips, 3 H. & C. 892, 35 L. J. Ex. 84. See also Doe *d.* Palk *v.* Marchetti, 1 B. & Ad. 715.

(*j*) The words of the sect. are:—That when the reversion expectant on a lease, made either before or after the passing of this act, of any tenements or hereditaments, of any tenure shall, after the said first day of October one thousand eight hundred and forty-five, be surrendered or merge, the estate which shall, for the time being, confer as against the tenant under the same lease the next vested right to the same tenements or hereditaments, shall, to the extent and for the purpose of preserving such incidents to and obligations on the same reversion, as, but for the surrender or merger thereof, would have subsisted, be deemed the reversion expectant on the same lease.

(*k*) Webb *v.* Russell, 3 T. R. 393; Stokes *v.* Russell, ib. 678; Woolley *v.* Gregory, 2 Y. & J. 536.

covenants *in deed* as are not *express* covenants. There are many implied covenants which are not covenants in law, and which differ only from express covenants by reason of the obscurity with which the intention of the parties is expressed (*l*).

A covenant in law " is an agreement which the law infers or implies from the use of certain words having a known legal operation in the creation of an estate; so that, after they have had their primary operation in creating the estate, the law gives them a secondary force, by implying an agreement on the part of the grantor to protect and preserve the estate so by those words already created " (*m*).

Such covenants cease with the estate of the lessor (*n*), but during the continuance of the estate, the covenant will run with the land (*o*).

It is a maxim of the law that "*expressum facit cessare tacitum*," and therefore an express covenant will control an implied covenant of the same nature (*p*).

Covenants may be implied from what appears to be the general intent of the parties. Thus a recital in a

(*l*) Williams *v*. Burrell, 1 C. B. 429.
(*m*) *Per* Tindal, C.J., in Williams *v*. Burrell, 1 C. B. 429.
(*n*) Swan *v*. Stransham, Dyer, 257 a, 1 Leon. 179, cited 6 Bing. 666; Penford *v*. Abbott, 32 L. J. Q. B. 67.
(*o*) Bac. Abr. tit. Covenant (E)

5; Vyvyan *v*. Arthur, 1 B. & C. 410.
(*p*) Merrill *v*. Frame, 4 Taunt. 329; Line *v*. Stephenson, 5 Bing. N. C. 183; Standen *v*. Chrismas, 10 Q. B. 135, 141; Deering *v*. Farriugton, 1 Ld. Raym. 14, 19; Mathew *v*. Blackmore, 1 H. & N. 762.

CH. IV.] HOW DEMISES ARE MADE. 137

deed may amount to an implied covenant upon which an action may be maintained (*q*).

In the case of a lease of lands in which are the words " yielding and paying " so much rent, this is an agreement for the payment of rent which amounts to a covenant, and an action lies for the non-payment (*r*). Payment of rent.

In the absence of any express covenant, an implied one arises, on the part of the lessee, that he will use the buildings demised in a tenant-like and proper manner (*s*). Repairs.

An express covenant to repair will control an implied one (*t*); but, if not inconsistent with each other, both may stand (*u*). As to its effect upon an implied covenant to farm, &c., according to the custom of the country, see *infra*.

It was said in Smith *v*. Marrable, that it was an implied condition in the letting of a house that it should be fit for habitation (*v*); but it has since been decided that that is not so, nor is there any implied condition that it should be fit for the purposes for which it is let (*w*). But where a

(*q*) Severn *v*. Clark, 2 Leon. 122; Hollis *v*. Carr, 2 Mod. 87; Barfoot *v*. Freswell, 3 Keb. 465; Sampson *v*. Easterby, 9 B. & C. 505, in error, 6 Bing. 644; Saltoun *v*. Houston, 1 Bing. 433; Farrall *v*. Hilditch, 5 C. B. N.S. 840. See also Lay *v*. Mottram, 19 C. B. N. S. 479; Aspdin *v*. Austin, 5 Q. B. 671; Sharp *v*. Waterhouse, 7 E. & B. 816.

(*r*) Hellier *v*. Casbard, 1 Sid. 266; Porter *v*. Swetnam, Styles, 406. See also Giles *v*. Hooper, Carth. 135.

(*s*) Leach *v*. Thomas, 7 C. & P. 327; Harnett *v*. Maitland, 16 M. & W. 287; Yellowby *v*. Gower, 11 Exch. 294; Morrison *v*. Chadwick, 7 C. B. 266; White *v*. Nicholson, 4 M. & G. 95.

(*t*) See *ante*, Covenant for Quiet Enjoyment, pp. 130, 136.

(*u*) White *v*. Nicholson, 4 M. & G. 95.

(*v*) 11 M. & W. 5.

(*w*) Hart *v*. Windsor, 12 M. & W. 68; Sutton *v*. Temple, Id. 52.

furnished house was let, subject to an express condition that it was fit for occupation, the condition was held broken by the house being infested by bugs (x).

So also there is no implied covenant on the part of the lessor that he will do any repairs whatever (y); and if the landlord contract to do the repairs, there is no implied agreement that upon breach the tenant may quit (z), or that the tenant may do the repairs and deduct the amount from his rent (a).

Husbandry.

There is also an implied covenant on the part of the lessee that he will manage and cultivate the lands demised in a good and husbandlike manner, according to the custom of the country (b).

If, however, there is an express covenant in the lease, such a covenant will control the implied covenant to farm according to the custom (c).

Where the covenant is not inconsistent with the custom, both may stand (d), and it is question of law

---

(x) Campbell $v.$ Lord Wenlock, 4 F. & F. 716.
(y) Arden $v.$ Pullen, 10 M. & W. 321; Gott $v.$ Gandy, 2 E. & B. 845.
(z) Surplice $v.$ Farnsworth, 7 M. & G. 576.
(a) Howlett $v.$ Strickland, Cowp. 56; Smith $v.$ Mapleback, 1 T. R. 446.
(b) Powley $v.$ Walker, 5 T. R. 373; Legh $v.$ Hewitt, 4 East. 154; Angerstein $v.$ Hanson, 1 C. M. & R. 789; Earl of Falmouth $v.$ Thomas, 1 Cr. & M. 89; Hallifax $v.$ Chambers, 4 M. & W. 662; Martin $v.$ Gilham, 7 A. & E. 540; Bickford $v.$ Parson, 5 C. B. 920; Wilkins $v.$ Wood, 17 L. J. Q. B. 319.
(c) Webb $v.$ Plummer, 2 B. & C. 746; Roberts $v.$ Barker, 1 Cr. & M. 808; Clarke $v.$ Roystone, 13 M. & W. 752.
(d) Hutton $v.$ Warren, 1 M. & W. 466; Holding $v.$ Pigott, 7 Bing. 465; Sutton $v.$ Temple, 12 M. & W. 63; Faviel $v.$ Gaskoin, 7 Exch. 273; Muncey $v.$ Dennis, 1 H. & N. 216; White $v.$ Nicholson, 4 M. & G. 95; Martyn $v.$ Clue, 18 Q. B. 661, 682.

for the Court whether the custom is excluded by the terms of the covenant (e.)

An agreement to grant a lease contains an implied For title. undertaking on the part of the intended lessor that he has title to grant such lease; and, if he has not, he is liable to an action at the suit of the intended lessee (f). So also upon an agreement to sell an existing lease, the seller impliedly engages to make out the lessor's title to demise (g); but upon the sale of an agreement for a lease, it seems to be otherwise (h), for it is not a sale of an interest in the land, but only a sale of an agreement.

A tenant has a right to have his estate secured to Quiet enjoyhim, and he has a right to have the quiet enjoyment ment. of it secured to him (i). Hence arises an implied covenant upon the part of the landlord for quiet enjoyment by the mere use of the word "demise" (j), and that even upon a parol demise (k).

The word "let" or "lease," or any other word creating an actual demise, will have the same force as the word "demise" in creating a covenant for quiet enjoyment (l).

(e) Parker v. Ibbetson, 4 C. B. N.S. 846. See *post*, Part 2, c. 3, s. 3.
(f) Stranks v. St John, L. R. 2 C. P. 376, 36 L. J. C. P. 118; Anthony v. Brecon Market Co., L. R. 2 Ex. 167.
(g) Hall v. Betty, 4 M. & G. 410; Souter v. Drake, 5 B. & Ad. 992; De Medina v. Norman, 9 M. & W. 820.
(h) Kintrea v. Perston, 1 H. & N. 357, 25 L. J. Ex. 287.
(i) Smith's L. & T. 480, 2d edit.

(j) Williams v. Burrell, 1 C. B. 429; Adams v. Gibney, 6 Bing. 656; Noke's case, 4 Co. Rep. 80 b; Fraser v. Skey, 2 Chit. Rep. 646; Burnett v. Lynch, 5 B. & C. 589.
(k) Bandy v. Cartwright, 8 Exch. 913; Messent v. Reynolds, 3 C. B. 194.
(l) Bandy v. Cartwright, 8 Exch. 913; Hall v. City of London Brewery Company, 2 B. & S. 737 31 L. J. Q. B. 257.

The word "give or "grant" had formerly a similar effect; but now by the 8 & 9 Vict., c. 106, s. 4, in a deed executed after the 1st of October 1845, these words will not imply a covenant, except by special Act of Parliament.

This implied covenant assures to the tenant quiet enjoyment of the demised premises during the continuance of the term, without any lawful interruption or disturbance by any person having title (*m*); but it does not extend to assure the tenant of quiet enjoyment, without any eviction from or by the party or parties entitled to the reversion of or in the demised premises expectant on the termination of the landlord's lease (*n*).

A mere agreement for a lease does not create an implied stipulation for quiet enjoyment during the term agreed to be granted (*o*).

An express covenant will control an implied one (*p*).

An implied covenant for quiet enjoyment runs with the land, and may be sued on by the assignee of the lessee (*q*).

Sometimes covenants are implied from the express

(*m*) Williams *v.* Burrell, *supra;* Hayes *v.* Bickerstaff, Vaugh. 118; Lucy *v.* Levington, Freem. 103, 3 Keb. 163.
(*n*) Granger *v.* Collins, 6 M. & W. 458. See Jackson *v.* Cobbin, 8 M. & W. 790. See p. 131.
(*o*) Drury *v.* Macnamara, 5 E. & B. 612, 25 L. J. Q. B. 5;

Brashier *v.* Jackson, 6 M. & W. 549; Coe *v.* Clay, 5 Bing. 440; Jinks *v.* Edwards, 11 Exch. 775; Parker *v.* Taswell, 2 De G. & J. 559, 27 L. J. Ch. 42.
(*p*) See *ante*, pp. 135, 137, 138.
(*q*) Williams *v.* Burrell, 1 C. B. 402.

CH. IV.] HOW DEMISES ARE MADE. 141

covenants which have been entered into, although the Other implied
Courts have recently shown a disposition not to imply covenants.
covenants which ought to have been expressed (r).

SECT. 8.—PROVISOS AND CONDITIONS.

After the covenants by the lessee, provisos and conditions by which the estate granted may be enlarged (s) or defeated are frequently inserted. A condition or proviso (t) is defined to be " some quality annexed to a real estate, by which it may be defeated, enlarged, or " created upon an uncertain event " (u).

No precise form of words is necessary for the purpose of creating a condition in a lease, as the construction of the clause will be governed by the apparent intention of the parties, to be collected from the instrument itself (v). Even if the word "condition" be used, it will be construed to mean contract or

(r) Aspdin v. Austin, 5 Q. B. 671; Dunn v. Sayles, Id. 685; Doe d. Marquis of Bute v. Guest, 15 M. & W. 160; Pilkington v. Scott, Id. 657; Smith v. Mayor of Harwich, 2 C. B. N.S. 651; Sharp v. Waterhouse, 7 E. & B. 816. See, however, Emmens v. Elderton, 4 H. of L. Cases, 624; Whittle v. Frankland, 2 B. & S. 49, 31 L. J. M. C. 81.

(s) It is unnecessary to advert to conditions *precedent*, or those upon which an estate may come into *esse*. See Bac. Abr. Conditions (I); Shep. Touch. 133. The question whether any provision in a contract is a condition *precedent*, depends upon the intention of the parties, as apparent on the contract, and not upon any formal arrangement of the words. See Boone v. Eyre, 1 H. M. 273,

note (a) : Tidey v. Mollett, 16 C. B. N.S. 298; Notes to Pordage v. Cole, 1 Wms. Saund. 320 a; and to Cutter v. Powell, 2 Smith's L. C. 5th edit. ; Com. Dig. Condition (B).

(t) A condition is called a proviso, merely on account of the word with which it usually begins.

(u) Co. Litt. 201 a.' See also Litt. S. S. 328, 329; Bac. Abr. Conditions (A) ; Lord Cromwell's case, 2 Rep. 69 b. As to the distinction between conditions in law, *i.e.*, implied conditions, and conditions in deed, see Litt. 325, 380; Co. Litt. 214 b; Mary Portington's case, 10 Rep. 41 ; Shep. Touch. 117.

(v) Doe d. Henniker v. Wall, 8 B. & C. 308.

stipulation, in order to effectuate the intention of the parties (w).

And where words both of covenant and condition are used, both will operate (x). Where a power of re-entry is expressly given, or may be gathered from the words of the instrument, a condition, and not a covenant, will in general be created (y).

A condition may be indorsed on the instrument, or may be contained in another executed the same day (z).

Provisos or conditions which do not concern the thing demised, but are merely collateral, do not run with the land, so as to entitle an assignee of the reversion to sue (a).

Leases usually contain provisos and conditions not to assign without license, with powers of re-entry for any breach of such conditions (b).

Not to assign. We have already stated the general nature and effect of a covenant not to assign or underlet, and also the nature of provisos and conditions in

(w) Hayue v. Cummings, 16 C. B. N.S. 421.
(x) Shep. Touch. 122 ; Co. Litt. 146 ; Co. Litt. 203 (B) ; Doe d. Henniker v. Wall, 8 B. & C. per Bailey, J., 315.
(y) Doe d. Wilson v. Phillips, 2 Bing. 13 ; Doe d. Gardner v. Kennard, 12 Q. B. 244. In Shaw v. Coffin, 14 C. B. N.S. 372, it was held that the following words in an agreement for letting did not create a condition :—" The said tenant hereby agrees that he will not underlet the said premises without the consent in writing of the landlord."
(z) Com. Dig. Condition (A) 9 ; Griffin v. Stanhope, Cro. Jac. 456; Goodright d. Nicholls v. Mark, 4 M. & S. 30.
(a) Stevens v. Copp, L. R. 4, Ex. 20, 38 L. J. Ex. 31. See *post*, Part 3, c. 1, Covenants Running with the Land.
(b) See *infra*, ss. 8 and 9, pp. 141, 147; and also *supra*, Covenants not to Assign, p. 125.

general (c), and we shall now proceed to explain what is a breach of a covenant not to assign, and how it may be waived.

It has been held in several cases that a condition not to assign is not broken by an assignment by operation of law (d). But if special words are inserted in the condition to include such case, a forfeiture will ensue (e).

A covenant not to assign is broken by the execution of a deed assigning the whole of the term, although the deed purports to be merely an under-lease, reserving rent with powers of re-entry (f). In order to create a forfeiture, the assignment must be valid in point of law (g). So an advertisement to underlet or assign is no breach (h). A covenant contained in the lease of a chophouse not to grant any under-lease or leases, or let, set, assign, transfer, set over, or otherwise part with the premises demised, or the indenture of lease, is not broken by depositing the lease with the brewers of the lessee as a security for money advanced by them (i).

Whether a bequest, or, as the books call it, the

(c) See *ante*, p. 141.
(d) See Doe d. Goodbehere v. Bevan, 3 M. & S. 353; Doe d. Mitchinson v. Carter, 8 T. R. 57; Doe d. Lord Anglesea v. Rugeley, 6 Q. B. 107; Croft v. Lumley, 5 E. & B. 648, 682, and 6 H. of L. Cas. 672; Slipper v. Tottenham Junction Railway Co., L. R. 4 Eq. 112; 36 L. J. Ch. 841; Bailey v. De Crespigny, L. R. 4 Q. B. 180.
(e) Roe d. Hunter v. Galliers, 2 T. R. 133; Rex v. Topping, M'Cel. & J. 544; Davis v. Eyton, 7 Bing. 154; Rouch v. The Great Western Railway Co., 1 Q. B. 51; Doe d.
Wyndham v. Carew, 2 Q. B. 317; Doe d. Lloyd v. Ingleby, 15 M. & W. 465.
(f) Parmenter v. Webber, 8 Taunt. 593; Pierce v. Corrie, 5 Bing. 24; Wollaston v. Hakewill, 3 M. & G. 297; Thorne v. Woollcombe, 3 B. & Ad., 586.
(g) Doe d. Lloyd v. Powell, 5 B. & C. 308.
(h) Gourlay v. Duke of Somerset, 1 V. & B. 68.
(i) Doe d. Pitt v. Laming, 1 Ry. & M. 36; Doe d. Pitt v. Hogg, 4 Dow. & Ry. 226. See Doe d. Goodbehere v. Bevan, 3 M. & S. 353.

devise of a term without the landlord's assent is a breach of a covenant not to assign without license, appears doubtful. The law on the subject continued uniform up to the time of James I., namely, that a devise was a breach of the condition (*j*). But in the time of Charles I., a contrary doctrine was established, and this doctrine appears to have been since adhered to (*k*). In this doubtful state of the law, it would be as well to provide for the case of a devise by express words in the covenant. If the covenant contain an exception in favour of assignment by will, it would seem that the executors are not within the exception, and therefore not at liberty to sell for payment of debts without license of the lessor (*l*).

A letting of part of the demised premises is a breach of a covenant not to let the demised premises, or any part or parcel thereof (*m*). So where the covenant was not to assign the whole or any part, and the lessor himself entered upon part, and the lessee afterwards assigned, it was held to be a breach of the covenant (*n*).

License. At common law it was held that if a lessor licensed one assignment, the condition not to assign without license was at an end for ever, and the assignee might afterwards assign without license (*o*). And this has

(*j*) Lord Windsor *v*. Bury, Dyer, 45 b; Knight *v*. Mory, Cro. Eliz. 60; Barry *v*. Stanton, Cro. Eliz. 330; Berry *v*. Taunton, Cro. Eliz. 331; Parry *v*. Harbert, Dyer, 45 b; Dumpor *v*. Syms, Cro. Eliz. 817; Huton *v*. Huton, Cro. Jac. 74.

(*k*) Fox *v*. Swann, Stg. 482, 483; Crusoe *d*. Blencowe *v*. Bugby, 3 Wils. 237. See the judgment of Bailey, J., in Doe *d*. Goodbe-

here *v*. Bevan, 3 M. & S. 361. In Doe *d*. Evans *v*. Evans, 9 A. & E. 719, the point was raised, but not decided.

(*l*) *Per* Mansfield, C.J., in Lloyd *v*. Crisp, 5 Taunt. 249.

(*m*) Roe *d*. Dingley *v*. Sales, 1 M. & S. 297.

(*n*) Collins *v*. Sillye, Style, 265.

(*o*) Dumpor's case, 1 Smith's L. C. 5th edit. 28. See notes 31.

been held to be the case even where the license was to assign to a particular person (*p*). This law is still in force with reference to covenants and licenses contained in leases made before August 1859 (*q*). But the license, in order to put an end to the condition, must be such a license as is contemplated by the instrument. Thus where the condition is not to assign without license in writing, a parol license is no dispensation (*r*), unless such parol license is used as a snare, in which case equity would relieve (*s*). So also where there is an exception in favour of assignment by will, the condition is still in force after an assignment by will (*t*).

According to the general principle of law that long acquiescence in any adverse claim of right is good ground on which a jury may presume that the claim had a legal commencement, it has been held that a license may be presumed to have been given according to the terms of the condition. Thus upon proof of an uninterrupted sub-lease of the premises for more than twenty years, to the knowledge of the lessor, and contrary to the condition of the lease, the Court held that the jury ought to be directed to presume that a license in writing had been duly given (*u*).

Now, however, by 22 & 23 Vict., c. 35, s. 1 (*v*), it is enacted that " Where any license to do any act which, without such license, would create a for-

(*p*) Brummel *v.* Macpherson, 14 Ves. 173.
(*q*) See 22 & 23 Vict. c. 35, *infra.*
(*r*) Roe *v.* Harrison, 2 T. R. 425; Macher *v.* Foundling Hospital, 1 V. & B. 191.
(*s*) Richardson *v.* Evans, 3 Madd. 218.

(*t*) Lloyd *v.* Crispe, 5 Taunt. 249, 254; Mason *v.* Corder, 7 Taunt. 9.
(*u*) Gibson *v.* Doeg, 2 H. & N. 615. See also Doe *d.* Sheppard *v.* Allen, 3 Taunt. 78; Doe *d.* Boscawen *v.* Bliss, 4 Taunt. 735.
(*v*) See also 23 & 24 Vict. c. 38, as to waiver, Part 3, c. 3, s. 2.

K

feiture, or give a right to re-enter, under a condition or power reserved in any lease heretofore granted, or to be hereafter granted, shall at any time after the passing of this Act be given to any lessee or his assigns, every such license shall, unless otherwise expressed, extend only to the permission actually given, or to any specific breach of any proviso or covenant made or to be made, or to the actual assignment, under-lease, or other matter thereby specifically authorised to be done, but not so as to prevent any proceeding for any subsequent breach (unless otherwise specified in such license) ; and all rights under covenants, and powers of forfeiture and re-entry in the lease contained, shall remain in full force and virtue, and shall be available as against any subsequent breach of covenant or condition, assignment, under-lease, or other matter not specifically authorised, or made dispunishable by such license, in the same manner as if no such license had been given ; and the condition or right of re-entry shall be and remain in all respects as if such license had not been given, except in respect of the particular matter authorised to be done."

By sect. 2 :—" Where in any lease heretofore granted, or to be hereafter granted, there is or shall be a power or condition of re-entry on assigning or underletting, or doing any other specified act without license, and a license, at any time after the passing of this Act, shall be given to one of several lessees or co-owners to assign or underlet his share or interest, or to do any other act prohibited to be done without license, or shall be given to any lessee or owner, or any one of several lessees or owners, to assign or underlet part only of the property, or to do any other such act as aforesaid, in respect of part only of such property, such license shall not operate to destroy or extinguish the right of re-entry in case of any breach of the covenant or condition by the co-lessee or co-lessees, or owner or owners, of the other shares or interests in the property, or by the lessee or owner of the rest of the property (as the case may be), over or in respect of such shares or interests or remaining property, but such right of re-entry shall remain in full force over or in respect of the shares or interests or property not the subject of such license."

Sometimes a condition is inserted that the lessor shall not withhold his license to assign unreasonably or vexatiously, and he will be bound by such a condition (*w*). As to a waiver of the forfeiture by the lessor, see *infra*, Part 3, c. 3, s. 2.

9. POWERS OF RE-ENTRY.

All leases should contain a proviso for re-entry, for the purpose of enforcing the payment of the rent and the performance of the covenants.

Powers of re-entry.

The form is usually as follows :—

Provided always, and it is expressly agreed, that if the rent hereby reserved, or any part thereof, shall be unpaid for (fifteen) days after any of the days on which the same ought to have been paid (although no formal demand shall have been made thereof), or in case of the breach or non-performance (*x*) of any of the covenants and agreements herein contained on the

(*w*) Lehmann *v.* McArthur, L. R. 3 Eq. 746, 3 Ch. Ap. 496.
(*x*) Where the words were "in case the lessee should fail in the observance or performance of the covenants," it was doubted whether such words would apply to the breach of a negative covenant, such as a covenant not to assign. West *v.* Dodd, L. R. 5 Q. B. Ex. Ch. 460, 39 L. J. Q. B. 190.

part of the said tenant, his executors, administrators, and assigns, then and in either of such cases it shall be lawful for the said (landlord), his (heirs or executors, administrators) or assigns, at any time thereafter, into and upon the said demised premises, or any part thereof in the name of the whole, to re-enter, and the same to have again, repossess, and enjoy as of his or their former estate, anything herein contained to the contrary notwithstanding (y).

Such provisos are construed according to the intention of the parties, to be collected from the words used (z). Thus where there was the following proviso, that if buildings should not be completed by a certain day, it should " be lawful for the lessor into the demised premises, or any part thereof in the name of the whole, and repossess, retain, and enjoy the same," it seems to have been held that the lessor had a right of re-entry, although the word "re-enter" had been omitted (a). But where the intention of the parties cannot be collected from the words used, the Court will not force a meaning into words which are insensible (b). Where the proviso for re-entry was to take effect upon breach of any of the covenants "thereinafter" contained, and there were none, except a covenant by the lessor for quiet enjoyment, provided the lessee performed the covenants "thereinbefore" mentioned, the Court would not reject the word "thereinafter" (c).

Although in general the Court will construe a pro-

(y) As to forfeiture, re-entry, and waiver generally, see *post*, Part 3, c. 3, ss. 1, 2.
(z) Doe *d*. Davis *v*. Elsam, M. & M. 189 ; Doe *d*. Muston *v*. Gladwin, 6 Q. B. 953, 961 ; Croft *v*. Lumley, 5 E. & Bl. 667, 27 L. J. Q. B. 321 ; Perry *v*. Davis, 3
C. B. N.S. 769 ; Baylis *v*. Le Gros, 4 C. B. N.S. 537, 539, 552.
(a) Hunt *v*. Bishop, 8 Exch. 675.
(b) Doe *d*. Wyndham *v*. Carew, 2 Q. B. 317 ; but see Doe *d*. Darke *v*. Bowditch, 8 Q. B. 973.
(c) Doe *d*. Spencer *v*. Godwin, 4 M. & S. 265.

viso most strictly as against the covenantor, yet a proviso that if, after thirty days' notice, the tenant should make default in performance of any covenant, the landlord might re-enter, was held not to apply to alterations of buildings made by the tenant without leave, and contrary to the covenant, but only to acts to be performed by the tenant upon notice given (*d*).

So a proviso for re-entry if the lessee "should do, or cause to be done, any act," &c., does not apply to a mere omission, as non-repair (*e*).

A proviso that upon breach the lessor may re-enter upon the premises, and hold them "as if the said lease had never been made," or other similar words, does not preclude an action upon the covenants accruing before the re-entry (*f*). Where there is a proviso in a lease that, upon breach of covenant, it shall be lawful for the landlord to re-enter, the landlord may elect whether to avail himself of the proviso or not (*g*), and the lessee cannot elect to treat the lease as void (*h*). A lease contained a covenant, amongst others, that the tenant should not carry away any hay, &c., under a penalty. Then followed a clause enumerating all the other covenants except

(*d*) Doe *d*. Palk *v*. Marchetti, 1 B. & Ad. 715.
(*e*) Doe *d*. Abdy *v*. Stevens, 3 B. & Ad. 299. See West *v*. Dodd, *supra*, p. 147.
(*f*) Hartshorne *v*. Watson, 4 Bing. N. C. 178, 6 Dowl. 404; Load *v*. Green, 15 M. & W. 216; Selby *v*. Browne, 7 Q. B. 620; Davies *v*. Underwood, 2 H. & N. 573; Att.-Gen. *v*. Cox, 3 H. L. Cas. 240.
(*g*) Reid *v*. Parsons, 2 Chit. 247; Doe *d*. Green *v*. Baker, 8 Taunt. 241; Rede *v*. Farr, 6 M. & S. 121;

Doe *d*. Bryan *v*. Bancks, 4 B. & A. 401; Arnsby *v*. Woodward, 6 B. & C. 519; Doe *d*. Nash *v*. Birch, 1 M. & W. 402; Roberts *v*. Davey, 4 B. & Ad. 667; Jones *v*. Carter, 15 M. & W. 718; Pennington *v*. Cardale, 3 H. & N. 356; Baylis *v*. Le Gros, 4 C. B. N.S. 537; Hayne *v*. Cummings, 16 C. B. N.S. 421.
(*h*) Rede *v*. Farr, 6 M. & S. 121; Doe *d*. Bryan *v*. Bancks, 4 B. & Ad. 401; Roberts *v*. Davey, 4 B. & Ad. 664; Doe *d*. Nash *v*. Birch, 1 M. & W. 402.

this, and providing that upon breach of "any of the covenants" the lessor might re-enter; and it was held that the words of the proviso were large enough to include the omitted covenant (*i*).

As to forfeiture, re-entry, and waiver generally, see *post*, Part 3, c. 3, ss. 1 and 2.

Void and voidable leases. Sometimes the clause for re-entry, instead of providing that in case of breach of covenant it shall be lawful for the lessor to re-enter, states that "the lease shall cease, determine, and become void and of no effect."

A proviso that upon non-payment of rent, &c., the lease shall become utterly void, or similar words, only means that it may be made so by some act of the lessor showing an intention to avoid the lease (*j*), and the lessee cannot elect to make the lease void (*k*).

Where a fraudulent representation is made with respect to a collateral matter, in order to procure the granting of the lease, it will not avoid the lease (*l*); but a plea of fraud or illegality may be a good answer to an action for not granting a lease under such circumstances (*m*).

Where there is an express covenant against using a

(*i*) Doe d. Antrobus v. Jepson, 3 B. & Ad. 402.
(*j*) Hartshorne v. Watson, 4 Bing. N. C. 178; Davies v. Underwood, 2 H. & N. 573; Roberts v. Davey, 4 B. & Ad. 664; Pennington v. Cardale, 3 H. & N. 656; Hughes v. Palmer, 19 C. B. N.S. 393; Arnsby v. Woodward, 6 B. & C. 519; Baylis v. Le Gros, 4 C. B. N.S. 537.
(*k*) Rede v. Farr, 6 M. & S. 121; Doe d. Bryan v. Bancks, 4 B. & Ad. 401; Roberts v. Davey, 4 B. & Ad. 664; Doe d. Nash v. Birch, 1 M. & W. 402.
(*l*) Feret v. Hill, 15 C. B. 207.
(*m*) Calvaleiro v. Puget, 4 F. & F. 537; Cowan v. Milburn, L. R. 2 Ex. 230, 36 L. J. Ex. 124.

house for immoral purposes, yet if the lessor permits a breach of the covenant, and derives gain from it, he cannot afterwards recover upon his covenant (*n*).

Arrears of rent accruing before the lease is made void may be sued for; and so also with respect to breaches of other covenants, even if the lessor is to hold the premises upon re-entry "as if the lease had never been made" (*o*).

10. LEASES UNDER POWERS.

The general nature and effect of powers, and what is or is not a valid execution of a particular power, is too wide a subject to be treated of here. There are, however, certain leading cases and principles which should be stated. The subject is fully treated of in other works more particularly devoted to this branch of the law (*p*). It may, in general, be stated, that the creation of the power and its execution will be construed according to the intention of the parties, collected from the words of the instrument, according to their ordinary and common acceptation (*q*).

The Court will, if possible, support an appointment under a power, if it is not exercised from improper motives (*r*).

(*n*) Smith *v*. White, 35 L. J. Ch. 454. See also Gas Light Co. *v*. Turner, 5 Bing. N. C. 666, where the purpose is illegal.
(*o*) See Hartshorne *v*. Watson, 4 Bing. N. C. 178. And see the cases cited *ante*, p. 149, n. (*f*), as to re-entry.
(*p*) See Sugden on Powers, 711–835; Woodfall, L. & T. 153, 10th edit.; Chance on Powers; Powell on Powers.
(*q*) Ren *d*. Hall *v*. Bulkeley, 1

Doug. 293; Pomeroy *v*. Partington, 3 T. R. 665; Goodtitle *d.* Clarges *v*. Funucan, 2 Doug. 573; Hawkins *v*. Kemp, 3 East. 441; Doe *d*. Bartlett *v*. Rendle, 3 M.'& S. 99; Griffith *v*. Harrison, 4 T. R. 737; Jagon *v*. Vivian, L. R. 2 C. P. 422, 3 H. L. Cas. 285, 36 L. J. C. P. 145, 37 ib. 313.
(*r*) See *per* Turner, L.J., in Carver *v*. Richards, 29 L. J. Ch. 360.

It is also a general principle that a man having a power may do less than such power enables him to do; or if he do more, it shall be good to the extent of his power (s).

If a tenant for life make a lease without taking notice of a power, it shall be taken to be an execution of the power, for otherwise the lease shall not have an effectual continuance (t).

If a man charge his estate, and then execute his power of leasing, the lessee will take subject to the charge (u).

Upon a general power to make leases, the law adjudges that the leases ought to be leases in possession, and not in reversion (v). And if a man have a power to make leases in possession *or* reversion, having exercised his power in one way, he cannot afterwards exercise it in another (w).

Where the power makes no mention of covenants, any covenants may be inserted or omitted, provided such insertion or omission be not a fraud which may lessen the value of the reversion (x).

Where the power requires that the leases should be made under the "usual covenants," the question what are such is a question for the jury, and they must

(s) Isberwood v. Oldknow, 3 M. & S. 382; Easton v. Pratt, 2 H. & C. 676, 33 L. J. Ex. 233; Edwards v. Milbank, 4 Drew, 606, 29 L. J. Ch. 45; Sug. Pow, 746, pl. 26.
(t) 1 Vent. 228.
(u) Sabbarton v. Sabbarton, Cas. Temp. Hardw. 415.
(v) Sheecomb v. Hawkins, Cro. Jac. 318, Yelv. 222.
(w) Winter v. Loveday, 1 Ld. Raym. 267.
(x) Goodtitle d. Clarges v. Funucan, 2 Doug. 575.

consider what were such at the time of the creation of the power (y).

By the 13 Vict., c. 17, s. 2, where upon or before the acceptance of rent under any such invalid lease, any receipt, memorandum, or note in writing, confirming such lease, is signed by the person accepting such rent, or some other person by him thereunto lawfully authorised, such acceptance shall, as against the person so accepting such rent, be deemed a confirmation of such lease.

These acts do not apply to leases granted by a mere stranger to the leasing power (z).

With respect to the mode of executing a lease under a power, it is provided by the 22 & 23 Vict., c. 35, s. 12, that such a lease may now be executed and attested in the manner in which deeds are ordinarily executed and attested, notwithstanding any express provision in the power to the contrary. But if the consent of any particular person be required by the power, such consent is necessary to a valid execution (a), or if any act is required to be performed, it must be performed (b). The statute does not make invalid the execution of the deed according to the terms of the power (c).

Defects in leases under powers are in many cases

(y) Goodtitle v Funncan, 2 Doug. 565 ; Doe d. Earl of Egremont v. Stephens, 6 Q. B. 208 ; Smith v. Doe d. Earl of Jersey, 7 Price, 281, 2 B. & B. 473 ; Doe d. Earl of Egremont v. Williams, 11 Q. B. 688.
(z) *Ex parte* Cooper *in re* the North London Railway Co., 34 L. J. Ch. 373. See also Robson v. Flight, 34 L. J. Ch. 226.
(a) Freshfield v. Reed, 9 M. & W. 404.
(b) Fryer v. Coombes, 11 A. & E. 403.
(c) See the proviso, 22 & 23 Vict. c. 35, s. 12.

now cured by the 12 & 13 Vict., c. 26, and the 13 Vict., c. 17.

By the 12 & 13 Vict., c. 26, s. 2, it is enacted, that where in the intended exercise of any such power of leasing as aforesaid, whether derived under an Act of Parliament, or under any instrument lawfully creating such power, a lease has been, or shall hereafter be, granted, which is, by reason of the non-observance or omission of some condition or restriction, or by reason of any other deviation from the terms of such power, invalid as against the person entitled, after the determination of the interest of the person granting such lease, to the reversion, or against other the person who, subject to any lease lawfully granted under such power, would have been entitled to the hereditaments comprised in such lease, such lease, in case the same have been made *bona fide*, and the lessee named therein, his heirs, executors, administrators, or assigns (as the case may require), have entered thereunder, shall be considered in equity as a contract for a grant at the request of the lessee, his heirs, executors, administrators, or assigns (as the case may require), of a valid lease under such power, to the like purport and effect as such invalid lease as aforesaid, save so far as any variation may be necessary in order to comply with the terms of such power; and all persons who would have been bound by a lease lawfully granted under such power shall be bound in equity by such contract: Provided always that no lessee under any such invalid lease as aforesaid, his heirs, executors, administrators, or assigns, shall be entitled by virtue of any such equitable contract as aforesaid to obtain any variation of such lease, where the persons who would have been bound by such contract are willing to confirm such lease without variation.

Sect. 3 of the Act is repealed by the 13 Vict., c. 17 (a).

By sect. 4, where a lease granted in the intended exercise of any such power of leasing as aforesaid is invalid by reason that, at the time of the granting thereof, the person granting the same could not lawfully grant such lease, but the estate of such person in the hereditaments comprised in such lease shall have continued after the time when such or the like lease might have been granted by him, in the lawful exercise of such power, then, and in every such case, such lease shall take effect, and be as valid as if the same had been granted at such last-mentioned time, and all the provisions herein contained shall apply to every such lease.

By sect. 5, when a valid power of leasing is vested in, or may be exercised by, a person granting a lease, and such lease, by reason of the determination of the estate or interest of such person, or otherwise, cannot have effect and continuance according to the terms thereof, independently of such power, such lease shall, for the purposes of this Act, be deemed to be granted in the intended exercise of such power, although such power be not referred to in the lease.

By sect. 6, the rights of lessees under covenants for title and quiet enjoyment, and the lessor's right of re-entry, and other rights for breach of covenant, are saved.

By sect. 7, the Act does not extend to ecclesiastical, college, hospital, or charitable leases, or where a lease has been surrendered, &c., by reason of its invalidity.

(d) See *post*, p. 156.

By the 13 Vict., c. 17, s. 2, it is enacted, that where, upon or before the acceptance of rent under any such invalid lease, as in the said first-recited Act mentioned, any receipt, memorandum, or note in writing, confirming such lease, is signed by the person accepting such rent, or some other person by him thereunto lawfully authorised, such acceptance shall, as against the person so accepting such rent, be deemed a confirmation of such lease.

By sect. 3, where, during the continuance of the possession taken under any such invalid lease, as in the said first-recited Act mentioned, the person for the time being entitled (subject to such possession as aforesaid) to the hereditaments comprised in such lease, or to the possession, or the receipt of the rents and profits thereof, is able to confirm such lease without variation, the lessee, his heirs, executors, or administrators (as the case may require), or any person who would have been bound by the lease, if the same had been valid, shall, upon the request of the person so able to confirm the same, be bound to accept a confirmation accordingly; and such confirmation may be by memorandum, or note in writing, signed by the persons confirming and accepting respectively, or by some other persons by them respectively thereunto lawfully authorised; and after confirmation and acceptance of confirmation, such lease shall be valid, and shall be deemed to have had from the granting thereof the same effect as if the same had been originally valid.

11. LEASES BY ESTOPPEL.

The creation of a lease by estoppel is of a singular character, and is therefore reserved for a separate section. It arises from the general doctrine of estoppel that a man is not permitted to allege or prove anything in contradiction or contravention of his own deed (*e*). Thus a lessor is estopped by the lease which he has made from denying his competency to make it, and the tenant, upon the other hand, is estopped from disputing his lessor's title, and hence the relation of landlord and tenant is created between them by law (*f*). "And if one makes a lease for years by indenture of lands wherein he hath nothing at the time of such lease made, and after purchases those very lands, this shall make good and unavoidable his lease, as well as if he had been in the actual possession and seisin thereof at the time of such lease made; because he having by indenture expressly demised those lands, is, by his own act, estopped and concluded to say he did not demise them, then there is nothing to take off or impeach the validity of the indenture, which expressly affirms that he did demise them; and consequently the lessee may take advantage thereof whenever the lessor comes to such an estate in those lands as is capable to sustain and support that lease" (*g*). And when the estoppel becomes good in point of interest —that is, when the lessor acquires the land by purchase or otherwise—the heir of the lessor, and persons claiming by assignment from the lessor, are bound by the estoppel (*h*). The law of estoppel also creates a reversion in fee-simple by estoppel in the lessor, which passes by descent to his heir, and by purchase to his assignee or devisee (*i*). But if, upon the face

(*e*) Lyon *v.* Reed, 13 M. & W. 285.
(*f*) Darlington *v.* Pritchard, 4 M. & G. 783; Green *v.* James, 6 M. & W. 656. But if the lessor is trustee for the public under a public Act which does not give him power to act, he will not be estopped. Fairtitle *v.* Gilbert, 2 T. R. 169.

(*g*) Bac. Abr. tit. Lease (O).
(*h*) Trevivan *v.* Lawrence, 1 Salk. 276; Goodtitle *v.* Morse, 3 T. R. 371; Doe *d.* Downe *v.* Thomson, 9 Q. B. 1043.
(*i*) Cuthbertson *v.* Irving, 4 H. & N. 758, 28 L. J. Ex. 306, 29 ib. 485.

of the lease, the real title or want of title of the lessor appears, or any interest passes, there will be no estoppel (*j*).

So also the tenant, so long as he retains possession, is estopped from denying his lessor's title (*k*); but in an action against him by the landlord, the tenant may show that the landlord's title has expired (*l*). So, if he is actually evicted by the title paramount of a third party, such eviction is pleadable in bar to a demand of rent by the lessor (*m*).

An under-lease made by a lessee who had no legal interest operates as an estoppel (*n*).

As to the effect of recitals in a lease in creating an estoppel, see *ante*, Recitals.

(*j*) Cuthbertson *v.* Irving, *supra;* Pargeter *v.* Harris, 7 Q. B. 708; Greenaway *v.* Hart, 14 C. B. 340; but see Morton *v.* Woods, 3 Q. B. 658, 37 L. J. Q. B. 242.

(*k*) Cuthbertson *v.* Irving, *supra;* Dolby *v.* Isles, 11 Ad. & E. 335; Phipps *v.* Sculthorpe, 1 B. & Ad. 50; Levy *v.* Lewis, 28 L. J. C. P. 144, 30 ib. 42; Wood *v.* Day, 7 Taunt. 646; Beckett *v.* Bradley, 7 M. & G. 994; Delaney *v.* Fox, 1 C. B. N.S. 166.

(*l*) Claridge *v.* Mackenzie, 4 M. & G. 143; Doe *d.* Leeming *v.* Skirrow, 7 A. & E. 157; Downes *v.* Cooper, 2 Q. B. 263; Neave *v.* Moss, 1 Bing. 363; Doe *d.* Jackson *v.* Ramsbottom, 3 M. & S. 516.

(*m*) Delaney *v.* Fox, 2 C. B. N. S. 768.

(*n*) Doe *d.* Prior *v.* Ongley, 10 C. B. 25.

PART II.

CONTINUATION OF TENANCY.

DIVISION I.—RIGHTS OF LANDLORD.

CHAPTER I.

PAYMENT OF RENT.

	PAGE		PAGE
1. TIME WHEN PAYABLE,	... 159	DEDUCTIONS —*continued.*	
2. MODE OF PAYMENT,	... 162	*sewers' rates,* ...	... 167
		poor-rates, ...	... 167
3. DEDUCTIONS—		*other rates,* ...	... 168
land tax,	... 164	*tithe rent-charge,*	... 169
income-tax,	... 166	4. APPORTIONMENT,	... 170

1. TIME WHEN PAYABLE.

WITH respect to the certainty of the time when rent Time of payment. is to be paid, where the reservation is half-yearly or quarterly, but no specific days are mentioned, the time of payment must be computed by the habendum; and in a case in which rent was payable by a parol demise "from Ladyday following," evidence of the custom of the country was admitted to show that, by "Ladyday," Old Ladyday was intended (*a*). If the reservation be general, and no mention be made of half-yearly or quarterly payments, nothing is due till the end of the year (*b*); and where a reservation was general in the written agreement of demise, but the landlord afterwards asked the tenant how he would like to pay the rent, and the tenant replied quarterly, it was held that the rent was still due annually, and not quarterly, although rent had been actually paid quarterly (*c*). Where rent is payable quarterly, it will be intended to be payable by equal portions (*d*), and will be due on the first of the days mentioned in order of time, without regard to the arrangement of the words (*e*). Where the reservation was "quarterly or half-quarterly, if desired," it was held that the landlord, having received the rent quarterly for the first twelve months, could not distrain for a half-quarter's rent without notice (*f*).

An agreement was entered into on the 31st of January, by which the tenant agreed to become tenant at the customary time of entry (which was the 12th of May), and to pay the annual rent at the usual time (which was Michaelmas), as agreed upon; and it was held that this did not necessarily mean that the rent should be payable at the end of the year from the time of entry, but at the customary time of Michaelmas (*g*).

(*a*) Doe *d*. Hall *v*. Benson, 4 B. & A. 588.
(*b*) Cole *v*. Sury, Latch. 264. See also Comber *v*. Howard, 1 C. B. 440; Turner *v*. Allday, Tyr. & Gr. 819; Collett *v*. Curling, 10 Q. B. 785.
(*c*) Turner *v*. Allday, Tyr. & Gr. 819; Comber *v*. Howard, 1 M. & Gr. 440.

(*d*) Com. Dig. Rent (B) 8; Hutchins *v*. Scott, 2 M. & W. 809.
(*e*) Hill *v*. Grange, Plowd. 171.
(*f*) Mallam *v*. Arden, 10 Bing. 299.
(*g*) Gore *v*. Lloyd, 12 M. & W. 463.

Sometimes rent is reserved payable in advance. When this is the case, it should be clearly expressed whether the payment in advance is intended to refer to the current quarter at the time of the reservation, or to each successive quarter during the term (*h*). A rent may also be reserved to commence before the lessee is to enter on all the land demised, as where there is a lease to commence *in futuro* of Blackacre, and *in præsenti* of Whiteacre, rendering rent payable before the commencement of the term in Blackacre. Here the rent, being an entire thing, is payable according to the reservation (*i*).

Rent reserved upon a lease is not payable until the midnight of the day specified in the lease for payment of it (*j*). Though where, in order to create a forfeiture, it is necessary to make a *demand*, the demand must be made before sunset (*k*).

Where the terms of the reservation were, "The yearly rent to be £110, and the rent shall be payable in advance if the landlord require the same," and no days of payment were specified, but at the end of the quarter the landlord demanded the quarter's rent, and, upon non-payment, distrained for the whole yearly rent, it was ruled that he was only entitled to distrain for the quarter's rent (*l*).

(*h*) Holland *v.* Palser, 2 Stark, 161; Hopkins *v.* Helmore, 8 A. & E. 463. See M'Leish *v.* Tate, Cowp. 781.
(*i*) Gilb. on Rents, 25.
(*j*) Cutting *v.* Derby, 2 Wm. Bl. 1077; Leftley *v.* Mills, 4 T. R. 170.
(*k*) Duppa *v.* Mayo, 1 Wm. Saund. 287; Tinckler *v.* Prentice, 4 Taunt. 549; Clun's case, 10

Co. 127. See also Com. Dig. Pleader (2 W. 49), Maund's case, 7 Co. R. 28 b; Fabian's case, 1 Leon. 305; Wood & Chiver's case, 4 Leon. 179; Acocks *v.* Phillips, 5 H. & N. 183; Collier *v.* Nokes, 2 C. & K. 1012. See also *post*, Part 3, c. 3, s. 1, pp. 257, 258.
(*l*) Clarke *v.* Holford, 2 C. & K. 540.

L

Where the tenant was to pay the last half-year's rent in advance, which was to be considered as reserved and due on a certain day preceding, if the landlord should see cause for such a demand, it was held that he might demand the rent and distrain for it between the day named and the expiration of the tenancy, without demand previous to the day named (*m*).

If the tenant pay his rent before it is due, it is voluntary and not satisfactory (*n*). The statute of Anne, which does away with attornment (*o*), protects the tenant from any claim by an assignee of the reversion where no notice has been given; but where the tenant paid rent to his landlord before it was due, and before it was due received notice from the assignee, it was held that the tenant was still liable to the assignee for the rent (*p*).

2. MODE OF PAYMENT.

Rent is to be paid on the land (*q*), except in the case of a covenant to pay rent, for then the covenantor must pay or tender the money to the covenantee, according to his covenant (*r*).

It is said that, like any other species of debt, rent may be paid by a remittance through the post (*s*).

(*m*) Witty *v.* Williams, 12 W. R. 755, 10 L. T. N.S. 457, Q. B.
(*n*) Clun's case, *supra.*
(*o*) See Attornment, Part 4, c. 1, s. 1, p. .
(*p*) *Re* Nichols, L. R. 5 C. P. 589, 39 L. J. C. P. 296.
(*q*) Rowe *v.* Young, 2 B. & B. 234; Crouch *v.* Fastolfe, Sir T. Raymond, 418, Com. Dig. Pleader (2 W. 49).
(*r*) Haldane *v.* Johnson, 8 Exch. 689.
(*s*) See Woodfall, L. & T. 9th edit. 359; Smith, L. & T. 2d edit. 168.

A demand for rent is even higher than a demand upon a bond or other specialty, although in case of death it ranks against the executor with specialty debts (*t*). So when the landlord takes a bond, bill, or note, this will not bar him of his remedies for rent (*u*).

Receipts for rent, like any other receipt, require a penny stamp if the sum amounts to £2 and upwards (*v*).

3. DEDUCTIONS.

Although no set-off or claim for damages sustained by the lessee can be set-off against a claim for rent due to the lessor, unless by some express agreement, yet there are several payments in the nature of cross demands which the lessee is entitled to have deducted from the amount of the rent, and to have considered as payment *pro tanto*. The general rule, however, is that the lessee can treat as a discharge of the rent only those payments to third parties which are made in satisfaction of a charge on the land or of a debt of the lessor (*w*). In Graham *v.* Allsopp (*x*), Rolfe, B., in giving the judgment of the Court, said, "The principle upon which these cases rest is this—the immediate landlord is bound to protect his tenant from all paramount claims; and when, there-

---

(*t*) Thompson *v.* Thompson, 9 Price, 471; Buller's N. P. 182.

(*u*) Davis *v.* Gyde, 2 A. & E. 624; Worthington *v.* Wigley, 3 Bing. N. C. 454; Murray *v.* King, 5 B. & A. 165; Parrott *v.* Anderson, 7 Exch. 93; Drake *v.* Mitchell, 3 East. 251.

(*v*) See the 33 & 34 Vict. c. 97, s. 120, and schedule "Receipt."

(*w*) Taylor *v.* Zamira, 6 Taunt. 524; Sapsford *v.* Fletcher, 4 T. R. 511; Johnson *v.* Jones, 9 A. & E. 809; Carter *v.* Carter, 5 Bing. 406; Boodle *v.* Campbell, 7 M. & G. 386.

(*x*) 3 Exch. 186-198.

fore, the tenant is compelled, in order to protect himself in the enjoyment of the land in respect of which his rent is payable, to make payments which ought, as between himself and his landlord, to have been made by the latter, he is considered as having been authorised by the landlord so to apply his rent due or accruing due. All such payments, if incapable of being treated as actual payment of rent, would certainly give the tenant a right of action against his landlord as for money paid to his use, and so would, in an action of debt for the rent, form a legitimate subject of set-off. And though in a replevin a general set-off cannot be pleaded, yet the Courts have given to the tenant the benefit of a set-off as to payments of this description, by holding them to be in fact payments of the rent itself or of part of it."

The ground upon which the landlord is presumed to authorise these payments is that he impliedly undertakes to protect the tenant against claims in respect of them (*y*). But a mere claim by a mortgagee to the rent is not sufficient to raise a presumption of an authority from the lessor to pay the rent (*z*).

Land-tax. By the 38 Geo. III., c. 5, s. 17, it is enacted, "That the several and respective tenant or tenants of all houses, &c., which shall be rated by virtue of this Act, are hereby required and authorised to pay such sum or sums of money as shall be rated upon such houses, &c., and to deduct out of the rent so much of the said rate as, in respect of the said rents of any such houses, &c., the landlord should and ought to pay and bear; and the said landlords, both mediate and immediate, according to their respective interests,

(*y*) Jones *v*. Morris, 3 Exch. 742.   (*z*) Wilton *v*. Dunn, 17 Q. B. 294.

are hereby required to allow such deductions and payments upon the receipt of the residue of the rents."

By sect. 18, "Every tenant paying the said assessment or assessments last mentioned shall be acquitted and discharged of so much money as the said assessment or assessments shall amount unto, as if the same had actually been paid unto such person or persons to whom his rent shall have been due and payable;" with power to the commissioners of land-tax, or any two of them, to settle, as they shall think fit, any differences between landlord and tenant, or any other, concerning the said rates. When they have decided any such difference, the Court of Chancery will not re-examine it.

Sect. 35 provides, "That nothing in this Act contained shall be construed to alter, change, or determine, or make void, any contracts, covenants, or agreements whatsoever between landlord and tenant, or any other persons, touching the payment of taxes and assessments in England, Wales, and Berwick-upon-Tweed, anything herein contained to the contrary notwithstanding."

By sect. 4 of the above statute, the tax is to be rated upon all hereditaments, &c., and upon "all and every person or persons, &c., having or holding, &c., such premises in respect thereof" (*a*). As between the tenant and the public, it is a tenant's tax (*b*); but the tenant is entitled to deduct out of the current or accruing rent, at the time when it is payable, so much of the amount

---

(*a*) See *per* Bayley, J., Ward *v.* Const, 10 B. & C. 647; Chelsea Waterworks *v.* Bowley, 17 Q. B. 358, 20 L. J. Q. B. 520.

(*b*) R. *v.* Mitcham, Cald. 276 a; Watson *v.* Home, 7 B. & C. 285; Ward *v.* Const, 10 B. & C. 469

payable for the tax as the landlord would have to pay upon the rent reserved (*c*); and this is so even where the premises have been improved in value,—the tenant having to pay the tax upon the increased value, but being only entitled to deduct the old deduction upon the rent reserved (*d*).

As to the effect of special clauses in a lease as to the payment of taxes, see *ante*, p. 122, Part 1, c. 4, s. 7, Covenant to Pay Rates and Taxes.

Income-tax. By the Property-Tax Act (*e*), occupiers of lands, &c., paying the duty of seven pence in the pound on the annual value of lands, &c., in respect of the property thereof, may deduct seven pence in the pound on the amount of their rent out of the first payment afterwards made on account of it, and the landlords are to allow the deduction under a penalty of £50, and any stipulation made or to be made for payment in full, without allowing such deduction, will be void (*f*); and it is by the same statute enacted, " That no contract, covenant, or agreement between landlord and tenant, or any other person, touching the payment of taxes and assessments to be charged on their respective premises, shall be deemed or construed to extend to the duties charged thereon under this Act, nor be binding contrary to the intent and meaning of this Act; but that all such duties shall be charged upon and paid

(*c*) Andrew *v.* Hancock, 1 B. & B. 37.
(*d*) Yeo *v.* Leman, 2 Str. 1191, 1 Wils. 21; Hyde *v.* Hill, 3 T. R. 377; Graham *v.* Wade, 16 East. 29; Whitfield *v.* Brandwood, 2 Starkie, 441; Watson *v.* Holme, 7 B. & C. 285; Ward *v.* Const, 10 B. & C. 649, 657; Smith *v.* Humble, 15 C. B. 321.

(*e*) 5 & 6 Vict. c. 35, s. 60, Rule 4-9.
(*f*) Id. s. 103. See Fuller *v.* Abbott, 4 Taunt. 105; Tinkler *v.* Prentice, 4 Taunt. 549; Howe *v.* Synge, 15 East. 440; Att.-Gen. *v.* Shield, 3 H. & N. 834, 28 L. J. Ex. 49; Festing *v.* Tayler, 3 B. & S. 231, 32 L. J. Q. B. 41. See also Abadam *v.* Abadam, 33 Beavan, 475, 33 L. J. Ch. 593.

by the respective occupiers, subject to such deductions and repayments as are by this Act authorised and allowed, and all such deductions and repayments shall be made and allowed accordingly, notwithstanding such contracts, covenants, or agreements " (*g*).

The property-tax, like the land-tax, is a tenant's tax, as between the tenant and the public (*h*); and if he omit to deduct it in his next payment of rent, he cannot afterwards recover it as money paid to the use of the landlord (*i*). By the 27 Vict., c. 18, s. 15, he may now deduct it during the period through which the rent was accruing due.

A payment of income-tax by the tenant operates as a payment *pro tanto* of the rent (*j*).

The sewers' rate, though not imposed directly by Act of Parliament, and therefore not to be considered as a parliamentary tax, may be levied on the tenant or occupier of the premises subject to it. And after he has paid it, he is entitled to deduct from the next payment of his current rent so much of the rate as the landlord ought to bear, in like manner as in respect to land-tax (*k*).

Sewers' rates.

The poor-rate is not a tax on the land, but a personal charge in respect of the land. In general, the occupier is liable to pay this tax, for the rate is a charge on the occupier in respect of his possession, and not

Poor-rates.

(*g*) 5 & 6 Vict. c. 35, s. 73.
(*h*) Cumming *v.* Bedborough, 15 M. & W. 438.
(*i*) Ibid.
(*j*) Franklin *v.* Carter, 1 C. B. 750, cited 15 M. & W. 441.

(*k*) See *ante*, Land-tax, p. 164.
Smith *v.* Humble, 15 C. B. 321;
Palmer *v.* Earith, 14 M. & W. 428;
Brewster *v.* Kitchell, 2 Salk. 616;
Waller *v.* Andrews, 3 M. & W. 312.

upon the lessor in respect of the rent received (*l*). A landlord cannot be rated to the poor, even in respect of houses let to tenants who have been excused their rates on account of their poverty (*m*). By the Small Tenements' Rating Act (*n*), however, the landlord may be rated instead of the occupier, where the rateable value of the premises does not exceed £6. By sect. 7, such occupiers (whether paying such rates voluntarily or by compulsion) may deduct the amount, together with all costs and charges they may have incurred on account thereof, from the rent payable in respect of such tenements, and such amounts shall be deemed debts due from such owners to such occupiers, and be recoverable by action. With respect to tenements in parishes wholly or partly in a parliamentary borough, the liability of the landlord in this respect has ceased under the Reform Act of 1867, except as therein mentioned (*o*). By the proviso of sect. 6, it is enacted, that where the occupier under a tenancy subsisting at the time of the passing of this Act of any dwelling-house or other tenement, which has been let to him free from rates, is rated and has paid rates in pursuance of this Act, he may deduct from any rent due, or accruing due, from him in respect of the said dwelling-house or other tenement, any amount paid by him on account of the rates to which he may be rendered liable by this Act.

Other rates. Besides the poor-rate, there are various rates charged upon the occupiers of premises rateable to the

(*l*) Rowls *v.* Gells, Cowp. 452, 1 Dougl. 304, 43 Eliz. c. 2, s. 1.
(*m*) Rex *v.* The Hull Dock Co., 3 B. & C. 516.
(*n*) 13 & 14 Vict. c. 99.
(*o*) 30 & 31 Vict. c. 102, s. 6. This Act does not apply to any place where owners are made liable to be rated to the relief of the poor, under the provisions of any local Act. See also Davis on the Law of Registration and Elections, p. 233, note.

relief of the poor. The chief of these are the paving, watching, lighting, and water rates, the highway rates, the county and borough rates. These and others are, in general, regulated by the principles which govern the assessment to the poor-rates.

Under the Tithe Commutation Acts, the rent-charge, which is substituted in lieu of the tithes, is charged upon the land, and may be recovered by distress. Neither the landlord nor the tenant is, under these statutes, personally liable to pay it; but if the latter pays it, he may deduct it from his rent, unless he has agreed with his landlord to take the charge upon himself (*p*). By the 14 & 15 Vict. c. 25, however, a convenient remedy is given to the landlord or succeeding tenant who is obliged to pay the rent-charge which ought to have been paid by the previous tenant. It is provided by sect. 4 of this Act, that " if any occupying tenant of land shall quit, leaving unpaid any tithe rent-charge for or charged upon such land, which he was by the terms of his tenancy or holding legally or equitably liable to pay, and the tithe-owner shall give or have given notice of proceeding by distress upon the land for recovery thereof, it shall be lawful for the landlord, or the succeeding tenant or occupier, to pay such tithe rent-charge, and any expenses incident thereto, and to recover the amount or sum of money which he may so pay over against such first-named tenant or occupier, or his legal representatives, in the same manner as if the same were a debt by simple contract, due from such first-named tenant or occupier to the landlord or tenant making such payment."

Tithe rent-charge.

(*p*) See the 6 & 7 Will. IV. c. 71, ss. 67, 80, 81; and Griffin-hoofe *v.* Daubaz, 4 E. & B. 230, S. C. in error, 5 E. & B. 746.

4. APPORTIONMENT.

The lessee's liability to pay rent according to his agreement may be altered either by act of the parties or by act of law:—1. Where the reversion of the lessor becomes severed by alienation. 2. Where the lessee's interest in part of the estate is destroyed, and the rent is payable only in respect of the residue. 3. Where the interest of the lessee expires before his rent becomes due. 4. Where the lessor dies before the rent becomes due, but the lessee's interest does not thereby expire.

1. As the rent is incident to the reversion, whenever the reversion is severed by act of the parties, the rent shall be apportioned (*q*) ; but the lessee's concurrence to the apportionment is necessary, unless it be settled by a jury (*r*). The rent will also be apportioned in the case of a severance of the reversion by act of law (*s*).

2. Rent will be apportioned where the lessee's interest in part of the thing demised is extinguished either by the act of parties, the act of law, or the act of God. If the tenant surrender a portion of his estate, or if the lessor enters upon part of the tenant's land for a forfeiture, or if part of the land be recovered in an action for waste, the rent shall be apportioned (*t*). If the tenant be evicted out of a part of the land by force of a paramount title, the rent

---

(*q*) Co. Litt. 148 a ; Collins *v.* Harding, 1 Rolls Abr. 234 ; Doe *d.* Vaughan *v.* Meyler, 2 M. & S. 276.
(*r*) Bliss *v.* Collings, 5 B. & Ald. 876.
(*s*) Moody *v.* Garnon, 1 Rolls Abr. 237, 1. 3, 1. 12; Rushen's case, Dyer, 4 B ; Ewer *v.* Moyle, Cro. Eliz. 771.
(*t*) Smith *v.* Malings, Cro. Jac. 160 ; Fishe *v.* Campion, 1 Rolls Abr. 234, 1. 48, 235, 1. 20 ; Walker's case, 3 Rep. 22, 1 Rolls Abr. 325, 1. 23, 25.

will be apportioned; but if he be evicted wrongfully by the landlord, the rent will be suspended for the whole, and will not be apportioned (*u*).

Where a lease, not under seal, was made of lands, a portion of which was already leased to another in possession for a longer period, it was held that the lease was void as to the portion before leased, and that the rent could not be apportioned (*v*). But where the second lease was under seal, the case was held to be different, because such a lease passed the reversion with the rent thereon (*w*).

Where the lessor fails to fulfil his agreement in the chief object which had induced the lessee to become a party to it (as where he fails to give the exclusive privilege of sporting), the lessee cannot be said to have enjoyed under the agreement; and in an action for use and occupation, the tenant may show an eviction of part of the premises, and the amount of rent which the tenant ought to pay may be ascertained by a jury (*x*).

It seems that where part of land is lost to the lessee by the act of God, he may insist that the rent be apportioned,—as if the sea break in and overflow a part of the land, the rent shall be apportioned (*y*). Where lands and goods are let at an entire rent, and the

(*u*) Smith *v.* Malings, Cro. Jac. 160; Walker's case, 3 Rep. 22; Stevenson *v.* Lambard, 2 East. 575; Boodle *v.* Campbell, 7 M. & G. 386. See also Morrison *v.* Chadwick, 7 C. B. 283; Newton *v.* Allin, 1 Q. B. 518.
(*v*) Neale *v.* Mackenzie, in error, 1 M. & W. 747; Holgate *v.* Kay, 1 C. & K. 341; Eccl. Com-

missioners of Ireland *v.* O'Connor, 9 Ir. Com. L. R. 242.
(*w*) Eccl. Commissioners of Ireland *v.* O'Connor, 9 Ir. Com. L. R. 242.
(*x*) Tomlinson *v.* Day, 2 B. & B. 680. See the judgment of the Court by Lord Denman in Neale *v.* Mackenzie, 1 M. & W. 764.
(*y*) 1 Rolls Abr. 256, l. 46.

tenant is evicted from the lands, no apportionment of the rent can be made for the goods, as rent issues from the land alone (*z*). In Salmon *v.* Matthews, 8 M. & W. 827, however, it appears to have been thought that the rent might be apportioned; but the case was decided on the ground that there was evidence for the jury to infer a fresh agreement to pay for the use of the goods.

3. Where the interest of the lessee expires before his rent becomes due, it cannot be apportioned (*a*). But by the 11 Geo. II., c. 19, s. 15, after reciting "that where any lessor or landlord having only an estate for life in the lands, tenements, or hereditaments demised, happens to die before or on the day on which any rent is reserved or made payable, such rent, or any part thereof, is not by law recoverable by the executors or administrators of such lessor or landlord, nor is the person in reversion entitled thereto, any other than for the use and occupation of such lands, tenements, or hereditaments, from the death of the tenant for life, of which advantage hath been often taken by the under-tenants, who thereby avoid paying anything for the same;" it is enacted, "That where any tenant for life shall happen to die before or on the day on which any rent was reserved or made payable upon any demise or lease of any lands, tenements, or hereditaments, which determined on the death of such tenant for life, the executors or administrators of

---

(*z*) Emott's case, Dyer, 212 b, in margin; Collins *v.* Harding, Cro. Eliz. 606; Cadogan *v.* Kennett, Cowp. 432; Gilb. Rents, 175; Williams *v.* Haywood, 1 E. & E. 1040, 28 L. J. Q. B. 374.

(*a*) Countess of Plymouth *v.* Throgmorton, 1 Salk. 65; Clun's case, 10 Rep. 127 b; Jenner *v.* Morgan, 1 P. W. 392; Edwards *v.* Countess of Warwick, 2 P. W. 176; Hay *v.* Palmer, ib. 502; Lord Strafford *v.* Lady Wentworth, 1 P. W. 180; Lord Rockingham *v.* Penrice, ib. 177; Slack *v.* Sharp, 8 A. & E. 366.

such tenant for life shall and may, in an action on the case, recover of and from such under-tenant or under-tenants of such lands, &c., if such tenant for life die on the day on which the same was made payable, the whole, or if before such day, then a proportion, of such rent, according to the time such tenant for life lived, of the last year, or quarter of a year, or other time in which the said rent was growing due as aforesaid, making all just allowances, or a proportionable part thereof respectively."

A tenant in tail is within the statute, and his executors are entitled to an apportionment (*b*). No apportionment of rent takes place as between the heir and the personal representatives of a tenant in fee, but the heir is entitled to the whole rent (*c*). Nor does the statute apply to a case where a tenancy from year to year has been originally created by the owner of the fee, and the tenant for life claiming under the lessor dies; for his death does not determine the tenancy (*d*). Where a lease made by a tenant for life or in tail does not terminate with his death, as if made in pursuance of a power or conformably with a statute, the rent is not apportioned; but if it terminate with his death, an apportionment takes place (*e*).

By 4 & 5 Will. IV., c. 22, s. 1, " Rents reserved and made payable on any demise or lease of lands,

(*b*) Whitfield *v.* Pindar, cited in 2 Bro. C. C. 662, 8 Ves. 311.
(*c*) *Re* Clulow, 3 K. & J. 689, 26 L. J. Ch. 513 ; Lord Rockingham *v.* Penrice, 1 P. W. 177.
(*d*) Catley *v.* Arnold, 28 L. J. Ch. 352; Mills *v.* Trumper, L. R. 4 Ch. Ap. 320.

(*e*) Symons *v.* Symons, Madd. & Geld. 207 ; Clarkson *v.* Earl of Scarborough, 1 Swans. 354, note ; Strafford *v.* Wentworth, Prec. Ch. 555; *ex parte* Smythe, 1 Swans. 337. See further notes to 2 Chitty's Statutes, "Landlord and Tenant," p. 1122.

tenements, or hereditaments, and which have been and shall be made, and which leases or demises determined or shall determine on the death of the person making the same (although such person was not strictly tenant for life thereof), or on the death of the life or lives for which such person was entitled to such hereditaments, shall, so far as respects the rents reserved by such leases, and the recovery of a proportion thereof by the person granting the same, his or her executors or administrators (as the case may be), be considered within the provisions of the said recited Act" (11 Geo. II., c. 19).

By sect. 2, " All rents-service reserved on any lease by a tenant in fee, or for any life interest, or by any lease granted under any power (and which leases shall have been granted after the passing of this Act), and all rents-charge, and other rents, annuities, pensions, dividends, moduses, compositions, and all other payments of every description in the United Kingdom of Great Britain and Ireland, made payable or coming due at fixed periods, under any instrument that shall be executed after the passing of this Act, or (being a will or testamentary instrument), that shall come into operation after the passing of this Act, shall be apportioned so, and in such manner, that on the death of any person interested in any such rents, annuities, pensions, dividends, moduses, compositions, or other payments as aforesaid, or in the estate, fund, office, or benefice from or in respect of which the same shall be issuing or derived, or on the determination by any other means whatsoever of the interest of any such person, he or she, or his or her executors, administrators, or assigns, shall be entitled to a proportion of such rents, annuities, pensions, dividends, moduses, compositions, and other payments, according to the time which shall have elapsed from the commencement or last period of payment thereof respectively (as the case may be), including the day of the death of such person, or of the determination of his or her interest, all just allowances and deductions in respect of charges on such rents, annuities, pensions, dividends, moduses, compositions, and other payments being made; and every such person, his or her executors, administrators, and assigns, shall have such and the same remedies at law and in equity for recovering such apportioned parts of the said rents, annuities, pensions, dividends, moduses, compositions, and other payments, when the entire portion of which such apportioned parts shall form part shall become due and payable, and not before, as he, she, or they would have had for recovering and obtaining such entire rents, annuities, pensions, dividends, moduses, compositions, and other payments, if entitled thereto, but so that persons liable to pay rents reserved by any lease or demise, and the lands, tenements, and hereditaments comprised therein, shall not be resorted to for such apportioned parts specifically as aforesaid, but the entire rents of which such portion shall form part shall be received and recovered by the person or persons who, if this Act had not passed, would have been entitled to such entire rents, and such portions shall be recoverable from such person or persons by the parties entitled to the same under this Act in any action or suit at law, or in equity."

By sect. 3, "The provisions herein contained shall not apply to any case in which it shall be expressly stipulated that no apportionment shall take place, or to annual sums made payable in policies of assurance of any description."

The provisions of this Act are extended to rent-charges payable under 6 & 7 Will. IV., c. 71, s. 86, and to rent-charges payable under 4 & 5 Vict., c. 35, s. 50.

The statute extends the doctrine of apportionment to rents, annuities, dividends, and other payments coming due at fixed periods (*f*). It also applies to rents, &c., reserved by leases granted after the Act under a power given before the Act (*g*). It only applies to rents reserved by instruments in writing (*h*). The statute does not apply where the party entitled to the rent himself determines the lease during a current quarter (*i*). A testator gave the residue of his real and personal estate to trustees upon trust to receive and accumulate the rents and profits till his nephew should attain twenty-one, when he was to be put into possession for his life. It was held that the trustees were entitled to an apportionment of the rents up to that period (*j*).

By the Apportionment Act, 1870 (*k*), after reciting the 11 Geo. II., c. 19, the 4 & 5 Will. IV., c. 22, the 6 & 7 Will. IV., c. 72, 14 & 15 Vict., c. 25, and the 23 & 24 Vict., c. 154, it is enacted by sect. 2, that from and after the passing of this Act, all rents, annuities, dividends, and other periodical payments in the nature of income (whether reserved or made payable under an

(*f*) St Aubyn *v.* St Aubyn, 30 L. J. Ch. 917.
(*g*) Plummer *v.* Whitely, 1 Johns. 585, 29 L. J. Ch. 247; Wardroper *v.* Cutfield, 33 L. J. Ch. 605; Llewellyn *v.* Rous, L. R. 2 Eq. 27, 35 Beav. 591.
(*h*) *In re* Markby, 4 M. & Craig, 484; Cattley *v.* Arnold, 1 John. & Hemming, 651, 28 L. J. Ch. 353; Mills *v.* Trumper, L. R. 4 Ch. Ap.
320. But see *infra*, 33 & 34 Vict. c. 35.
(*i*) Oldershaw *v.* Holt, 12 A. & E. 590; Hall *v.* Burgess, 5 B. & C. 332. But see Bridges *v.* Potts, 17 C. B. N.S. 314, 33 L. J. C. P. 338.
(*j*) Wheeler *v.* Tootel, L. R. 3 Eq. 571, following St Aubyn *v.* St Aubyn, 1 Dr. & Sm. 611.
(*k*) 33 & 34 Vict. c. 35.

instrument in writing or otherwise), shall, like interest on money lent, be considered as accruing from day to day, and shall be apportionable in respect of time accordingly.

By sect. 3, the apportioned part of any such rent, annuity, dividend, or other payment, shall be payable or recoverable, in the case of a continuing rent, annuity, or other such payment, when the entire portion of which such apportioned part shall form part shall become due and payable, and not before ; and in the case of a rent, annuity, or other such payment determined by re-entry, death, or otherwise, when the next entire portion of the same would have been payable, if the same had not so determined, and not before.

By sect. 4, all persons, and their respective heirs, executors, administrators, and assigns, and also the executors, administrators, and assigns respectively of persons whose interests determine with their own deaths, shall have such or the same remedies at law and in equity for recovering such apportioned parts as aforesaid, when payable (allowing proportionate parts of all just allowances), as they respectively would have had for recovering such entire portions as aforesaid, if entitled thereto respectively; provided that persons liable to pay rents reserved out of or charged on lands, or other hereditaments of any tenure, and the same lands, or other hereditaments, shall not be resorted to for any such apportioned part forming part of an entire or continuing rent as aforesaid specifically, but the entire or continuing rent, including such apportioned part, shall be recovered and received by the heir, or other person, who, if the rent had not been apportionable under this Act, or otherwise, would have been entitled to such entire or continuing rent, and such

M

apportioned part shall be recoverable from such heir, or other person, by the executors or other parties entitled under this Act to the same, by action at law or suit in equity.

By sect. 5, in the construction of this Act :—

The word "rents" includes rent-service, rent-charge, and rent-seck, and also tithes, and all periodical payments or renderings in lieu of, or in the nature of rent or tithe.

By sect. 7, the provisions of this Act shall not extend to any case in which it is, or shall be expressly stipulated, that no apportionment shall take place.

4. Where the lessor dies before the rent becomes due, but the lessor's interest does not thereby expire, the rent is payable to the heir or remainder-man. If the lessor dies after the rent has become due, it is payable to his executor (*l*) ; and so of tenant for life, where the lease is not determined by his death (*m*); for the statutes above cited do not apply to cases where the lease is not determined by the death of the lessor (*n*).

The proper action in which to apportion rent between a lessor and lessee is an action of debt, and it cannot be apportioned in an action of covenant by lessor against lessee, the action being personal ; but in covenant against an assignee whose obligation

---

(*l*) Duppa *v.* Mayo, 1 Saund. 287.
(*m*) Norris *v.* Harrison, 2 Mad. Ch. R. 269 ; Barwick *v.* Foster, Cro. Jac. 227, 233 ; Lord Strafford *v.* Lady Wentworth, 9 Mod. 21 ; 1 P. Wms. 180.
(*n*) *Ante*, p. 172.

arises from privity of estate, and not of contract, the case is different against him, therefore the rent may be apportioned in an action of covenant (*o*).

(o) Stevenson *v.* Lambard, 2 East. 575.

CHAPTER II.

REMEDIES FOR NON-PAYMENT.

	PAGE		PAGE
1. ACTION—		(c) WHAT MAY NOT BE DISTRAINED—	
use and occupation	180	things absolutely privileged	196
debt	182	things conditionally privileged	201
2. DISTRESS—			
definition of	183	(d) WHERE THE DISTRESS MAY BE MADE	201
(a) WHO MAY DISTRAIN—			
joint-tenants	185	(e) WHEN THE DISTRESS MAY BE MADE	204
coparceners	186		
tenants in common	186	(f) HOW A DISTRESS SHOULD BE MADE	207
husband and wife	187		
tenant pur autre vie	188	(g) WHAT TO BE DONE WITH IT	211
tenant by elegit	188		
mortgagee	188	(h) TENANT'S REMEDIES—	
agents, bailiffs, and receivers	189	when no rent is due	221
executors and administrators	190	distraining for more rent than is due	221
sequestrators	192	twice for the same rent	221
		for excessive distress	222
(b) WHAT MAY BE DISTRAINED—		things not the subject of distress	223
general rule	192	for other illegal acts	224
growing crops, hay, straw, &c.	193	rescue	225
		replevin	225

1. ACTION.

Action. In order to enforce payment of the rent in arrear, the landlord may bring an action of either debt for use and occupation or covenant (*a*). If the demise is not by deed, an action of covenant (*b*) will not lie (*c*); but the landlord may bring an action of debt on simple contract (*d*), or of assumpsit for the use and

(*a*) Since the Common Law Procedure Act, 1852, an action for use and occupation may be considered either as an action on the case, founded on 11 Geo. II. c. 19, s. 14 (see *infra*), or as an action of debt at common law.

(*b*) As to what words constitute a covenant, see *ante*, pp. 114, 116.

(*c*) If there is a mere agreement by deed to demise, an action for use and occupation may be maintained. Elliot *v.* Rogers, 4 Esp. 59; Gudgen *v.* Bessett, 6 E. & B. 986.

(*d*) Wilkins *v.* Wingate, 6 T. R. 62; Stroud *v.* Rogers, 6 T. R. 63 n; Elger *v.* Marsden, 5 Taunt. 25; Gibson *v.* Kirk, 1 Q. B. 850.

occupation of the premises. The remedies by debt and covenant existed at common law, but the action of assumpsit is given by statute, 11 Geo. II., c. 19, s. 14 (*e*).

By 11 Geo. II., c. 19, s. 14, "To obviate some difficulties that many times occur in the recovery of rents, where the demises are not by deed, it shall and may be lawful to and for the landlord or landlords, where the agreement is not by deed, to recover a reasonable satisfaction for the lands, tenements, or hereditaments, held or occupied by the defendant or defendants in an action on the case, for the use and occupation of what was so held or enjoyed; and if in evidence on the trial of such action, any parol demise, or any agreement (not being by deed), whereon a certain rent was reserved, shall appear, the plaintiff in such action shall not therefore be nonsuited, but may make use thereof as an evidence of the *quantum* of the damages to be recovered."

Use and occupation.

An action for use and occupation is always founded on some contract, express or implied (*f*), and the defendant must have occupied the premises under such express or implied contract (*g*). Thus a tenant who agrees to take lodgings, but does not enter, is not liable for use and occupation (*h*). But where there is no express or implied contract, and the defendant is a mere wrong-doer or trespasser, this action will not

(*e*) See Selwyn's *Nisi Prius*, tit. Use and Occupation.
(*f*) Birch *v.* Wright, 1 T. R. 378, 387; Beverley *v.* Lincoln Gas Light and Coke Co., 6 A. & E. 829; Gibson *v.* Kirk, 1 Q. B. 850; Churchward *v.* Ford, 2 H. & N. 446, 26 L. J. Ex. 354.
(*g*) Marquis of Camden *v.* Batterbury, 5 C. B. N.S. 808, 7 Id. 864, 28 L. J. C. P. 335; Levi *v.* Lewis, 6 C. B. N.S. 766, 9 Id. 872; Hall *v.* Burgess, 5 B. & C.

333; Hellier *v.* Silcox, 19 L. J. Q. B. 295, explained in Churchward *v.* Ford, 2 H. & N. 446, 449, 450; Smith *v.* Elridge, 15 C. B. 236; Smith *v.* Twoart, 2 M. & G. 841; Bailey *v.* Bradley, 5 C. B. 396.
(*h*) Edge *v.* Strafford, 1 C. & J. 391; Lowe *v.* Ross, 19 L. J. Ex. 318, 5 Exch. 553; Towne *v.* D'Heindrich, 13 C. B. 892, 22 L. J. C. P. 219.

lie (*i*); nor will such an action lie if it be proved that the plaintiff's title expired after the demise, and before the period in respect of which the action is brought, although there has not been any eviction, and the possession has not been given up to the plaintiff (*j*).

In order to support this action under the statute, it is sufficient if there is an actual holding on the part of the tenant, and if he has the power to occupy the premises so far as depends on the landlord. Thus the tenant would be liable for use and occupation, although the premises were destroyed by fire (*k*). And it is sufficient if the tenant allow another person to occupy (*l*). If a lease is made to two persons, and one holds over at its expiration, without the assent of the other, they are not both liable for use and occupation (*m*).

Rent payable in advance must be declared for specially (*n*).

Debt. The action of debt for rent is founded upon privity of contract, express or implied (*o*), or sometimes upon privity of estate (*p*). Unlike the action for use and occupation, it can be brought where the demise is by

(*i*) Marquis of Camden *v.* Batterbury, *supra;* Churchward *v.* Ford, *supra;* Tew *v.* Jones, 13 M. & W. 12; Turner *v.* Cameron's Coalbrook Co., 5 Exch. 932, 20 L. J. Ex. 71; Levi *v.* Lewis, *supra.*

(*j*) Mountnoy *v.* Collier, 1 E. & B. 630.

(*k*) See Pindar *v.* Ainsley, cited in the judgment in Belfour *v.* Weston, 1 T. R. 312; Baker *v.* Holtzappel, 4 Taunt. 45; Leeds *v.* Cheetham, 1 Sim. 146; Izon *v.* Gorton, 5 Bing. N. C. 501; Packer *v.* Gibbins, 1 Q. B. 421; Surplice *v.* Farnsworth, 7 M. & G.

576; Loft *v.* Dennis, 1 E. & E. 856.

(*l*) Bull *v.* Sibbs, 8 T. R. 327; Bertie *v.* Beaumont, 16 East. 33; Christy *v.* Tanaed, 7 M. & W. 127, 9 M. & W. 438, 12 M. & W. 316; Waring *v.* King, 8 M. & W. 571.

(*m*) Draper *v.* Crofts, 15 M. & W. 166.

(*n*) Angell *v.* Randal, 16 L. T. N.S. 489.

(*o*) Bull, N. P. 167.

(*p*) Lord Ward *v.* Lumley, 5 H. & N. 87, 656, 29 L. J. Ex. 322.

deed (*q*). At common law, this action did not lie for rent reserved on a freehold lease (*r*). But by the 8 Anne, c. 14, s. 4, any persons entitled to rent in arrear on a lease for life or lives, may have an action of debt during the existence of the life, as on a lease for years during the term. An entry by the tenant on the premises demised is not necessary to support this action, as in the action for use and occupation (*s*). So an assignee of the term, who has never entered to take possession as assignee, may be liable to an action for the rent (*t*), but not to an action for use and occupation (*u*). So a husband is not liable in an action for use and occupation to pay for the enjoyment of a house by his wife *dum sola* ; such occupation not having been by him, nor at his request (*v*); but he would be liable to an action for the rent, the declaration being framed specially according to the facts.

By 3 & 4 Will. IV., c. 42, s. 3, a limitation of twenty years is imposed on actions of debt for rent upon an indenture of demise.

Rent when due, but not accruing rent, may be attached under the 17 & 18 Vict., c. 125, s. 61 (*w*).

2. DISTRESS.

A distress is the taking of a personal chattel out of the possession of the wrong-doer, into the custody of

Definition of Distress.

(*q*) Gibson *v*. Kirk, 1 Q. B. 850, 474.
(*r*) Bishop of Winchester *v*. Wright, 2 Lord Raymond, 1056; Kelly *v*. Clubbe, 3 B. & B. 130.
(*s*) Bellasis *v*. Burbrick, 1 Salk. 209 ; Bull *v*. Sibbs, 8 T. R. 327 ; Smith *v*. Scott, 6 C. B. N.S. 781, *per* Willes, J. See also Alexander *v*. Dyer, Cro. Eliz. 169.
(*t*) Ringer *v*. Cann, 3 M. & W. 343 ; Burton *v*. Barclay, 7 Bing.

745, 761; Williams *v*. Bosanquet, 1 B. & B. 238.
(*u*) How *v*. Kennett, 3 A. & E. 659 ; Lowe *v*. Ross, 5 Exch. 556; Clarke *v*. Webb, 1 C. M. & R. 29 ; Jones *v*. Reynolds, 7 C. & P. 335.
(*v*) Richardson *v*. Hall, 1 B. & B. 50.
(*w*) Mitchell *v*. Lee, 8 B. & S. 92, L. R. 2 Q. B. 259 ; Jones *v*. Thompson, 27 L. J. Q. B. 234.

the party injured, to procure a satisfaction for the wrong committed (*x*), and is the remedy most frequently resorted to by landlords for obtaining payment of rent in arrear. Inasmuch as, strictly speaking, rent can issue out of real property only, there can be no distress for payments made for the use of personal property, which are sometimes also called rents. When, however, personal and real property are let together, there may be a distress for the rent, because it issues wholly out of the real part of the property demised (*y*).

The thing taken, as well as the process, is sometimes called a distress.

The rent must be certain, and not subject to conditional deductions, or the landlord will not be entitled to distrain (*z*). Neither can he distrain where the amount of rent is not fixed by the demise, although he may do so as soon as it has been ascertained, whether by the actual payment of a certain rent, or in any other manner (*a*).

(a.) WHO MAY DISTRAIN.

Who may distrain.

In order to warrant a distress, the relation of landlord and tenant must exist. If, therefore, a termor parts with the whole of his interest in the term, whether by assignment or in any other way, reserving a rent, he has no power of distress without a special

---

(*x*) 3 Bl. Com. 6.
(*y*) Newman *v*. Anderton, 2 N. R. 224. And see Baynes *v*. Smith, 1 Esp. N. P. 206.
(*z*) Regnart *v*. Porter, 7 Bing. 451.
(*a*) Knight *v*. Bennett, 3 Bing. 361; Riseley *v*. Ryle, 11 M. & W. 16; Watson *v*. Waud, 8 Exch.

335; Hancock *v*. Austin, 14 C. B. N.S. 634. See Daniel *v*. Gracie, 6 Q. B. 145; Doe *d*. Edney *v*. Benham, 7 Q. B. 976. The right to distrain may exist by express agreement, although not reserved upon what is strictly a rent. See Pollitt *v*. Forrest, 11 Q. B. 949.

clause of distress, because there is no tenancy (*b*); and if he underlet, so as to reserve a reversion to himself, yet when his own term is expired, his remedy by distress against his under-tenant is gone (*c*). A tenant from year to year, however, underletting from year to year, has such a reversion as will entitle him to distrain (*d*). Where a party is in possession in contemplation only of a tenancy, there is no demise, and consequently no reversion to which the power of distress can attach (*e*); but, as soon as a tenancy is constituted, and rent is in arrear, the landlord may distrain (*f*). So also where the landlord has elected to treat the party in possession of his land as a trespasser, he cannot distrain, although the possession be continued up to the day of the distress (*g*), nor can he distrain after the expiration of a notice to quit, without some evidence, at least, of a renewal of the tenancy (*h*). As to the effect of the bankruptcy of the tenant upon the landlord's right to distrain, see *post*, Part 4, c. 2, s. 2.

Joint-tenants are seised *per my et per tout*; and therefore, as every joint-tenant has an estate in every part of the rent, he may distrain alone for the whole, although he must afterwards avow jointly with his co-

Who may distrain—Joint-tenants.

(*b*) Butt's case, 7 Rep. 101; Lord Mountjoy's case, 5 Rep. 4; Earl of Stafford *v.* Buckley, 2 Ves. 170; Turner *v.* Turner, 1 Bro. Ch. Rep. 316; Bro. Abr. Debt, pl. 39; Pouletney *v.* Holmes, Str. 405; —— *v.* Cooper, 2 Wils. 375; Smith *v.* Mapleback, 1 T. R. 441; Hoby *v.* Roebuck, 7 Taunt. 157; Jalentine *v.* Deunion, Cro. Jac. 111; Parmenter *v.* Webber, 8 Taunt. 593; Preece *v.* Corrie, 5 Bing. 25; Palmer *v.* Edwards, 1 Doug. 187.

(*c*) Burne *v.* Richardson, 4 Taunt. 720.

(*d*) Curtis *v.* Wheeler, 1 M. & M. 493.

(*e*) Hegan *v.* Johnson, 2 Taunt. 148.

(*f*) Cox *v.* Bent, 5 Bing. 182, 2 Moo. & P. 281; Mann *v.* Lovejoy, 1 Ry. & M. 355; Doe *d.* Westmoreland *v.* Smith, 1 Man. & R. 137; Braithwaite *v.* Hitchcock, 10 M. & W. 494.

(*g*) Bridges *v.* Smyth, 2 Moo. & P. 740, 5 Bing. 410.

(*h*) Jenner *v.* Clegg, 1 Moo. & R. 213.

tenants, or make cognisance as their bailiff, and account to them for their respective shares; and it is immaterial whether he make the distress by his own hand or the hand of another, and, therefore, he may appoint a bailiff to distrain for the whole rent (*i*), without the assent of his fellows (*j*). So the survivor may distrain for the arrears accrued in the lifetime of his deceased co-tenant (*k*).

Who may distrain—Co-parceners.

Co-parceners before partition are considered in law but as one heir (*l*), and therefore must join in making a distress (*m*), but after partition they may make several distresses (*n*). The same rule governs co-heirs in gavelkind, who are parceners by custom (*o*). One, however, may distrain for rent due to him and his fellows without an actual authority from them, and avow in his own right, and make cognisance as their bailiff (*p*).

Who may distrain— Tenants in common.

Tenants in common, not holding by one title, and possessing several estates, although they may join in an action for rent (*q*), yet, if they distrain, must make several distresses, and avow separately (*r*). And where one, holding under two tenants in common, paid the whole rent to one of them, after notice from the other not to do so, it was held that he who gave the notice might distrain for his share of the rent (*s*). But it seems that, upon a lease by tenants in common,

(*i*) Pullen *v.* Palmer, 3 Salk. 207.
(*j*) Leigh *v.* Shepherd, 2 B. & B. 465; Robinson *v.* Hofman, 4 Bing. 562.
(*k*) 2 Rol. Abr. 86.
(*l*) Co. Litt. 163 b.
(*m*) Stedman *v.* Page, 1 Salk. 390, Gilb. Distress, 161.
(*n*) Co. Litt. 174 b, 195 b.

(*o*) Litt. ss. 241, 265.
(*p*) Leigh *v.* Shepherd, 2 B. & B. 465.
(*q*) Midgley *v.* Lovelace, Carth. 289.
(*r*) Litt. s. 317; Whitley *v.* Roberts, 1 M'Clel. & Y. 107; Pullen *v.* Palmer, 3 Salk. 207.
(*s*) Harrison *v.* Barnby, 5 T. R. 246.

CH. II.] REMEDIES FOR NON-PAYMENT. 187

the survivor may distrain for the whole rent, although the reversion be to the lessors, according to their respective interests (*t*); and one tenant in common may lease his share to another, rendering rent, for which he may distrain as if he had demised to a stranger (*u*).

With regard to the lands of a married woman, the wife can in no case whatever distrain alone, but the husband may in all cases distrain, and even avow alone, during the life of the wife, for rent accruing during the coverture (*v*). Further, by the 32 Hen. VIII., c. 37, s. 3, if a man have, in the right of his wife, any estate in fee-simple, fee-tail, or for term of life, of or in any rents or fee-farms, and the same be due, behind, and unpaid in the wife's life, then the husband, after the death of the wife, may distrain for the said arrearages in like manner and form as he might have done if his wife had been then living. It has been held that this statute enables the husband not only to distrain for arrears accrued during the coverture, for which, at the common law, he could have sued in his own name (*w*), but also for arrears accrued before coverture (*x*), which, previously to the statute, could only have been recovered in an action brought by the husband, not in his own name, but as his wife's personal representative (*y*). It will be observed that the remedy by distress is given to the husband alone, and is not extended to his executors and administrators (*z*).

Who may distrain— Husband and wife.

(*t*) Wallace *v*. M'Laren, 1 Man. & Ryl. 516.
(*u*) Snelgar *v*. Henston, Cro. Jac. 611.
(*v*) North *v*. Wyard, 2 Bulst. 233; Bowles *v*. Poore, Cro. Jac. 282; Wise *v*. Bellent, ib. 442; Pullen *v*. Palmer, 3 Salk. 207.
(*w*) Co. Litt. 162 b, 351 b, Ognel's Case, 4 Rep. 51.
(*x*) Co. Litt. 162 b.
(*y*) Sharp *v*. Pool, Bendl. 457.
(*z*) See Osborn *v*. Wickenden, 1 Saund. 197; Ankerstein *v*. Clarke, 4 T. R. 617; Parry *v*. Hindle, 2 Taunt. 181.

Who may distrain— Tenant pur autre vie.

At the common law tenant *pur autre vie* could of course distrain in the lifetime of the *cestui que vie;* and by the 32 Hen. VIII., c. 37, s. 4, he may distrain for rent in arrear at the death of the *cestui que vie.*

Who may distrain— Tenant by elegit.

Tenant by *elegit* may distrain without attornment so long as the debt is unpaid, and the interest of his execution debtor continues (*a*); but as he is not within the 32 Hen. VIII., c. 37, his power of distress is gone as soon as the interest of the execution debtor is determined. Thus a tenant by *elegit* cannot distrain after the death of the tenant for life for arrears accrued in his lifetime (*b*).

Who may distrain— Mortgagee.

A mortgagee can distrain upon the mortgagor in possession only where a tenancy has been created between them, and the rent ascertained (*c*). And it was held that even where there was a stipulation in the mortgage deed, that, upon a certain event happening, the mortgagee should become tenant to the mortgagor, which event happened, yet the mortgagee could not distrain until he had given notice of his intention to treat the mortgagor as tenant (*d*). Where the property mortgaged has been leased before the mortgage, the mortgagee may distrain, immediately after giving notice of the mortgage to the tenant, for rent in arrear *at the time of the notice,* as well as for that which accrues afterwards; for the attornment of the tenant is rendered unnecessary by the 4 Anne, c. 16, s. 9, and the notice to the tenant has relation back to the date of the mortgage (*e*). Where the mortgaged premises

(*a*) Lloyd *v.* Davies, 2 Exch. 103. Bro. Distr. pl. 72.
(*b*) Pool *v.* Neel, 2 Sid. 29; Pool *v.* Duncomb, Bull. N. P. 56.
(*c*) Morton *v.* Woods, L. R. 3 Q. B. 658, 37 L. J. Q. B. 242.
(*d*) Clowes *v.* Hughes, L. R. 5 Ex. 160, 39 L. J. Ex. 62.
(*e*) Moss *v.* Gallimore, Doug. 279; Rogers *v.* Humphreys, 4 Ad. & El. 299.

are let by the mortgagor after the execution of the mortgage, the mortgagee cannot distrain on the tenant until a new tenancy has been created between them, as by the mortgagee accepting rent from the tenant (*f*), or giving the tenant notice to pay him the rent, in which the tenant has acquiesced (*g*). In such a case, the rents that have accrued between the commencement of the lease from the mortgagor, and of the new tenancy between the tenant and the mortgagee, cannot be recovered by the mortgagee by distress; but if the tenant refuse to pay, the mortgagee may evict him, and recover it in the form of mesne profits (*h*).

The distress is generally effected by means of a bailiff on behalf of the lessor, or other person entitled to distrain. The bailiff need not be a sworn bailiff under the 13 Edward I., c. 37 (*i*). He may be authorised to distrain by word of mouth (*j*), except in the case of a corporation aggregate, not having a superior (*k*); and a subsequent ratification of his act by the landlord will be equivalent to a previous appointment (*l*). If a landlord direct a bailiff to distrain, and then die, and the distress is made after his death, his executors may ratify the act of the bailiff (*m*). A mere authority to receive the rent will not, however, without

Who may distrain—Agents, bailiffs, receivers.

(*f*) Rogers *v.* Humphreys, 4 Ad. & El. 299.
(*g*) Doe *d.* Chawner *v.* Boulter, 6 Ad. & El. 675; Partington *v.* Woodcock, ib. 680; Evans *v.* Elliott, 9 A. & E. 342; Brown *v.* Storey, 1 Man. & G. 117; Wilton *v.* Dunn, Q. B.
(*h*) Pope *v.* Biggs, 9 B. & C. 421; Evans *v.* Elliot, 9 Ad. & E. 342.
(*i*) Begbie *v.* Hayne, 2 Bing. N.S. 124; Child *v.* Chamberlain, 6 Car. & P. 213.

(*j*) Cary *v.* Matthews, Salk. 191; Manby *v.* Long, 3 Leo. 107.
(*k*) Randal *v.* Dean, 2 Lutw. 149 b; Vin. Ab. vol. 3, p. 538.
(*l*) Trevillian *v.* Pyne, 11 Mod. 112; Anon. Goodb. 109, 4 Vin. Ab. Bailiff (D), pl. 7; Whitehead *v.* Taylor, 10 Ad. & El. 212.
(*m*) Whitehead *v.* Taylor, 10 Ad. & E. 212.

more, authorise a distress for rent in arrear (*n*). A receiver of rents appointed by the Court of Chancery may distrain for arrears in the name of the lessor without the order of the Court (*o*). If, however, there is a doubt who is the lessor, he should obtain such an order for his own protection (*p*), as he can only distrain in the name of the person having the legal right to do so (*q*). Of course, if he is himself the actual lessor, he may distrain in his own name, and this although it appears on the face of the lease that he is a receiver only, and the rent is reserved to him in that capacity (*r*).

Similarly, a guardian making leases in his own name may also distrain in his own name (*s*).

Who may distrain— Executors and administrators.

By the common law, upon the death of a lessor possessed of a freehold estate, the remedy by distress was gone, because the land went to the heir or remainder-man, while the rent in arrear at the time of the lessor's death went to his executor or administrator (*t*). Where, however, tenant for years underlet for years and died, the executor, or his representative *in infinitum*, so long as the term remained in them, could distrain for the arrears, for they were never separated from the reversion, and both belonged to the executor (*u*).

The power to distrain was first extended to the

(*n*) Ward *v*. Shew, 9 Bing. 608, 2 M. & Sc. 756.
(*o*) Pitt *v*. Snowden, 3 Atk. 750.
(*p*) Hughes *v*. Hughes, 3 Bro. C. C. 87. See Rickman *v*. Johns, L. R. 6 Eq. 488.
(*q*) Hughes *v*. Hughes, 3 Bro. C. C. 87 ; Pitt *v*. Snowden, *supra*.

(*r*) Dancer *v*. Hastings, 4 Bing. 2, S. C. 12 Moore, 34.
(*s*) Shopland *v*. Radler, Cro. Jac. 55, 98 ; Bredell *v*. Constable, Vaugh. 179 ; Bennett *v*. Robins, 5 Car & P. 379.
(*t*) Co. Litt. 162 a.
(*u*) Wade *v*. Marsh, Latch. 211 1 Rol. Abr. 672, l. 35.

executors and administrators of the lessor in the case of a lease for lives of freehold lands (*v*), by the 32 Hen. VIII., c. 37, s. 1 (*w*), which empowers them to distrain for the arrearages upon the lands charged while such lands are in the possession of the tenant, or of any one claiming by and from him by purchase, gift, or descent (*x*), in like manner and form as the testator might have done in his lifetime (*y*); and now, by the 3 & 4 Will. IV., c. 42, s. 37, the executors or administrators of any lessor or landlord may distrain upon the lands demised for any term, or at will, for the arrearages of rent due to such lessor or landlord in his lifetime, in like manner as he himself might have done. By sect. 38, the arrearages may be distrained for after the end or determination of the term or lease at will, in the same manner as if the term or lease had not been ended or determined; but the distress must be made within six calendar months after the determination of the term or lease, and during the continuance of the possession of the tenant from whom the arrears became due, and all the powers and provisions in the several statutes relating to distresses for rent will be applicable to distresses so made.

An administrator cannot distrain before administration, nor justify the detention of goods distrained by the intestate for rent, and remaining under distress at his death; an executor, however, may distrain before probate (*z*). If an administrator makes

---

(*v*) Appleton *v.* Doily, Yelv. 135.
(*w*) Co. Litt. 162 b. Prescott *v.* Boucher, 2 B. & Ad. 859; Hool *v.* Bell, Lord Raym. 572, S. C.; Howell *v.* Bell, 3 Salk. 136.
(*x*) Ognel's case, 5 Rep. 50 b; Eldridge's case, 5 Rep. 118; Lambert *v.* Austin, Cro. Eliz.

332; Lord Fairfax *v.* Lord Derby, 2 Vern. 612; Anon. 1 Leon. 302, pl. 418.
(*y*) Co. Litt. 162, b ; Ognel's case, 4 Rep. 50 b.
(*z*) Dejoncourt *v.* Rogers, 8 Ir. L. Rep. 450. See Whitehead *v.* Taylor, 10 A. & E. 210.

an under-lease of a term of years of the deceased, reserving rent to himself, his executors, &c., it has been held that his executors, and not the administrator *de bonis non*, shall have the rent; but it would seem that, at common law, they cannot distrain for it (*a*), because the reversion belongs to the administrator *de bonis non*, and a reversion is necessary to found the remedy by distress (*b*); there seems, however, no sufficient reason why the executors may not distrain under the 3 & 4 Will. IV., c. 42.

Sequestrators.

By the 12 & 13 Vict., c. 67, a sequestrator is empowered to levy a distress in his own name for the recovery of tithes, rents-charge, or rents, &c., payable to the incumbent of the sequestrated estate.

(b.) WHAT MAY BE DISTRAINED.

What things may be distrained— General rule.

The general rule is that all personal chattels found on the premises demised may be distrained for rent, whether they be the chattels of the tenant or of a third person (*c*). But to this general rule there are

---

(*a*) Drue *v.* Baylie, 1 Freem. 402, 2 Leo. 100.
(*b*) Brawley *v.* Wade, 1 M'Clel. 664; Preece *v.* Corrie, 2 Bing. 24; Pluck *v.* Digges, 2 Dow. & C. 180; Burne *v.* Richardson, 4 Taunt. 720.
(*c*) Gilb. Distr. 33; 3 Bl. Com. 7. Cattle of a stranger upon the land are immediately liable to be distrained, Read *v.* Burley, Cro. Eliz. 549; Gill *v.* Gawin, 2 Rol. Rep. 124, except when they are turned in for the night, with the privity of the lessor or lessee, on their way to market. Tate *v.* Gleed, 2 Wms. Saund. 290 (n) 7. If a stranger's cattle, by default of their owner, or by breaking the fences, escape, they are distrainable without being *levant* and *couchant*. Hargreaves, Co. Litt. 47 b, note 301; Poole *v.* Longueville, 2 Saunds. 290, note 7; Kemp *v.* Cruwes, 2 Lutw. 1580; Reynolds *v.* Oakley, 1 Brownl. 170. But if they escape through default of the tenant, they cannot be distrained by the landlord for rent-service until they have been *levant* and *couchant*; nor even afterwards for rent reserved, unless the owner of the cattle, after notice, fail to remove them. Gill *v.* Gawin, *supra*.

several exceptions; for (1.) some things which are not personal chattels have been rendered distrainable by different statutes; and (2.) certain personal chattels are protected from distress either absolutely or conditionally.

By the common law, things fixed to the freehold, as doors, windows, furnaces, and the like, not being personal chattels, cannot be distrained (*d*); nor will a mere temporary disunion render them distrainable, though it will be otherwise if the separation is entire and permanent (*e*).

By the 11 Geo. II., c. 19, s. 8, an exception to this rule is created in the case of growing crops, the words being, "All sorts of corn and grass, hops, roots, fruits, pulse, or other product whatsoever which shall be growing, &c., and the same to cut, gather, make, cure, carry, and lay up when ripe," &c. (*f*). The landlord, however, is not bound to resort to growing crops to satisfy the distress before taking things conditionally privileged, such as beasts of the plough, &c. (*g*).

What things may be distrained—Growing crops, hay, straw, &c.

The 2 Will. & Mary, sess. 1, c. 5, s. 3, gives power to any person having rent in arrear, and due upon any demise, lease, or contract whatsoever (see sect. 2), to seize any sheaves or cocks of corn, or corn loose or in the straw, or hay lying or being in any barn or granary, or upon any hovel, stack, or rick, or other-

(*d*) Co. Litt. 47 b; Niblet *v.* Smith, 4 T. R. 504; Winn *v.* Ingleby, 5 B. & Ald. 625; Duck *v.* Braddyl, 13 Price, 459, S. C. M'Clel. 217.
(*e*) Year Book, 14 Hen. VIII. 25 b.
(*f*) Trees growing in the grounds of a nurseryman are not within the words "other product," for they are not subject to the process of becoming ripe, &c. Clark *v.* Gaskarth, 8 Taunt. 431.
(*g*) Piggott *v.* Birtles, 1 M. & W. 441.

N

wise upon any part of the land, &c., for or in the nature of a distress.

Under this Act and the 4 Geo. II., c. 28, s. 5, the grantee of a rent-charge may distrain hay or straw, loose or in the stack (*h*). But under the 11 Geo. II., c. 19, the grantee of an annuity cannot distrain growing crops, even under an express power in the deed, for that Act only applies to landlords, and not to " any person having rent in arrear " (*i*).

If the corn be sold before it is ripe, the sale is void (*j*), though not the distress. Where the defendant seized the plaintiff's growing wheat, and sold it while growing for its full value to a purchaser, who cut it, and the surplus of the sale, after satisfying the rent, was paid over to the plaintiff, and he sustained no damage, it was held that the plaintiff was not entitled to recover even nominal damages (*k*).

Growing corn sold under an execution could not formerly be distrained unless the purchaser allowed it to remain an unreasonable time on the ground after it was ripe (*l*). But now, by the 14 & 15 Vict., c. 25, s. 2, growing crops seized and sold by the sheriff under an execution are liable, as long as they remain on the land, to be distrained for the rent which becomes due after the seizure and sale, provided there is no other sufficient distress.

(*h*) Johnson *v.* Faulkner, 2 Q. B. 925.
(*i*) Miller *v.* Green, 2 Cr. & J. 142, 8 Bing. 92 (in error).
(*j*) Owen *v.* Legh, 3 B. & A. 470. See Proudlove *v.* Twemlow, 1 Cr. & M. 326.
(*k*) Rodgers *v.* Parker, 18 C. B. 112.
(*l*) Peacock *v.* Purvis, 2 B. & B. 362; Wright *v.* Dewes, 1 A. & E. 641; Hutt *v.* Morrell, 11 A. & E. 425.

The 56 Geo. III., c. 50, s. 1 (*m*), provides, that no sheriff or other officer in England or Wales shall, by virtue of any process of any court of law, carry off or sell, or dispose of for the purpose of being carried off from any lands let to farm, any straw threshed or unthreshed, or any straw of crops growing, or any chaff, colder, or any turnips, or any manure, compost, ashes, or seaweed, in any case whatsoever, nor any hay, grass, or grasses, whether natural or artificial, nor any tares or vetches, nor any roots or vegetables, being produce of such lands, in any case where, according to any covenant or written agreement, entered into and made for the benefit of the owner or landlord of any farm, such hay, grass, or grasses, tares and vetches, roots or vegetables, ought not to be taken off or withholden from such lands, or which, by the tenor or effect of such covenants or agreements, ought to be used or expended thereon, and of which covenants or agreements such sheriff or other officer shall have received a written notice before he shall have proceeded to sale.

By sect. 3 it is provided, that the sheriff may dispose of produce, subject to an agreement to expend it on the land (*n*).

By sect. 6, in all cases where any purchaser or purchasers of any crops or produce hereinbefore mentioned shall have entered into any agreement with such sheriff or other officer, touching the use and expenditure thereof on lands let to farm, it shall not be lawful for the owner or landlord of such lands to distrain for any rent on any corn, hay, straw, or other

---

(*m*) See *post*, Part 2, c. 3, Repairs and Cultivation.
(*n*) It has been doubted whether this section is more than directory. See Wright *v.* Dewes, 1 Ad. & E. 644.

produce thereof, which, at the time of such sale and the execution of such agreement entered into under the provisions of this Act, shall have been severed from the soil, and sold, subject to such agreement, by such sheriff or other officer; nor on any turnips, whether drawn or growing, if sold according to the provisions of this Act; nor on any horses, sheep, or other cattle, nor on any beast whatsoever, nor on any waggons, carts, or other implements of husbandry, which any person or persons shall employ, keep, or use on such lands, for the purpose of threshing out, carrying, or consuming any such corn, hay, straw, turnips, or other produce, under the provisions of the Act, and the agreement or agreements directed to be entered into between the sheriff or other officer and the purchaser or purchasers of such crops and produce as hereinbefore mentioned.

When hay or straw are seized under a distress, and the tenant is under covenant to expend them upon the premises, the landlord cannot sell them at a less price, subjecting them to a condition that the purchaser shall expend them according to the covenant (*o*).

(c.) WHAT MAY NOT BE DISTRAINED.

Things absolutely privileged at common law.
1. Things annexed to the freehold. 2. Things of third persons on the tenant's premises in the way of his trade. 3. Things which cannot be restored in the same plight, as sheaves of corn, &c. 4. Things in actual use.

(*o*) Ridgway *v.* Lord Stafford, 6 Exch. 404; Frusher *v.* Lee, 10 M. & W. 709. In Abbey *v.* Petch, 8 M. & W. 419, which was an earlier case, the contrary was decided.

CH. II.] REMEDIES FOR NON-PAYMENT. 197

1. Whatever is part of the freehold is exempted from distress; thus kilns, furnaces, cauldrons, windows, doors, and the like, affixed to the freehold, cannot be distrained (*p*). There appear to be three reasons for this rule: first, that fixtures are not personal chattels, but form part of the thing demised; secondly, that they cannot be taken away without damage to the freehold (*q*); and thirdly, that they would be injured by severance and removal, and could not be restored in the same condition as they were in when taken (*r*); and this is a rule still in force, subject to some statutory exceptions as to growing crops and matters of this nature (*s*). This privilege extends also to such things as would be removable as between landlord and tenant (*t*). Thus, kitchen-ranges, stoves, coppers, and grates are not distrainable, although they may be removed by the tenant during the term (*u*); and a mere temporary removal of fixtures for the purpose of repairing, &c., will not destroy the privilege (*v*).

A question has often arisen as to the degree of annexation required to bring the particular thing within the rule which excepts fixtures from distress. In Wiltsheer *v.* Cottrell (*w*) it was held that a granary,

(*p*) Co. Litt. 47 b; Simpson *v.* Hartopp, Willes, 515, 1 Smith's L. C., notes, p. 373; Niblett *v.* Smith, 4 T. R. 504; Darby *v.* Harris, 1 G. & D. 234; Dalton *v.* Whittem, 3 G. & D. 260; Gorton *v.* Falkner, 4 T. R. 567.
(*q*) See the judgment in Hellawell *v.* Eastwood, 6 Exch. 311.
(*r*) Termes de la Ley, Distress, 69 a; Co. Litt. 47 a.
(*s*) Morley *v.* Pincombe, 2 Exch. 101. See *ante*, p. 193.
(*t*) There is a distinction in this respect between a distress and an execution; for under the latter, fixtures which would be removable by the tenant as between him and his landlord, may be seized. Poole's case, 1 Salk. 368.
(*u*) Darby *v.* Harris, 1 Q. B. 895; Pitt *v.* Shew, 4 B. & A. 208; Dalton *v.* Whittem, 3 G. & D. 260.
(*v*) Gorton *v.* Falkner, 4 T. R. 567; Bro. Abr. tit. Distress, pl. 23; Niblet *v.* Smith, 4 T. R. 504, 11 Co. R. 50.
(*w*) 1 E. & B. 674.

resting by its mere weight upon straddles built into the land, was not a fixture within the meaning of a deed by which all the fixtures appertaining to a farm were conveyed. In Duck v. Braddyll (x) it was doubted whether machinery bolted to the floor of a factory was distrainable. Besides the test of being easily removed without injury to itself or the premises, it is also to be considered whether the annexation is for the permanent and substantial improvement of the premises, or merely for a temporary purpose (y).

2. Things delivered to the tenant to be wrought, worked up, or managed in the way of his trade or employment, are not distrainable (z). So goods sent to an auctioneer for sale were held to be privileged from being distrained for his rent (a), and the carcass of a beast sent to a butcher to be slaughtered was also held to be privileged (b).

A cab in the hands of an agent for the sale of carriages is privileged (c). Goods in possession of a pawnbroker as security for money advanced are also privileged (d). Where, however, the goods of a third party are upon the premises, but not for the purpose of being wrought up, or having anything done to them by the tenant in the way of his trade, they are not

(x) Duck v. Braddyll, M'Clel. 217, S. C. 13 Price, 455. See also Trappes v. Harter, 2 Cr. & M. 177.

(y) Hellawell v. Eastwood, 6 Exch. 311 ; Walmsley v. Milne, 7 C. B. N.S. 115. See also Lane v. Dixon, 3 C. B. 776 ; Wood v. Hewett, 8 Q. B. 913 ; Waterfall v. Penistone, 6 C. & B. 876. See *post*, Fixtures, Part 3, c. 7.

(z) 1 Inst. 47 a ; Gisbourn v. Hurst, 1 Salk. 249 ; Gilman v. Elton, 3 B. & B. 75 ; Thompson v. Mashiter, 1 Bing. 283 ; Matthias v. Mesnard, 2 C. & P. 353, Co. Litt. 47 a ; Gibson v. Ireson, 3 Q. B. 39.

(a) Adams v. Grane, 1 Cr. & M. 380; Brown v. Arundell, 10 C. B. 54 ; Williams v. Holmes, 8 Exch. 861.

(b) Brown v. Shevill, 2 A. & E. 138.

(c) Findon v. M'Laren, 6 Q. B. 891.

(d) Swire v. Leech, 18 C. B. N. S. 479.

privileged, as in the case of a carriage sent in order to convey goods, or casks containing beer, &c. (*e*).

In the case of Parsons *v.* Gingell (*f*), Wilde, C.J., in delivering judgment, said, " If the goods are sent to the premises for the purpose of being dealt with in the way of the party's trade, and are to remain upon the premises until that purpose is answered, and no longer, the case falls within one class; but if they are sent for the purpose of remaining there merely at the will of the owner, there being no work to be done upon them, it falls within a totally distinct consideration. The case of a horse sent to a livery-stable *merely* to be cleaned and fed is very different from one where he is sent to remain during the owner's pleasure, the feeding and grooming (in the latter case) being only incident to the principal object."

In Muspratt *v.* Gregory (*g*) it was said that the cases of exemption from distress ought not to be extended; and it seems doubtful whether a carriage actually containing privileged goods is distrainable or not (*h*).

3. Things which cannot be restored in the same plight, as sheaves and cocks of corn, &c., are privileged (*i*); but as to sheaves and cocks of corn, &c., see now the 2 Will. & Mary, sess. 1, c. 5, s. 3, *ante*, p. 193, and the 56 Geo. III., c. 50, ss. 1, 3, 6, *ante*, p. 195.

(*e*) Muspratt *v.* Gregory, 1 M. & W. 633; Joule *v.* Jackson, 7 M. & W. 450; Wood *v.* Clarke, 1 Tyrwh. 314, 1 C. & J. 484; Fenton *v.* Logan, 9 Bing. 676; Parsons *v.* Gingell, 4 C. B. 545.
(*f*) *Supra.*
(*g*) See *supra,* and see Joule *v.* Jackson, 7 M. & W. 457.

(*h*) See Rede *v.* Burley, Cro. Eliz. 596; and see the judgment of Alderson, B., in Muspratt *v.* Gregory, 1 M. & W. 646. See also Smith L. C. 5th edit. 376.
(*i*) Wilson *v.* Duckett, 2 Mod. 61; Johnson *v.* Faulkner 2 Q. B. 925.

And now, with respect to growing crops taken in execution, it is enacted by the 14 & 15 Vict., c. 25, s. 2, that in case all or any part of the growing crops of the tenant of any farm or lands shall be seized and sold by any sheriff, or other officer by virtue of any writ of *fieri facias*, or other writ of execution, such crops, so long as the same shall remain on the farms or lands, shall, in default of sufficient distress of the goods and chattels of the tenant, be liable to the rent which may accrue and become due to the landlord after any such seizure and sale, and to the remedies by distress for recovery of such rent, and that notwithstanding any bargain and sale or assignment which may have been made or executed of such growing crops by any such sheriff or other officer. Upon this principle it has been decided that butcher's meat cannot be distrained (*j*).

4. Things while in actual use are privileged from distress in order to prevent a breach of the peace (*k*).

Besides these classes of things, there are also two others which are privileged, viz., firstly, things in which there can be no valuable property, such as animals *feræ naturæ* (*l*); and secondly, goods in the custody of the law (*m*).

(*j*) Morley *v.* Pincombe, 2 Exch. 101.
(*k*) Simpson *v.* Hartopp, 1 Smith's L. C. 377, 5th edit.; Field *v.* Adams, 12 A. & E. 652; Bond *v.* Kennington, 1 Q. B. 679.
(*l*) As to deer, see Davies *v.* Powell, Willes, 47; Morgan *v.* Earl of Abergavenny, 8 C. B. 768. As to dogs, which it seems are distrainable, see 2 Bl. Com. 391; Davies *v.* Powell, *supra*, and 1 Smith's L. C. 378, 5th edit.
(*m*) Such as property taken damage, feasant, or in execution. See 1 Inst. 47 a; Eaton *v.* Southby, Willes, 181; Peacock *v.* Purvis, 2 B. & B. 362; Wright *v.* Dewes, 1 A. & E. 641; Wharton *v.* Naylor, 12 Q. B. 673.

The goods of a guest at a public inn are in general not distrainable upon principles of public convenience (*n*).

There are some species of property conditionally privileged, provided there be other sufficient distress upon the premises (*o*). Of these there are three classes :—1. Beasts of the plough and instruments of husbandry (*p*). 2. The instruments of a man's trade or profession (*q*). 3. Beasts which improve the land, as sheep (*r*). {Things conditionally privileged.}

(d.) WHERE THE DISTRESS MAY BE MADE.

The distress can only be made on some part of the demised premises out of which the rent issues (*s*), except in the case of the Crown, and except in the case of fraudulent removals to prevent a distress, as to which see *infra ;* so that if the landlord go to distrain cattle, and they escape out of the lands {Where the distress may be made.}

(*n*) Robinson *v.* Walter, 3 Bulst. 269. But see Francis *v.* Wyatt, 3 Burr. 1499 ; Adams *v.* Grane, 1 C. & M. 381, Bayley, J.; Brown *v.* Shevil, 4 N. & M. 283, Paterson, J.; Crozier *v.* Tomlinson, Barnes, 472, cited in 3 Burr. 1500 ; Muspratt *v.* Gregory, 3 M. & W. 681, Lord Denman, C.J.
(*o*) Co. Litt. 47 a; Fenton *v.* Logan, 9 Bing. 676 ; Gorton *v.* Falkner, 4 T. R. 565. It should be observed that even if there is a sufficient distress without resorting to things privileged *sub modo*, yet if that distress consists of growing crops, which are only distrainable by statute, and are not immediately productive, the landlord may distrain the things privileged *sub modo*. Piggott *v.* Birtles, 1 M. & W. 441.
(*p*) Colts, steers, and heifers, do not fall within this class, as they do not gain the land. Keen *v.* Priest, 4 H. & N. 236.
(*q*) Nargett *v.* Nias, 1 E. & E. 439; Gorton *v.* Falkner, *supra ;* Fenton *v.* Logan, *supra*.
(*r*) Keen *v.* Priest, *supra*.
(*s*) 1 Rol. Abr. 671, l. 37 ; Co. Litt. 161 a ; Gilb. Distress, 40 ; Capel *v.* Buzzard, 6 Bing. 150 ; Com. Dig. Distress (A) 3, (B) 1 ; Rogers *v.* Birkmire, 2 Strange, 1040. The statute of Marlebridge (52 Hen. III. c. 15) confirmed the common law in this respect. See 2 Inst. 131, and Gilb. Dist. 40. It seems sufficient if the distress be made not absolutely on the premises, although practically so. Gillingham *v.* Gwyes, 16 L. T. N.S. 640, Lush., J. ; Hodges *v.* Lawrence, 18 Just. Peace, 347 Ex.

demised, or into any highway within his view, he cannot pursue them (*t*), neither can he if they be driven off the lands in his sight for any lawful purpose (*u*); but where they are driven off in the view of the landlord, for the express purpose of avoiding the distress, the landlord may make fresh pursuit, and seize them in the highway, or in any other place off the lands demised (*v*). But at common law, if before the landlord had view of the cattle, they were driven off the lands, even for the express purpose of avoiding a distress, the landlord could not pursue or follow them (*w*). By the 11 Geo. II., c. 19, s. 1, however, if the tenant fraudulently or clandestinely (*x*) remove his goods from the demised premises, in order to prevent a distress, the landlord is within thirty days allowed to follow and distrain them, wherever they may be found, provided they have not been previously sold for valuable consideration to a *bonâ fide* purchaser. To entitle the landlord to pursue the goods of the tenant under this statute, it was held by Eyre, C.J., that the removal must have taken place after the rent actually became due, and was in arrear (*y*). And although in a subsequent case, where the goods had been removed from the premises the night before the rent became due, Lord Ellenborough, C.J., declared (*z*) that upon this point he entertained some considerable doubts, and, but that the case before him turned upon another point, would have reserved it for the opinion of the Court; yet the law, as laid down by Chief-Justice Eyre, has since been recognised

---

(*t*) Co. Litt. 161 a; 2 Inst. 131.
(*u*) Ibid. 1 Rol. Abr. 671 l 45.
(*v*) Ibid.
(*w*) Co. Litt. 161 a.
(*x*) Watson *v*. Main, 3 Esp. 15; Opperman *v*. Smith, 4 D. & R.

33. The landlord must show that the goods were removed to elude the distress. Parry *v*. Duncan, 7 Bing. 243.
(*y*) Watson *v*. Main, 3 Esp. 15.
(*z*) Furneaux *v*. Fotherby, 4 Camp. 136.

and confirmed on argument by the Court of Common Pleas (a).

The statute applies to the goods of the tenant only (b). By sect. 4, an additional (c) remedy is given to the landlord by complaint to two justices, where the goods do not exceed the value of £50.

By sect. 7 of the 11 Geo. II., c. 19, when goods are fraudulently removed, and placed in any house or place locked up or otherwise secured, the landlord or his agent may, with the assistance of a peace-officer (and in the case of a dwelling-house, after oath being made before a magistrate of a reasonable ground to suspect that the goods are in it), break open the house, &c., in the day-time, and distrain the goods as if they had been in any open place.

By the 8th sect. of the same statute, 11 Geo. II., c. 19, the landlord may distrain cattle (of the tenants) depasturing upon any common or way appertaining to the premises demised, a privilege too reasonable to require comment. The language of this section is, that the landlords or their agents may "take and seize, as a distress for arrears of rent, any cattle or stock of their respective tenant or tenants, feeding or depasturing upon any common appendant or appurtenant, or any way belonging, to all or any part of the premises demised or holden."

(a) Rand v. Vaughan, 1 Bing. N. C. 767.
(b) Thornton v. Adams, 5 M. & S. 38; Portman v. Harrell, 6 C. & P. 225.
(c) Bromley v. Holden, 1 Moo. & M. 175. On the construction of this section, see Stanley v. Wharton, 9 Price, 301, 10 Id. 138; Coster v. Wilson, 3 M. & W. 411.

(e.) WHEN THE DISTRESS MAY BE MADE.

When the distress may be made.
As rent is not in arrear till the last minute of the day on which it becomes payable has elapsed, the landlord cannot distrain until the day after it becomes due (*d*), except by express agreement (*e*). Nor can he distrain in the night-time, *i.e.*, from sunset to sunrise (*f*).

At common law a landlord could not have distrained for rent after the determination of the tenancy (*g*). But by 8 Anne, c. 14, ss. 6, 7, " Any person or persons having any rent in arrear or due upon any lease for life or lives, or for years, or at will, ended or determined, may distrain for such arrears after the determination of the said respective leases, in the same manner as they might have done if such lease or leases had not been ended or determined; provided that such distress be made within the space of six calendar months after the determination of such lease, and during the continuance of such landlord's title or interest (*h*), and during the possession of the tenant (*i*) from whom such arrears became due (*j*).

(*d*) Duppa *v.* Mayo, 1 Saund. 287.
(*e*) Buckley *v.* Taylor, 2 T. R. 600; Giles *v.* Spencer, 3 C. B. N.S. 244, 26 L. J. C. P. 237.
(*f*) Co. Litt. 142 a; Aldenburgh *v.* Peaple, 6 C. & P. 212; Tutton *v.* Darke, 5 H. & N. 647; Nixon *v.* Freeman, 5 H. & N. 647; Keen *v.* Priest, 4 H. & N. 240, per Watson, B.
(*g*) Pennant's case, 3 Co. Rep. 64; Williams *v.* Stiven, 9 Q. B. 14.
(*h*) Burne *v.* Richardson, 4 Taunt. 720.
(*i*) Taylorson *v.* Peters, 7 A. & E. 110; Doe *d.* David *v.* Williams, 7 C. & P. 322; Nuttall *v.* Staunton, 4 B. & C. 51; Braithwaite *v.* Cooksey, 1 H. Bl. 465; Turner *v.* Barnes, 2 B. & S. 435, 31 L. J. Q. B. 170. But as to possession continued beyond the expiration of the term under a custom of the country, see Beavan *v.* Delahay, 1 H. Bl. 5; Griffiths *v.* Puleston, 13 M. & W. 358.
(*j*) Before this statute it was not unusual, and may still be expedient, to insert in leases a provision that the last half year's rent shall be paid on some day prior to the determination of the lease, so as to enable the landlord to distrain before the removal of the tenant. See Co. Litt. 47 b.

Where a landlord intends to rely on a forfeiture, he should not distrain under or by virtue of this Act, for such distress may operate as a waiver of the forfeiture (*k*).

The distress must be made within six years from the time when the rent becomes payable; for by 3 & 4 Will. IV., c. 27, s. 42, no arrears of rent, or any damages in respect of such arrears, shall be recovered by any distress, action, or suit, but within six years next after the same respectively shall have become due, or next after an acknowledgment of the same in writing shall have been given to the person entitled thereto, or his agent, signed by the person to whom the same was payable, or his agent. Under this statute the landlord can distrain for the last six years' rent, so long as he has a reversion, but when his right to the land is at an end, as there is no longer any tenancy or any reversion, his right to distrain likewise ceases (*l*).

By sect. 2 of this Act it is provided, that no person shall make an entry or distress, or bring an action to recover any land or rent, but within twenty years next after the right of entry, distress, or action has first accrued. But this section has been held not to apply to rents reserved on a demise, but to be confined to rents existing as an inheritance distinct from the land, and for which before this Act the party entitled to them might have had an assize. The only way, therefore, in which it can affect the right of making a distress is by its operation in destroying the right to recover the land itself after the period of limitation which it mentions (*m*).

(*k*) Ward *v.* Day, 4 B. & S. 337, 33 L. J. Q. B. 254.
(*l*) See 3 & 4 Will. IV. c. 27, ss. 2, 3, 8.
(*m*) See Paget *v.* Foley, 2 Bing. N. C. 679; Grant *v.* Ellis, 9 M. & W. 113; Doe *d.* Angell *v.* Angell, 9 Q. B. 328; The Dean of Ely *v.*

Generally speaking a second distress cannot lawfully be made where the first has been abandoned, nor can it be divided and taken part at one time and part at another (*n*), if there is a fair opportunity for making the distress in the first instance. But where the tenant by his own misconduct prevents the first distress, or where a mistake has arisen with respect to the value of the goods seized (*o*), then a second distress would be lawful (*p*).

By the 17th Car. II., c. 7, s. 4, it is provided, that "in all cases (aforesaid) where the value of the cattle distrained as aforesaid shall not be found to be to the value of the arrears distrained for, the party to whom such arrears were due, his executors and administrators, may from time to time distrain again for the residue of the said arrears."

Although there can in general be no second distress, yet where there has been no abandonment, there may be a recontinuance of a distress, and then even an outer-door may be broken open (*q*). It is a question for the jury whether there has been an abandonment or not (*r*).

Cash, 15 M. & W. 617; Owen *v.* De Beauvoir, 16 M. & W. 547, S. C. 5 Exch. 166. And see the notes to Nepean *v.* Doe, 2 Smith's L. C. 577, 5th edit.; and see 3 Chit. St. tit. Limitation of Actions, pp. 25-62.

(*n*) Com. Dig. Distress (A) 1; Bagge, *v.* applt., Mawby, respondt., 8 Ex. 641; Gambull *v.* Earl of Falmouth, 4 A. & E. 73; Lear *v.* Caldecott, 4 Q. B. 123; Owens *v.* Wynne, 4 E. & B. 579; Smith *v.* Goodwin, 4 B. & Ad. 413; Dawson *v.* Cropp, 1 C. B. 961;

Nash *v.* Lucas, L. R. 2 Q. B. 590.

(*o*) Hutchins *v.* Chambers, 1 Burr. 579, 1 Wms. Saund. 201, n (1).

(*p*) Lee *v.* Cooke, 2 H. & N. 584, 3 H. & N. 203; Woolaston, applt., *v.* Stafford, respondt., 15 C. B. 278.

(*q*) Bannister *v.* Hyde, 2 E. & E. 627, 29 L. J. Q. B. 141; Eldridge *v.* Stacey, 15 C. B. N.S. 458.

(*r*) Eldridge *v.* Stacey, *supra*. See also Russell *v.* Rider, 6 C. & P. 416; Kerby *v.* Harding, 6 Exch. 234.

(f.) HOW A DISTRESS SHOULD BE MADE.

A distress for rent is made by the landlord or his agent entering upon some part of the demised premises (*s*) and seizing some portions of the goods there in the name of the whole, or of so much as may be necessary to satisfy the rent (*t*); but a very slight act amounts, in contemplation of law, to such a seizure, if the intention of the party distraining is manifest. Thus walking round the premises, making an inventory of the articles there, and declaring that they were seized as a distress for the rent due, or merely saying " These things shall not be removed until the rent is paid," has been held to amount to a distress, although no seizure was made (*u*).

How a distress should be made.

The breaking open of an outer-door, window, gate, inclosure, or the unfastening of a hasp, will render the distress illegal and void *ab initio* (*v*).

So, in order to make an entry for distress, the landlord or his agent may not put his hand through a hole in a door or through a broken pane of glass and remove a bar, window, latch, or other fastening where such a mode of entering is not the usual mode (*w*).

But if the outer-door be open, an inner-door or lock may be forced open in order to find distrainable

(*s*) As to fraudulent removals, see *supra*, p. 202.
(*t*) Dodd *v.* Morgan, 6 Mod. 215; Draper *v.* Thompson, 4 C. & P. 84, Bullen, 131.
(*u*) Wood *v.* Nunn, 5 Bing. 10; Swan *v.* Earl of Falmouth, 8 B. & C. 456; Hutchins *v.* Scott, 2 M. & W. 809; Cramer *v.* Mott, L. R. 5 Q. B. 357, 39 L. J. Q. B. 172.
(*v*) Lemayne's case, 5 Co. R.; Duke of Brunswick *v.* Slowman, 8 C. B. 317; Brown *v.* Glenn, 16 Q. B. 254, 9 Vin. Abr. 128, Distress (E) 2, pl. 6, Co. Litt. 161 a; Attack *v.* Bramwell. 3. B. & S. 520, 32 L. J. Q. B. 146; Hancock *v.* Austin, 14 C. B. N.S. 634, 32 L. J. C. P. 252; Nash *v.* Lucas, L. R. 2 Q. B. 590, 8 B. & S. 531.
(*w*) Fitz. Abr. tit. Distress, pl. 21; Hancock *v.* Austin, 14 C. B. N.S. 634, 32 L. J. C. P. 252. See Ryan *v.* Shilcock, 7 Exch. 72, 21 L. J. Ex. 55.

goods (*x*). So the party distraining may climb over a fence to gain access to the house by an open door (*y*), and may open an outer-door which is fastened to keep the door shut, and not to keep people out, if he use the ordinary means, as lifting the latch, withdrawing a bolt, or turning a key; or he may enter through an open window (*z*).

Where a room occupied by the landlord was over a mill demised to the tenant, and there being no ceiling the landlord entered through the floor by raising the boards, it was held a lawful entry (*a*).

Where a distress has been lawfully begun, but there is an interruption not amounting to an abandonment, an outer-door may be broken open in order to continue the distress (*b*). So also in order to get out and remove the distress (*c*). Where it is necessary, a police officer may be called in (*d*).

In order that the tenant may know what goods the landlord intends to distrain, the party distraining must make an inventory of as many goods as are sufficient to cover the rent distrained for, and the expenses of the distress and the inventory should not be vague and uncertain (*e*).

Notice of the distress having been made, and of the time when the goods will be appraised and sold

(*x*) Browning *v.* Dann, Bull. N. P. 81, Co. Litt. 161 a.
(*y*) Eldridge *v.* Stacey, 15 C. B. N.S. 458.
(*z*) Ryan *v.* Shilcock, 7 Exch. 72, 21 L. J. Ex. 55; Nixon *v.* Freeman, 5 H. & N. 647, 653.
(*a*) Gould *v.* Bradstock, 4 Taunt. 562

(*b*) See Bannister *v.* Hyde, *supra*, p. 206.
(*c*) Pugh *v.* Griffiths, 7 A. & E. 827.
(*d*) Skidmore *v.* Booth, 6 C. & P. 777.
(*e*) See Wakeman *v.* Lindsay, 14 Q. B. 625.

unless replevied or the rent or charges satisfied, should be given; and it is convenient to write such notice at the bottom of the inventory (*f*). The notice should state the amount of rent due (*g*).

It must be served with a true copy of the inventory on the tenant, or left at the house or other most notorious place charged with the rent (*h*). The place to which the goods are removed must be mentioned in the notice (*i*). The notice, unless personal, must be in writing (*j*). It must not be vague and uncertain as to the goods distrained (*k*).

A defect or want of notice does not render the distress illegal, but makes it irregular to proceed to sell (*l*).

The notice need not state when the rent became due, nor the amount (*m*). Any defect in the notice is generally immaterial, for a man may distrain for one cause and avow or justify for another (*n*).

It frequently happens that when a distress is commenced, the tenant makes a tender of the rent in arrear. The common-law rule upon this subject is thus laid down by Lord Coke, in the Six Carpenters'

(*f*) Lyon *v.* Tomkies, 1 M. & W. 606, 2 W. & M. sess. 1, c. 5, s. 2.
(*g*) Taylor *v.* Henniker, 12 A. & E. 488.
(*h*) 2 W. & M. c. 5, s. 2.
(*i*) 11 Geo. II. c. 19, s. 9.
(*j*) Wilson *v.* Nightingale, 8 Q. B. 1034; Walter *v.* Rumball, 1 Lord Raymond, 53.
(*k*) Kerby *v.* Harding, 6 Exch. 234, 20 L. J. Ex. 163; Wakeman *v.* Lindsey, 14 Q. B. 625.
(*l*) Trent *v.* Hunt, 9 Exch. 14; Lucas *v.* Tarleton, 3 H. & N. 116;

Wilson *v.* Nightingale, *supra;* Robinson *v.* Waddington, 13 Q. B. 753.
(*m*) Moss *v.* Gallimore, 1 Doug. 279, 1 Smith's L. C. 5th edit. 542; Tancred *v.* Leyland, 16 Q. B. 669.
(*n*) Crowther *v.* Ramsbottom, 7 T. R. 654; Etherton *v.* Popplewell, 1 East. 139; Wootley *v.* Gregory, 2 J. & J. 536; Trent *v.* Hunt, 9 Exch. 14, 22 Exch. 318; Phillips *v.* Whitsed. 2 E. & E. 804, 29 L. J. Q. B. 164.

O

case (*o*) :—" Tender upon the land, before the distress, makes the distress tortious; tender after the distress, and before the impounding, makes the detainer, and not the taking, wrongful. Tender after the impounding makes neither the one nor the other wrongful, for then it comes too late, because then the case is put to the trial of the law to be there determined."

If, however, the tender is made within the five days allowed by the statute (*p*) for the tenant to replevy, a special action on the case may be maintained against the landlord, if he proceed to sell the distress, although the goods were impounded before tender (*q*). A tender of the rent without expenses after a warrant of distress has been delivered to the broker, is a good tender (*r*). Whether the distress be "impounded" before the tender or not, is a question depending on the circumstances of the case (*s*). A tender may be made to the landlord himself, even where he has placed the matter in his broker's hands (*t*). So it may be made to any agent of the landlord having authority to receive the rent (*u*). But a tender to a man who is merely in possession is bad (*v*). The tenant must tender the full amount of the rent due, except actual or constructive payments on account of rent (*w*). He must also tender a sufficient sum for

---

(*o*) 8 Rep. 146.

(*p*) 2 W. & M. sess. 1, c. 5, s. 2.

(*q*) Johnson *v.* Upham, 2 E. & E. 250, 28 L. J. Q. B. 252, overruling Ellis *v.* Taylor, 8 M. & W. 415.

(*r*) Bennett *v.* Bayes, 5 H. & N. 391.

(*s*) Thomas *v.* Harries, 1 M. & G. 695; Swan *v.* Earl of Falmouth, 8 B. & C. 456; Tennant *v.* Field, 8 E. & Bl. 336; Brown *v.* Powell. 4 Bing. 230; Pepper-

corn *v.* Hoffman, 9 M. & W. 618.

(*t*) Smith *v.* Goodwin, 4 B. & Ad. 413.

(*u*) Bennett *v.* Bayes, 5 H. & N. 391, 29 L. J. Ex. 224; Hatch *v.* Hale, 15 Q. B. 10; Brown *v.* Powell, 4 Bing. 230.

(*v*) Boulton *v.* Reynolds, 2 E. & E. 369, 29 L. J. Q. B. 11; Pilkington *v.* Hootings, Cro. Eliz. 813.

(*w*) See *ante*, Deductions, p. 163.

the lawful expenses of the distress (x). The tender must be made unconditionally (y).

(g.) What to be done with it.

As soon as the distress (z) is made, the landlord or his agent must impound the goods in a pound (a) suitable to the nature of the distress. Thus, if the articles distrained are of a perishable nature, the landlord should secure them in a pound *covert* or weather-proof; if they are cattle, in an open pound (b). At common law, if the distrainer put the cattle distrained into a *public* pound, they lay there at the tenant's risk, and if they starved, the distrainer was not answerable (c).

What to be done with it.

By 12 & 13 Vict., c. 92, s. 5, " Every person who shall impound or confine, or cause to be impounded or confined, in any pound or receptacle of the like nature any animal, shall provide and supply, during such confinement, a sufficient quantity of fit and wholesome food and water to such animal; and every such person who shall refuse or neglect to provide and supply such animal with such food and water as aforesaid, shall, for every such offence, forfeit and pay a penalty of twenty shillings."

(x) See *infra*, pp. 217, 219.
(y) Finch *v.* Miller, 5 C. B. 428; Bowen *v.* Owen, 11 Q. B. 130; Bull *v.* Parker, 2 Dow. N.S. 345; Manning *v.* Lunn, 2 C. & K. 13; Jennings *v.* Major, 8 C. & P. 61; Foord *v.* Noll, 2 Dow. N.S. 617; Laing *v.* Meandor, 1 C. & P. 257.
(z) At common law the distress was only a pledge for the rent in arrear, and the landlord was entitled to keep it as a security until his rent was satisfied. If he sold it, he became a trespasser *ab initio*, and the proceedings were void. See Six Carpenters' case, 1 Smith's L. C. 132; Gilbert on Distress, 67.
(a) Co. Litt. 47 b.
(b) See Wilder *v.* Speer, 8 A. & E. 547; Gilbert on Dist. 62, 2 Inst. 106, Co. Litt. 37 b, Bac. Abr. Distress (D); Bignell *v.* Clark, 5 H. & N. 485.
(c) Bac. Abr. Distress (D).

By sect. 6, "In case any animal shall at any time be impounded or confined as aforesaid, and shall continue confined without fit and sufficient food and water for more than twelve successive hours, it shall and may be lawful to and for any person whomsoever, from time to time, and as often as shall be necessary, to enter into and upon any pound or other receptacle of the like nature, in which any such animal shall be so confined, and to supply such animal with fit and sufficient food and water during so long a time as such animal shall remain and continue confined as aforesaid, without being liable to any action of trespass, or any other proceeding by any person whomsoever, for or by reason of such entry for the purposes aforesaid; and the reasonable cost of such food and water shall be paid by the owner of such animal, before such animal is removed, to the person who shall supply the same, and the said cost may be recovered in like manner as herein provided for the recovery of penalties under this Act," *i.e.*, by summary proceedings before a justice.

By 17 & 18 Vict., c. 60, s. 1," Every person who, since the passing of the said Act of the 12th and 13th years of Her Majesty, has impounded or confined, or hereafter shall impound or confine, as in the said Act mentioned, any animal, and has provided and supplied, or shall hereafter provide and supply, such animal with food and water as therein mentioned, shall and may, and he is hereby authorised, to recover of and from the owner or owners of such animal, not exceeding double the value of the food and water so already or hereafter to be supplied to such animal, in like manner as is by the said last-mentioned Act provided for the recovery of penalties under the same Act; and every person who has supplied or shall hereafter supply such food and water, shall be at liberty, if he shall so think fit, instead of proceeding for the recovery of the value thereof as last aforesaid, after the expiration of seven clear days from the time of impounding the same, to sell any such animal openly at any public market (after having given three days' public printed notice thereof), for the most money that can be got for the same, and to apply the produce in discharge of the value of such food and water so supplied as aforesaid, and the expense of and attending such sale, rendering the overplus (if any) to the owner of such animal " (*d*).

When the distress is taken, the distrainer cannot use or work it, except it seems where the user is necessary for its preservation; and if any injury happens to the distress from any act of the distrainer, who is responsible for the state of the pound, he must answer for it to the tenant (*e*).

At common law a distress could be impounded by removing it from the place at which it was taken and placing it in a common pound anywhere under the custody of the pound-keeper (*f*). But the 52 Hen. III. (statute of Marlebridge), c. 4, prohibited the person distraining from driving the distress out of the county. The 1 & 2 Philip & Mary, c. 12, directed that no distress of cattle should be driven out of the hundred, rape, wapentake, or lathe where it was taken, except to an open pound in the same shire not above three miles from the place of taking it. By the 11 Geo. II., c. 19, s. 10,

(*d*) See Mason *v.* Newland, 7 C. & P. 575; Layton *v.* Hurry, 8 Q. B. 811.
(*e*) Wilder *v.* Speer, 8 A. & E. 547; Vaspar *v.* Edwards, 1 Salk. 248; Dodd *v.* Morgan, 6 Mod. 216; Duncomb *v.* Reeve, Cro.
Eliz. 783; Chamberlayn's case, 1 Leon. 220; Bagshawe *v.* Gilliard, 1 Roll. Abr. 673, l. 26, 32; Smith *v.* Wright, 6 H. & N. 821.
(*f*) Thomas *v.* Harries, 1 M. & Gr. 707, n. (*a*).

it was enacted, " That it shall be lawful for any person or persons lawfully taking any distress for any kind of rent, to impound or otherwise secure the distress so made, of what nature or kind soever it may be, in such place, or on such part of the premises chargeable with the rent, as shall be most fit and convenient for the impounding and securing such distress."

The goods seized should, if convenient, be put into one room, unless the consent of the owner is given to the contrary, and very slight evidence is necessary to prove such consent (*g*).

But by 2 Will. & Mary, sess. 1, c. 5, s. 2, " Where any goods or chattels shall be distrained for any rent reserved and due upon any demise, lease, or contract whatsoever, and the tenant or owner of the goods so distrained shall not, within five days next after such distress taken, and notice thereof (with the cause of such taking) left at the chief mansion-house, or other most notorious place on the premises charged with the rent distrained for, replevy the same, with sufficient security to be given to the sheriff according to law, then in such case, after such distress and notice as aforesaid, and expiration of the said five days, the person distraining shall and may, with the sheriff or under-sheriff of the county, or with the constable of the hundred, parish, or place where such distress shall be taken (who are hereby required in aiding and assisting therein), cause the goods and chattels so distrained to be appraised by two sworn appraisers (whom such sheriff, under-sheriff, or constable are hereby empowered to swear) to appraise the same truly according to the best of their understandings; and after such

---

(*g*) Washbourn *v.* Black, 11 East. 405 n ; Cox *v.* Painter, 7 C. & P. 767 ; Woods *v.* Durant, 16 M. & W. 149.

appraisement, shall and may lawfully sell the goods and chattels so distrained for the best price that can be gotten for the same, towards satisfaction of the rent for which the said goods and chattels shall be distrained, and of the charges of such distress, appraisement, and sale, leaving the overplus (if any) in the hands of the said sheriff, under-sheriff, or constable, for the owner's use."

Although it is in most cases optional with the party distraining to impound the distress either on or off the premises, yet where sheaves or cocks of corn, or corn loose or in the straw, or hay lying in a barn or granary, or on a hovel, stack, or rick, or otherwise, are distrained under the statute 2 Will. & Mary, sess. 1, c. 5, a removal from the premises where seized is prohibited. Growing crops seized under 11 Geo. II., c. 19, ss. 8 and 9, can only be removed when they have become ripe and are cut, and there is no barn or proper place on the premises wherein they may be placed (*h*).

The distress being considered merely as a pledge, could not at common law have been sold.

The notice having been given, and the five days having expired, the landlord may proceed with the appraisement and sale, except in the case of growing crops, which are not appraiseable until after they are ripe and severed (*i*). The five days mentioned in the statute are exclusive of the day of taking and notice, and also of the day of sale (*j*). But the landlord has a reasonable time after the expiration of the five days

(*h*) Piggott *v.* Birtles, 1 M. & W. 448.
(*i*) 11 Geo. II. c. 19, s. 8; Owen *v.* Legh, 3 B. & A. 470. See *supra*.

(*j*) Robinson *v.* Waddington, 13 Q. B. 753; Harper *v.* Taswell, 6 C. & P. 166. In Lucas *v.* Tarleton, 3 H. & N. 116, it was held, in action for selling the goods within

for the purpose of appraising and selling (*k*). During such reasonable time the goods distrained are in *custodiâ legis*, and are protected from seizure under an execution (*l*). It is usual, however, for the tenant to consent that the landlord should remain beyond the five days. If such consent is given, it is prudent to have it in writing.

The two appraisers (*m*), who must be persons having no interest, and should not be the broker or party distraining (*n*), should then be sworn by the sheriff or under-sheriff of the county, or constable of the parish where it is taken (*o*) before the appraisement is made. The constable should be present when the appraisement is made; he usually indorses a memorandum of the administration of the oath and attendance upon the inventory. Such memorandum does not require a stamp (*p*). The appraisers must not be sworn by the constable of an adjoining parish, although the proper constable cannot be found (*q*). But if the tenant, to save expense, dispenses with the formalities required by the statute, he will be estopped from insisting on an irregularity occasioned at his own instance (*r*).

For stamp upon appraisement, see the Stamp Act, 1870, 33 & 34 Vict., c. 97, s. 38, and the schedule.

the five days that plaintiff was not entitled to a verdict unless he had sustained actual damage. See also Rodgers *v.* Parker, 18 C. B. 112.

(*k*) Pitt *v.* Shew, 4 B. & A. 208; Griffin *v.* Scott, 2 Ld. Raymond, 1424; Winterbourne *v.* Morgan, 11 East. 395, 2 Camp. 117 n; Etherton *v.* Poppleton, 1 East. 139; Harrison *v.* Barry, 7 Price, 690; Fisher *v.* Algar, 2 C. & P. 274.

(*l*) Bac. Abr. Execution (C) 4; Harrison *v.* Barry, 7 Price, 690.

(*m*) Even where the rent does not exceed £20 there must be two. See 57 Geo. III. c. 93; Allen *v.* Flicker, 10 A. & E. 640; Bishop *v.* Bryant, 6 C. & P. 484.

(*n*) Andrews *v.* Russell, Bull. N. P. 81; Lyon *v.* Weldon, 2 Bing. 334; Westwood *v.* Cowne, 1 Strange, 172.

(*o*) Avenell *v.* Crocker, Moo. & M. 172.

(*p*) See Dunn *v.* Lowe, 4 Bing. 193.

(*q*) Kenney *v.* May, 1 M. & Rob. 56; Wallace *v.* King, 1 H. Bl. 13.

(*r*) Bishop *v.* Bryant, 6 C. & P. 448.

CH. II.] REMEDIES FOR NON-PAYMENT. 217

The goods having been appraised, must be sold for the best price that can be got for them, unless they have been replevied, or the rent and the charges have been paid. Where the goods are sold at their appraised value, the law will intend that they have been sold at the best price (*s*). It is not unusual for the appraisers to buy them at their own valuation, but the landlord cannot sell the goods to himself even at their appraised value (*t*). The produce of the sale must be applied in satisfaction of the rent and the expenses of the distress, and if the produce is more than sufficient for that purpose, the overplus must be left in the hands of the sheriff (*u*).

There is no statutory regulation as to the costs of a distress for rent above £20, except the 1 & 2 Philip & Mary, c. 12, which fixes a sum of fourpence for impounding a distress; but this statute has been held not to extend to cases where goods are impounded on the premises under the 11 Geo. II., c. 19 (*v*). The charges must, however, be reasonable (*w*); the general practice appears to be to charge one or two guineas for the levy, and three shillings and sixpence *per diem* for the man in possession. Where the sum distrained for does not exceed £20, the costs (*x*) are regulated by the 57 Geo.

(*s*) Walter *v*. Rumball, 1 Ld. Raymond, 53; Pointer *v*. Buckley, 5 C. & P. 512.
(*t*) King *v*. England, 4 B. & S. 782; 33 L. J. Q. B. 145.
(*u*) See *infra*, p. 219.
(*v*) Child *v*. Chamberlain, 5 B. & Ad. 1049.
(*w*) Lyon *v*. Tomkies, 1 M. & W. 603; Hills *v*. Street, 5 Bing. 37.
(*x*) The schedule of expenses at the end of the statute is as follows :—

Levying distress £0 3 0

Man in possession per day 0 2 6
Appraisement, whether by one broker or more, sixpence in the pound on the value of the goods.
Stamp, the lawful amount thereof. See Stamp Act, 1870 (33 & 34 Vict., c. 97-99).
All expenses of advertisement (if any such) 0 10 0
Catalogues, sale, and commission, and delivery of goods, one shilling in the pound on the net produce of the sale.

III., c. 93, whereby it is enacted, "That no person whatsoever making any distress for rent, where the sum demanded and due shall not exceed the sum of £20 for and in respect of such rent, nor any person whatsoever employed in any manner in making such distress, or doing any act whatsoever in the course of such distress, or for carrying the same into effect, shall have, take, or receive out of the produce of the goods and chattels distrained upon and sold, or from the tenant distrained on, or from the landlord, or from any other person whatsoever, any other or more costs and charges for and in respect of such distress, or any matter or thing done therein, than such as are fixed and set forth in the schedule hereunto annexed, and appropriated to each act which shall have been done in course of such distress; and no person or persons whatsoever shall make any charge whatsoever for any act, matter, or thing mentioned in the said schedule, unless such act shall have been really done."

By sect. 2, a party aggrieved by a distress may apply to justices for redress, who may order treble the amount of monies unlawfully taken to be paid to the party complaining, together with full costs. The words of the section are, "If any person, &c., shall take, &c., any other or greater costs or charges than are set down in the schedule, or make any charge whatsoever for any act, matter, or thing mentioned in the schedule and not really done;" and it was held that these words did not apply to the case of a person *bonâ fide* thinking that he ought to have an appraisement, and other matters of detail, and charging for them, although such charges were not strictly lawful (*y*).

(*y*) Nott *v.* Bound, L. R. 1 Q. B. 405.

There is in sect. 6 of the above statute an enactment applicable to every distress, whether the sum distrained for be above or under £20. It is, "That every broker or other person who shall make and levy any distress whatsoever, shall give a copy of his charges, and of all the costs and charges of any distress whatsoever, signed by him, to the person or persons on whose goods and chattels any distress shall be levied, although the amount of rent demanded shall exceed the sum of £20." A landlord who does not personally interfere in the distress is not liable for the neglect of the broker employed by him to make a distress in not delivering a copy of the charges required by the statute (z).

A bailiff has no right to go on with a distress and sale for his expenses after his authority has been withdrawn by the landlord (a).

After appraisement and sale, the landlord is, under the 2 Will. & Mary, sess. 1, c. 5, s. 2, to leave " the overplus (b) (if any) in the hands of the said sheriff, under-sheriff, or constable, for the owner's use." If he does not do so, and actual damage ensues, a special action on the case is maintainable (c). The proper course is to leave the overplus money with the sheriff, &c., and to return the surplus goods to the premises from whence they were taken (d).

(z) Hart $v.$ Leach, 1 M. & W. 560.
(a) Harding $v.$ Hall, 14 W. R. 646, 14 L. T. N.S. 410.
(b) After payment of rent and reasonable expenses of distress. Lyon $v.$ Tomkies, 1 M. & W. 603.
(c) Rodgers $v.$ Parker, 18 C. B. 112; Lyon $v.$ Tomkies, 1 M. & W. 603; Yates $v.$ Eastwood, 6 Exch. 805. See Evans $v.$ Wright, 2 H. & N. 527, 27 L. J. Ex. 50.
(d) Evans $v.$ Wright, *supra*.

(h.) Tenant's Remedies.

Tenant's remedies.

A distress is said to be wrongful when no rent is due at the time, or not so much rent as is distrained for, or where an excessive distress is taken, or where goods are distrained which are not by law the subject of a distress. It is said to be irregular where, although the distress itself is legal, some of the proceedings thereon are not in conformity with the statutes by which they are regulated.

At common law any irregularity committed in the course of a distress rendered the party distraining a trespasser *ab initio* (e). But by 11 Geo. II., c. 19, s. 19, "When any distress shall be made for any rent justly due, and any irregularity or unlawful act shall be afterwards done by the party distraining or his agent, the distress shall not be deemed unlawful, nor the distrainer a trespasser *ab initio*, but the party grieved may recover satisfaction in an action of trespass on the case."

This statute does not apply to the case of a distress unlawfully made, as where a landlord, in distraining, breaks an outer-door (f).

The nature of the irregularity determines the form of action. If the irregularity be in the nature of an act of trespass, the landlord must bring trespass; and if it be in itself the subject-matter of an action on the case, he must bring case (g).

(e) Six Carpenters' Case 8 Co. Rep. 290.

(f) Attack v. Bramwell, 3 B. & G. 520, 32 L. J. Q. B. 146, per Blackburn, J., 149.

(g) Messing v. Kemble, 2 Camp. 115; Winterbourne v. Morgan, 11 East. 395; Etherton v. Popplewell, 1 East. 139; Wallace v. King, 1 H. Bl. 13.

At common law if a landlord distrained for rent where no rent was due, the tenant's remedy was by action of trespass. *When no rent is due at the time.*

But by 2 Will. & Mary, sess. 1, c. 5 (which first enabled a landlord to sell a distress taken for rent), it is provided and enacted, by sect. 5, "That in case any such distress and sale as aforesaid shall be made, by virtue or colour of this present Act, for rent pretended to be arrear and due, where in truth no rent is in arrear or due to the person or persons distraining, or to him or to them in whose name or names or right such distress shall be taken as aforesaid, that then the owner of such goods or chattels distrained and sold as aforesaid, his executors or administrators, shall and may, by action of trespass or upon the case, to be brought against the person or persons so distraining, any or either of them, his or their executors or administrators, recover double of the value of the goods or chattels so distrained and sold, together with full costs of suit."

In order to support an action under this statute, the goods distrained must have been sold (*h*).

The tenant may at common law bring an action on the case where the distress was made for more rent than was due (*i*), even though the goods actually distrained are of less value than the rent really due (*j*). *Distraining for more rent than is due.*

If several distresses are made for one entire rent, and it can be shown that there were sufficient goods on the premises which might have been taken under *Distraining twice for the same rent.*

(*h*) Salter *v.* Bunsden, 4 Mod. 231; Masters *v.* Farris, 1 C. B. 715.
(*i*) Carter *v.* Carter, 5 Bing. 406.
(*j*) Taylor *v.* Henniker, 12 A. & E. 488.

the first distress to satisfy the rent distrained for, the landlord will be liable at common law in an action on the case for distraining twice for the same rent, or the tenant may bring trespass, at his option (*k*).

<small>For an excessive distress.</small> The remedy for an excessive distress by the statute of Marlebridge, 52 Hen. III., c. 4, is an action on the case founded on the statute (*l*). A count in trover is often added in case the tenancy or the distress should be denied, or some goods should be taken away which are not in the inventory (*m*).

Whether a distress is excessive or not is a question for the jury (*n*); and if it be excessive, the plaintiff is entitled to recover the fair value of the goods, deducting for rent and expenses of distress (*o*).

The mere distraining of the goods to an excessive value above the rent due, without sale or removal, is sufficient to maintain the action on the statute (*p*). The measure of damages, where the goods are removed and impounded, is the loss of the use and enjoyment of the surplus of the goods; and if they are not restored before action, the plaintiff may claim the full value of the surplus (*q*). He may recover substantial damages even if he retain the use of the goods under the distress (*r*), and nominal if he cannot prove substantial damages (*s*).

(*k*) See *supra*, p. 206; Lear *v.* Caldicott, 4 Q. B. 123.
(*l*) Hutchinds *v.* Chambers, 1 Burr. 589.
(*m*) Bishop *v.* Bryant, 6 C. & P. 484; Spargo *v.* Brown, 9 B. & C. 935.
(*n*) Smith *v.* Ashforth, 29 L. J. Ex. 259. See Walter *v.* Rumbald, 1 Lord Raymond, 53.
(*o*) Wells *v.* Moody, 7 C. & P. 59;

Biggins *v.* Goode, 2 C. & J. 364; Knight *v.* Egerton, 7 Exch. 407.
(*p*) Sells *v.* Hoare, 1 Bing. 401; Swann *v.* Earl of Falmouth, 8 B. & C. 456.
(*q*) Piggott *v.* Birtles, 1 M. & W. 441, 448.
(*r*) Bayliss *v.* Foster, 7 Bing. 153.
(*s*) Chandler *v.* Doulton, 3 H. & C. 553, 34 L. J. Ex. 89.

Trespass is the ordinary form of action where fixtures have been taken; but trover may be brought, although in that form of action the things converted are treated as goods and chattels, and their value as such only can be recovered (t). The measure of damages is the value of the fixtures as between the outgoing and incoming tenant (u). *For distraining things not the subject of distress.*

An action of trespass, trover, or case lies for distraining things delivered to the tenant to be dealt with in the way of his trade (v).

So also such actions will lie for distraining implements of trade, &c., even though not in actual use at the time, if there be other sufficient distrainable goods upon the premises (w). When beasts of the plough or sheep are unlawfully distrained, the tenant may either rescue them or bring trespass under the 51 Hen. III., c. 4 (x). The plaintiff may recover the full value of the beasts notwithstanding the other goods on the premises liable to distress belonged to him (y).

If the appraisement shows that there is not sufficient distress without taking beasts of the plough, the action will not lie even if the sale shows the reverse, and the sale is not a test of value; but the plaintiff may show that the appraisement was too low, and that there was sufficient distress without resorting to the beasts of the plough (z). There is no order in the

(t) Dalton v. Whittem, 3 Q. B. 961; Harvey v. Pocock, 11 M. & W. 740; Thompson v. Pettitt, 10 Q. B. 101. See *supra*, p. 192.
(u) Moore v. Drinkwater, 1 F. & F. 134.
(v) See *supra*, p. 192.
(w) See *supra*, p. 192.
(x) Co. Litt. 161 a, Com. Dig. Distress (D) 5; Keen v. Priest, 4 H. & N. 240; Porphrey v. Legingham, 2 Keble, 290. See Davies v. Aston, 1 C. B. 746.
(y) Keen v. Priest, *supra*.
(z) Jenner v. Yolland, 6 Price, 3; Smith v. Ashforth, 29 L. J. Ex. 259.

sale of the distress, and therefore beasts may be sold before the other goods distrained (*a*).

Action for other illegal proceedings. The tenant may bring trespass or case, or may rescue the distress, where the landlord distrains or impounds after tender (*b*).

An action on the case may be brought under the 52 Hen. III., c. 4, and the 1 & 2 Philip & Mary, c. 12, s. 1 (*c*), for driving a distress out of the hundred, &c.

If the landlord remain an unreasonable time after the five days allowed by the statute (2 Will. & Mary, sess. 1, c. 5, s. 2; and see 11 Geo. II., c. 19, s. 10) (*d*), the tenant may bring an action of trespass (*e*) or case, at his option.

The tenant may bring an action on the case for selling before the expiration of the five days allowed after the distress has been taken, and also if the landlord sell without notice (*f*).

Actions on the case for selling without appraisement (*g*), for not selling at the best price (*h*), and for not returning the surplus after distress (*i*), may be brought by the tenant. An action of trespass will not lie for a mere omission (*j*).

(*a*) Jenner *v.* Yolland, 6 Price, 3.
(*b*) Six Carpenters' case, 8 Co. 147 a, Co. Litt. 160 b; Smith *v.* Goodwin, 4 B. & Ad. 113; Branscomb *v.* Bridges, 1 B. & C. 445. See p. 209.
(*c*) See p. 214.
(*d*) See p. 214.
(*e*) Winterbourne *v.* Morgan, 2 Camp. 117, 11 East. 395; Etherington *v.* Popplewell, 1 East. 139; *per* Lord Denman in Ladd *v.* Thomas, 12 Ad. & E. 117.
(*f*) See the 2 W. & M. sess. 1, c. 5, s. 2, *supra*, p. 214; and see also 11 Geo. II. c. 19, s. 9.
(*g*) See *supra*, p. 214.
(*h*) See *supra*, p. 214.
(*i*) See *supra*, p. 214. In this action the reasonableness of the charges of distraining may be disputed. Lyon *v.* Tomkies, 1 M. & W. 603.
(*j*) Messing *v.* Kemble, 2 Camp. 115.

CH. II.] REMEDIES FOR NON-PAYMENT.

The tenant may have his remedy for excessive charges under an action for not returning the surplus (*k*).

In some cases a rescue of the goods seized is justifiable. A rescue is where the owner, or some person on his behalf, takes away the things distrained by force, after they have been actually in possession of the person distraining (*l*). This may lawfully be done before the goods are impounded, if the distress be wrongful, but not after (*m*). Whenever a distrainer abandons a distress, the retaking of it by the tenant or owner is not a rescue (*n*). The owner may prevent the distrainer from abusing a distress by working it, and it is no rescue (*o*).

Rescue.

By the 2 Will. & Mary, sess. 1, c. 5, s. 4, on any pound-breach, or rescue of goods distrained for rent, the person grieved thereby shall, in a special action on the case, recover with damages and costs (*p*) against the offender, or against the owner of the goods, if they afterwards be found to come into his use or possession (*q*).

Wherever personal (*r*) goods or chattels have been wrongfully (*s*) taken under a distress, the tenant or

Replevin.

(*k*) See *supra*, Expenses of Distress, p. 214, 217.
(*l*) Buller's *Nisi Prius*, 84; Co. Litt. 160.
(*m*) Co. Litt. 47 b, 161 a; Buller's *Nisi Prius*, 61 a ; Bevil's case, 4 Co. Rep. 11 b; Keen *v*. Priest, 4 H. & N. 240 ; Cotesworth *v*. Bettison, 1 Salk. 247, 1 Lord Raymond, 105.
(*n*) Dodd *v*. Morgan, 6 Mod. 216 ; Smith *v*. Wright, 6 H. & N. 821, 30 L. J. Ex. 313 ; Knowles *v*. Blake, 5 Bing. 499.

(*o*) Smith *v*. Wright, *supra*.
(*p*) But now, in lieu of treble costs, a reasonable indemnity may be recovered. See 5 & 6 Vict. c. 97, s. 2.
(*q*) See as to cattle impounded, damage feasant, 6 & 7 Vict. c. 30.
(*r*) Dalton *v*. Whittem, 3 Q. B. 961 ; Niblett *v*. Smith, 4 T. R. 504. Replevin lies for growing corn, &c., taken under a distress, under 11 Geo. II. c. 19, s. 8.
(*s*) See *supra*, p. 220.

P

owner, if he do not rescue them, but suffer them to be impounded, may replevy them, that is, he may retake his goods out of the pound upon giving security to the officer that he will bring an action of replevin against the landlord for the seizure, and if judgment be given against him, restore the goods. So long as the goods remain unsold, the tenant may replevy, although after the five days allowed by the statute (*t*). Goods under an execution or other process of law cannot be replevied (*u*).

Replevin cannot be joined with any other cause of action (*v*). The plaintiff is only entitled to recover (beyond the goods replevied) the expenses incurred by him in obtaining the replevy, including the fees paid at the County Court, and his costs of the action (*w*). The object of the action is to procure the restitution of the goods themselves, and to have the use of them while the right to them is being tried in the action (*x*). After obtaining judgment, the plaintiff cannot maintain another action for irregularities in the same distress (*y*).

Formerly the sheriff, upon the application of the owner and the execution of a replevin bond, took the goods from the distrainer and re-delivered them to the owner; but now by the 19 & 20 Vict., c. 108, these

(*t*) Jacob *v*. King, 5 Taunt. 451; Anon. 1 Chitty's Rep. 196 a; Griffiths *v*. Stephens, ib.

(*u*) Wiunard *v*. Forster, 2 Lutch. 1190; Cannon *v*. Smallwood, 3 Lev. 204; George *v*. Chambers, 11 M. & W. 149; 2 Chitty's Archbold, 1071, 11th edit.; Allen *v*. Sharp, 2 Ex. 352; Marshall *v*. Pitman, 9 Bing. 595; Wilson *v*. Weller, 1 B. & B. 57; Wootton *v*. Harvey, 6 East. 75; Rex *v*. Hoseaston, 14 East. 605.

(*v*) County Court Rules, No. 177, 15 & 16 Vict. c. 76, s. 41.

(*w*) Ros. Ev. 683, 11th edit.; Pease *v*. Chaytor, 3 B. & S. 634, 32 L. J. M. C. 121; Connor *v*. Bentley, 1 Jebb & S. 246.

(*x*) Mennic *v*. Blake, 6 E. & B. 846.

(*y*) Phillips *v*. Berryman, 3 Doug. 286; White *v*. Willis, 2 Wils. 87; Pease *v*. Chaytor, 1 B. & S. 658, 662, 3 ib. 620, 634, 647, 32 L. J. M. C. 121.

powers are transferred to the registrar of the County Court of the district in which the distress is taken (z). By sects. 65 and 66 of this Act, the replevin may be commenced in any superior Court in the form applicable to personal actions therein, upon such security being given to the registrar as therein mentioned, provided a question of title is involved, or the rent exceeds £20 (a). Even where a question of title is involved, or the damage exceeds £20, the action may be brought in the County Court, subject to a power of removal by the defendant under sect. 67.

If the plaintiff obtains a verdict, he is, in ordinary cases, entitled to small damages for the detention of the goods, and he also is entitled to retain the goods which he has replevied. If the defendant obtains a verdict, he is entitled to a return of the goods, and to recover his rent and costs (b). And in the County Court the defendant may require the Court to find the value of the distress. If the value is less than the rent, judgment must be given for the amount of such value; if the rent is less than the value, judgment must be given for the amount of the rent (c).

See further Woodfall's "Landlord and Tenant," Replevin, 9th edition, pp. 791 to 854.

(z) Sects. 63–66, 71.
(a) By s. 22 of the Common Law Procedure Act, 1860 (23 & 24 Vict. c. 126), the provisions of 19 & 20 Vict. c. 108, are extended to all cases of replevin.
(b) 17 Car. II. c. 7, s. 2.
(c) See County Court Rules, 1857, Reg. 180.

CHAPTER III.

REPAIRS AND CULTIVATION.

	PAGE		PAGE
1. WASTE—		2. FIRE ...	232
without impeachment of waste	228	3. CULTIVATION	... 233

1. WASTE.

THERE is an obligation on the part of the lessee to see that no injury is done to the inheritance by his own wilful or negligent conduct, and a breach of such obligation will render him liable to be punished for waste (*a*). Whatever does lasting damage to the freehold or inheritance, or anything which alters the nature of the property, so as to render the evidence of ownership more difficult, or to destroy or weaken the proof of identity, or diminish the value of the estate, or increase the burden upon it, is waste (*b*). It is either voluntary or permissive,—the one an offence of commission, as pulling down a house; the other of omission, as allowing a house to fall for want of necessary repairs. It may be incurred in respect of—
1. The soil; 2. The buildings; 3. The trees, fences, &c.; 4. The live stock (*c*).

A tenant in fee-simple or fee-tail has power to deal with the property as he pleases (*d*). But it is otherwise with regard to tenants of lesser estates, although they are entitled to reasonable *estovers* and *botes* for

(*a*) Co. Litt. 53 a.
(*b*) 4 Co. Rep. 64, Co. Litt. 68 a; Huntley *v.* Russell, 13 Q. B. 572, judgment of Patterson, J. 588; Doe *d.* Grubb *v.* Lord Burlington, 5 B. & Ad. 507, 517; Lord Darcy *v.* Askwith, Hob.
234; Phillips *v.* Smith, 14 M. & W. 589, 593.
(*c*) It is also voluntary waste to destroy heirlooms, 1 Cruise's Dig. tit. 3, s. 14.
(*d*) 11 Co. 50 a, Plowden, 259.

purposes of repairs, &c. The rules, however, vary in their application according to the particular estate, since there was a distinction at common law between the tenants of estates created by the act of law, and tenants of estates created by the contract of parties (*e*). With regard to voluntary waste, a tenant for years stands in the same situation as a tenant for life (*f*); but it would seem that the liability of the tenant for years for permissive waste is less than that of a tenant for life (*g*). With regard to a tenant strictly at will, it is laid down by Littleton, s. 71, that he cannot commit waste at all (*h*).

1. To the soil. Voluntary waste may be committed if the tenant in any manner essentially varies the nature of the soil or produce, or changes its face. Thus to convert arable land into pasture, to sow grain in hop-grounds, or to build a house upon the land, is waste (*i*); or to dig and carry away the soil, or to open mines or pits, but not to work those already open, provided that they have not been abandoned by the owner of the inheritance for the permanent advantage of the estate (*j*). Nor is it waste to take the soil for the purpose of reparation or improvement, as to dig a trench to drain the water (*k*). Permissive waste to

(*e*) See statutes of Marlebridge (52 Hen. III. c. 13) and of Gloucester (6 Edw. I. c. 5), Lord Coke's 2d Inst. 299.
(*f*) See Viner's Abr. Waste (S).
(*g*) Gibson *v.* Wells, 1 New. Rep. 290; Herne *v.* Benbow, 4 Taunt. 764; Jones *v.* Hill, 7 Taunt. 392. But see Co. Litt. 53, 2 Inst. 298; Harnett *v.* Maitland, 16 M. & W. 257; Yellowby *v.* Gower, 11 Ex. 294; Notes to Greene *v.* Cole, 2 Wms. Saund. 252.
(*h*) See Harnett *v.* Maitland, *supra*.

(*i*) Co. Litt. 53 a; Harrow School *v.* Alderton, 2 Bos. & P. 86; Wetherell *v.* Howells, 1 Camp. 227, Bac. Abr. Waste (C) 3; Simmons *v.* Norton, 7 Bing. 640; Hutton *v.* Warren, 1 M. & W. 472.
(*j*) Co. Litt. 53 a; Bagot *v.* Bagot, 32 Beavan, 509, 33 L. J. Ch. 116; Huntley *v.* Russell, 13 Q. B. 572.
(*k*) Moyle *v.* Moyle, Owen, 67; Altham's case, [2 Rol. Abr. 820, l. 23.

the soil may be committed if the tenant by his negligence suffer the land to be surrounded or overflowed with water, but not if the overflow be caused by tempest, unless he omit to repair the damage (*l*).

2. Voluntary waste to buildings may be committed by the tenant if he pull them down, unroof or alter them (*m*). So it was waste if the tenant removed anything affixed to the freehold, even if he originally put it there (*n*). But this rule is now considerably relaxed in favour of the tenant (*o*). Permissive waste to buildings may be committed if the tenant omit to keep them in tenantable repair, and he will be liable if, owing to such neglect, damage be occasioned by the act of God; but if the buildings are destroyed by the act of God or the Queen's enemies, it is not waste (*p*). Before the 6 Anne, c. 31, tenants in whose houses accidental fires commenced were liable for waste (*q*).

3. Voluntary waste may also be committed if the tenant cuts down or lops timber so as to occasion its decay (*r*). It is, however, not waste if the tenant cut them down and use them for the necessary and actual repairs of the buildings which existed when he entered. But if the decay had been occasioned by his own default, and he cuts down timber for the repair,

(*l*) Co. Litt. 53 b; Viner's Abr. Waste, 1; Reg. *v.* Leigh, 10 A. & E. 398. See Paradine *v.* Jane, Aleyn, 27.
(*m*) Co. Litt. 53 a; Doe d. Grubb *v.* Burlington, 5 B. & Ad. 511.
(*n*) Co. Litt. 53 a.
(*o*) See *infra*, Part 3, c. 7, Fixtures, p. 298.
(*p*) Co. Litt. 53 a; Reg. *v.* Leigh, 10 A. & E. 398.

(*q*) See *infra*, Fire, p. 232.
(*r*) Co. Litt. 53 a. Trees must be above twenty years old to be timber. Oak, ash, and elm of that age are always considered timber; 2 Inst. 643; Aubrey *v.* Fisher, 10 East. 431. Others may by local custom be accounted timber; see the judgment of the Court in Phillips *v.* Smith, 14 M. & W. 589, 593, citing Lord Darcy *v.* Askwith, Hob. 234.

he will be liable for double waste (*s*). To cut down trees, not being timber, if they are growing, in defence of the house, is also waste (*t*). So is the doing of any act which causes a decay of the wood. So destroying fruit-trees in the garden or orchard is waste (*u*).

The tenant, however, may cut down timber-trees that are dead (*v*); he may also cut such trees as are not timber, and do not grow, in defence of the house (*w*); but if he grub up the trees, hedges, &c., he will be guilty of waste (*x*).

4. Voluntary waste may be done in respect of animals, by taking or destroying so many of them as to unstock the dovecote, warren, park, or fishpond, in which they are kept (*y*); and it is waste if the tenant stop the pigeon-holes so that the pigeons cannot build (*z*). It is permissive waste if the tenant suffer the park-paling to be decayed, so that the deer stray and are lost (*a*).

A tenant for life, "without impeachment of waste," may cut down trees and open mines, and is entitled to the timber when they are cut down (*b*); but he will be restrained by injunction from pulling down houses, and cutting down ornamental or sheltering

Without impeachment of waste.

(*s*) Co. Litt. 53 b; Darcy *v*. Askwith, Hob. 238; Gorges *v*. Stanfield, Cro. Eliz. 593; Simmons *v*. Norton, 7 Bing. 640, Com. Dig. Waste (D) 5; Doe *d*. Foley *v*. Wilson, 11 East. 56.
(*t*) Co. Litt. 53 a; Phillips *v*. Smith, *supra*.
(*u*) Co. Litt. 53 a; Id. note (6). See Wetherell *v*. Howells, 1 Camp. 227.

(*v*) Co. Litt. 53 b.
(*w*) Gage *v*. Smith, 2 Roll. Abr. 817, 1. 17.
(*x*) Co. Litt. 53 b.
(*y*) Ibid.
(*z*) Moyle *v*. Moyle, Owen, 66.
(*a*) Ibid.
(*b*) Pyne *v*. Dor, 1 T. R. 55; Gordon *v*. Woodford, 27 Beav. 603, 29 L. J. Ch. 222.

timber (c), and from taking the lead and tiles off a house (d).

An action of trespass for waste cannot be maintained by one tenant in common against another (e).

2. FIRE.

Fire.

If the premises were accidentally or negligently destroyed by fire, the tenant would not at common law have been guilty of waste if he neglected to rebuild them (f). By the statute of Gloucester (6 Edw. I., c. 5), tenants for life or years were made liable for waste without any exception, and were therefore rendered answerable for destruction by fire (g). But by 14 Geo. III., c. 78, s. 86 (h), " No action, suit, or process whatsoever shall be had, maintained, or prosecuted against any person in whose house, chamber, stable, barn, or other buildings, or on whose estate any fire shall accidentally begin," provided "that no contract or agreement made between landlord and tenant shall be hereby defeated or made void."

The statute does not apply to fires produced by malice or negligence (i). This statute is not "local and personal," and extends to the whole kingdom (j).

The statute specially excepts all express contracts as to waste by fire; and, therefore, where the tenant covenants to repair the premises and to leave them in

(c) See *post*, Injunction, p. 239.
(d) Vane v. Lord Barnard, 1 T. R. 56 n.
(e) Jacob v. Seward, L. R. 4 C. P. 518.
(f) Co. Litt. 53 b.
(g) Countess of Salop's case, 5 Rep. 13, Co. Litt. 57 a (n), 377.
(h) Repealing 6 Anne, c. 31.

See Chitty's Statutes, vol. 2, tit. Fire.
(i) Filliter v. Phippard, 11 Q. B. 355; Vaughan v. Taff Vale Ry. 5 H. & N. 679; Vaughan v. Manlove, 4 Scott, 244.
(j) Richards v. Easto, 15 M. & W. 244; *ex parte* Goreley, *in re* Barker, 34 L. J. Bkt. 1.

repair, and accidents by fire are not excepted, the tenant will be compelled to rebuild the premises if they are burnt down (*k*), and even to pay the rent (*l*), unless his covenant can be construed to exempt him (*m*).

3. CULTIVATION.

Although it is waste to change the face or character Cultivation. of the soil (*n*), yet it is not waste to neglect to cultivate it (*o*). But we have seen, *ante*, Part 1, c. 4, s. 7, pp. 124, 138, that covenants to farm according to the custom of the country, in a husband-like manner, are either expressly made in most leases, or arise from the mere relation of landlord and tenant (*p*). Where the custom is not excluded by the terms of the agreement, it is not necessary to prove that such custom is immemorial, if a reasonable usage can be shown (*q*).

By 56 Geo. III., c. 50, s. 1 (*r*), no sheriff shall, by virtue of any process, " carry off, or sell, or dispose of, for the purpose of being carried off from any lands let to farm, any stacks, thrashed or unthrashed, or any straw of crops growing, or any chaff, colder, or any turnips, or any manure, compost, ashes, or sea-weed, in any case whatsoever; nor any hay, grass, or

(*k*) Earl of Chesterfield *v.* Duke of Bolton, Comyn, 267; Poole *v.* Archer, Skin. 210; Bullock *v.* Dommitt, 6 T. R. 650.
(*l*) Weigall *v.* Waters, 6 T. R. 488; Izon *v.* Gorton, 5 Bing. N. C. 501; Holtzappel *v.* Baker, 4 Taunt. 45; Packer *v.* Gibbins, 1 Q. B. 421; Loft *v.* Dennis, 1 E. & E. 474.
(*m*) Bennett *v.* Ireland, 1 E. B. & E. 326.
(*n*) See *ante*, p. 228, 229.

(*o*) Hutton *v.* Warren, 1 M. & W. 472, *per* Parke, B.
(*p*) See *infra*, Part 3, c. 6, Emblements.
(*q*) Dalby *v.* Hirst, 1 B. & B. 224; Legh *v.* Hewitt, 4 East. 154; Earl of Falmouth *v.* Thomas, 1 C. & M. 89. If a particular custom is alleged, it must be proved as alleged. See Angerstein *v.* Handson, 1 C. M. & R. 789.
(*r*) See *ante*, p. 195, Distress.

grasses, whether natural or artificial, nor any tares or vetches, nor any roots or vegetables, being produce of such lands, in any case where, according to any covenant or written agreement entered into and made for the benefit of the owner or landlord of any farm, such hay, &c., ought not to be taken off or withholden from such lands, or which, by the tenor or effect of such covenants or agreements, ought to be used or expended thereon, and of which covenants or agreements such sheriff shall have received a written notice before he shall have proceeded to sale." Sect. 2 provides, that the tenant shall give notice to the sheriff of the existence of such covenants, and of the name and residence of the landlord; that the sheriff shall give notice to the landlord of the seizure of the crops; and that, if he hears nothing from him, he shall put off the sale as long as he legally can. Subsequent sections provide, however, that such produce may be sold, subject to an agreement to expend it on the land, according to the custom of the country, where there is no covenant or agreement, and according to such contract, where there is. In case of such qualified sale, the purchasers may use all such necessary barns, buildings, yards, and fields, for the purpose of consuming such produce, as the sheriff shall assign for the purpose, and which the tenant would have been entitled to, and ought to have used for the like purpose. By sect. 11, the assignees of bankrupt or insolvent tenants, together with all purchasers whatsoever, are prevented from disposing of the crops in any other manner than the bankrupt, &c., himself might do (s). The Bankrupt Act, 12 & 13 Vict., c. 106, s. 144, contains a similar enactment. By 14 & 15 Vict., c. 25, s. 2, growing crops seized and sold under

---

(s) Wilmot v. Rose, 3 E. & E. 563.

an execution, are liable for accruing or subsequent rent.

The remedies for the breach of such contracts to farm according to the course of husbandry are—an action of covenant where the contract is under seal, an action of assumpsit where it is not under seal, and an action of ejectment where the breach works a forfeiture of the estate (*t*).

(*t*) See *post*, Remedies for Non-repair, p. 236.

CHAPTER IV.

REMEDIES FOR NON-REPAIR AND WASTE.

	PAGE		PAGE
1. ACTION—		2. ENTRY OR EJECTMENT	... 238
action for non-repair	... 236	3. INJUNCTION ...	... 239
action for waste	... 237		

FOR the breach of a covenant to repair, the landlord has two remedies—one by action, and another by entry or ejectment. For waste the landlord has a remedy by action and by injunction.

1. ACTION.

Action for non-repair.

An action of covenant may be brought by the landlord against the tenant for non-repair where the lease is under seal (*a*); but where it is not under seal, the action must be in the form of assumpsit for breach of the promise to repair, or case for the breach of duty (*b*).

An action for non-repair may be maintained before the expiration of the lease, where a lessee has cove-

---

(*a*) A covenant to repair must be express, but an implied one of a similar nature arises from the relation of landlord and tenant. See *supra*, c. 4, s. 7, sub-sects. (a.) and (b.)

(*b*) Kinlyside *v.* Thornton, 2 W. Bl. 1111; Marker *v.* Kenrick, 13 C. B. 188. See also Elliott *v.* Johnson, 8 B. & S. 38, L. R. 2 Q. B. 120, 36 L. J. Q. B. 44.

nanted to repair, and keep in repair, during the continuance of the term (c); and in such action, the landlord may recover damages commensurate with the injury to the reversion, and not the amount required to put the premises in repair (d). But where the lease is determined, as by forfeiture, it is otherwise (e). The landlord may also recover a compensation for the loss of the use of the premises while the repairs are being effected (f); but he cannot recover the costs of alterations necessary to enable him to carry on his business in new premises, nor their rent, nor the cost of restoring them to their original state (g).

The amount of damages also depends upon the condition of the premises at the time of the demise (h).

An action on the case for non-repair of fences will lie, as such repair is a duty which is cast upon the tenant (i). Tenants from year to year, or at will, however, do not seem to be liable for non-repair of fences or permissive waste (j).

An action on the case in the nature of waste is now a common remedy, even if an action for covenant will *Action for waste.*

(c) Luxmore v. Robson, 1 B. & A. 584.
(d) Worcester School Trustees v. Rowlands, 9 C. & P. 734; Smith v. Peat, 9 Ex. 161; Turner v. Lamb, 14 M. & W. 412.
(e) Davies v. Underwood, 27 L. J. Ex. 113, 2 H. & N. 570.
(f) Woods v. Pope, 1 Bing. N. C. 467.
(g) Green v. Eales, 2 Q. B. 225.
(h) Stanley v. Towgood, 3 Bing. N. C. 4; Burdett v. Withers, 7 A. & E. 136; Payne v. Haine, 16 M. & W. 541.
(i) Cheetham v. Hampson, 4 T. R. 318; Russell v. Shenton, 3 Q. B. 449; Chauntler v. Robinson, 4 Ex. 163; Whitfield v. Weedon, 2 Chit. R. 685.
(j) See *ante*, p. 229, Waste, and *per* Lord Kenyon in Cheetham v. Hampson, *supra*.

also lie (*k*). But the action does not lie for permissive waste (*l*).

It will lie for acts done by a tenant while holding over after the expiration of a notice to quit (*m*).

An action on the case for waste would lie against a tenant's executor for waste committed within six months before the tenant's death (*n*).

In an action on the case for commissive waste, the plaintiff may claim a writ of injunction (*o*).

2. ENTRY OR EJECTMENT.

Entry or ejectment.

A breach of a covenant to repair will not justify a re-entry for a forfeiture, unless there is in the lease or agreement (*p*) a proviso for re-entry in case of non-repair; nor will such a breach support an action of ejectment; but if there be such a proviso, the landlord may re-enter or maintain ejectment upon breach at any time during the term (*q*).

The courts of equity will not decree the specific performance of a general covenant to repair, but will leave the party to his remedy at law (*r*).

(*k*) Kinlyside *v.* Thornton, 2 W. Bl. 1111; Marker *v.* Kenrick, 13 C. B. 188.
(*l*) Herne *v.* Benbow, 4 Taunt. 764; Gibson *v.* Wells, 1 Bos. & P. N. R. 290; Martin *v.* Gilham, 7 A. & E. 540; Harnett *v.* Maitland, 16 M. & W. 257.
(*m*) Burchell *v.* Hornsby, 1 Camp. 360.
(*n*) 3 & 4 Will. IV. c. 42, s. 2.
(*o*) See *post*, p. 239.

(*p*) See Hayne *v.* Cummings, 16 C. B. N.S. 421.
(*q*) Doe *d.* Hills *v.* Morris, 11 L. J. Ex. 313; Bennett *v.* Herring, 3 C. B. N.S. 370; Baylis *v.* Le Gros, 4 C. B. N.S. 537.
(*r*) Hill *v.* Barclay, 16 Ves. 405; City of London *v.* Nash, 1 Ves. 12; Lucas *v.* Commerford, 3 Bro. C. C. 166; Paxton. *v.* Newton, 2 Sm. & Giff. 437.

No injunction will be granted by a court of equity to restrain an action of ejectment for not repairing (s).

3. INJUNCTION.

1. The plaintiff in an action on the case for commissive waste may claim a writ of injunction against the repetition or continuance of the act complained of (t). The writ of summons must be indorsed with a notice in the prescribed form of the intention to claim a writ of injunction (u). The injunction must also be claimed in the declaration (v). The application for the injunction must be to the Judge at chambers, or the Court *in banc*, supported by affidavits.

Injunction at common law.

2. The party to whom the reversion belongs may apply to the Court of Chancery for an injunction to restrain commissive waste (w), and this is a most efficient remedy, as the Court interferes to prevent the injury from being done, and does not merely grant a remedy for it when done.

Injunction in Chancery.

An injunction was given to restrain injury to fishponds (x). Tenants are usually restrained from re-

(s) Hill v. Barclay, 16 Ves. 405; Gregory v. Wilson, 9 Hare, 683; Job v. Banister, 2 Kay & J. 374, 26 L. J. Ch. 125. See, however, Bargent v. Thompson, 4 Giff. 473; Bamford v. Creasy, 3 Giff. 675.
(t) See the 17 & 18 Vict. c. 125, ss. 79-82.
(u) Reg. Mich. Vac. 1854, No. 36, 4 E. & B. 384.
(v) Bull & L. l. 343, 3d edit.; De la Rue v. Fortescue, 2 H. & N. 324, 26 L. J. Ex. 339.
(w) Com. Dig. Chancery (D) 11; Smith v. Carter, 18 Beav. 78; Duke of Beaufort v. Bates, 31 L. J. Ch. 481; Farrant v. Lovel, 3 Atk. 723; Jackson v. Cator, 5 Ves. 688; Mayor of Loudon v. Hedger, 18 Ves. 355; Norway v. Rowe, 19 Ves. 154; Hindley v. Emery, L. R. 1 Eq. 52, 35 L. J. Ch. 6; Onslow v. ——, 16 Ves. 173; Pratt v. Brett, 2 Madd. 62; Drury v. Molins, 6 Ves. 328; Lord Grey de Wilton v. Saxon, 6 Ves. 106; Kimpton v. Eve, 2 V. & B. 349.
(x) Earl of Bathurst v. Burden, 2 Bro. C. C. 64.

moving hay, straw, dung, &c., contrary to their express covenants, and from removing fixtures attached to the freehold (*y*). Where the lease contained no express covenant not to plough the pasture, but a covenant to manage pasture in a husband-like manner, an injunction was granted to restrain the tenant from ploughing the pasture (*z*).

In granting an injunction to restrain the tenant from breaking up a meadow for the purpose of building, contrary to an express covenant in the lease, Eldon, L.Ch., said that he did so upon the ground of the covenant not to convert the meadow, otherwise he should doubt whether it would do upon the ground of waste, without any affidavit that it was ancient meadow (*a*).

The Court will not grant an injunction against a tenant for having done an act of waste for which merely nominal damages would be given, where it appears that he has not the least intention to commit further waste (*b*).

The Court will restrain a tenant from committing acts in the nature of waste against the wish of the landlord, even if they be to the landlord's advantage (*c*), but not if the landlord stand by at first and see the act done and approve of it (*d*).

A mortgagor may have an injunction to stay waste

(*y*) Kimpton *v*. Eve, 2 V. & B. 352 ; Pratt *v*. Brett, 2 Madd. 62; Fleming *v*. Snook, 5 Beav. 250.
(*z*) Drury *v*. Molins, 6 Ves. 328.
(*a*) Lord Grey de Wilton *v*. Saxon, 6 Ves. 106.

(*b*) Doran *v*. Carroll, 11 Ir. Ch. R. 379.
(*c*) Smyth *v*. Carter, 18 Beav. 78.
(*d*) See Brydges *v*. Kilbourne, cited in Jackson *v*. Cator, 5 Ves. 688.

against a mortgagee for cutting down timber, and not applying the proceeds of the sale in sinking the principal and interest; and so likewise may a mortgagee where a mortgagor commits waste (*e*). A tenant in common may have an injunction to restrain his co-tenant from committing destructive waste (*f*); but not from farming contrary to the custom of the country, because the relation of landlord and tenant does not exist between them (*g*).

A covenant to repair and leave in good condition will not prevent the landlord from claiming an injunction (*h*), nor will a right of re-entry (*i*).

In order to obtain an injunction, some actual waste, or some act showing an intention to commit actual waste, must appear by affidavit (*j*), as sending a surveyor out to mark trees, or threatening or insisting upon the right to commit waste (*k*).

Where a lease is made " without impeachment of waste," the tenant will not be restrained from cutting timber, ploughing pasture land, opening mines, &c. (*l*), but he will be restrained from pulling down houses, defacing seats, or cutting down ornamental or sheltering timber (*m*).

(*e*) Farrant *v.* Lovel, 3 Atk. 723.
(*f*) Arthur *v.* Lamb, 2 D. & S. 428.
(*g*) Bailey *v.* Hobson, L. R. 5 Ch. 180, 39 L. J. Ch. 270.
(*h*) Mayor of London *v.* Hedger, 18 Ves. 355.
(*i*) Parker *v.* Whyte, 1 H. & M. 167, 32 L. J. Ch. 520.
(*j*) Amos on Fixtures, 284 (2d edit.)
(*k*) Jackson *v.* Cator, 5 Ves. 688; Gibson *v.* Smith, 2 Atk. 182, Barnard, 491, 497; Tipping *v.* Eckersley, 2 K. & J. 264.

(*l*) Com. Dig. tit. Chancery, (D) 11.
(*m*) Williams *v.* Day, 2 Cas. Ch. 32; Packington's case, 3 Atk. 215; Garth *v.* Cotton, Id. 756; Chamberlayne *v.* Dumorier, 1 Bro. C. C. 166, 3 Id. 549; Marquis of Downshire *v.* Lady Sandys, 6 Ves. 107; Ford *v.* Tynte, 31 L. J. Ch. 177. As to "ornamental" timber, see Williams *v.* M'Namara, 8 Ves. 70; and Coffin *v.* Coffin, Jacob. 70.

Q

DIVISION II.—RIGHTS OF TENANT.

CHAPTER I.

POSSESSION AND QUIET ENJOYMENT.

	PAGE		PAGE
1. Right to Possession and Quiet Enjoyment	242	2. Remedies for Disturbance	243
		3. Right to a Lease	244

1. Right to Possession and Quiet Enjoyment.

Right to possession and quiet enjoyment.
As we have seen, the rights of the landlord are chiefly —first, to have his rent paid; and, secondly, to restrain his tenant from committing waste, or damaging the property by neglect. Upon the other hand, the principal rights which a tenant possesses are—first, a right to have and retain possession during the term, and peaceably and quietly to enjoy the property without disturbance.

The subject of quiet enjoyment is treated of *ante*, pp. 131–132, as far as relates to covenants, whether implied or expressed, as well as to breaches of such covenants.

With respect to the right to possession, it only remains to be said, that in Messent v. Reynolds (a), it was doubted whether a contract for quiet enjoyment could be implied from a mere agreement to let; but in Coe v. Clay it was held that he who lets agrees to give possession, and not merely to give a chance of a lawsuit, so that the lessees may recover damages for a breach of such agreement, and is not left to a remedy by ejectment (b).

2. REMEDIES FOR DISTURBANCE.

For the breach of covenants for quiet enjoyment, where the lease is under seal, an action of covenant will lie (c). If the demise be not under seal, and there be an express agreement for quiet enjoyment, the tenant upon breach may bring *assumpsit* (d) or case (e).

Remedies for disturbance.

In cases of implied contract of indemnity against distress, the proper form of remedy is an action of tort (f).

With respect to the damages for a breach of a covenant for quiet enjoyment, where the lessor had not power to grant the lease, but the tenant obtained a fresh lease of less value from the person having power, it was held that the tenant was entitled to be indemnified for his loss by breach of the covenant, and,

---

(a) 3 C. B. 194.
(b) 5 Bing. 440; Jinks v. Edwards, 11 Ex. 775. See Hawkes v. Orton, 5 A. & E. 367; and see Locke v. Furze, 19 C. B. N.S. 96, L. R. 1 C. P. 441, 34 L. J. C. P. 201, 35 Id. 141.
(c) Dawson v. Dyer, 5 B. & Ad. 584.
(d) Granger v. Collins, 6 M. & W. 458; Hancock v. Caffyn, 8 Bing. 358.
(e) Burnet v. Lynch, 8 D. & R. 368; Hancock v. Caffyn, *supra*.
(f) Hancock v. Caffyn, *supra*.

therefore, in this case, to the difference in value of the void lease and of the valid lease (*g*).

The tenant may also have a remedy by injunction. The Court of Chancery will restrain a landlord from cutting down ornamental trees which he has allowed the tenant to plant (*h*); so the tenant may restrain the landlord from committing a nuisance (*i*), obstructing lights (*j*), or a sea view, contrary to agreement (*k*), and in many other cases.

3. Right to a Lease.

Right to a lease.

Somewhat akin to the right of the tenant to have the peaceable enjoyment of his property, is his right to compel his landlord, under certain circumstances, to grant him a lease. Thus, if the landlord covenant or agree in writing to grant a lease, the Court of Chancery will decree specific performance of the agreement (*l*).

So also where the tenant is in possession under a mere oral agreement, and has been permitted by the landlord to expend money on the faith of a contract; in reasonable pursuance of such contract, he will be entitled to have a lease granted to him (*m*); but if

---

(*g*) Locke *v*. Furze, *ante*, p. 243, note (b). See Rolph *v*. Crouch, L. R. 3 Ex. 44, 37 L. J. Ex. 8.

(*h*) Jackson *v*. Cator, 5 Ves. 688; Nicholson *v*. Rose, 4 De Gex & J. 10.

(*i*) Tipping *v*. Eckersley, 2 Kay & J. 264; Lingwood *v*. Stowmarket Co. L. R. 1 Eq. 77.

(*j*) Fox *v*. Purcell, 3 Sm. & Giff. 242.

(*k*) Piggott *v*. Stratton, 1 De Gex. F. & J. 33, 44.

(*l*) Martin *v*. Pycroft, 2 De G. M. & G. 798; Rankin *v*. Lay, 29 L. J. Ch. 734; Parker *v*. Taswell, 27 ib. 812; Middleton *v*. Greenwood, 2 De G. J. & S. 142.

(*m*) Powell *v*. Thomas, 6 Hare, 304; Pain *v*. Coombs, 3 Sm. & G. 464; Nunn *v*. Fabian, L. R. 1 Ch. 35; Farrall *v*. Davenport, 3 Giff. 363; Wills *v*. Stradling, 3 Ves. 378; Stockley *v*. Stockley, 1 V. & B. 23; Sutherland *v*. Briggs, 1 Hare, 26; Surcombe *v*. Pinniger, 3 De G. M. & G. 571;

the expenditure be merely such as is incidental to his oral agreement—as, for instance, in the ordinary course of husbandry—he would not be entitled to have a lease granted to him (*n*).

Where there was an understanding between the landlord and tenant that, so long as the tenant was a good customer in using a canal, he should have the use of the waste water for his works, it was held that he was not entitled to a decree for specific performance of such understanding; but if the water was essential, or anything like essential, to the works, he might have been entitled to a decree (*o*).

Price *v.* Salusbury, 32 Beav. 446.
And see Frame *v.* Dawson, 14 Ves. 380; Lindsay *v.* Linch, 2 Sch. & Lef. 1.

(*n*) Brennan *v.* Bolton, 2 Dru. & W. 349.
(*o*) Bankark *v.* Tennant, L. R. 10 Eq. 141, 39 L. J. Ch. 809.

PART III.

DETERMINATION OF TENANCY.

CHAPTER I.

EFFLUXION OF TIME.

Effluxion of time.
WHEN the lease is for a term of years certain, the tenancy is determined upon the expiration of the term, and the landlord is entitled to possession. Should the tenant hold over, he becomes a tenant on sufferance; or should there be any circumstances, such as the payment and acceptance of rent, indicating an intention to create a yearly tenancy, he will be a tenant from year to year, upon such of the terms of the original lease as are applicable to such a tenancy (*a*).

Where the term is limited conditionally upon the happening of some event, the term will cease at the expiration of the time, or on the happening of the event (*b*). But "if a house be letten to one to hold at will, by force whereof the lessee entereth into the house, and brings his household stuff into the same,

(*a*) Doe d. Hollingworth *v.* Stennett, 2 Esp. 717; Bishop *v.* Howard, 2 B. & C. 100; Doe d. Thomson *v.* Amey, 12 A. & E. 746; Hyatt *v.* Griffiths, 17 Q. B. 505.

(*b*) Hughes & Crowther's case, 13 Co. R. 66; Brudnell's case, 5 Co. R. 9; Doe d. Lockwood *v.* Clarke, 8 East. 185.

and after the lessor puts him out, yet he shall have free entry, egress, and regress into the said house, by reasonable time to take away his goods and utensils" (c). And a stipulation in a weekly tenancy that, after the expiration of the tenancy, the tenant should have a reasonable time to remove his goods, has been held to be good (d).

(c) Litt. s. 69, Co. Litt. 56 a.

(d) Cornish v. Stubbs, L. R. 5 C. P. 334, 39 L. J. C. P. 202.

CHAPTER II.

SURRENDER.

	PAGE		PAGE
1. EXPRESS AT COMMON LAW, AND SINCE THE STATUTE OF FRAUDS—	248	2. BY OPERATION OF LAW— *taking a new lease* ... *other acts* ... *by merger* ...	250 251 252
who may surrender ...	249		
to whom surrender may be made	249	3. EFFECT OF A SURRENDER ON UNDER-LEASES—	254
in what words	249	*operation of merger* ...	255

1. EXPRESS AT COMMON LAW, AND SINCE THE STATUTE OF FRAUDS.

Express at common law, and since the Statute of Frauds.

A SURRENDER is the yielding up an estate for life, or years, to him who has the immediate estate in reversion or remainder, either in fee or for any less estate (*a*), and may be either in express terms, that is, by deed, or note in writing, signed by the party surrendering, or his agent thereunto lawfully authorised by writing, or by act and operation of law (*b*). The surrender, if made after the 1st day October 1845, must be by deed, unless the interest surrendered is copyhold, or of such a nature that it could by law have been created without writing (*c*), in which cases the surrender may be in writing. Where the term

(*a*) Com. Dig. Surrender (H); Bac. Abr. Leases, (S) 1-3; Co. Litt. 337; Challoner *v.* Davis, 1 Lord Raymond, 402; Hughes *v.* Rowbotham, Cro. Eliz. 302.
(*b*) 29 Car. II. c. 3. s. 3.
(*c*) 8 & 9 Vict. c. 106, s. 3.
(*d*) Wms. Saund. 236 c, note (*n*).

could not have been created except by deed, it cannot be otherwise surrendered, unless indeed it be surrender by the operation of law (*d*).

In order to effect an express surrender, the surrenderor must have an estate in possession at the time of the surrender. There can be no express surrender, therefore, before entry, for the lessee has not the possession until he has entered. His assignee, however, can surrender without actual entry, for the entry of the lessee severs the possession from the reversion, and the assignment transfers it to the assignee (*e*). It is otherwise with a surrender in law. If, therefore, the lessee takes a second lease before the first has commenced, this will operate as a surrender in law of the first lease (*f*). *Who may surrender.*

A surrender can only be made to him who has the immediate reversion or remainder expectant on the interest to be surrendered, and consequently there must be no intervening interest between the term to be surrendered and the estate of the surrenderee, which must also be of a higher and greater nature than the interest of the surrenderor. It is also necessary that there should be a privity of estate between the surrenderor and surrenderee, who must have the estate in his own right and not in that of another, and be seized solely and not as joint-tenant (*g*). *To whom the surrender may be made.*

The words most commonly used in surrenders are "surrender and yield up;" but any words expressing an immediate intention of giving up the estate, if *In what words the surrender should be made.*

(*d*) Cole Eject. 225; M'Garth *v.* Shannon, 17 Ir. Com. L. R. 128.
(*e*) Bac. Abr. Leases (S) 2.
(*f*) Shep. Touch. 302; Jez *v*
Sams, Cro. Eliz. 521; Hutchins *v.* Martin, Cro. Eliz. 605.
(*g*) Shep. Touch. 303; 2 Black. Com. 336. See, however, Shep. Touch. 308.

accepted by the landlord, will be sufficient (*h*). The Court, however, will not construe an informal document as a surrender where there is no intention to surrender at all (*i*), or where there is merely an intention to surrender upon a condition which has not been performed (*j*).

2. SURRENDER BY OPERATION OF LAW.

Taking a new lease.

A surrender by operation of law is where the lessee, with some object other than that of surrendering his lease, is party to some act which cannot be effected while the lease continues, and the validity of which he is estopped from disputing (*k*). If, therefore, the tenant accept a new lease, to take effect during the continuance of a previous lease, this is a surrender in law of the latter lease, for the two leases are incompatible, and the acceptance of the second shows that the lessee contemplated the destruction of the first (*l*). There must, however, be an actual and valid demise. A mere agreement for a lease (*m*), and *a fortiori* an agreement between the lessor and a stranger that the lessee shall have a new lease (*n*), or a void or voidable lease (*o*), will not operate as a surrender of the sub-

(*h*) Farmer *v.* Rogers, 2 Wils. 26 ; Smith *v.* Mapleback, 1 T. R. 441 ; Weddall *v.* Copes, 1 M. & W. 50 ; Shep. Touch, 306 ; Lloyd *v.* Langford, 2 Mod. 175 ; Williams *v.* Sawyer, 3 Brod. & Bing. 70 ; Parmenter *v.* Webber, 8 Taunt. 593 ; Doe *d.* Wyatt *v.* Stagg, 5 Bing. N. C. 564.

(*i*) Lyon *v.* Reed, 13 M. & W. 285 ; Doe *d.* Murrell *v.* Milward, 3 M. & W. 328 ; Bessell *v.* Landsberg, 7 Q. B. 638 ; Weddall *v.* Copes, 1 M. & W. 50.

(*j*) Coupland *v.* Maynard, 12 East. 134.

(*k*) Lyon *v.* Reed, 13 M. & W.

285 ; Bessell *v.* Landsberg, 7 Q. B. 368 ; Com. Dig. Surrender, (I) ; 20 Vin. Abr. Surrender, (F), (G).

(*l*) Davison *d.* Bromley *v.* Stanley, 4 Burr. 2110 ; Crowley *v.* Vitty, 7 Ex. 319, 21 L. J. Ex. 136 ; Furnivall *v.* Grove, 8 C. B. N.S. 496, 30 L. J. C. P. 3 ; Roll. Abr. Surrender.

(*m*) John *v.* Jenkins, 1 Cr. & M. 227 ; Foquet *v.* Moore, 7 Ex. 870 ; Cannon *v.* Hartley, 9 C. B. 634, 19 L. J. C. P. 323 ; Badeley *v.* Vigurs, 23 L. J. Q. B. 297.

(*n*) Porris *v.* Allen, Cro. Eliz. 173.

(*o*) Zouch *d.* Abbot *v.* Parsons, 3 Burr. 1807 ; Wilson *v.* Sewell,

sisting lease, nor will the acceptance of a new lease by the lessee in trust for another (*p*). If the new lease is for part only of the land included in the old, the old lease will be surrendered as to that part, but will continue to exist as to the residue (*q*).

If there be two lessees, and one take a new lease, it is a surrender of his moiety (*r*).

The new lease must also take effect during the continuance of the old lease (*s*), for if the new lease is not to begin until the happening of some future event, it will not operate as a surrender of the first lease until the event takes place (*t*).

A surrender will also be effected where the tenant accepts some interest in the property demised inconsistent with the existence of the lease, as a grant of common or rent, provided always that such interest commences during the term (*u*). It is otherwise, however, if the grant is consistent with the continuance of the lease (*v*). Not only the acceptance of a new lease by the lessee, but the granting of a new lease by the lessor to a stranger, or to the old tenant and a stranger (*w*), with

Other acts.

4 Burr. 1980, 1 W. Blac. 617; Roe *d*. Earl Berkeley *v*. Archbishop of York, 6 East. 86, 2 Smith, 166; Davison *d*. Bromley *v*. Stanley, 4 Burr, 2210, Com. Dig. Estate (G), 13; Doe *d*. Biddulph *v*. Poole, 11 Q. B. 713: Doe *d*. Earl Egremont *v*. Courtenay, 11 Q. B. 702. See, however, Doe *d*. Murray *v*. Bridges, 1 B. & Ad. 847.

(*p*) Com. Dig. Surrender, (H, L) 1.

(*q*) Earl of Carnarvon *v*. Villibois, 13 M. & W. 342; per Alderson, B. Morrison *v*. Chadwick, 7 C. B. 266, Bac. Abr. Leases, (D) 3.

(*r*) Shep. Touch. 302.

(*s*) Ive *v*. Sams, Cro. Eliz. 522; Hutchins *v*. Martin, Cro. Eliz. 604.

(*t*) Bac. Abr. Leases, (S) 53; Doe *d*. Gray *v*. Stanion, 1 M. & W. 695; Juste *v*. Darby, 15 M. & W. 601.

(*u*) Gybson *v*. Searle, Cro. Jac. 84, 177; Com. Dig. Surrender, (I) 1; Mellows *v*. May, Cro. Eliz. 874; Peter *v*. Kendal, 6 B. & C. 703.

(*v*) Gie *v*. Rider, 1 Sid. 75; Earl of Arundel *v*. Lord Gray, 2 Dyer, 200 b; Woodward *v*. Aston, 1 Ventr. 296.

(*w*) Hamerton *v*. Stead, 3 B. & C. 478.

the assent of the lessee, will operate as a surrender of the old lease (*x*), and so will an agreement by the landlord to accept a third person in the place of the tenant, provided the agreement is in writing, or the third person actually takes possession (*y*). But the mere quitting by the tenant with the assent of the landlord will not (*z*) unless the lessor accepts possession (*a*).

By merger. A lease for years may be determined by merger, that is, by the union of the term with the immediate reversion (*b*), both being vested (*c*) in one person at the same time and in the same right (*d*). Where the particular estate and that in immediate reversion are both legal and both equitable, and they become vested in one person, they will merge; but it seems that the conveyance of the reversion in fee to a trustee expressly to avoid the merger will have the effect of preventing a merger (*e*). In order to effect a merger, it is not necessary that the reversion should be of a duration greater than or even equal to that of the term

(*x*) Nickells *v.* Atherstone, 10 Q. B. 944; Walls *v.* Atcheson, 3 Bing. 462; Davison *v.* Gent, 1 H. & N. 744, 26 L. J. Ex. 122; Thomas *v.* Cook, 2 B. & Ad. 119; Wilson *v.* Sewell, 4 Burr. 1975; Hall *v.* Burgess, 5 B. & C. 332; Woodcock *v.* Nuth, 8 Bing. 170; Bees *v.* Williams, 2 C. M. & R. 581; Lyon *v.* Reid, 13 M. & W. 285; Phipps *v.* Sculthorpe, 1 B. & A. 50; Hyde *v.* Moakes, 5 C. & P. 42.

(*y*) Taylor *v.* Chapman, Peake, Add. Cas. 19; Stouc *v.* Whiting, 2 Stark. 235; Nickells *v.* Atherstone, 10 Q. B. 944; Walker *v.* Richardson, 2 M. & W. 882.

(*z*) Mollett *v.* Brayne, 2 Camp. 103; Thompson *v.* Wilson, 2 Stark, 379; Doe *d.* Huddleston *v.* Johnson, 1 M'Clel. & G. 141;

Johnson *v.* Huddleston, 4 B. & C. 922; Doe *d.* Murrell *v.* Milward, 3 M. & W. 328; Cannan *v.* Hartley, 9 C. B. 634, 19 L. J. C. P. 323.

(*a*) Bac. Abr. Leases, 211; Grimman *v.* Legge, 8 B. & C. 324; Brown *v.* Burtinshaw, 7 D. & R. 603; Furnivall *v.* Grove, 8 C. B. N.S. 496, 30 L. J. C. P. 3; Reeve *v.* Bird, 1 C. M. & R. 31; Dodd *v.* Acklom, 6 M. & G. 672.

(*b*) Burton *v.* Barclay 7 Bing. 745.

(*c*) Vested, that is, in estate; a mere *interesse termini* will not merge in the freehold. Doe *d.* Rawlings *v.* Walker, 5 B. & C. 111.

(*d*) Bac. Abr. Leases (R); Salmon *v.* Swan, Cro. Jac. 619.

(*e*) Belaney *v.* Belaney, L. R. 2 Ch. Ap. 138, 36 L. J. Ch. 265.

merged (*f*). With respect to estates not vested in the same right, it appears to have been thought by Lord Coke (*g*) that a man might have a term of years in *autre droit*, and a freehold in his own right, but that he could not by possibility have a term of years in his own right and a freehold in *autre droit* to consist together. The latter position, however, cannot be maintained after the decision in Platt *v.* Sleap (*h*), and Jones *v.* Davies (*i*), in which it was held that the husband being termor, and the fee descending upon or being devised to his wife, there was no merger. A distinction has been drawn, in the case of estates in different rights, between cases in which the second estate is acquired by the act of the husband himself, and those in which it comes to him without any act on his part; and it has been contended that in the former class of cases a merger takes place in law though not in equity (*j*). In Lishden *v.* Winsmore (*k*), however, it was said—though no decision was finally had upon it—that where the lessee granted his estate to the husband of the reversioner, the two estates did not merge, as the husband held them in different rights—the term in his own right, and the reversion in right of his wife. Whichever may be the true opinion, it is clear that neither in the case of a devise of the fee to the wife of the termor (*l*), nor in that of the marriage of the man seized of the freehold with the lessee (*m*), is there such an act on the part of the husband as to cause a merger

(*f*) Hughes *v.* Robotham, Cro. Eliz. 302, Poph. 30; Stephens *v.* Bridges, 6 Madd. 66.
(*g*) Co. Litt. 338 b.
(*h*) Cro. Jac. 275.
(*i*) 5 H. & N. 766, S. C.; on appeal, 7 H. & N. 507.
(*j*) Shep. Touch. p. 303, note (a); Cruise Dig. tit. xxxix. Merger, s. 49, p. 53; Webb *v.* Russell, 3 T. R. 393.

(*k*) 2 Roll. Rep. 472. See also the opinion of Lord Holt in Gage *v.* Acton, 1 Salk. 326, and of Hobart, C. J. in Young *v.* Bradfroot, Hob.; and the case of Jones *v.* Davies, 5 H. & N. 777.
(*l*) Jones *v.* Davies, 5 H. & N. 766.
(*m*) Bracebridge *v.* Cook, Plow. Com. 417.

of the term. Whether a termor, who is also tenant by the courtesy after the death of his wife holds both estates in his own right so as to cause a merger, has not been decided; but it has been held that, at any rate, during the life of the wife, the tenancy by the courtesy initiate is not such an estate, or is not held in such a right, as will merge a term possessed by the husband in his own right (*n*).

3. EFFECT OF A SURRENDER ON UNDER-LEASES.

Effect of a surrender.

The surrender of a lease will not prejudice an under-lease (*o*), or any other interest or right created by the lessee before the surrender—as, for instance, a mortgage of the tenant's fixtures (*p*). Formerly, if a lessee who had created an under-lease surrendered his term, the reversion on the under-lease being gone, the rent reserved and the covenants contained in the under-lease were gone also (*q*). This inconvenience was remedied by the 4 Geo. II., c. 28, s. 6; and now by the 8 & 9 Vict., c. 106, s. 9, if a reversion expectant on a lease is surrendered, the estate which confers, as against the tenant, the next vested right to the tenement, shall be deemed the reversion for the purpose of preserving the incidents to, and obligations on, the reversion.

By the surrender the lease, with all its incidents, is entirely gone, so that no action can be maintained for

(*n*) Jones *v.* Davies, 5 H. & N. 766, 29 L. J. Ex. 374.
(*o*) Doe *d.* Beaden *v.* Pyke, 5 M. & S. 146; Pleasant *v.* Benson, 14 East. 232; Torriano *v.* Young, 6 Car. & P. 8; Pigott *v.* Stratton, 1 De G. F. & J. 44, 29 L. J. Ch. 1, 8.

(*p*) London and Westminster Loan and Discount Co. Limited *v.* Drake, 6 C. B. N.S. 798.
(*q*) Shep. Touch. 301; Threr *v.* Barton, Moor. 94; Webb *v.* Russell, 3 T. R. 393; Burton *v.* Barclay, 7 Bing. 756.

rent previously due, except where there is a personal covenant for its payment, in which case an action may be brought on the covenant (*r*). Rent accruing at the time the surrender is made is entirely lost (*s*).

The operation of a merger was similar to that of a surrender (*t*), and was similarly remedied by the 8 & 9 Vict., c. 106, s. 9 (*u*).

Operation of merger.

(*r*) Att.-Gen. *v.* Cox, 3 H. L. Cas. 240.
(*s*) Grimman *v.* Legge, 8 B. & C. 324; Slack *v.* Sharp, 8 A. & E. 366; Dodd *v.* Acklom, 6 M. & G. 973; Doe *d.* Philip *v.* Benjamin, 9 A. & E. 644; Furnivall *v.* Grove, 8 C. B. N.S. 496.
(*t*) Webb *v.* Russell, 3 T. R. 393; Thorne *v.* Woolcombe, 3 B. & Ad. 586.
(*u*) *Ante*, p. 254.

CHAPTER III.

FORFEITURE.

	PAGE		PAGE
1. RE-ENTRY FOR—	... 256	2. WAIVER	259
by whom	... 256	3. DISCLAIMER	262
for non-payment of rent	257		

1. RE-ENTRY.

Re-entry for. A LEASE may be determined by entry or ejectment for a forfeiture incurred by breach of an express or implied condition, but not for a mere breach of covenant without proviso for re-entry (*a*). If the tenant do any act unequivocally (*b*) inconsistent with his character as tenant (*c*); as if, being tenant for years, he make a feoffment, or give up possession to a party claiming an adverse title to the lessor (*d*); or if he be guilty of a breach of any express condition in the lease, a forfeiture will be incurred for which the landlord may enter (*e*).

By whom. In general no one can re-enter for a forfeiture but the person legally entitled to the reversion (*f*). A

(*a*) Doe *d*. Wilson *v.* Phillips, 2 Bing. 13; Doe *d*. Rudd *v.* Golding, 6 Moo. 231; Doe *d.* Rains *v.* Kneller, 4 C. & P. 3; Doe *d*. Darke *v.* Bowditch, 8 Q. B. 973.
(*b*) See Ackland *v.* Lutley, 9 A. & E. 879.
(*c*) Bac. Abr. Leases, (T) 2, Co. Litt. 215 a.

(*d*) Doe *d*. Ellerbroch *v.* Flynn, 1 C. M. & N. 137.
(*e*) Rees *v.* Ervington, Cro. Eliz. 322; Fenn *d*. Matthews *v.* Smart, 12 East. 444; Goodright *d.* Walters *v.* Davids, Cowp. 803.
(*f*) Doe *d*. Barney *v.* Adams, C. & J. 232; Doe *d.* Barker *v.* Goldsmith, 2 C. & J. 674; Doe *d*.

reversioner who has parted with his reversion, either absolutely or by way of mortgage, cannot enter or maintain ejectment for a forfeiture (*g*). But where a termor demised his whole interest, subject to a right of re-entry on the breach of a condition, it was held that he might enter for the condition broken, although he had no reversion (*h*).

By the 32 Hen. VIII., c. 34, all grantees of the reversion, their heirs, executors, successors, and assigns, shall have the like advantage (as their grantors had) against the lessees by entry for non-payment of rent, or for doing waste or other forfeiture.

As to the construction of this Act, see *infra*, Part 4, " Change of Parties," c. 1, s. 3.

In order to make an effectual re-entry for a forfeiture, the lessor must do some act showing an intention to enter for the forfeiture (*i*); and where he brings ejectment for a forfeiture, the onus of proving the forfeiture lies upon him (*j*).

Where there is a condition of re-entry upon non-payment of the rent, the landlord must make a formal demand, unless there are express words in the lease or agreement dispensing with such demand (*k*), or the

For non-payment of rent.

Barber *v.* Lawrence, 4 Taunt. 23, Litt. *s.* 347, Co. Litt. 414 b; Moore *v.* Earl of Plymouth, 3 B. & Ald. 66.

(*g*) Fenn *d.* Matthews *v.* Smart, 12 East. 443; Doe *d.* Marriott *v.* Edwards, 5 B. & Ad. 1065; Doe *d.* Price *v.* Ongley, 10 C. B. 25; Webb *v.* Russell, 3 T. R. 393, 402.

(*h*) Doe *d.* Freeman *v.* Bateman, 2 B. & Ald. 168, Litt. s. 325.

(*i*) Fenn *d.* Matthews *v.* Smart,

12 East. 444, 451; Arnsby *v.* Woodward, 6 B. & C. 519; Roberts *v.* Davey, 4 B. & Ad. 664; Baylis *v.* Le Gros, 4 C. B. N.S. 537, 6 Id. 552.

(*j*) Doe *d.* Bridger *v.* Whitehead, 8 A. & E. 571; Toleman *v.* Portbury, L. R. 5 Q. B. Ex. Ch. 288, 39 L. J. Q. B. 136.

(*k*) See Doe *d.* Harris *v.* Masters, 2 B. & C. 490.

R

case falls within 15 & 16 Vict., c. 76, s. 210 (*l*). 1. Such demand must be made by the landlord or his agent duly authorised (*m*). 2. It must be made precisely on the day when the rent is due and payable. Thus where the proviso is that if the rent shall be behind and unpaid by the space of thirty days after the day of payment, it shall be lawful for the lessor to re-enter, the demand must be made on the thirtieth day (*n*). 3. The demand must be made a convenient time before sunset(*o*). 4. It must be made at the most notorious place on the land (*p*); or if a place is appointed for the payment of the rent, it must be made there (*q*). 5. It must be of the *precise* sum *then* payable (*r*).

By the 15 & 16 Vict., c. 76, s. 210 (*s*), a formal demand of the rent is unnecessary when one half-year's rent is in arrear, and the landlord hath by law right to re-enter for the non-payment thereof, and when no sufficient distress is to be found in the premises countervailing the arrears then due. Where neither the value of the premises, nor the rent payable in respect of them, exceeds £50 by the year, proceedings may be taken, and possession may be recovered, in the County Court (*t*).

The decisious upon the earlier statute, 4 Geo. II.,

(*l*) See *infra*.
(*m*) Roe *d*. West *v*. Davis, 7 East. 363 ; Toms *v*. Wilson, 32 L. J. Q. B. 33 Id. 382.
(*n*) Doe *d*. Dixou *v*. Roe, 7 C. B. 134 ; Doe *d*. Forster *v*. Wandlass, 7 T. R. 117 ; Smith & Bustard's case, 1 Leon. 142; Duppa *v*. Mayo, 1 Wms. Saund. 287.
(*o*) See *ante*, p. 161; Tinkler *v*. Prentice, 4 Tannt. 555 ; Doe *d*. Wheeldon *v*. Paul, 3 C. & P. 613 ; Doe *d*. Murray *v*. Brydges, 2 D. & N. 29 ; Alcocks *v*. Phillips, 5 H. & N. 183.
(*p*) Co. Litt. 201 b ; Maunde's case, 7 Rep. 28 ; Kidwelly *v*. Brand,

Plowd. 70 a, b ; Scot *v*. Scot, Cro. Eliz. 73 ; Wood & Chiver's case, 4 Leon. 180.
(*q*) Co. Litt. 202 a.
(*r*) Fabian & Windsor's case, 6 Leon. 305.
(*s*) Re-enacting s. 2 of 4 Geo. II. c. 28, with certain differences rendered necessary by the effect of new procedure in ejectment. On the construction of this Act, see Doe *d*. Hitchings *v*. Lewis, 1 Burr. 614 ; Doe *d*. Forster *v*. Wandlass, 7 T. R. 117, 1 Wms. Saunds. 287 a.
(*t*) See 19 & 20 Vict. c. 108, s. 52.

c. 28, s. 2, still apply in the construction to be placed on the above statutes. The 4 Geo. II., c. 28, s. 2, does not apply unless the landlord has actually a right of re-entry in respect of the non-payment of half a year's rent at the time of issuing the writ (*u*); nor where the right of re-entry is not absolute, as if the landlord is only to re-enter and hold the premises until the rent is satisfied (*v*). To proceed under these statutes, it must be proved that no sufficient distress was found on the premises (*w*). Therefore every part of the premises should, if possible, be searched with reasonable diligence (*x*). But if the tenant prevent the landlord from entering to distrain, it is not necessary to show that no sufficient distress was on the premises (*y*). If more than half a year's rent is due, it is sufficient to prove that there is no distress sufficient to countervail the arrears of rent (*z*).

2. WAIVER.

As the landlord must do some distinct act showing an intention to claim a forfeiture (*a*), so likewise, upon the other hand, he must not do anything which may operate as a waiver of the forfeiture, if he wishes to determine the lease (*b*); thus he must not distrain for rent after the forfeiture (*c*); but the receipt of rent due

Waiver.

(*u*) Doe *d*. Dixon *v*. Roe, 7 C. B. 134. See Cotesworth *v*. Spokes, 10 C. B. N.S. 103.
(*v*) Doe *d*. Darke *v*. Bowditch, 8 Q. B. 973.
(*w*) Doe *d*. Smelt *v* Fuchau, 15 East. 286.
(*x*) Rees *d*. Powell *v*. King, cited in the judgment in Smith *v*. Jersey, 2 Bro. & Bing. 514; Wheeler *v*. Stevenson, 6 H. & N. 155. See Doe *d*. Haverson *v*. Franks, 2 Car. & Kir. 678.
(*y*) Doe *d*. Chippendale *v*. Dyson, 1 Moo. & M. 77.
(*z*) Cross *v*. Jordan, 8 Ex. 149.

But see Doe *d*. Powell *v*. Roe, 9 Dowl. 548; Doe *d*. Gretton *v*. Roe, 4 C. B. 576; and notes to Day's Common Law Procedure Acts, 3d edit., p. 164.
(*a*) See *ante*, p. 257.
(*b*) Dendy *v*. Nicholl, 4 C. B. N. S. 376, 27 L. J. C. P. 220.
(*c*) Pellatt *v*. Boosey, 31 L. J. C. P. 281; Ward *v*. Day, 4 B. & S. 337, 5 Id. 359, 32 L. J. Q. B. 254; Doe *d*. Griffith *v*. Pritchard, 5 B. & Ad. 765; Cottesworth *v*. Spokes, 10 C. B. N.S. 103, 30 L. J. C. P. 220.

before the happening of the forfeiture will not operate as a waiver (*d*). The receipt of rent due since the forfeiture, or the bringing of an action for it with knowledge of the forfeiture, operates as a waiver (*e*).

Where there was a lease for life rendering rent, with a clause for re-entry on non-payment, and the lessor brought his action for rent in arrear, yet it was adjudged he might still enter for the forfeiture; for the action for the rent did not affirm the lease, because it should be intended to be brought for a duty due upon the contract; but if the lessor had distrained for the rent it would have been otherwise (*f*).

Where there was a covenant to keep in repair, and to repair three months after notice, and a clause for re-entry, the landlord gave notice, and it was held to be a waiver of the forfeiture under the general covenant to keep in repair (*g*).

An insufficient distress for rent has been said to be no bar to an entry for forfeiture (*h*), but it seems that this must be limited to cases arising under the 4 Geo. II., c. 28 (*i*), and that at common law such a distress would operate as a waiver (*j*).

The mere receipt of subsequent rent does not of itself

(*d*) Marsh *v*. Curteys, Cro. Eliz. 528; Price *v*. Worwood, 4 H. & N. 512, 28 L. J. Ex. 329.
(*e*) Anon. 3 Salk. 3; Croft *v*. Lumley, 5 E. & B. 648, 27 L. J. Q. B. 321; Dendy *v*. Nicholl, 4 C. B. N.S. 376, 27 L. J. C. P. 220.
(*f*) Anon. 3 Salk. 3.
(*g*) Doe *d*. Morecraft *v*. Meux, 4 B. & C. 606. See also Doe *d*. Rutzen *v*. Lewis, 5 A. & E. 277;

Roe *d*. Goatley *v*. Paine, 2 Camp. 520.
(*h*) Doe *d*. Taylor *v*. Johnson, 1 Starkey, 411; Brewer *d*. Onslow *v*. Eaton, 3 Doug. 233, cited in Goodright *d*. Charter *v*. Cordwent, 6 T. R. 220, and in Cottesworth *v*. Spokes, *supra*.
(*i*) And see the Common Law, Procedure Act, 1852, s. 210.
(*j*) See Adams on Ejectment, p. 174, 3d edit.

operate as a waiver, it is only evidence which may be rebutted of the election of the lessor not to enter for a forfeiture. The question is, whether the money is received by the lessor as rent *eo nomine* due under the lease (*k*).

After the lessor has by some unequivocal act, as by bringing ejectment, expressed his election to treat the lease as void, a receipt of rent cannot operate to revive it (*l*).

The receipt of rent is no waiver of a forfeiture recurring by reason of a continuing breach of covenant (*m*).

In order to render acceptance of rent, or any other act, a waiver of forfeiture, the lessor must have notice or knowledge of the forfeiture at the time of the acceptance of rent (*n*).

It has been laid down that where the estate or lease is *ipso facto* void by the condition or limitation, no acceptance of the rent after can make it to have a continuance; it is otherwise of an estate or lease voidable by entry (*o*).

By the 23 & 24 Vict., c. 38, s. 6, "where any actual waiver of the benefit of any covenant or condition in any lease on the part of any lessor, or his heirs, exe-

(*k*) See *per* Parke, J., Doe *d.* Griffith *v.* Pritchard, 5 B. & Ad. 776; Doe *d.* Cheney *v.* Batten, Cowp. 243; 1 Smith's Leading Cases, Notes to Dumpor's case, pp. 37, 38.
(*l*) Jones *v.* Carter, 15 M. & W. 718.
(*m*) Doe *d.* Baker *v.* Jones, 5 Ex. 498.

(*n*) Pennant's case, 3 Co. R. 636; Duppa *v.* Mayo, 1 Wms. Saund. 288 a, b, note (16); Goodright *d.* Walker *v.* Davids, 2 Cowp. 803; Roe *d.* Gregson *v.* Harrison, 2 T. R. 425.
(*o*) 1 Co. Inst. 214 b; Pennant's case, *infra*; Finch *v.* Throckmorton, Cro. Eliz. 221. See Void and Voidable Leases, *ante*, p. 150.

cutors, administrators, or assigns, shall be proved to have taken place after the passing of this Act in any one particular instance, such actual waiver shall not be assumed or deemed to extend to any instance, or any breach of covenant or condition, other than that to which such waiver shall specially relate, nor to be a general waiver of the benefits of any such covenant or condition, unless an intention to that effect shall appear."

As to forfeiture upon assigning or underletting and license, see *ante*, Part I., c. 4, ss. 8 and 9.

3. Disclaimer.

Disclaimer. The tenant may commit a forfeiture by disclaiming or denying the landlord's title (either by setting up a title in some third person, or by claiming title in himself) (*p*). Except in cases of tenancies from year to year, or at will, a mere verbal disclaimer will not create a forfeiture (*q*), nor will payment of rent to a third person (*r*), but the disclaimer must be by matter of record. In one case, however, the term was held forfeited by a fraudulent giving up of possession to a third party (*s*).

A disclaimer by tenant from year to year operates as a waiver of notice to quit, and, in effect, determines the tenancy at the election of the landlord (*t*).

(*p*) Bac. Abr. Leases (T) 2; Doe d. Williams *v.* Cooper, 1 M. & G. 139.
(*q*) Doe d. Graves *v.* Wells, 10 Ad. & E. 427.
(*r*) Doe d. Dillon *v.* Parker, Gow. 180; Doe d. Williams *v.* Pasquali, Peake, 196.
(*s*) Doe d. Ellenbrock *v.* Flynn, 1 C. M. & R. 137.

(*t*) Doe d. Bennett *v.* Long, 9 C. & P. 773; Doe d. Grubb *v.* Grubb, 10 B. & C. 816; Doe d. Phillips *v.* Rollings, 4 C. B. 188; Doe d. Davies *v.* Evans, 9 M. & W. 48; Doe d. Lansell *v.* Gower, 17 Q. B. 589; Doe d. Calvert *v.* Frowd, 4 Bing. 560.

In order to constitute a disclaimer, the expressions used must amount to a denial of the existence of the relation of landlord and tenant (*u*).

A tenant or assignee who brings ejectment against his landlord, and attempts to prove a freehold title, makes a disclaimer (*v*).

A disclaimer may be waived by any act of the landlord acknowledging the party disclaiming as his tenant, as by distraining for subsequent rent in arrear (*w*).

(*u*) Doe *d.* Calvert *v.* Frowd, *supra.* And see the numerous cases in Woodfall's "Landlord and Tenant," pp. 326–328, 9th edit.

(*v*) Doe *d.* Jeffries *v.* Whittick, Gow. 195.

(*w*) Doe *d.* David *v.* Williams, 7 C. & P. 322.

CHAPTER IV.

NOTICE TO QUIT.

	PAGE		PAGE
1. Form of Notice	264	4. How Served	272
2. When to be Given	268	5. Waiver of	272
3. By and to Whom Given	270		

1. Form of Notice.

Form of notice. In the absence of any express stipulation it is not necessary that the notice should be in writing (*a*).

A notice to quit will be taken to be a good notice if the tenant could not mistake its nature; but the Court will not construe a notice in a manner at variance with its express language even if the effect of adhering to such language would be to make the notice bad. So notices dated in the wrong year (*b*), or misdescribing the premises (*c*), or their situation, have been held good (*d*). A notice was given in October 1833 to quit premises held under a yearly tenancy from February, " at the expiration of half a year from the delivery of this notice, or at such other time or times

---

(*a*) Timmins *v.* Rowlinson, 3 Burr. 1603; Doe *d.* Lord Macartney *v.* Crick, 5 Esp. 196.
(*b*) Doe *d.* Duke of Bedford *v.* Kightley, 7 T. R. 63. In this case there was evidence of a parol notice.
(*c*) Doe *d.* Cox *v.* —, 4 Esp. 185.
(*d*) Doe *d.* Armstrong *v.* Wilkinson, 12 A. & E. 743.

as your *present* year's holding of the premises shall expire after the expiration of half a year from the delivery of this notice." It was held that this would operate as a notice to quit in February 1835, although the notice was inaccurate, and that the word "*present*" might be rejected as surplusage (*e*).

Upon the other hand, the Courts have declined to give a meaning contrary to the words used, in order to support a notice. Where the notice was given in October 1842, to quit in May next, "or upon such other day or time as the *current* year for which you now hold will expire," which would be in November 1842, it was held a bad notice, for it could not be intended to refer to November 1843. Pateson, J., said, "That if the notice were read as if the words were the 'current year next ending half a year after this notice,' it would be within the case of Doe *d.* Williams *v.* Smith (*f*), and the notice would be good" (*g*).

The notice must not be ambiguous or optional, as, for instance, " I desire you to quit, or else that you agree to pay double rent" (*h*); but a notice to quit at the end of the current year, "on failure whereof I shall require you to pay me double former rent, or value for so long as you detain possession," was held good (*i*).

The time at which the notice requires the tenant to quit must be the expiration of the term of his tenancy (*j*).

(*e*) Doe *d.* Williams *v.* Smith, 5 Ad. & El. 350. See Doe *d.* Mayor of Richmond *v.* Morphett, 7 Q. B. 577; Doe *d.* Lord Huntingtower *v.* Culliford, 4 D. & R. 248.
(*f*) Cited *supra*, note (*e*).
(*g*) Doe *d.* Mayor of Richmond *v.* Morphett, *supra ;* Mills *v.* Goff, 14 M. & W. 72.

(*h*) Doe *d.* Matthews, *v.* Jackson, 1 Doug. 175, *per* Lord Mansfield.
(*i*) Doe *d.* Lyster *v.* Goldwin, 2 Q. B. 143 ; Doe *d.* Matthews *v.* Jackson, *supra.*
(*j*) Roe *d.* Jordon *v.* Ward, 1 H. Bl. 97; Doe *d.* Rawlings *v.* Walker, 7 T. R. 478 ; Doe *d.* Pitcher *v.* Donovan, 1 Taunt. 555 ; Kemp *v.* Derrett, 3 Camp. 510 ;

As to the effect of a notice to quit on Michaelmas Day, &c., and the interpretation put upon such a notice with respect to new or old style, the question turns upon whether the tenant is misled by the terms of the notice or not, and what the parties meant at the time of making the agreement (*k*). Where the agreement is by deed, new Michaelmas Day must be intended (*l*); but where the agreement is by parol, extrinsic evidence may be given of the intention of the parties (*m*).

The notice must extend to all the premises demised, and not merely to a part (*n*); but the Court will incline to construe a notice as a notice to quit the whole of the premises rather than hold it a bad notice (*o*).

A joint-tenant, or tenant in common, may give notice to quit " all his part or share of the demised premises " (*p*).

A notice to quit and give up possession was held not to be bad notwithstanding it did not state to whom the possession was to be given up (*q*).

The notice need not state the day upon which the tenant is to quit, but it is sufficient to give notice to quit " at the expiration of the current year " (*r*), even

Doe *d*. Eyre *v*. Lambley, 2 Esp. 635. And a notice to quit at twelve o'clock at noon on the proper day is bad; Page *v*. More, 15 Q. B. 684.

(*k*) Furley *d*. Mayor of Canterbury *v*. Wood, 1 Esp. 198 ; Doe *d*. Hinde *v*. Vince, 2 Camp. 256.

(*l*) Doe *d*. Spier *v*. Lea, 11 East. 312; Smith *v*. Walton, 8 Bing. 233.

(*m*) Denn *d*. Peters *v*. Hopkinson, 3 D. & R. 507 ; Doe *d*. Hall *v*. Benson, 4 B. & Ald. 588.

(*n*) Right *d*. Fisher *v*. Cuthell, 5

East. 498 ; Doe *d*. Rodd *v*. Archer, 14 East. 245.

(*o*) Doe *d*. Rodd *v*. Archer, *supra* ; Doe *d*. Morgan *v*. Church, 3 Camp. 71.

(*p*) Doe *d*. Whayman *v*. Chaplin, 3 Taunt. 120 ; Cutting *v*. Derby, 2 W. Bl. 1075 ; Doe *d*. Robertson *v*. Gardner, 12 C. B. 323.

(*q*) Doe *d*. Bailey *v*. Foster, 3 C. B. 215.

(*r*) Doe *d*. Lord Huntingtower *v*. Culliford, 4 D. & R. 248 ; Doe *d*. Williams *v*. Smith, 5 A. & E. 350 ;

although upon the face of the notice it does not appear that it was given within the proper time (*s*).

When the date of commencement of the tenancy is unknown, the notice should be to quit on a specified quarter-day, " or at the expiration of the current year of your tenancy which shall expire next after the end of one half year from the service of this notice " (*t*).

So also where different parts of the demised premises are let at different times, the notice should be to quit at the corresponding periods, or at the expiration of the year of the tenancy which will expire next after the expiration of half a year from the delivery of this notice (*u*). A notice to quit which refers to the day of entry on the substantial part of a holding, determines the tenancy as to the other parts of the holding (*v*.)

A notice by an agent is good, without stating the authority of the landlord, provided it is such a notice as the tenant may act upon with safety, and has reason to believe to be binding upon the landlord (*w*).

It is not necessary that the notice should be directed to the tenant, if it be delivered to him as tenant (*x*); and if it be directed to the tenant by a wrong Christian name, and he keeps it, he waives the objection, and will be bound by the notice (*y*).

Doe *d*. Mayor of Richmond *v*. Morphett, 7 Q. B. 577.
(*s*) Doe *d*. Gorst *v*. Timothy, 2 C. & K. 351.
(*t*) Doe *d*. Digby *v*. Steel, 3 Camp. 117; Hirst *v*. Horn, 6 M. & W. 393.
(*u*) Doe *d*. Williams *v*. Smith, 5 A. & E. 350; Woodfall, L. & T. 316, 9th edit.

(*v*) Doe *d*. Davenport *v*. Rhodes, 11 M. & W. 602, 606, and the cases there cited.
(*w*) Jones *v*. Phipps, 37 L. J. Q. B. 198. See also Doe *d*. Lyster *v*. Godwin, 2 Q. B. 143.
(*x*) Doe *d*. Matthewson *v*. Wrightman, 4 Esp. 5.
(*y*) Doe *v*. Spiller, 6 Esp. 70.

A notice to quit need not be attested, and it may be proved by an examined copy or duplicate without notice to produce the original (z).

2. When to be Given.

When to be given.

In general, a tenancy may be determined by half a year's notice expiring at the end of the first or any subsequent year (a), and in the case of a yearly tenancy uncontrolled by custom or special stipulation, such a notice is necessary (b).

The parties may, however, stipulate for a longer or shorter notice, and in that case the notice stipulated for must be given (c), or, under certain circumstances, they may agree that the tenant may quit without giving notice (d). But a stipulation depriving either party of the right of giving notice is bad (e).

Where a "six months'" notice is to be given, it was held by Wood, V.C., that a six lunar months' notice was sufficient (f).

Where the tenancy created is for two or three years at least (g), it cannot be determined by notice to quit before the expiration of that term (h).

(z) Doe d. Fleming v. Somerton, 7 Q. B. 58.
(a) Doe d. Clarke v. Smaridge, 7 Q. B. 957; Doe d. Plumer v. Mainby, 10 Q. B. 473.
(b) Parker d. Walker v. Constable, 3 Wils. 58; Right d. Flower v. Darby, 1 T. R. 159.
(c) Doe d. Green v. Baker, 8 Taunt. 241; Doe d. Robinson v. Dobell, 1 Q. B. 806.
(d) Bethel v. Blencowe, 3 M. & G. 119; Shirley v. Newman, 1

Esp. 266; Sparrow v. Hawkes, 2 Esp. 505.
(e) Doe d. Warner v. Browne, 8 East. 165.
(f) Rodgers v. Dock Company at Kingston-upon-Hull, 34 L. J. Ch. 165.
(g) See *ante*, c. 4, s. 5, Duration of Term, p. 105.
(h) Doe d. Chadborn v. Green, 9 A. & E. 658; Jones v. Nixon, 1 H. & C. 48, 31 L. J. Ex. Ch. 505.

When a lease is determinable upon a certain event, or at a particular period, no notice to quit is necessary, because both parties are equally apprised of the determination of the term (i).

So where a demise is for one year (j), for a number of years (k), till a particular day (l), during joint lives (m), during the continuance of a partnership (n), or during service (o), no notice is necessary. So where a tenant holds under a mere agreement for a lease for a term, no notice to quit is necessary at the end of the term (p). With respect to lodgings, &c., if the tenancy be for a quarter, month, or week, no notice to quit is necessary; but if from quarter to quarter, month to month, week to week, then the corresponding notice must be given.

If there is no custom or stipulation as to the notice, some reasonable notice must be given, even in the case of a weekly tenancy (q).

No notice is necessary in the case of a mere tenancy

(i) *Per* Lord Mansfield, C.J., in Right *v.* Darby, 1 T. R. 162.
(j) Cobb *v.* Stokes, 8 East. 358, 361; Johnstone *v.* Huddlestone, 4 B. & C. 937; Strickland *v.* Maxwell, 2 Cr. & M. 539.
(k) Messenger *v.* Armstrong, 1 T. R. 54; Doe *d.* Godsell *v.* Inglis, 3 Taunt. 54.
(l) Doe *d.* Leeson *v.* Sayer, 3 Camp. 8.
(m) Doe *d.* Bromfield *v.* Smith, 6 East. 530.
(n) Doe *d.* Waithman *v.* Miles, 1 Stark. 181.
(o) Doe *d.* Hughes *v.* Corbett, 9 C. & P. 494.
(p) Doe *d.* Tilt *v.* Stratton, 4 Bing. 446; Doe *d.* Davenish *v.* Moffatt, 15 Q. B. 257; Tress *v.* Savage, 4 E. & B. 36. The case of Chapman *v.* Towner, 6 M. & W. 100, seems to be to the contrary. It is not referred to in the two cases last above cited, nor is the case of Doe *d.* Tilt *v.* Stratton referred to in Chapman *v.* Towner.
(q) Huffel *v.* Armistead, 7 C. & P. 56; Jones *v.* Mills, 10 C. B. N.S. 788, 31 L. J. C. P. 66. Williams, J., thought a week's notice necessary; but the rest of the Court merely stated that there should be some reasonable notice. See also *ante*, pp. 266, 267.

at will (*r*), but some demand of possession or entry must be made on or before ejectment brought (*s*).

A tenant at sufferance, or an intruder, is not even entitled to a demand of possession (*t*).

And so also in the case of a mortgagor who has been allowed to remain in possession (*u*).

Yearly tenants of a mortgagor, who were tenants before the mortgage, are entitled to notice; but those who became tenants after the mortgage are not even entitled to a demand of possession (*v*).

Where the plaintiff claims the lands by a title paramount to the landlord of the defendant, no notice to the defendant is necessary (*w*).

A disclaimer operates as a waiver of notice (*x*).

3. By Whom and to Whom Given.

By whom and to whom given.

A notice to quit should be given by a landlord to his immediate tenant, and not to a mere under-tenant (*y*); and the tenant should give a similar notice to his

(*r*) Doe *d*. Tomes *v*. Chamberlaine, 5 M. & W. 14; Doe *d*. Jones *v*. Jones, 10 B. & C. 718.
(*s*) Goodtitle *d*. Galloway *v*. Herbert, 4 T. R. 680; Denn *d*. Brune *v*. Rawlings, 10 East. 261; Doe *d*. Jacobs *v*. Phillips, 10 Q. B. 130.
(*t*) Doe *d*. Moore *v*. Lawder, 1 Starkie, 308; Doe *d*. Leeson *v*. Sayer, 3 Camp. 8; Doe *d*. Knight *v*. Quigley, 2 Camp. 505.
(*u*) Doe *d*. Roby *v*. Maisey, 8 B.

& C. 767; Doe *d*. Fisher *v*. Giles, 5 Bing. 421; Doe *d*. Snell *v*. Tom, 4 Q. B. 615.
(*v*) Keech *v*. Hall, 1 Doug. 21; 1 Smith, L. C. 505, 5th edit.
(*w*) Doe *d*. Putland *v*. Hilder, 2 B. & A. 782.
(*x*) *Per* Best, C.J., in Doe *d*. Calvert *v*. Frowd, 4 Bing. 560.
(*y*) Pleasant *d*. Hayton *v*. Benson, 14 East. 234; Burn *v*. Phelps, 1 Stark. 94.

under-tenants; although, if they refuse to give up possession, the tenant will still be liable to ejectment (*z*).

A notice to quit given by the tenant should be given to his immediate landlord; and if he is dead, or has assigned, the notice should be given to the person legally entitled to the immediate reversion (*a*).

Notice given to or by an agent properly authorised at the time of giving the notice is sufficient (*b*). So a receiver duly appointed, and with a general authority to let lands from year to year, has implied authority to give notice to quit (*c*). But a mere receiver of rents has no such authority (*d*).

One of several executors or administrators may give notice on behalf of all (*e*).

Joint-tenants and tenants in common, upon giving notice, may severally recover their respective shares which they have jointly demised (*f*); and a notice to quit, signed by one on behalf of all, is sufficient to determine the tenancy as to all (*g*).

A notice to quit, given by a tenant in common, may be to quit his undivided part or share (*h*).

(*z*) Roe *v.* Wiggs, 2 B. & P. N. R. 330.
(*a*) Cole Eject. 46.
(*b*) Doe *d.* Prior *v.* Ongley, 10 C. B. 25; Papillon *v.* Brunton, 5 H. & N. 518, 29 L. J. Ex. 265; Doe *d.* Mann *v.* Walters, 10 B. & C. 626; Doe *d.* Lyster *v.* Godwin, 2 Q. B. 143.
(*c*) Wilkinson *v.* Colley, 5 Burr. 2696; Doe *d.* Marsack *v.* Read, 12 East. 57; Doe *d.* Earl Manvers *v.* Mizem, 2 Moo. & R. 56.
(*d*) Doe *d.* Mann *v.* Walters, *supra, per* Parke, J.
(*e*) Cole Eject. 43.
(*f*) Doe *d.* Whayman *v.* Chaplin, 3 Taunt. 120, Cole. Eject. 44.
(*g*) Doe *d.* Aslin *v.* Somerset, 1 B. & Ad. 135; Doe *d.* Kindersley *v.* Hughes, 7 M. & W. 139.
(*h*) Cutting *v.* Derby, 2 Wm. Bl. 1075; Doe *d.* Robertson *v.* Gardiner, 12 C. B. 323.

4. How Served.

How served.

The notice must be served at the dwelling-house on the party himself, or to his wife or servant (*i*).

But a notice left at the tenant's house merely, there being no evidence of its having come to the hand of the tenant, his wife, or servant, is not sufficient (*j*).

It seems to have been doubted in one case whether service on the wife of the tenant, but not on the premises, was sufficient (*k*).

Where a notice to quit was placed under the door of the tenant's house, and his wife proved that the notice was received by the tenant in due time, it was held a sufficient service (*l*).

So a notice to quit may be sent by post; and where a notice to quit at Michaelmas was sent through the post by the tenant on the morning of the 25th of March, to the place of business of the landlord's agent, and the jury found that the letter was delivered that evening during the hours of business (*m*), although the agent did not find it till the following morning, it was held sufficient (*n*).

5. Waiver of Notice.

Waiver of notice.

By a notice to quit the tenancy is put an end to by

(*i*) Smith *v.* Clarke, 9 Dowl. 202; Jones *d.* Griffiths *v.* Marsh, 4 T. R. 464; Roe *d.* Blair *v.* Street, 2 A. & E. 329; Doe *d.* Neville *v.* Dunbar, M. & M. 10.

(*j*) Doe *d.* Buross *v.* Lucas, 5 Esp. 153.

(*k*) Roe *d.* Blair *v.* Street, 2 A. & E. 329.

(*l*) Alford *v.* Vickery, Car. & M. 280.

(*m*) *Per* Bramwell, B.

(*n*) Papillon *v.* Brunton, 5 H. & M. 518, 29 L. J. Ex. 265.

the agreement of the parties, who can also agree to waive the notice, and so to create a new tenancy (*o*).

Where the landlord has given notice, but the tenant holds over, the landlord cannot waive the notice, and distrain for rent subsequently accruing; for there is no "agreed rent" to distrain for until a new tenancy arises (*p*).

A waiver of notice will be presumed from a receipt of rent as such, subsequently to the expiration of the notice (*q*); but a mere demand is a question of intention, which must be left to the jury (*r*).

So a second notice will operate as a waiver of the first (*s*), unless it be clear that it is not intended to have that effect (*t*).

A good parol notice, however, will not be waived by a subsequent insufficient notice in writing (*u*).

As is stated above, the parties may mutually agree to waive a notice to quit which has been given, but the tenant will not be allowed to take advantage of a mere indulgence on the part of a landlord, and treat it as a waiver (*v*).

A disclaimer operates as a waiver of notice (*w*).

(*o*) Blyth *v.* Dennett, 13 C. B. 180; Dendy *v.* Nicholl, 4 C. B. N.S. 381; Tayleur *v.* Wildin, 37 L. J. Ex. 173.
(*p*) Jenner *v.* Clegg, 1 Moo. & R. 213; Alford *v.* Vickery, 1 Car. & M. 280.
(*q*) Goodright *d.* Charter *v.* Cordwent, 6 T. R. 219; Croft *v.* Lumley, 5 E. & B. 648, 6 H. L. Cas. 672; Blyth *v.* Dennett, 13 C. B. 180.
(*r*) Blyth *v.* Dennett, *supra.*
(*s*) Doe *d.* Brierley *v.* Palmer, 16 East. 53.

(*t*) Doe *d.* Williams *v.* Humphreys, 2 East. 237; Doe *d.* Godsell *v.* Inglis, 3 Taunt. 54; Messenger *v.* Armstrong, 1 T. R. 53.
(*u*) Doe *d.* Lord Macartney *v.* Crick, 5 Esp. 196.
(*v*) Whiteacre *d.* Boult *v.* Symonds, 10 East. 13, 17; Doe *d.* Lord Macartney *v.* Crick, 5 Esp. 196; Doe *d.* Marquis of Hertford *v.* Hunt, 1 M. & W. 690.
(*w*) See *ante*, 262.

CHAPTER V.

HOLDING OVER.

	PAGE		PAGE
1. SMALL TENEMENTS ACT	... 275	3. DOUBLE VALUE ...	284
2. DESERTION BY TENANT	... 281	4. DOUBLE RENT ...	287

UPON the determination of the tenancy, the landlord is entitled to receive the full and complete possession from his tenant, who must therefore deliver up to his landlord the peaceable and quiet possession of the demised premises, together with all fixtures (*a*), except what he is entitled to remove; and also all growing crops, unless there be an agreement or custom (*b*) to the contrary (*c*). If the tenant holds over after the expiration of the notice to quit, whereby the landlord is prevented from delivering possession to a party to whom he had agreed to let the premises, the landlord can recover the reasonable damages and costs that he has sustained (*d*). Where it is impossible for the tenant to give up possession, by reason of the ill-will or obstinacy of his under-tenant, to whom he has let the whole or part of the premises, the original tenant will still be liable (*e*). The landlord, however, may discharge him by accepting the under-tenant as his

(*a*) See Fixtures, p. 298.
(*b*) See Emblements, p. 288.
(*c*) Hyatt *v.* Griffiths, 17 Q. B. 505; Newson *v.* Smythies, 3 H. & N. 840, 28 L. J. Ex. 97; Caldecott *v.* Smythies, 7 C. & P. 808; Henderson *v.* Squire, L. R. 4 Q. B. 170.
(*d*) Bramley *v.* Chesterton, 2 C. B. N.S. 592, 27 L. J. C. P. 23.

(*e*) Harding *v.* Crethorn, 1 Esp. 57; Ibbs *v.* Richardson, 9 A. & E. 849. See also Christy *v.* Tancred, 7 M. & W. 127, 9 M. & W. 433; Tancred *v.* Christy, 12 M. & W. 316; Draper *v.* Crofts, 15 M. & W. 166; Jones *v.* Shears, 4 A. & E. 832, 835; Gray *v.* Bompas, 11 C. B. N.S. 520; Waring *v.* King, 8 M. & W. 571.

tenant. Where the tenant holds over, the landlord may enter on the demised premises peaceably and without action, if he can succeed in doing so (*f*); but if he break in forcibly, so as to endanger a breach of the peace, he may be liable to the risk of an indictment (*g*). It is safer, therefore, to sue in trespass for the recovery of damages, or in ejectment for the recovery of the premises.

1. SMALL TENEMENTS ACT.

In order to save the landlords of small tenements the expense and delay of a proceeding by ejectment to recover possession, where a tenant refuses to quit on the determination of his interest in the premises, the statute 1 & 2 Vict., c. 74, s. 1, enacts, that " When and so soon as the term or interest of the tenant of any house, land, or other corporeal hereditaments held by him at will, or for any term not exceeding seven years, either without being liable to the payment of any rent, or at a rent not exceeding the rate of £20 a year, and upon which no fine shall have been reserved or made payable, shall have ended, or shall have been duly determined by a legal notice to quit or otherwise, and such tenant or (if such tenant do not actually occupy the premises, or only occupy a part thereof) any person by whom the same, or any part thereof, shall be then actually occupied, shall neglect or refuse to quit and deliver up possession of the premises, or of such part thereof respectively, it shall be lawful for the landlord of the said premises, or his agent, to cause the person so neglecting or

(*f*) Taylor *v.* Cole, 1 Smith's L. C. 5th edit., 111.
(*g*) R. *v.* Smyth, 1 M. & R. 155, judgment of Lord Tenterden. See Newton *v.* Harland, 1 M. & Gr. 664, where it was held that the landlord may be liable to an action at the suit of the tenant, but that point is not decided; Harvey *v.* Brydges, 14 M. & W. 437; Wright *v.* Burroughes, 3 C. B. 699; Davison *v.* Wilson, 11 Q. B. 890; Davis *v.* Burrell, 10 C. B. 825.

refusing to quit and deliver up possession to be served (in the manner hereinafter mentioned) with a written notice in the form set forth in the schedule in this Act, signed by the said landlord or his agent, of his intention to proceed to recover possession under the authority and according to the mode prescribed in this Act; and if the tenant or occupier shall not thereupon appear at the time and place appointed, and show to the satisfaction of the justices hereinafter mentioned reasonable cause why possession should not be given under the provisions of this Act, and shall still neglect or refuse to deliver up possession of the premises, or of such part thereof of which he is then in possession, to the said landlord or his agent, it shall be lawful for such landlord or agent to give to such justices proof of the holding, and of the end or other determination of the tenancy, with the time and manner thereof; and where the title of the landlord has accrued since the letting of the premises, the right by which he claims the possession; and upon proof of service of the notice and of the neglect or refusal of the tenant or occupier, as the case may be, it shall be lawful for the justices acting for the district, division, or place within which the said premises, or any part thereof, shall be situate, in petty sessions assembled, or any two of them, to issue a warrant under their hands and seals to the constables and peace-officers of the district (*h*), division, or place within which the said premises, or any part thereof, shall be situate, commanding them within a period to be therein named, not less than twenty-one nor more than thirty clear days from the date of such warrant, to enter (by force if needful) into the premises, and give possession of the same to such landlord or agent: provided always that entry upon any such warrant

(*h*) Jones *v.* Chapman, 14 M. & W. 124.

shall not be made on a Sunday, Good Friday, or Christmas Day, or at any time except between the hours of nine in the morning and four in the afternoon: provided also, that nothing herein contained shall be deemed to protect any person on whose application and to whom any such warrant shall be granted, from any action which may be brought against him by any such tenant or occupier, for or in respect of such entry and taking possession, where such person had not, at the time of granting the same, lawful right to the possession of the same premises: provided also, that nothing herein contained shall affect any rights to which any person may be entitled as outgoing tenant by the custom of the country or otherwise."

A like remedy is given to the valuer under the Inclosure Acts in respect of encroachments, and recent inclosures of land subject to the provisions of those Acts (*i*). By " The Charitable Trusts Act, 1860 " (*j*), a like remedy is given to the trustees against a schoolmaster wrongfully holding over.

By the 59 Geo. III., c. 12, ss. 24, 25, churchwardens and overseers of hereditaments belonging to the parish (*k*) can, in the mode therein provided, obtain a warrant from the justices for the possession of hereditaments belonging to the parish which are wrongfully held over (*l*), and the justices may inquire into the matter although a claim of title arises (*m*).

(*i*) 15 & 16 Vict. c. 79, s. 13; Chilcote *v.* Youlden, 29 L. J. M. C. 197.
(*j*) 23 & 24 Vict. c. 136, s. 13. As to land vested in the Secretary of State for War, see 22 Vict. c. 12, s. 5.
(*k*) See *ante*, Part 1, c. 1, p. 20.
(*l*) As to cottage allotments, see 2 & 3 Will. IV. c. 42, ss. 5, 11.
(*m*) *Ex parte* Vaughan, 7 B. & S. 902, L. R. 2 Q. B. 114, 36 L. J. M. C. 17.

By 19 & 20 Vict., c. 108, s. 50 (*n*), "When the term and interest of the tenant of any corporeal hereditament, where neither the value of the premises nor (*o*) the rent payable in respect thereof shall have exceeded £50 by the year, and upon which no fine or premium shall have been paid, shall have expired or shall have been determined, either by the landlord or the tenant by a legal notice to quit, and such tenant, or any person holding or claiming by, through, or under him, shall neglect or refuse to deliver up possession accordingly, the landlord may enter a plaint, at his option, either against such tenant or against such person so neglecting or refusing, in the County Court of the district in which the premises lie, for the recovery of the same, and thereupon a summons shall issue to such tenant or such person neglecting or refusing; and if the defendant shall not, at the time named in the summons, show good cause to the contrary, then, on the proof of his still neglecting or refusing to deliver up the possession of the premises, and of the yearly value and rent of the premises, and of the holding, of the expiration or other determination of the tenancy, with the time and manner thereof, and of the title of the plaintiff, if such title has accrued since the letting of the premises, and of the service of the summons on the defendant thereto, the judge may order that possession of the premises mentioned in the plaint be given by the defendant to the plaintiff, either forthwith or on or before such day as the judge shall think fit to name; and if such order be not obeyed, the registrar, whether such order can be proved to have been served or not, shall, at the

---

(*n*) This section is an amendment of 9 & 10 Vict. c. 95, s. 122. The cases on the latter section are *In re* Earl of Harrington *v.* Ramsay, 8 Ex. 879; Fearon *v.*

Norvall, 5 D. & L. 445; Crowley *v.* Vitty, 7 Ex. 319.

(*o*) The word "or" was used in sect. 122 of 9 & 10 Vict. c. 95. See *supra*, note (*n*).

instance of the plaintiff, issue a warrant authorising and requiring the high bailiff of the Court to give possession of such premises to the plaintiff."

The relation of landlord and tenant must exist to enable the Court to have jurisdiction.

Where plaintiff claimed as a mortgagee, and the defendant, who held under a demise from the mortgagor subsequent to the mortgage, had never attorned to the plaintiff, it was held that the statute did not apply (*p*). Where defendant was let into possession of premises under an agreement to purchase, and he agreed to pay 8s. a week rent, to be afterwards deducted from the purchase-money, and he had paid, under this agreement, sums of money which, with a set-off, equalled the amount of the purchase-money, it was held that the relation of landlord and tenant did not exist (*q*).

If a *bona fide* claim of title is set up and proved to exist, the County Court judge has no jurisdiction to decide the case (*r*) except by the written consent of the parties or their attorneys (*s*). But the tenant is estopped from denying his landlord's title (*t*). Under sect. 51, plaintiff may add a claim for rent or mesne profits as against his tenant down to the day of leaving, so that his claim does not exceed £50 (*u*).

By 19 & 20 Vict., c. 108, s. 52, " When the rent of

(*p*) Jones *v.* Owen, 5 D. & L. 669.
(*q*) Banks *v.* Rebbeck, 2 L. M. & P. 452.
(*r*) Lilley *v.* Harvey, 5 D. & L. 648; Fearon *v.* Norvall, Id. 439; Marwood *v.* Waters, 13 C. B. 820; Latham *v.* Spedding, 17 Q. B. 440; Lloyd *v.* Jones, 6 C. B. 81, 5 D. & L. 784; Pearson *v.* Glaze-brook, 37 L. J. Ex. 15, L. R. 3 Ex. 27.
(*s*) 19 & 20 Vict. c. 108. s. 25.
(*t*) See Leases by Estoppel, *ante*, p. 156. *In re* Emery *v.* Barnett, 27 L. J. C. P. 216, 4 C. B. N.S. 423; Lloyd *v.* Jones 6 C. B. 81.
(*u*) See Campbell *v.* Loader, 8 H. & C. 520.

any corporeal hereditament, where neither the value of the premises nor the rent payable in respect thereof exceeds £50 by the year, shall for one half year be in arrear, and the landlord shall have right by law to re-enter for the non-payment thereof, he may, without any formal demand or re-entry, enter a plaint in the County Court of the district in which the premises lie for the recovery of the premises; and thereupon a summons shall issue to the tenant, the service whereof shall stand in lieu of a demand or re-entry; and if the tenant shall, five clear days before the return-day of such summons, pay into Court all the rent in arrear, and costs, the said action shall cease; but if he shall not make such payment, and shall not at the time named in the summons show good cause why the premises should not be recovered, then, on proof of the yearly value and rent of the premises, and of the fact that one half-year's rent was in arrear before the plaint was entered, and that no sufficient distress was then to be found on the premises to countervail such arrear, and of the landlord's power to re-enter, and of the rent being still in arrear, and of the title of the plaintiff, if such title has accrued since the letting of the premises, and of the service of the summons, if the defendant shall not appeal thereto, the judge may order that possession of the premises mentioned in the plaint be given by the defendant to the plaintiff on or before such day, not being less than four weeks from the day of hearing, as the judge shall think fit to name, unless within that period all the rent in arrear and costs be paid into Court, and if such order be not obeyed, and such rent and costs be not so paid, the registrar shall, whether such order can be proved to have been served or not, at the instance of the plaintiff, issue a warrant authorising and requiring the high bailiff of the court to give possession of such premises to the plaintiff, and the plaintiff shall, from the time of the execution of such warrant, hold the premises discharged of the tenancy, and the defendant, and all persons claiming by, through, or under him, shall, so long as the order of the Court remains unreserved, be barred from all relief in equity or otherwise."

2. DESERTION BY TENANT.

By 11 Geo. II., c. 19, s. 16, " If any tenant holding any lands, tenements, or hereditaments, at a rackrent, or where the rent reserved shall be full three fourths of the yearly value of the demised premises, who shall be in arrear for one year's rent (extended by 57 Geo. III., c. 52, to one half year's rent), shall desert the demised premises, and leave the same uncultivated or unoccupied, so as no sufficient distress can be had to countervail the arrears of rent, it shall and may be lawful to and for two or more justices of the peace of the county, riding, division, or place (having no interest in the demised premises), at the request of the lessor or landlord, lessors or landlords, or his, her, or their bailiff or receiver, to go upon and view (*v*) the same, and to affix or cause to be affixed on the most notorious part of the premises, notice in writing, what day (at the distance of fourteen days at least) (*w*) they will return to take a second view thereof, and if, upon such second view, the tenant or some person on his or her behalf shall not appear and pay the rent in arrear, or there shall not be sufficient

(*v*) Where the premises are within the Metropolitan Police District the police magistrate need not view the premises, but can, upon proof given to his satisfaction of the arrear of rent and desertion of the premises by the tenant, issue his warrant, requiring a constable to view the premises; 3 & 4 Vict. c. 84, s. 13.

(*w*) *i.e.*, fourteen clear days; Creak *v.* the Justices of Brighton, 1 F. & F. 110.

distress upon the premises, then the said justices may put the landlord or landlords, lessor or lessors, into the possession of the said demised premises, and the lease thereof to such tenants, as to any demised therein contained only, shall from thenceforward become void."

By sect. 17, such proceedings of the justices are examinable in a summary way by the judge going the circuit in his individual capacity, and not as a justice of assize (*x*). He may order restitution to be made to the tenant, together with the expenses and costs. If the judge affirms the act of the justices, he can award costs not exceeding five pounds.

The 57 Geo. III., c. 52, extended the powers of the 11 Geo. II., c. 19, s. 16 (*y*), to the case of tenants "who shall hold such lands and tenements or hereditaments under any demise or agreement, either written or verbal, and although no right or power of re-entry be reserved or given to the landlord in case of non-payment of rent."

The above statutes apply to all demises, whether written or oral, however long may be the term and however large may be the amount of rent reserved (*z*). It matters not that the lease or agreement contains no condition or proviso for re-entry for non-payment of rent (*a*); and, therefore, this mode of proceeding may sometimes be adopted where no action of ejectment could be supported, nor any remedy obtained in the County Court. But the following circumstances must

(*x*) Reg. *v.* Sewell, 8 Q. B. 161.
(*y*) Where by the terms of the lease the landlord had not a right of re-entry, it was held that this statute did not apply; *Ex parte* Pilton, 1 B. & A. 369 a.
(*z*) *Ex parte* Pilton, see *supra*.
(*a*) Edward *v.* Hodges, 15 C. B. 477.

concur, viz. :—1. The rent reserved must be rackrent, or full three-fourths of the yearly value of the demised premises. 2. One half a year's rent at the least must be in arrear. 3. The premises must have been deserted and left uncultivated or unoccupied, so as no sufficient distress may be had to countervail the arrear of rent. No information or complaint on oath need be made before the justices; a mere request is sufficient (*b*). But upon an application to a metropolitan police magistrate, proof must be made to his satisfaction of the rent in arrears and desertion of the premises by the tenant (*c*). The justices are upon their own view to determine whether the premises are deserted or not (*d*). Also whether they have been left uncultivated or unoccupied, so as no sufficient distress can be had to countervail the arrears of rent; also, whether the rent reserved is a rack-rent, or full three-fourths of the yearly value of the demised premises. It has been decided, where a tenant ceased to reside on the premises for several months, and left them without any furniture or sufficient other property to answer the year's rent, that the landlord might properly proceed under the statute to recover the possession, although he knew where the tenant then was, and although the justices found a servant of the tenant on the premises when they first went to view the same (*e*). On the other hand, in a case where the wife and children of the tenant remained on the premises, but there was no furniture in the house except three or four chairs, which were stated by the wife to belong to a neighbour : it was held, on appeal (reversing the decision of the justices), that the premises had not

---

(*b*) Basten *v.* Carew, 3 B. & C. 649, *Re* Perham, 5 H. & N. 30.
(*c*) See *supra*, 3 & 4 Vict. c. 84, s. 13.
(*d*) Basten *v.* Carew, *supra*.
(*e*) *Ex parte* Pilton, *supra*. See Taylorson *v.* Peters, 7 A. & E. 110.

been deserted within the meaning of the Act (*f*). Where magistrates had given possession of a dwelling-house as deserted and unoccupied, and the judges of assize on appeal made an order for restitution with costs, and the tenant brought an action of trespass for the eviction against the magistrates, the constable, and the landlord, it was held that the record of the proceedings before the magistrate was an answer to the action on behalf of all the defendants (*g*).

3. DOUBLE VALUE.

Double value. By 4 Geo. II., c. 28, s. 1 (*h*), " In case any tenant, or tenants for life, lives, or years, or other person or persons who are or shall come into possession of any lands, tenements, or hereditaments, by, from, or under, or by collusion with, such tenant or tenants, shall wilfully hold over any lands, tenements, or hereditaments after (*i*) the determination of such term or terms, and after demand made, and notice in writing given, for delivering the possession thereof by his or their landlords or lessors, or the person or persons to whom the remainder or reversion of such lands, &c., shall belong, his or their agent (*j*), or agents thereunto lawfully authorised, then and in such case such person or persons so holding over, shall for and during the time he, she, or they, shall so hold over, or keep the person or persons entitled out of possession of the said lands, tenements, or hereditaments as aforesaid, pay to the person or per-

(*f*) Ashcroft *v.* Bourne, 3 B. & Ad. 684.
(*g*) Ashcroft *v.* Bourne, *supra;* Basten *v.* Carew, 3 B. & C. 649.
(*h*) As to the construction of this statute, which is a remedial law, see Wilkinson *v.* Colley, 5 Burr. 2694.

(*i*) Page *v.* More, 15 Q. B. 684.
(*j*) A receiver appointed by the Court of Chancery in a suit depending, is a sufficient agent to give notice; Wilkinson *v.* Colley, 5 Burr. 2694. See Goodtitle *ex dem* Read *v.* Badtitle, 1 B. & P. 385; Poole *v.* Warren, 8 A. & E. 582.

sons so kept out of possession, their executors, administrators, or assigns, at the rate of double the yearly value of the lands, tenements, and hereditaments (*k*) so detained, for so long as the same are detained, to be recovered in any of His Majesty's courts of record by action of debt (*l*), whereunto the defendant or defendants shall be obliged to give special bail (*m*), against the recovering of which said penalty there shall be no relief in equity."

The Act does not apply unless the holding over is wilful and contumacious. If the tenant, therefore, retains the possession under a fair claim of right, or there is a real dispute as to the landlord's title, the tenant is not liable to pay double value (*n*).

Where there had been a treaty for a further term between the landlord and tenant, but which afterwards went off, the tenant held over during the treaty; an action having been brought for double value under the statute, it was held by Lord Mansfield that the action was not maintainable (*o*). The remedy under the Act, that is, an action of debt, is given only to the landlord, or person entitled to the reversion. A new lessee, therefore, whose term is to begin on the ending of the first lease, having

(*k*) Where the owner of a woollen mill and steam-engine let a room with a supply of power from the engine, by means of a revolving shaft in the room, it was held, in estimating the double value of the premises, the value of the power supplied could not be included. Robinson *v.* Learoyd, 7 M. & W. 48.

(*l*) But not by distress; Timmins *v.* Rawlinson, 3 Burr. 1605. A demand for double value under this statute is a plea of personal action, and may be sued for in the County Court; Wickham *v.* Lee, 12 Q. B. 521, 18 L. J. Q. B. 21.

(*m*) See Wheeler *v.* Copeland, 5 T. R. 364.

(*n*) Wright *v.* Smith, 5 Esp. 203; Swinfen *v.* Bacon, 5 H. & C. 184, 846, 30 L. J. Ex. 33. *Per* Lord Ellenborough in Soulsby *v.* Neving, 9 East. 313.

(*o*) Doe *d.* Cheney *v.* Batten, Cowp. 243 M. S. 9 East. 315.

only an *interesse termini*, cannot sue for double value (*p*). This action will lie even after recovery of the premises by ejectment, where there was no real *bona fide* defence to the ejectment (*q*).

This statute requires that there should be a " demand made, and notice in writing given for delivering the possession" of the premises. A notice to quit (*r*), when regular, will operate also as a demand of the possession under the Act, without any more specific demand; and notices to deliver up the possession under the statute are not construed strictly (*s*). But where a notice required the tenant to give up the possession at twelve at noon on the day on which the tenancy was determinable, at which time the landlord would attend to receive the keys and the rent, and the notice stated that in the event of his not so surrendering, the landlord would demand a certain daily rent mentioned in the notice, which exceeded, in fact, double the amount of the original rent, it was held that this notice was insufficient, the tenant being required to give up the possession before the expiration of the tenancy (*t*).

A weekly tenant is not within the Act (*u*), neither is a tenant from quarter to quarter (*v*).

(*p*) Blatchford *v.* Cole, 5 C. P. N.S. 514, 28 L. J. C. P. 140.
(*q*) Soulsby *v.* Neving, 9 East. 310; Wright *v.* Smith, 5 Esp. 203.
(*r*) See c. 4, Notice to Quit, *ante.*
(*s*) Doe *d.* Matthew *v.* Jackson, 1 Dougl. 175; Poole *v.* Warren, 8 A. & E. 582; Doe *d.* Lister *v.* Goldwin, 2 Q. B. 143; Page *v.* Moore, 15 Q. B. 684; Messenger *v.* Armstrong, 1 T. R. 53; Hirst *v.* Horn, 6 M. & W. 393. If a sufficient notice is given to a female tenant, who afterwards marries, the action for not delivering up possession may be maintained against her husband without any new demand; Lake *v.* Smith, 1 B. & P. N. R. 174.
(*t*) Page *v.* More, 15 Q. B. 684.
(*u*) Lloyd *v.* Rosbee, 2 Camp. 453; but see Co. Litt. 54 b.
(*v*) Sullivan *v.* Bishop, 2 C. & P. 359; Wilkinson *v.* Hall, 3 Bing. N. C. 508.

4. DOUBLE RENT.

By 11 Geo. II., c. 19, s. 18, " In case any tenant or tenants shall give notice of his, her, or their intention to quit the premises by him, her, or them, holden at a time mentioned in such notice, and shall not accordingly deliver up the possession thereof at the time in such notice contained, then the said tenant or tenants, his, her, or their executors or administrators, shall from thenceforward pay to the landlord or landlords, lessor or lessors, double the rent or sum which he, she, or they should otherwise have paid, to be levied, sued for, and recovered at the same time and in the same manner as the single rent or sum before the giving such notice could be levied, sued for, or recovered, and such double rent or sum shall continue to be paid during all the time such tenant or tenants shall continue in possession as aforesaid." The landlord, therefore, may either distrain for the double rent, or bring an action for it upon the statute (*w*). The statute applies only to cases where the tenant has the power of determining the tenancy by a notice, and has given a valid notice to that effect (*x*). It is immaterial whether the tenancy is in writing or by parol, and the notice to quit need not be in writing (*y*). The statute does not extend to weekly tenants (*z*). A tenant who has given notice, and paid double rent, may quit at any time, without giving a fresh notice (*a*); and the landlord may waive his claim to double rent by accepting single rent (*b*).

(*w*) Johnstone *v.* Huddlestone, 4 B. & C. 922.
(*x*) Ibid. See Farrance *v.* Elkington, 2 Camp. 591.
(*y*) Timmins *v.* Rawlinson, 3 Burr. 1603.
(*z*) Sullivan *v.* Bishop, 2 C. & P. 359.
(*a*) Booth *v.* Macfarlane, 1 B. & Ad. 904.
(*b*) Doe *d.* Cheney *v.* Batten, Cowp. 243.

CHAPTER VI.

EMBLEMENTS.

	PAGE		PAGE
1. WHERE THERE IS NO CONTRACT—		entry to take them ...	292
where they may be claimed	288	2. WHERE THERE IS A CONTRACT	292
out of what claimed ...	291		

1. WHERE THERE IS NO CONTRACT.

Where they may be claimed. THE right to emblements is a right to the corn growing upon the land on the determination of an uncertain estate by no act of the tenant. Emblements are allowed in order to encourage agriculture, for it would be obviously unjust to deprive the tenant of the benefit of the crop which he sowed at a time when he might reasonably expect to reap it (*a*).

Thus where the tenant for life dies before harvest, his executors will be entitled to the crop, for that is the act of God (*b*). So the personal representatives of the incumbent of a benefice were held to be entitled to emblements of the glebe lands (*c*).

Where the tenancy is at will, or from year to

(*a*) Co. Litt. 55 b ; 2 Bl. Com. 146.
(*b*) Co. Litt. 55 b.
(*c*) Williams on Exors. 603, 4th edit. See 28 Hen. VIII. c. 11.

year (*d*), or for an uncertain term of years, as a term for so many years if the tenant should so long live (*e*), the executor is entitled to the emblements (*f*). So also tenants by statute-merchant and recognizance under extent or elegit, are entitled to emblements where, by some sudden and casual profit arising between seed-time and harvest-time, the tenancy is determined by the judgment being satisfied (*g*). So upon the death of a tenant by the courtesy, the executors are entitled to emblements (*h*).

So also a tenant in dower, and a woman who has lands for her jointure, are entitled to emblements; but the latter is not entitled to the crop which was sown at the time of her husband's death (*i*).

If a lease be made to husband and wife during the coverture, and afterwards they are divorced *causâ præcontractus*, the husband shall have the emblements, for the sentence which dissolves the marriage is the judgment of the law (*j*).

Where the uncertain event upon which the determination of the estate depends is the death or cessor of estate of the landlord, the common-law right has been qualified by the 14 & 15 Vict., c. 25, s. 1, which enables the tenant, in lieu of emblements, to hold over till the end of the current year. The section is as follows :—" Where the lease or tenancy of any farm or

(*d*) Kingsbury *v.* Collins, 4 Bing. 207 ; Haines *v.* Welch, L. R. 4 C. P. 91, 38 L. J. C. P. 118.
(*e*) 1 Roll. Abr. 727, pl. 12.
(*f*) 1 Inst. 55 b ; Co. Litt. 56 a ; Knevett *v.* Poole, Cro. Eliz. 463 ; Vin. Abr. Emblements; Kingsbury *v.* Collins, 4 Bing. 207 ; Barden's case, 2 Leon. 54.

(*g*) 1 Roll. Abr. 727, pl. 12 ; Barden's case, 2 Leon. 54.
(*h*) 1 Roper's "Husband and Wife," 25, 2d edit.
(*i*) 2 Inst. 80 ; 20 Hen. III. c. 2 (Stat. of Merton) ; 1 Wms. Exors. 677, 6th edit. ; Fisher *v.* Forbes, Vin. Abr. tit. Emblements, pl. 82.
(*j*) Oland's case, 5 Coke, 116.

T

lands held by a tenant at a rack-rent shall determine by the death or cessor of the estate of any landlord entitled for his life, or for any other uncertain interest, instead of claims to emblements, the tenant shall continue to hold and occupy such farm or lands until the expiration of the then current year of his tenancy, and shall then quit, upon the terms of his lease or holding, in the same manner as if such lease or tenancy were then determined by effluction of time or other lawful means during the continuance of his landlord's estate; and the succeeding landlord or owner shall be entitled to recover and receive of the tenant, in the same manner as his predecessor or such tenant's lessor could have done if he had been living or had continued the landlord or lessor, a fair proportion of the rent for the period which may have elapsed from the day of the death or cessor of the estate of such predecessor or lessor to the time of the tenant so quitting, and the succeeding landlord or owner, and the tenant respectively, shall, as between themselves and as against each other, be entitled to all the benefits and advantages, and be subject to the terms, conditions, and restrictions to which the preceding landlord or lessor, and such tenant respectively, would have been entitled and subject in case the lease or tenancy had determined in manner aforesaid at the expiration of such current year: Provided always that no notice to quit shall be necessary or required by or from either party to determine any such holding and occupation as aforesaid."

Upon the other hand, where the estate is for a term certain, so that the tenant would sow at his own risk, or where the tenant voluntarily determines the lease by his own act, he or his executors will not be entitled to the emblements. So where a tenant at will himself determines the estate, he will not be entitled (*k*). And where the estate is to determine upon some act of the tenant—as if he does waste (*l*), or if he incur a debt upon which judgment is signed (*m*)—and he does the act provided against, he will not be entitled to the emblements.

So where a clergyman resigns his living, he is not entitled to emblements, for it is his own act (*n*). And where a woman copyholder of certain land *durante viduitate suâ*, according to the custom of the manor, sowed the land, and before severance of the emblements took a husband, it was adjudged that the lord should have the emblements, because the estate determined by the act of the lessee herself (*o*).

If the person claiming the crop be not the sower of the crop, or his representative, he will not be entitled to the crop. Thus where a person who sows the land afterwards creates a life estate, the reversionor, and not the executor of the tenant for life, shall have the crop; and if a tenant for life sows land, and afterwards grants over his estate, the executor of the grantee shall not have the crop (*p*).

As between an executor and a devisee, the emblements belong to the devisee, unless especially bequeathed to the executor (*q*).

The doctrine of emblements extends to roots planted and other *annual artificial* profits (*r*). It will not, *Out of which claimed.*

(*k*) Litt. s. 68, 5 Coke, 116; Bulwer *v.* Bulwer, 2 B. & A. 470.
(*l*) Oland's case, 5 Coke, 116; Com. Dig. Bieus, (G) 2; Wigglesworth *v.* Dallison, 1 Doug. 207.
(*m*) Davis *v.* Eyton, 7 Bing. 154.
(*n*) Bulwer *v.* Bulwer, 2 B. & Ald. 470.
(*o*) Oland's case, 5 Coke, 116 a.
(*p*) 1 Roll Abr. 727, pl. 21; Knevett *v.* Poole, Cro. Eliz. 463; Grantham *v.* Hawley, Hob. 132.
(*q*) Cooper *v.* Woolfit, 2 H. & N. 122; Shep. Touch. by Preston, 472.
(*r*) Latham *v.* Attwood, Cro. Car. 515, Co. Litt. 55 b, note (*l*);

therefore, extend to fruit-trees, oak, elm, and other trees, as these are not planted in anticipation of present immediate profit, and take more than a year to come to perfection (*s*); and so it was held not to extend to clover of which the crop was not to be taken within a year from the time of sowing it (*t*); nor will it extend to growing grass, for that is not an *artificial* product (*u*), unless it be artificial grass, such as clover and the like (*v*).

Entry to take them.

Where the tenant is entitled to emblements, he is also entitled to free ingress and egress to take them (*w*), and if he sell them, the vendor will have the same right (*x*). But this right of entry does not involve a right of occupation, and it is doubtful whether a personal representative of the tenant is not liable for rent, or to pay for the use and occupation if he occupies the land until the corn be ripe (*y*).

2. Where there is a Contract.

Where there is a contract.

The right to take what is called the away-going crop may become a matter of express contract between the parties, or the subject of an implied contract arising from the custom of the country (*z*). Where the terms of the lease are inconsistent with the custom

Evans *v.* Roberts, 5 B. & C. 829, 832. It has been held to extend to teazles, Kingsbury *v.* Collins, 4 Bing. 202.
(*s*) Co. Litt. 55 b; Com. Dig. Liens, (G) 1.
(*t*) Graves *v.* Weld, 5 B. & Ad. 105.
(*u*) Co. Litt. 56 a; 1 Roll. Abr. 728; Com. Dig. Biens, (G) 1.
(*v*) Smith's L. & T. 2d edit. 349; and see Graves *v.* Weld, *supra*.

(*w*) Co. Litt. 56 a; Hayling *v.* Okey, 8 Ex. 531, 545.
(*x*) Shep. Touch. 244.
(*y*) Plowden's Queries, No. 239; 1 Wms. Exors. 679, 6th edit. See Strickland *v.* Maxwell, 2 Cr. & M. 539; but see Beavan *v.* Delahay, 1 H. Bl. 5; Griffiths *v.* Puleston, 13 M. & W. 358, *post*, p. 293.
(*z*) Wigglesworth *v.* Dallison, 1 Doug. 201; 1 Smith L. C. 520, 6th edit.

of the country, they will exclude it (*a*); but where they are not inconsistent, the custom may entitle the tenant to take the crop and to do everything which is necessary for that purpose (*b*), even when the lease is under seal (*c*).

The custom will operate, unless it can be collected from the instrument, either expressly or impliedly, that the parties do not mean to be governed by it (*d*).

If the lease contains no stipulation as to the mode of quitting the premises, the off-going tenant is entitled to his away-going crop according to the custom of the country, even though the terms of the *holding* be inconsistent with such custom, for the custom does not operate until the holding is determined (*e*).

Where the custom of the country was that the tenant should have the way-going crop on the regular expiration of a Ladyday tenancy, the tenant entered on Ladyday, but the tenancy was determined on the 1st of June, it was held that the custom would not operate (*f*).

The tenant's interest in his way-going is not a mere easement, but a *possession*, which continues until the crop is carried away (*g*).

(*a*) See *ante*, Covenants, part i., c. 4, s. 7.
(*b*) Beavan *v*. Delahay, 1 H. Bl. 5; Boraston *v*. Green, 16 East. 71; Caldecott *v*. Smithies, 7 C. & P. 808.
(*c*) Wigglesworth *v*. Dallison, 1 Doug. 201.
(*d*) Hutton *v*. Warren, 1 M. & W. 466, 477, where the authorities are collected; Clarke *v*. Royston, 13 M. & W. 466; Wiltshear *v*. Cottrell, 1 E. & B. 674; Muncey *v*. Dennis, 1 H. & N. 216.
(*e*) Holding *v*. Pigott, 7 Bing. 465; Muncey *v*. Dennis, 1 H. & N. 216.
(*f*) Thorpe *v*. Eyre, 1 A. & E. 926.
(*g*) Beavan *v*. Delahay, 1 H. Bl. 5; Griffiths *v*. Puleston, 13 M. & W. 358.

A strictly legal custom which has immemorially existed is not necessary, for a common usage of the neighbourhood, collected from what is usually done in cases of tenancies from year to year, as well as from the usual course pursued where tenants hold under regular leases, is sufficient (*h*).

The tenant may either sue the landlord for the value of the tillages, manure, &c., which he is entitled to by the custom (*i*), or he may recover it from the incoming tenant if he has made a contract with him to that effect (*j*). Such a contract does not affect any of the existing rights of the landlord (*k*).

Under a clause that the tenant should be entitled to a way-going crop to be taken from the land, &c., and which way-going crop it was agreed should be left for the landlord or the incoming tenant at a valuation, it was held that the tenant had no right to reap the crop, he not having any interest distinct in that crop so as to be able to dispose of it, or to authorise any person but the landlord himself to take that crop. In reality the clause was nothing but a measure by which he might recoup himself (*l*).

If the outgoing tenant carries away the corn at the end of his term when he is not entitled to do so, the landlord may bring trover (*m*), but not the incoming tenant (*n*).

(*h*) Senior *v.* Armytage, Holt, 197, Woodfall L. & T. p. 989, 10th edit.
(*i*) Faviell *v.* Gascoigne, 7 Ex. 273 ; Mousley *v.* Ludlam, 21 L. J. Q. B. 64.
(*j*) Mouncey *v.* Dennis, 1 H. & N. 216.
(*k*) Petrie *v.* Daniel, 1 Smith R. 199.
(*l*) *Per* Bayley, B., in Strickland *v.* Maxwell, 2 Cr. & M. 539, 552.
(*m*) Davies *v.* Connop, 1 Price, 53.
(*n*) Borraston *v.* Green, 16 East. 80, 81, *per* Bailey, J.

The same remark which has been made, *ante*, pp. 124, 128, viz., that a custom which is not inconsistent with the terms of the lease may be incorporated with the lease, extends to a custom to leave hay, straw, manure, &c., upon the premises, and to receive a compensation for them (*o*). Sometimes by the terms of the agreement the outgoing tenant may dispose of them to the incoming tenant (*p*).

Where the tenant is entitled to be paid a fair price for the straw left, but nothing for the manure, he is only entitled to be paid for the straw at a fodder price, viz., one half the market price (*q*).

Where a tenant who was bound to bring back dung for all hay sold and sent by him off the premises, sold some hay to a purchaser without informing him of the contract by which he was bound, it was held that the incoming tenant might refuse to let the purchaser remove the hay (*r*).

Where the tenant is to bring back manure in lieu of hay or straw sold off the premises, it should be clearly expressed whether the manure is to be of the value of the straw, or only such a quantity as the straw sold would have produced (*s*).

Where the lessee covenanted that he "should not nor would, *during the last year* of the term thereby granted, sell, &c., any hay, straw, or fodder, which should arise and grow in the said farm and lands,"

(*o*) Roberts *v.* Barker, 1 Cr. & M. 808; Dalby *v.* Hirst, 1 Bro. & Bing. 224; Hutton *v.* Warren, 1 M. & W. 466.
(*p*) Legh *v.* Lillie, 6 H. & N. 165, 30 L. J. Ex. 25; Hurst *v.* Hurst, 4 Ex. 579; Massey *v.* Goodall, 17 Q. B. 310.
(*q*) Clarke *v.* Westrope, 18 C. B. 765, 25 L. J. C. P. 287.
(*r*) Smith *v.* Chance, 2 B. & A. 753.
(*s*) Lowndes *v.* Fountain, 11 Ex. 487, 25 L. J. Ex. 49.

the covenant was held to extend to hay, &c., which had arisen and grown at any time during the term (*t*).

A covenant to pay £10 per ton for "hay, straw, or other fodder," sold or taken away, was held to extend to hay unfit for food for cattle (*u*),

Where the outgoing tenant was to sell the manure to the incoming tenant at a valuation, it was held that the possession and property remained in him until the valuation was made, and the incoming tenant would be liable to an action of trespass if he removed it (*v*).

It is not inconsistent with a tenancy from year to year that the outgoing tenant shall be paid for the tillages on the determination of his tenancy (*w*).

In a strict tenancy at will, if the lessor enters before sowing, the lessee will not have the costs of ploughing and manuring (*x*).

Where the custom is that the incoming tenant shall pay for the tillages, and shall be paid back again upon leaving, he may recover the amount from the landlord, if there be no new tenant coming in (*y*). But where the tenant took a farm for fourteen years, and in the first year said he would leave, and the landlord said he might, it was held that he was not entitled to the tillages (*z*). It seems also that the custom would not

---

(*t*) Gale *v*. Bates, 3 H. & C. 84, 33 L. J. Ex. 235.
(*u*) Fielden *v*. Tattersall, 7 L. T. N.S. Ex. 718.
(*v*) Beaty *v*. Gibbons, 16 East. 116.
(*w*) Brocklington *v*. Saunders,
13 W. R. 46 Q. B.; Onslow *v*. ——, 16 Ves. 173.
(*x*) Co. Litt. 55 a, n. 4.
(*y*) Favicll *v*. Gascoigne, 7 Ex. 273.
(*z*) Whittaker *v*. Barker, 1 Cr. & M. 113.

apply where the term ceases upon the determination of the landlord's interest (a).

There is also another kind of compensation which a tenant may be entitled to claim, either by the custom of the country, or by express agreement, and that is for tillage bestowed upon the land, the benefit of which still remains unexhausted. As to this also, the same remark applies which has been made, *ante*, p. 293, viz., that the custom will operate where it is not inconsistent with the covenants of the lease.

A custom for the outgoing tenant to be paid a reasonable compensation for tillage is a reasonable custom (b).

(a) See Faviell *v.* Gascoigne, *supra;* Womersley *v.* Dally, 26 L. J. Ex. 219.
(b) Dalby *v.* Hirst, 1 B. & B. 224; Hutton *v.* Warren, 1 M. & W. 466; Senior *v.* Armytage, Holt, 197.

CHAPTER VII.

FIXTURES.

	PAGE		PAGE
1. WHERE THERE IS NO AGREE-		2. WHERE THERE IS AN AGREE-	
MENT—	298	MENT—	311
tenant's fixtures ...	300	*valuation*	315
trade fixtures	303		
agricultural fixtures ...	307		
when to be removed ...	310		

1. WHERE THERE IS NO AGREEMENT.

Where there is no agreement. WHEN personal inanimate chattels are affixed to the freehold, they are usually called fixtures : and, in general, whatever chattels are affixed to the realty become part of it, partaking of all its incidents and properties. Hence, where there is no agreement, fixtures are usually the property of the landlord and not of the tenant, although the tenant may have affixed them (*a*).

Where, at the time of making a demise, nothing is said respecting the chattels affixed to the premises, the tenant will be entitled to use of them during his

(*a*) See Amos and Ferard on Fixtures ; Judgments of Parke, B., & Martin, B., in Elliot *v.* Bishop, 10 Ex. 496, 11 Ex. 119; Elwes *v.* Maw, 2 Smith's L. C. 114 ; Co. Litt. 53 a. See Wiltshire *v.* Cotterell, 1 E. & B. 674 ; Sheen *v.* Rickie, 5 M. & W. 175 ; Lee *v.* Risdon, 7 Taunt. 191 ; Minshall *v.* Lloyd, 2 M. & W. 450–459 ; Walmsley *v.* Milne, 7 C. B. N.S. 115 ; Elwes *v.* Maw, 2 Smith's L. C. 114, and cases therein cited ; Horn *v.* Baker, 9 East. 215.

tenancy as part of the demise, and the landlord cannot afterwards, during the term, remove them or insist upon their being valued and paid for (*b*).

It is a question of fact in each case whether the chattel is sufficiently annexed to the realty so as to form part of it (*c*). This question depends principally upon two circumstances:—1. The mode of annexation to the soil or fabric of the house, and the extent to which it is united to them, whether it can easily be removed, *integrè*, *salvè*, *et commodè*, or not, without injury to itself or to the fabric of the building. 2. On the object and purpose of the annexation, whether it was for the permanent and substantial improvement of the dwelling (*d*), or merely for a temporary purpose, or the more complete enjoyment and use of it as a chattel (*e*). Machinery and other articles, and even buildings, may be so erected as not to be let into the soil nor annexed to it, or to any building, in such a manner as to become part of the freehold, and to lose their chattel character. Thus barns, granaries, sheds, or mills erected upon blocks, rollers, pattens, pillars, or plates, resting on brickwork, but not affixed to the freehold by being let into it or united to it by nails or otherwise, are not considered as fixtures, but as chattels removable by the tenant during the term, notwithstanding they may have sunk into the ground by their own weight (*f*). So a wooden mill or barn resting by its own weight on a brick foundation is not part of the freehold (*g*).

(*b*) Goff *v.* Harris, 5 M. & G. 573.
(*c*) Elwes *v.* Maw, 2 Smith's L. C. 14, and cases therein cited.
(*d*) 20 Hen. VII. c. 13.
(*e*) Hellawell *v.* Eastwood, 6 Ex. 295; Trappes *v.* Harter, 2 C. & M. 177; Turner *v.* Cameron, L. R. 5 Q. B. 306, 39 L. J. Q. B. 125.
(*f*) Huntly *v.* Russell, 13 Q. B. 572.
(*g*) Rex *v.* Otley, 1 B. & Ad. 161; Wansborough *v.* Maton, 4

Certain articles movable in their nature are sometimes considered to be constructively annexed to the structure to which they belong, such as the doors and windows of a house, or the gate of a field suspended on hooks, keys, winches, rings, and other detached appendages necessary for the convenient use of fixtures, which are deemed parcel of, and pass with, the fixtures to which they are appurtenant (*h*). Where a fixture is severed from the freehold for a special and temporary object, as for the purpose of being repaired, it does not lose its original character of a fixture. Thus a millstone taken from a mill for the purpose of being picked and hammered is not distrainable (*i*). If the roof of a building be annexed by a tenant to the freehold, although the roof is kept in its position merely by its own weight, and can be removed without injury to the walls on which it is sustained, yet, as the tenant has no right to remove the whole building, he cannot carry away the roof, which forms an essential part of the structure (*j*).

Tenant's fixtures.

Questions concerning fixtures in the case of landlord and tenant usually arise in the nature of exception to this general rule, viz., that whatever is affixed to the freehold becomes parcel of it. Tenant's fixtures are the property or privilege which a tenant, in the absence of any agreement, continues to possess, and the right of removal that belongs to him when he has, during his term, annexed anything to the demised premises which may be considered a fixture (*k*). This

---

A. & E. 884. See also Dean *v.* Allalley, 3 Esp. 11; Penton *v.* Robart, 4 Esp. 33; Fitzherbert *v.* Shaw, 1 H. Blac. 258; Martin *v.* Roe, 26 L. J. Q. B. 129.

(*h*) Liford's case, 11 Rep. 50 b; Pyot *v.* St John, Cro. Jac. 329, 2 Bulst. 102, Shep. Touch. 470.

(*i*) Wigstow's case, Year-book, 14 Hen. VIII. fo. 25, pl. 6; Gorton *v.* Falkner, 4 T. R. 567; Place *v.* Fagg, 4 M. & Ry. 277. See *supra*, tit. Distress, p. 197.

(*j*) Wansborough *v.* Maton, 6 A. & E. 884–889.

(*k*) Amos and Ferard on Fix-

property or privilege extends—(1.) to fixtures erected by the tenant for the purposes of trade and manufactures, and sometimes, if combined with other purposes, (2.) to fixtures erected by the tenant for ornament and convenience. As to the latter class, a tenant has been allowed to remove fixtures put up for convenience or ornament, and which are of such a description as to be capable of being disannexed without any permanent injury to the inheritance, such, for instance, as stoves and grates fixed into the chimney with brickwork, and marble chimneypieces and wainscot, fixed with screws (*l*). In Grymes *v*. Boweren (*m*), a tenant was allowed to take away a pump which was attached to a stout perpendicular plank resting on the ground at one end, and at the other end fastened to the wall by an iron pin, which had a head at one end and a screw at the other, and went completely through the wall. The judgment of the Lord Chief-Justice Tindal in that case contains a good summary of the law with regard to this class of fixtures :—" It is difficult to draw any very general, and, at the same time, precise and accurate, rule on this subject; for we must be guided, in a great degree, by the circumstances of each case, the nature of the article, and the mode in which it is fixed. The pump, as it is described to have been fixed in this case, appears to me to fall within the class of removable fixtures. The rule has always been more relaxed as between landlord and tenant than as between persons standing in other relations. It has been holden that stoves are removable during the term, and grates, ornamental chimneypieces, wainscots fastened with screws, coppers, and various other

tures, p. 18 ; Hallen *v*. Runder, 1 C. M. & N. 266 ; Elliot *v*. Bishop, 10 Ex. 508.
(*l*) See Lawton *v*. Lawton, 3 Atk. 13 ; R. *v*. St Dunstan, 4 B.
& C. 686 ; Colegrave *v*. Dias Santos, 2 B. & C. 76 ; Winn *v*. Ingilby, 5 B. & A. 625.
(*m*) 6 Bing. 437.

articles; and the circumstances that, upon a change of occupiers, articles of this sort are usually allowed by landlords to be paid for by the incoming tenant to the outgoing tenant, is confirmatory of this view of the question. Looking at the facts of this case, considering that the article in dispute was of domestic convenience, that it was slightly fixed, was erected by the tenant, could be moved entire, and that the question is between the tenant and his landlord, I think the rule should be made absolute."

There are five circumstances most material to be considered in ascertaining whether the tenant may remove fixtures which he has put up for ornament, or for the convenience of his occupation, viz., 1. That the article was one of domestic convenience. 2. That it was erected by the tenant. 3. That it could be moved entire. 4. That it was but slightly fixed. 5. That the question was between landlord and tenant.

The following articles have been held to fall within this class of tenants' fixtures:—Hangings, tapestry, pier-glasses, chimney-glasses, and iron backs to chimneys (*n*); beds fastened with ropes or nails to the ceiling (*o*); stoves, mash-tubs, locks, bolts, and blinds (*p*); cupboards standing on the ground and supported by holdfasts (*q*); coffee-mills and malt-mills (*r*); iron ovens, clock cases (*s*); carpets attached to the floor by nails, for the purpose of keeping them stretched out, curtains, pictures, and other like matters of an ornamental nature which are slightly

---

(*n*) Beck *v.* Rebow, 1 P. Wms. 94; Harvey *v.* Harvey, 2 Str. 1141.
(*o*) Noy's Maxims, 167, 9th edit.; Keilw. 88.
(*p*) Colegrave *v.* Dias Santos, 2 B. & C. 76.

(*q*) Reg. *v.* St Dunstan, 4 B. & C. 686.
(*r*) Reg. *v.* Inhabitants of Londonthorpe, 6 T. R. 377. The mill was clearly a chattel in this case.
(*s*) 4 Burns' Eccl. Law, 411, 9th edit.

attached to the walls of the dwelling-house as furniture (t). So where a rector erected in the garden of the rectory two hothouses apart from and unconnected with the rectory, and which consisted of a brick wall two feet from the ground, upon which was placed a frame and glasswork, it was held that the frame and glasswork being removable without injury to the freehold, passed as a personal chattel to his executors (u). But where a conservatory was erected by a tenant on a brick foundation attached to the dwelling-house, and communicating with it by windows opening into the conservatory, and a flue passing into the parlour chimney, it was held that it became part of the freehold, and could not be removed (v). Fruit trees and shrubs planted by the tenant, not in the way of his trade are not removable by him (w); nor even a border of box or flowers (x).

But it is to be noticed that tenants' fixtures, while they are annexed to the land or building, are not chattels, but form parcel of the realty. The right of removal does not alter the fact that the fixture constitutes part of the realty until severance (y).

The right of the tenant to remove fixtures set up by Trade fixtures.

(t) See judgment in Hellawell v. Eastwood, 6 Ex. 313; Bishop v. Elliott, 10 Ex. 496, in error, 11 Ex. 113.
(u) Martin v. Roe, 7 E. & B. 237, 26 L. J. Q. B. 129.
(v) Buckland v. Butterfield, 2 Bro. & Bing. 54. See the judgment of Dallas, C.J. See also Martin v. Roe, 7 E. & Bl. 237, 26 L. J. Q. B. 129; West v. Blakeway, 2 M. & G. 729; Penry v. Brown, 2 Starkie, 403; Jenkins v. Gething, 2 J. & H. 520.
(w) Wyndham v. Way, 4 Taunt. 316.
(x) Empson v. Soden, 4 B. & Ad. 65.
(y) Lee v. Risdon, 7 Taunt. 190. See Hellawell v. Eastwood, 6 Ex. 295, 20 L. J Ex. 154; Reg. v. North Staffordshire Railway Co., 30 L. J. M. C. 68; Reg. v. The Southampton Dock Co., 14 Q. B. 587; Reg. v. The Inhabitants of Lee, 35 L. J. M. C. 105.

him for the purposes of his trade, and the ground upon which this privilege was based, was plainly stated by Lord Holt, C.J., in Poole's case (z). It was there held that a soap-boiler might well remove vats set up by him for the purposes of his trade, and this he might do by the common law, and not by virtue of any special custom in favour of trade and to encourage industry (a).

This right of the tenant to remove fixtures which he has annexed to the demised premises for the purpose of carrying on his trade, has been indisputably established by subsequent cases, principally upon the ground of the benefit to the public (b). This right is of wider extent than the right that the tenant has to remove ornamental fixtures.

Thus in Lawton v. Lawton (c), where the question was whether a steam-engine set up for the benefit of a colliery, by a tenant for life, should at his death go to his executors or to the tenant in remainder, Lord Hardwicke in his judgment thus explains the principle of the rule respecting trade erections:—" To be sure, in the old cases, they go a great way upon the annexation; and so long ago as Henry VII.'s time, the Courts of law construed even a copper and furnace to be part of the freehold (d). Since that time, the general ground the Courts have gone upon of relaxing the strict construction of law is, that it is for the benefit of the public to encourage tenants for

(z) Salk. 368.
(a) *Per* Lord Holt, C.J., as to reasons given for this privilege in the earlier cases. See Amos on Fixtures, 22–27; 2 Smith's L. C. 5th edit. 161.
(b) See Amos on Fixtures, p. 32, and the cases there cited; Penton v. Roberts, 2 East. 90; Com. Dig. Waste, (D) 2, 2 Saund.

259 n. 11. *Per* Tindal, C.J., in Mansfield v. Blackburne, 6 Bing. N. C. 439; Elwes v. Maw, 3 East. 38, 54; Heap v. Barton, 12 C. B. 274; Fisher v. Dixon, 12 C. C. & F. 312.
(c) 3 Atk. 13.
(d) See Year-book, 42 Edw. III. p. 6, pl. 19; Year-book, 20 Hen. VII. p. 13.

life (*e*) to do what is advantageous to the estate during their term."

The next question is what trade fixtures a tenant may lawfully remove. He may lawfully remove vessels and utensils of trade, such as furnaces, coppers, brewing vessels, fixed vats, salt-pans, tables, partitions, and the like (*f*); machinery in breweries, colleries, mills, &c., as steam-engines, cider-mills, and the like (*g*). Also *certain* buildings for trade, such as a varnish-house, at least if they are built on plates laid on brickwork (*h*). So sheds or buildings, called Dutch barns, formed of uprights, rising from a foundation of brickwork may be removed (*i*). It has not been established that a tenant may remove substantial and extensive additions to the premises, although he may have built them for the convenience of his trade, such as limekilns (*j*), pottery or brick-kilns, workshops, storehouses, and other buildings; nor indeed is it clearly determined that trade erections of a less substantial kind are in all cases removable by the tenant. Cases, therefore, of this description are subject to doubt, wherever the removal of the article would deteriorate the freehold to which it is attached, or where the structure or substance of the thing itself would be

(*e*) Decisions in favour of executors of tenant for life in tail or in fee, as against the remainderman, reversioner, or heir, may be considered as governing authorities in support of a tenant's rights. See Amos on Fixtures. pp. 28, 29. See also Lord Dudley *v.* Lord Warde, Amb. 114; Lawton *v.* Salmon, 1 H. Black. 259, *in notis*, 3 Atk. 16, *in notis*, S. C.

(*f*) Poole's case, 1 Salk. 368; Lawton *v.* Lawton, 3 Atk. 13; Lord Dudley *v.* Lord Warde, Amb. 114; Lawton *v.* Salmon, 1 H. Black. 259; Elwes *v.* Maw, 3 East. 58; Mansfield *v.* Blackburne, 6 Bing. N. C. 439.

(*g*) 3 Atk. 12, Amb. 114, 3 East. 53; Davis *v.* Jones, 2 B. & Ald. 165.

(*h*) Penton *v.* Robart, 2 East. 88.

(*i*) Dean *v.* Allalley, 3 Esp. 11. See 3 East. pp. 47, 55, 56.

(*j*) See Thresher *v.* East London Waterworks Co., 2 B. & C. 608; Judgmt. of Lord Brougham in Fisher *v.* Dixon, 12 Cl. & F. 312; Niblett *v.* Smith, 4 T. R. 504.

U

destroyed in the removal (*k*). It would seem, however, that a building accessory to the principal thing —*e.g.*, an engine-house built to shelter a removable engine—might be removed (*l*).

There are other circumstances besides those that relate to the construction of the thing affixed, which it may sometimes be necessary to consider in order to judge of the right of the tenant to remove trade erections. Thus the existence of a custom in respect of the property in question (*m*), the intention of the party in making the erection, the injury occasioned to the freehold by its removal, and the comparative value to the respective claimants. Mr Amos, in his work on Fixtures (*n*), after examining the authorities, says, "The following rule, however, may perhaps be found to be most consistent with the adjudged cases. That things which a tenant has fixed to the freehold for the purposes of trade or manufacture may be taken away by him, wherever the removal is not contrary to any prevailing practice; where the articles can be removed without causing material injury to the estate; and where, in themselves, they were of a perfect chattel nature before they were put up, or at least have in substance that character, independently of their union with the soil; or, in other words, where they may be removed without being entirely demolished, or losing their essential character or value. If an erection, put up in relation to trade, can be severed without violating any one of these conditions, it may very safely be affirmed, that whatever be its magnitude, construction, or mode of annexation, it is

(*k*) See 12 Cl. & F. 312; Walmsley *v.* Milne, 29 L. J. C. P. 97; Whitehead *v.* Bennett, 27 L. J. Ch. 474; Foley *v.* Addenbrooke, 13 M. & W. 174.

(*l*) Elwes *v.* Maw, 3 East. 38.
(*m*) Culling *v.* Tuffnall, Bul. N. P. 34; Davis *v.* Jones, 2 P. & Ald. 165.
(*n*) Page 48.

a fixture which a tenant is privileged to remove. It is not, however, meant to be inferred, that because in any particular instance these circumstances do not all concur, therefore an article cannot be removed by the tenant. On the contrary, it is not inconsistent with some of the decisions to say, that things may be removable, although these requisites are not completely fulfilled. And, indeed, when the liberality with which the Courts have generally been disposed to construe the indulgence in favour of trade is considered, it is not improbable that they would extend the privilege even to cases where not one of these conditions is found to be satisfied. The rule, therefore, here proposed is only offered as an affirmative one, that wherever the above-mentioned circumstances do concur, there an article may confidently be pronounced to belong to the tenant. And although it may be thought that this rule is too narrow to be of much practical utility, still no other could safely be laid down; because, upon looking into the judgments of the Courts, it is impossible not to see that, in a disputed claim between landlord and tenant, the absence of any one of the requisites which have been mentioned might, with propriety, be urged against the exercise of the tenant's right."

At common law a tenant in husbandry has not the same privilege as a tenant in trade; for he cannot take away fixtures which he has affixed to the demised premises at his own expense, for purposes which are merely agricultural. Thus it has been held that a tenant cannot remove a beast-house, carpenter's shop, fuel-house, cart-house, pump-house, or fold-yard wall, erected for the use of his farm, even though he leaves the premises exactly in the same state as he

Agricultural fixtures.

found them on his entry (*o*). This rule, however, is confined to articles of a strictly agricultural nature. For if the object and purpose of an erection has also relation to a trade of any description, the tenant may take it away, notwithstanding it is the means of obtaining the profits of land, subject to the principles before stated in the case of trade fixtures. Thus a tenant may take away a mill for making cider (*p*); or machinery for working mines and collieries (*q*); or, it would seem, utensils set up by the tenant for *manufacturing* salt from springs on the demised premises (*r*). So a nurseryman or gardener is entitled to remove and dispose of young trees and shrubs which he has planted for the purpose of sale (*s*). So it would seem that a tenant might remove fruit-trees also, although of full bearing age, if they are nursery-trees, such as he might fairly deal with in his trade (*t*). But it has been held that a tenant of garden ground could not plough up *strawberry beds*, although he had purchased them, and although there was a practice to pay for such plants as between outgoing and incoming tenants (*u*).

Now by the 14 & 15 Vict., c. 25, s. 3, "If any tenant of a farm or lands shall, after the passing of this Act, with the consent in writing of the landlord for the time being, at his own cost and expense, erect

(*o*) Elwes *v.* Maw, 3 East. 38. See judgment of Lord Ellenborough, 2 Smith L. C. 164, and notes.
(*p*) Lawton *v.* Lawton, 3 Atk. 12.
(*q*) Lord Dudley *v.* Lord Warde, Amb. 113.
(*r*) Lawton *v.* Salmon, 1 H. Blac. 259, *in notis*. See Amos on Fixtures, 60-63.
(*s*) Wyndham *v.* Way, 4 Taunt. 316, *per* Heath, J. See Lee *v.*

Risdon, 2 East. 191; and Penton *v.* Robart, 7 Taunt. 91.
(*t*) Wardell *v.* Usher, 3 Scott's N. Rep. 508.
(*u*) Wetherell *v.* Howells, 1 Camp. 237. This case was decided on the ground that the ploughing up of the plants was an injury maliciously done to the reversion, and that the plants were not removed by the tenant for sale in his ordinary occupation.

any farm building, either detached or otherwise, or put any other building, engine, or machinery, either for agricultural purposes, or for the purposes of trade and agriculture (which shall not have been erected or put up in pursuance of some obligation in that behalf), then all such buildings, engines, and machinery shall be the property of the tenant, and shall be removable by him, notwithstanding the same may consist of separate buildings, or that the same, or any part thereof, may be built in, or permanently fixed to the soil, so as the tenant making any such removal do not in anywise injure the land or buildings belonging to the landlord, or otherwise do put the same in like plight and condition, or as good plight and condition, as the same were in before the erection of anything so removed: Provided, nevertheless, that no tenant shall, under the provision last aforesaid, be entitled to remove any such matter or thing as aforesaid, without first giving to the landlord, or to his agent, one month's previous notice in writing of his intention so to do; and thereupon it shall be lawful for the landlord, or his agent on his authority, to elect to purchase the matters and things so proposed to be removed, or any of them, and the right to remove the same shall thereby cease, and the same shall belong to the landlord; and the value thereof shall be ascertained and determined by two referees, one to be chosen by each party, or by an umpire to be named by such referees, and shall be paid or allowed in account by the landlord who shall have so elected to purchase the same."

In general, a tenant must remove his fixtures before the expiration of his tenancy (*v*). In Lyde *v.* Russell (*w*), this rule was expressly recognised and

When to be removed.

(*v*) Poole's case, 1 Salk. 368; *Ex parte* Quincey, 1 Atk. 477; Dudley *v.* Warde, Amb. 113; Year-books, 20 Hen. VII. 13, 21 Hen. VII. 26; Minshall *v.* Lloyd, 2 M. & W. 450; Pugh *v.* Arton, L. R. 8 Eq. 626.
(*w*) 1 B. & Ad. 394.

approved by Lord Tenterden, C.J., who added, "According to these authorities, then, the property in fixtures which would be in the tenant if he removed them during the term, vests in the landlord on the determination of the term." Sometimes a tenant under certain circumstances may retain his right of removing his fixtures, where he continues in possession after the expiration of his tenancy, and this would seem (x) to depend upon the question whether he had intended to abandon his property in the fixtures. But even in this case the tenant may be liable to an action at the suit of his landlord for being on the premises after his tenancy has expired (y). If the interest that the tenant has in the demised premises be uncertain, or if he is strictly a tenant at will, or tenant *pur autre vie*, he will be allowed a reasonable time to remove his fixtures after the actual determination of his tenancy (z). So where the tenancy is determined by the death of the lessor (a). But where steam-engines were removable by the lessee, and had not been removed previously to the lessor entering for a forfeiture, it was held that trover could not be maintained for them (b). So where a lessor re-enters for a forfeiture, by reason of the tenant having become a bankrupt, the bankrupt or his assignees cannot afterwards sever and remove any fixtures (c), except in pursuance of a special stipulation in that behalf (d). So where a lessor recovers possession under an ejectment for a forfeiture, the tenant has no

(x) See judgment of Lord Kenyon, C.J., in Penton $v.$ Robart, 2 East. 88; Hallen $v.$ Runder, 1 Cr. M. & N. 275.
(y) Penton $v.$ Robart, *supra*.
(z) Weeton $v.$ Woodcock, 7 M. & W. 14, *per* Parke, B., in Mackintosh $v.$ Trotter, 3 M. & W. 184.
(a) Heap $v.$ Barton, 12 C. B. 278; Martin $v.$ Roe, 7 E. & B. 237.

(b) Minshall $v.$ Lloyd, 2 M. & W. 450; Mackintosh $v.$ Trotter, 3 M. & W. 184. But see Sumner $v.$ Bromilow, 34 L. J. Q. B. 130.
(c) Weeton $v.$ Woodcock, 7 M. & W. 14; Pugh $v.$ Arton, L. R. 8 Eq. 626.
(d) Stansfield $v.$ The Mayor of Portsmouth, 4 C. B. N.S. 120, 27 L. J. C. P. 124; Sumner $v.$ Bromilow, *supra*.

right afterwards to sever and remove any fixtures (*e*). Where the purchaser of lands having brought an ejectment against the tenant from year to year, the parties entered into an agreement that judgment should be signed for the plaintiff, with a stay of execution till a given period; it was held that the tanant could not in the interval remove buildings, &c., from the premises which he had himself erected during his term, and before the action was brought (*f*). Where the landlord, during the term, by letter declined to buy the tenant's fixtures, but added, " I have no objection to your leaving them on the premises, and making the best terms you can with the incoming tenant;" such letter was held not to operate as a valid license (it not being under seal); and if the new tenant refuse to pay for the fixtures so left, or to permit them to be removed, no action of trover will lie for them, whilst they remain unsevered from the freehold (*g*).

2. WHERE THERE IS AN AGREEMENT.

If there is an express agreement between the landlord and tenant respecting fixtures, the rules and principles before stated will be overruled by that agreement. Thus if a tenant covenants to repair the demised premises and all erections built or that may be afterwards built thereon, such covenant will prevent the tenant from taking down an erection put up by himself for the purpose of his trade (*h*). So where the lessee has covenanted to deliver up the premises at the

<small>Where there is an agreement.</small>

(*e*) Minshall *v.* Lloyd, 2 M. & W. 450; Mackintosh *v.* Trotter, 3 M. & W. 184. But see Sumner *v.* Bromilow, 34 L. J. Q. B. 130.

(*f*) Fitzherbert *v.* Shaw, 1 H. Blac. 258; Heap *v.* Barton, 12 C. B. 274.

(*g*) Roffey *v.* Henderson, 17 Q. B. 574; Leader *v.* Homewood, 5 C. B. N.S. 546.

(*h*) See the following cases :—
Naylor *v.* Collinge, 1 Taunt. 19; Thresher *v.* East London Waterworks Co., 2 B. & C. 608;

end of the term, together with all dues, &c., and all other things which now are, or, any time during the said term shall be, fixed or fastened to the freehold, he has no right to remove trade fixtures (i). So custom may sometimes regulate the relative rights of landlord and tenant with regard to fixtures (j). But any such custom will be set aside by an express agreement inconsistent with it (k). Therefore, before a tenant severs an article from the freehold, it is necessary that he should examine his claim, not only with reference to the general law of fixtures, but also as it may be affected by any covenant or stipulation in his lease. If a tenant, at the expiration of his term, is desirous of renewing it, or if he enters into any fresh agreement respecting the premises, he should be careful to make a stipulation as to his fixtures, otherwise by making such fresh engagement he may lose his property therein (l). When a tenant, at the commencement of his term, purchases of the landlord articles affixed to the premises, his right of removal depends on the contract between them. In a contract which concerns

Dean v. Allalley, 3 Esp. 11; Earl of Mansfield v. Blackburne, 6 Bing. N. C. 426; Penry v. Brown, 2 Starkie, 403; West v. Blakeway, 2 M. & G. 729, 9 Dowl. 846; Haslett v. Burt, 18 C. B. 162, 893, 25 L. J. C. P. 201, 295; Wilson v. Whately, 1 J. & H. 436, 7 Jur. N.S. 908; Dumergue v. Rumsay, 2 H. & C. 777, 33 L. J. Ex. 88; Storer v. Hunter, 3 B. & C. 368; Clark v. Crownshaw, 3 B. & Ad. 804; Horn v. Baker, 9 East. 215, 2 Smith L. C. 161, 4th edit.; Fairburn v. Eastwood, 6 M. & W. 679; Foley v. Addenbrooke, 13 M. & W. 174, Amos on Fixt. 90; Reg. v. Topping, M'Clel. & You. 544; Martyr v. Bradley, 9 Bing. 24; Bishop v. Elliott (in error), 11 Ex. 113, 24 L. J. Ex. 229.

The Court below decided that the lessee had the right to sell only the trade fixtures; Elliott v. Bishop, 10 Ex. 496, 522, 24 L. J. Ex. 33; but the Judges were much divided in opinion; Drake v. Braddyll, M'Clel. 217, 13 Price, 455.

(i) Bidder v. Trinidad Petroleum Co., 17 W. R. 153.

(j) Trappes v. Harter, 4 Tyrwh. 603, S. C. 2 Cr. & M. 153; Davis v. Jones, 2 B. & A. 165; Wetherall v. Howells, 1 Camp. 227; Culling v. Tuffnall, Bull. N. P. 34; Wansborough v. Maton, 4 A. & E. 884.

(k) Wiltshear v. Cottrell, 1 E. & B. 674.

(l) See Amos on Fixtures, 117. Thresher v. East London Waterworks Co., 2 B. & C. 608.

realty as well as fixtures, if it is intended that the fixtures should be paid for separately, a stipulation to that effect should be inserted (*m*); for without such stipulation fixtures would pass to the vendee like timber upon land (*n*). Contracts for the sale of fixtures are not within the Statute of Frauds, as they are not goods or chattels within the meaning of the statute; nor do they, although annexed to the freehold, constitute an interest in land (*o*). But a memorandum of the actual sale of fixtures requires a conveyance stamp, and it makes no difference that it is in the past tense (*p*). A reversionary interest in trade fixtures will pass by an agreement in writing though not under seal (*q*). Where a lessee, who had power to remove a greenhouse fixed to the freehold, agreed to sell the lease, together with the greenhouse and furniture, plants and crops, for a certain sum, but was afterwards unable to obtain the lessor's consent to the assignment of the lease, which was necessary; it was held that the contract was an entire one, and that the lessee could not sue for the price of the greenhouse (*r*). A steam-engine erected for the purpose of working a colliery, to be used by the lessee of such colliery during his term, but to be held as the property of the landlord subject to such use, was held not to pass to the assignees of the tenant on his bankruptcy, on the ground that it did not come within the description of "goods and chattels" in the 12 & 13 Vict., c. 106, s. 125, nor had the bankrupt the actual or apparent ownership (*s*). In a later case it was held that fixtures,

(*m*) Colegrave *v.* Dias Santos, 2 B. & C. 76.
(*n*) Crockford *v.* Alexander, 15 Ves. 138; Boydell *v.* M'Michael, 1 C. M. & R. 177.
(*o*) Hallen *v.* Runder, 1 C. M. & R. 275; Lee *v.* Risdon, 7 Taunt. 191.
(*p*) Horsall *v.* Hey, 2 Ex. 778.
(*q*) Petrie *v.* Dawson, 2 C. & K. 138.
(*r*) Sleddon *v.* Cruikshank, 16 M. & W. 71.
(*s*) Coombes *v.* Beaumont, 5 B. & Ad. 72, *ex parte* Broadwood Id. 631.

part of which were erected before a mortgage and part afterwards, and which were by law removable as between landlord and tenant, as well as on the principle of the benefit of trade, passed to the mortgagee and not to the assignees of the bankrupt mortgagor under the same section (*t*). Where copper-roller manufacturers, being seised in fee of a mill and land, erected thereon steam-engines, machinery, &c., for the purpose of their trade, and then mortgaged in fee the mill and land, with all fixtures, &c., and afterwards became bankrupt; it was held that the mortgagees were entitled to all the machinery, &c., fixed to the freehold, and that the deed did not require to be registered as a bill of sale under the 17 & 18 Vict., c. 36 (*u*). But a mortgage of trade fixtures without the mill or land to which they are annexed is a mortgage of personal chattels within the meaning of 17 & 18 Vict., c. 36, as explained by sect. 7, which includes "fixtures and other articles capable of complete transfer by delivery" (*v*). And such fixtures will be deemed to be in the order and disposition of a mortgagor in the event of his bankruptcy, whilst he remains in possession thereof (*w*). The registration of the mortgage under the Bill of Sale Act (17 & 18 Vict., c. 36), makes no difference in this respect (*x*). By a mortgage of a mill, the stones, tackling, and implements pass to the mortgagee (*y*). So do looms and other machinery fixed to the floor (*z*). So do trade fixtures which before or after the mortgage have been affixed to the freehold by the mortagor for

(*t*) Ex parte Reynel, 2 Mont. D. & De G. 443.
(*u*) Mather v. Fraser, 2 K. & J. 536, 25 L. J. Ch. 361; Boyd v. Shorrock, L. R. 5 Eq. 72, 37 L. J. Ch. 154.
(*v*) Waterfall v. Penistone, 6 E. & Bl. 876, 26 L. J. Q. B. 100.
(*w*) Whitmore v. Empson, 23 Beav. 313, 26 L. J. Ch. 364.

(*x*) Badger v. Shaw, 2 E. & E. 472, 29 L. J. Q. B. 73; Re Daniel, ex parte Ashby, 25 L. T. R. 188.
(*y*) Place v. Fagg, 4 M. & R. 277; Ex parte Bentley re West, 2 Mont. D. & D.
(*z*) Boyd v. Shorrock, *supra*; Re Dawson, Tate, & Co., 16 W. R. 424.

the purpose of trade, and not for the improvement of the inheritance, and which are capable of being removed without damage to the freehold (*a*). An equitable mortgage of a leasehold public-house with the fixtures therein, consisting of ordinary house fixtures and trade fixtures, will be sufficient to prevent any of them being in the order and disposition of the lessee on his becoming bankrupt (*b*). Under an equitable mortgage, by the simple deposit of a lease unaccompanied by any memorandum, the tenant fixtures will be included (*c*).

Upon the demise of a house, it is usually agreed between the landlord and tenant that the fixtures shall be taken at a valuation—*i.e.*, such fixtures as a tenant would ordinarily be entitled to remove if he had put them up. It is expedient that such fixtures should be enumerated in the conveyance by schedule or otherwise, when it is intended that they should be paid for separately from the premises demised (*d*). If the landlord agrees to make an allowance for the fixtures at the end of the term, it would seem that those fixtures only should be valued which were paid for by the tenant at the commencement (*e*).

Valuation.

When it is agreed between an outgoing and incoming tenant that the fixtures on the premises are to be taken at a valuation, the broker should value such things to the incoming tenant as under the general law of fixtures are removable between a landlord and his tenant, and all fixed articles upon the premises

---

(*a*) Culwick *v.* Swindell, L. R. 3 Eq. 249, 37 L. J. Ch. 173; Climie *v.* Wood, L. R. 3 Ex. 257, 37 L. J. Ex. 158.
(*b*) *Ex parte* Barclay, 5 De G. M. & G. 403.
(*c*) Williams *v.* Evans, 23 Beav. 239.
(*d*) Colegrave *v.* Dias Santos, 2. B. & C. 76; Thresher *v.* East London Waterworks, 608.
(*e*) See Amos on Fixtures, 351.

falling within this description should be included in the valuation, although they may in fact have been originally purchased of the landlord by the outgoing tenant. But the outgoing tenant cannot insist on anything being appraised which, as against his landlord, he is not authorised by his lease to sever. If an incoming tenant agree with an outgoing tenant for the purchase of his fixtures, he should require that the landlord be made privy to the transaction, otherwise the incoming tenant may find that he has no right to remove them at the end of his tenancy (*f*). The rights of incoming and outgoing tenants are regulated in a great degree by custom (*g*). The valuation of the fixtures requires an appraisement stamp (*h*).

(*f*) Elliot *v.* Bishop, 10 Ex. 496, 11 Ex. 113 ; Burt *v.* Haslett, 18 C. B. 162, 893. See Minshall *v.* Lloyd, 2 M. & W. 450.

(*g*) See Davis *v.* Jones, 2 B. & Ald. 165 ; Wetherall *v.* Howells, 1 Camp. 227.

(*h*) Amos on Fixtures, 357. See Stamp Act, 1870, 33 & 34 Vict. c. 97.

PART IV.

CHANGE OF PARTIES.

CHAPTER I.

BY ACT OF THE PARTIES.

	PAGE		PAGE
1. By Landlord—	317	4. Covenants running	
attornment	318	with the Land—	
2. By Tenant	321	word 'assigns,' use of	326
3. Consequences—			
at common law	322	5. Assignment of part	328
by 32 Hen. VIII. c. 34	322		

A CHANGE of parties may take place either by the act of the parties themselves, as by assignment, attornment, or underletting, or by the operation of law, as through the death of either party, or through bankruptcy, marriage, or proceeding at law under a writ of execution.

1. BY LANDLORD.

A landlord may by deed assign his reversion (*a*), By landlord. and the consequences of such assignment as they affect the covenants will be considered, *post*, ss. 3-5. So also he may mortgage his property subsequently to the making of the lease, and such mortgage will ope-

(*a*) Beely *v.* Perry, 3 Lev. 155.

rate as an assignment of the reversion (*b*). So he may assign his property for the benefit of his creditors, but this will be considered under the title Bankruptcy, *post*, c. 2, s. 2.

We shall now consider the effect of attornment and acts amounting to attornment.

Attornment. Attornment is the consent of the vassal to the new lord upon alienation or transfer, and without this attornment a grant was in most cases void or incomplete (*c*).

By various Acts of Parliament restrictions against alienation have been removed, and principally by the Statute of *quia emptores* (18 Ed. I., c. 1), and the 12 Car. II., c. 24. The doctrine of attornment continued to a still later period, until, by the 4 & 5 Anne, c. 16, it was made no longer necessary to attorn in order to complete a grant or conveyance; and by the 11 Geo. II., c. 19, s. 11, the attornment of any tenant does not affect the possession of any lands, unless made with the consent of the landlord, or to a mortgagee after the mortgage is forfeited, or by direction of a court of justice.

By sect. 10 of the 4 & 5 Anne, c. 16, " No tenant shall be prejudiced or damaged by payment of any rent to any grantor or conusor, or by breach of any condition for non-payment of rent before notice shall be given to him of such grant by such grantee or conusee " (*d*).

(*b*) Rogers *v*. Humphrey, 4 A. & E. 299, 313. See *post*.
(*c*) Litt. s. 551.
(*d*) See Lumley *v*. Hodgson, 16 East. 99.

A payment of rent by a tenant to his landlord before the day when it becomes due is not a payment of rent within this section; therefore, where a tenant paid two quarters' rent in advance to his landlord, in ignorance of an assignment by the landlord of his interest in the premises to a third person, it was held that the assignee, after notice of the assignment to the tenant, was entitled to distrain (*e*).

The effect of the statute of Anne is, therefore, to substitute a giving of notice for attornment (*f*).

Where the party comes in by judgment of law—*e.g.*, as tenant by *elegit*—no attornment is necessary (*g*).

An assignee of the reversion by way of mortgage can sue for rent, &c., without attornment; but a mortgagee before the lease is not in the position of assignee of the reversion until attornment (*h*). After attornment he may distrain for arrears of rent thereby admitted to be due (*i*).

It seems, however, that, without attornment, a notice by the mortgagee to pay rent, if it is acquiesced in by the tenant, would operate as an attornment (*j*).

Payment of rent may be evidence of an attornment, but the circumstances of the case may rebut the presumption of an attornment; as where rent was

(*e*) De Nicols *v.* Saunders, 39 L. J. C. P. 296, L. R. 5 C. P. 589.
(*f*) See Moss *v.* Gallimore, 1 Smith L. C. 5th edit. 542.
(*g*) Lloyd *v.* Davies, 2 Ex. 103. As to where, in an avowry or cognisance, it is necessary to aver an attornment, see Vigers *v.* Dean and Chapter of St Paul's, 19 L. J. Q. B. 84.
(*h*) Evans *v.* Elliott, 9 A. & E. 342. See the notes to Moss *v.* Gallimore, 1 Smith L. C. 542.
(*i*) Gladman *v.* Plumer, 15 L. J. Q. B. 79.
(*j*) Brown *v.* Storey, 1 M. & G. 117.

paid after notice of an adverse claim, though the precise nature of the claim was unknown (*k*).

An instrument whereby the tenant merely puts one person in the place of another as his landlord, without varying the terms or conditions of his holding, is an attornment; but if it varies the terms, &c., it will amount to an agreement (*l*).

The tenant who attorns is generally estopped from denying the title of the person to whom he has attorned (*m*).

There is a distinction, however, between the case where a tenant has actually received possession from one who has no title, and the case where he has merely attorned by mistake or fraud. In the former case, the tenant cannot, except under very special circumstances, dispute the title; in the latter he may (*n*).

Where a person having possession of land under a good title inadvertently attorns and pays rent to a stranger, he is not estopped after the determination of the tenancy from setting up his own title in an ejectment by the landlord (*o*).

(*k*) Fenner *v.* Duploc, 2 Bing. 10; Gregory *v.* Doidge, 3 Bing. 474; Claridge *v.* Mackenzie, 4 M. & G. 143.
(*l*) Doe *d.* Lindsay *v.* Edwards, 5 A. & E. 95; Cornish *v.* Searell, 8 B. & C. 471; Doe *d.* Wright *v.* Smith, 8 A. & E. 255.
(*m*) Gravenor *v.* Woodhouse, 2 Bing. 71; Doe *d.* Marlow *v.* Wiggins, 4 Q. B. 367; Hill *v.* Saunders, 4 B. & C. 529; Cooke *v.* Loxley, 5 T. R. 4.
(*n*) Cornish *v.* Searell, 8 B. & C. 471, *per* Bayley, J., 475, citing Rogers *v.* Pitcher, 6 Taunt. 202, and Gravenor *v.* Woodhouse, 1 Bing. 38. See also Gregory *v.* Doidge, 3 Bing. 174; Doe *d.* Plevin *v.* Brown, 7 A. & E. 447; Brook *v.* Biggs, 2 Bing. N.C. 572.
(*o*) Accidental Death Insurance

2. BY TENANT.

A change of parties may take place by the tenant By tenant. assigning his term, and the consequences of such an assignment will be considered, *post*, ss. 3, 4, 5.

A change of possession takes place upon an underletting by the tenant; and with respect to underleases, it should be observed that the original lessee is liable upon the covenants entered into by him, although the under-lessee may have entered into similar covenants with the original lessee (*q*). It is the duty of the under-lessee to ascertain the contents of the original lease (*r*).

An under-lease should contain an express covenant on the part of the under-lessee to perform all the covenants and conditions, &c., in the original lease, except such as it is not intended he should perform. It is not sufficient to insert in the lease similar covenants, even if couched in the identical words of the covenants of the original lease, for the covenants may not after all be the same, as they may begin to operate at different times, and so may vary substantially in their operation (*s*).

3. CONSEQUENCES OF ASSIGNMENT.

At common law, when the landlord assigned the At common tenant became bound to pay rent to the assignee, but law.

Co. *v.* Mackenzie, 9 W. R. 713, 5 L. T. N.S. 20.
(*q*) Logan *v.* Hall, 4 C. B. 598, 613, 624.
(*r*) Cosser *v.* Collinge, 3 Myl. & K. 283; Grosvenor *v.* Green, 28 L. J. Ch. 173.
(*s*) See Logan *v.* Hall, *supra*.

X

the express covenants of the lease being distinct contracts, and only *choses in action*, did not pass, and neither lessee nor assignee could sue upon them (*t*).

By 32 Hen. VIII. c. 34.

By 32 Hen. VIII., c. 34, it was enacted, "That all persons being grantees or assignees to or by the King, or to or by any other persons than the King, and their heirs, executors, successors, and assigns, shall have like advantage against the lessees, their executors, administrators, and assigns, by entry for non-payment of the rent, or for doing of waste, or other forfeiture, and by action only for not performing other conditions, covenants or agreements expressed in the indentures of leases, and grants against the said lessees and grantees, their executors, administrators, and assignees, as the said lessors and grantors, their heirs, or successors, might have had."

Sect. 2 enacted, "That all lessees and grantees of lands or other hereditaments for terms of years, life, or lives, their executors, administrators, or assigns, shall have like action and remedy against all persons and bodies politic, their heirs, successors, and assigns, having any gift or grant of the King, or of any other persons, of the reversion of the lands and hereditaments so letten, or any parcel thereof, for any condition or covenant expressed in the indentures of their leases, as the same lessees might have had against the said lessors and grantors, their heirs and successors."

Since this statute the assignee of the reversion and of the term stand in nearly the same position as the

(*t*) Wms. Saund. 240 a, note 2; 1 Smith L. C. 51, 6th edit.; Martyn *v.* Williams, 1 H. & N. 817, 826, 26 L. J. Ex. 117.

CH. I.] BY ACT OF THE PARTIES. 323

heir-at-law (*u*) and tenant formerly did, both with respect to covenants in law (*v*) and express covenants (*w*), and can sue and be sued accordingly. The statute applies to grantees of part of the reversion (*x*). There are, however, some limitations to the operation of the statute.

Causes of action which accrued previous to the assignment of the reversion will not pass with it (*y*). The statute does not extend to mere collateral covenants, but to such as run with the land (*z*). The statute only applies to leases by deeds, so that the assignee of the reversion upon a lease not under seal cannot sue upon the lease (*a*), and the lessor in such case does not lose any of his rights of action against the lessee by assignment (*b*).

Where a lessee assigns his term, he enters into covenants that all has been done by him to maintain the lease, and the assignee, on his part, covenants to pay the rent, and perform the covenants in the lease, and save harmless the assignor (*c*).

A lessee continues liable in covenant to his lessor upon express (*d*) covenants, notwithstanding an as-

(*u*) See Webb *v.* Russell, 3 T. R. 393.
(*v*) See *ante*, tit. Covenants, p. 114.
(*w*) Ibid.
(*x*) Rawlings *v.* Morgan, 34 L. J. C. P. 185.
(*y*) Hunt *v.* Bishop, 8 Exch. 675, 22 L. J. Ex. 337; Hunt *v.* Remnant, 9 Exch. 635, 23 L. J. Ex. 135; Martyn *v.* Williams, 1 H. & N. 817, 26 L. J. Ex. 117.
(*z*) Webb *v.* Russell, 3 T. R. 393. See *post*, sect. 4, p. 324.
(*a*) Standen *v.* Christmas, 10 Q.
B. 135; Elliot *v.* Johnson, L. R. 2 Q. B. 120.
(*b*) Bickford *v.* Parson, 5 C. B. 920.
(*c*) Staines *v.* Morris, 1 V. & B. 10; Wolveridge *v.* Steward, 1 Cr. & M. 644; Harris *v.* Goodwyn, 2 M. & G. 405; Burnett *v.* Lynch, 5 B. & C. 589.
(*d*) It is said to be otherwise as to implied covenants. Batchelor *v.* Gage, 1 Sid. 447; Sir W. Jones 223; Auriol *v.* Mills, 4 T. R. 98; Williams *v.* Burrell, 1 C. B. 402.

signment of the term and acceptance of rent (*e*), as well as to his assignee (*f*).

There is an implied promise on the part of each successive assignee of a lease to indemnify the original lessee against breaches of covenants in the lease committed by such assignee during the continuance of his own term; and such promise will be implied although each assignee expressly covenants to indemnify his immediate assignor against all subsequent breaches (*g*).

An action of covenant will not lie against the assignee of a lessee for breaches committed after the assignee has assigned over to a third party (*h*), but he will be answerable for breaches committed before the assignment over (*i*).

Where the right of action is given to the assignee by the statute, the privity of contract is transferred, and it seems that the original covenantee cannot sue (*j*).

4. COVENANTS RUNNING WITH THE LAND.

Covenants running with the land.

The assignee of the reversion having by the statute (*k*) a right to sue the tenant, and the assignee of the term a right to sue the landlord upon covenants

---

(*e*) Barnard *v.* Godscall, Cro. Jac. 309; Norton *v.* Acland, Cro. Car. 579; Glover *v.* Cope, 4 Mod. 81; Marsh *v.* Bruce, Cro. Jac. 334; 1 Smith L. C. 56, 6th edit.
(*f*) Brett *v.* Cumberland, Cro. Jac. 521; Thursby *v.* Plant, 1 Wms. Saund. 241.
(*g*) Moule *v.* Garrett, L. R. 5 Ex. 132, 39 L. J. Ex. 69.
(*h*) Taylor *v.* Shum, 1 B. & P.
21; Le Keux *v.* Nash, Str. 1222; Odell *v.* Wake, 3 Camp. 394; Onslow *v.* Corrie, 2 Madd. 330. See *post*, c. 2, Death of Lessee.
(*i*) Harley *v.* King, 5 Tyrwh. 692.
(*j*) Beeley *v.* Parry, 3 Lev. 154; Green *v.* James, 6 M. & W. 656. See Thursby *v.* Plant, 1 Wms Saund. 240.
(*k*) *Ante*, p. 322.

which *run with the land* (*l*), or which *touch and concern the thing demised*, it is necessary to consider what these covenants are.

All covenants in law (*m*), generally called implied covenants, run with the land (*n*).

There are many express covenants which run with the land.

Express covenants for quiet enjoyment (*o*), for further assurance (*p*), for renewal (*q*), for repairs (*r*), and not to assign without license (*s*), run with the land.

So a covenant to maintain a sea-wall (*t*), that the lessee should constantly reside on the premises (*u*), that either party should have power to determine the lease (*v*), not to carry on a particular trade (*w*), to leave part of the land as pasture, or to cultivate in a particular manner (*x*), to produce title-deeds (*y*), to supply water to houses at a certain rate (*z*), runs with the land.

(*l*) Ante, p. 116.
(*m*) Ante, p. 135, et seq.
(*n*) Ante, p. 136.
(*o*) Campbell v. Lewis, 3 B. & A. 392; Williams v. Burrell, 1 C. B. 402.
(*p*) Middlemore v. Goodale, Cro. Car. 503.
(*q*) Roe v. Hayley, 12 East. 464; Brook v. Bulkeley, 2 Ves. Sen. 498; Simpson v. Clayton, 4 Bing. N. C. 758.
(*r*) Dean and Chapter of Windsor's case, 5 Co. 24; Lougher v. Williams, 2 Lev. 92; Buckley v. Pirk, 1 Salk. 317; Wakefield v. Brown, 9 Q. B. 209; Martyn v. Clue, 18 Q. B. 661.
(*s*) Williams v. Earle, L. R. 3 Q. B. 739, 37 L. J. Q. B. 231. It seems that this covenant will not run with the land unless "assigns" are mentioned. See Philpot v. Hoare, 2 Atk. 219, and the note to West v. Dobb, L. R. 4 Q. B. 637, per Blackburn, J.
(*t*) Morland v. Cook, L. R. 6 Eq. 212, 267, 37 L. J. Ch. 825.
(*u*) Tatem v. Chaplin, 2 H. Bl. 133.
(*v*) Roe v. Hayley, 12 East. 464.
(*w*) Per Lord Ellenborough, in Mayor of Congleton v. Pattison, 10 East. 130; Hunt v. Bishop, 8 Ex. 675, 9 Id. 635.
(*x*) Cockson v. Cock, Cro. Jac. 125.
(*y*) Barclay v. Raine, 1 Sim. & St. 449.
(*z*) Jourdain v. Wilson, 4 B. & A. 266.

A covenant to insure premises within the operation of 14 Geo. III., c. 78, s. 83 (*a*), enabling the owner to have the sum insured laid out upon the premises, was held to run with the land (*b*).

Where in the *reddendum* there was a stipulation for doing suit to the mill of the lessor by grinding there all such corn as should grow on the premises, it was held that this was in the nature of rent, and was a covenant which ran with the land (*c*).

A covenant to repair and leave in repair all buildings, &c., which should be erected, was held to run with the land (*d*).

So a covenant to build a new mill in lieu of an old one was held to run with the land (*e*).

Where there was a covenant that fixtures and movable things should be kept in repair and restored, it was held that, so far as it related to fixtures, it ran with the land, but as to mere movables, it was otherwise (*f*).

A covenant relating to a way or other profit appurtenant goes with the land (*g*).

Use of word "assigns."

In preparing covenants which are intended to run with the land, the "assigns" should always be men-

(*a*) See the 22 & 23 Vict. c. 35, s. 7.
(*b*) Vernon *v.* Smith, 5 B. & A. 1.
(*c*) Vyvian *v.* Arthur, 1 B. & C. 410.
(*d*) Minshull *v.* Oakes, 2 H. & N. 793, 27 L. J. Ex. 194. See *post*, p. 327.
(*e*) Easterly *v.* Sampson, 6 Bing.
644, 1 C. & J. 105. In this case "assigns" were named. See *infra*.
(*f*) Williams *v.* Earle, L. R. 3 Q. B. 739, 752. See also Gorton *v.* Gregory, 3 B. & S. 90, 31 L. J. Q. B. 302.
(*g*) Cole's case, 1 Show. 388, 1 Salk. 196.

tioned; for there is a class of cases in which assigns are bound if mentioned, but not otherwise; and it is prudent to provide for the possibility of a covenant being held to belong to this class (*h*).

There appears to be considerable doubt as to whether a covenant relating to something not *in esse* will run with the land or not (*i*). Such a covenant, according to Spencer's case, will not run with the land unless the "assigns" be named. This decision was followed in many cases, and, amongst others, in the case of Doughty *v.* Bowman (*j*). The Court of Exchequer, however, thought the question whether the "assigns" were named or not was wholly immaterial, and, according to their view of the law, the sole question was whether the thing covenanted to be done would touch or concern the thing demised, or be merely collateral or personal (*k*). In a subsequent case in equity, Turner, L.J., noticed that a covenant did not purport to bind the assigns, as though that would not be immaterial; but the case of Minshull *v.* Oakes does not appear to have been cited (*l*).

Covenants which are merely collateral or personal, or which relate only to the personal use and enjoyment of the land, and not to the permanent user of the land itself (*m*), do not run with the land, even if assigns are expressly named (*n*).

(*h*) Woodfall L. & T. 10th edit. 111. See note to West *v.* Dobb, L. R. 4 Q. B. 637.
(*i*) This question is discussed at length in the notes to Spencer's case. 1 Smith L. C. 46, 6th edit.
(*j*) Doughty *v.* Bowman, 11 Q. B. 444. See also Greenaway *v.* Hart, 1 C. B. 340, and Mayor of Congleton *v.* Pattison, 10 East. 130, *per* Lord Ellenborough, C.J.

(*k*) Minshull *v.* Oakes, 2 H. & N. 806, 27 L. J. Ex. 194.
(*l*) Wilson *v.* Hart, L. R. 1 Ch. Ap. 463, 466, 35 L. J. Ch. 569, 572.
(*m*) Wilson *v.* Hart, *supra*.
(*n*) Spencer's case, *supra ;* Bac. Abr. tit. Covenant, (E) 2, 5 ; Att.-Gen. *v.* Cox, 3 H. L. Cas. 240 ; Webb *v.* Russell, 3 T. R. 393 ; Stokes *v.* Russell, 3 T. R. 678 ; Russell *v.* Stokes, 1 H. Bl. 562;

Covenants which relate to mere movables do not run with the land (*o*).

A joint-covenant with tenants in common does not run with the land or with the reversion (*p*).

4. ASSIGNMENT OF PART.

Assignment of part.

An assignment may be made of a part of a reversion or term in the whole of the lands, or of the whole of the reversion or term as to part of the lands.

The 32 Hen. VIII., c. 34, has been held to apply to these cases, and an action of covenant will lie against the assignee (*q*).

An assignee of part of the estate demised, or the assignees of several parts jointly, or the assignee of five-sixths of the estate, being tenant in common with the assignee of the remaining sixth, may bring covenant (*r*).

The assignee of a part of the lands is not liable to be sued for the whole rent, but only for a proportional part (*s*).

Plight *v*. Glossop, 2 Bing. N. C. 125; Mayor of Congleton *v*. Pattison, 10 East. 130.

(*o*) Williams *v*. Earle, L. R. 3 Q. B. 739, 752; Gorton *v*. Gregory, 3 B. & S. 90, 31 L. J. Q. B. 302.

(*p*) Roach *v*. Wadham, 6 East. 289; Thompson *v*. Hakewill, 19 C. B. N.S. 713, 720.

(*q*) 1 Inst. 215 a; Congham *v*. King, Cro. Car. 221; Kidwelly *v*. Brand, Plowd. 69; Twynam *v*. Pickard, 2 B. & A. 105; Yates *v*. Cole, 2 Bro. & Bing. 660; Wollaston *v*. Hakewill, 3 M. & Gr. 297; Wright *v*. Burroughes, 3 C. B. 685; Badeley *v*. Vigurs, 4 E. & B. 71; Palmer *v*. Edwards, 1 Doug. 187 n.; Stevenson *v*. Lambard, 2 East. 575.

(*r*) Com. Dig. tit. Covenant, (B) 3; Simpson *v*. Clayton, 4 Bing. N. C. 758-780.

(*s*) Holford *v*. Hatch, 1 Doug. 183; Hare *v*. Cator, Cowp. 766; Curtis *v*. Spitty, 1 Bing. N. C. 756; Wollaston *v*. Hakewill, *supra*.

The lessee who assigns is still liable for the entire rent, for he cannot apportion it, and the covenant is personal as to him (*s*).

Although covenants could be apportioned, yet it was otherwise at common law with respect to conditions (*t*). It was, however, held that the assignee of part of the reversion in the whole of the land might avail himself of a condition, though the assignee of the whole reversion in a part of the land could not (*u*). But now, by the 22 & 23 Vict., c. 35, s. 3, where the reversion upon a lease is severed, and the rent or other reservation is equally apportioned, the assignee of each part of the reversion shall, in respect of the apportioned rent or other reservation allotted or belonging to him, have and be entitled to the benefit of all conditions or powers of re-entry for non-payment of the original rent, or other reservation, in like manner as if such conditions or powers had been reserved to him as incident to his part of the reversion in respect of the apportioned rent, or other reservation allotted or belonging to him.

(*s*) Broom *v.* Hore, Cro. Eliz. 633; Ards *v.* Watkin, Cro. Eliz. 637; Stevenson *v.* Lambard, 2 East. 575, 579.

(*t*) Twynam *v.* Pickard, 2 B. & A. 105.

(*u*) Wright *v.* Burroughes, 3 C. B. 685.

CHAPTER II.

BY ACT OF LAW.

	PAGE		PAGE
1. DEATH—		3. MARRIAGE—	
of lessor,	... 330	*of female lessor,*	... 342
of lessee,	... 331	*of female lessee,*	... 343
2. BANKRUPTCY,	... 334	4. WRITS OF EXECUTION,	348

A CHANGE of parties may take place by act of law as well as by the act of the parties themselves. Thus the death of the lessor or lessee, the bankruptcy or marriage (in certain cases) of either, and execution under a process of law, will effect a change of parties. These will be considered in their order.

1. DEATH.

Of lessor.

If the reversion descends to the heir, he is affected by such covenants as run with the land (*a*), and may sue for breaches committed after the death of the lessor.

The heir may sue for breaches committed after the death of the ancestor, although he is not named, and the covenant is made with the ancestor, his " executors, and administrators " (*b*).

So also the heir is liable to be sued, whether named or not (*c*). He is, however, not answerable for breaches committed by the ancestor during life, unless named, and then only to the extent of the assets which he has by descent (*d*).

(*a*) Lougher *v.* Williams, 2 Lev. 92; Com. Dig, Covenant, (B) 2, 3.
(*b*) Lougher *v.* Williams, 2 Lev. 92.
(*c*) Andrew's Case, 2 Leo n.104; Anon. Dyer 257 a.
(*d*) Co. Litt. 209 a; Anon. Dyer, 14 a; Giffard *v.* Young, 1 Lutw.; Dyke *v.* Sweeting,

For breaches of covenant by the lessee, whether running with the land or not, which were made before the death of the lessor, the executors and administrators are the proper persons to sue (*e*).

When the covenants run with the land and descend to the heir, he cannot sue for breaches which happened before the death of the ancestor, unless the substantial damage has taken place since the death (*f*).

If the reversion is a chattel, it passes to the executor or administrator, who is bound by and has the advantage of all the conditions and covenants (*g*).

The executor of the lessor may sue his lessee for a breach of covenant committed in the lifetime of the testator; and it is not necessary to aver any damage to the personal estate (*h*) unless it be a covenant upon which the heir alone can sue (*i*), or unless it be a mere personal contract (*j*).

Upon the death of the lessee, his personal representative may be sued, in his representative capacity, for rent, or for breach of express covenant, to the amount of the assets (*k*); but he is not liable for breaches of implied covenants (*l*) broken after the death of the testator (*m*).

Death of lessee.

Willes, 585; Buckley *v*. Nightingale, 1 Str. 665; Derisley *v*. Custance, 4 T. R. 75.
(*e*) See *post*, p. 331.
(*f*) Com. Dig. Administration (B) 13, Covenant, (B); Kingdon *v*. Nottle, 1 M. & G. 355; King *v*. Jones, 5 Taunt. 418; Orme *v*. Broughton, 10 Bing. 533; Raymond *v*. Fitch, 2 Cr. M. & R. 588; Ricketts *v*. Weaver, 12 M. W. 718.
(*g*) Co. Litt. 209 a; Com. Dig. tit. Covenant, (C) 1; Williams *v*. Burrell, 1 C. B. 402.

(*h*) Raymond *v*. Fitch, 2 Cr. M. & R. 588; Ricketts *v*. Weaver, 12 M. & W. 718.
(*i*) Kingdon *v*. Nottle, 1 M. & S. 355; King *v*. Jones, 5 Taunt. 418.
(*j*) Ricketts *v*. Weaver, *supra*.
(*k*) Tilney *v*. Norris, 1 Lord Raymond, 553; Williams on Executors, 1492; Wollaston *v*. Hakewill, 3 M. & Gr. 320; Kearsley *v*. Oxley, 2 H. & C. 896.
(*l*) See *ante*, Implied Covenants, p. 135.
(*m*) Adams *v*. Gibney, 6 Bing.

If, however, he be sued for rent as assignee, and the profits of the lease are less than the rent, and he has no other assets, he should plead that the premises are of less yearly value than the rent, that he has offered to surrender his lease to his landlord, and that he has no other assets (*n*), and should pay the actual value of the premises during the period into court (*o*).

He must not, however, have depreciated the value of the rent by his own acts (*p*), and he will be liable for the profit and advantage which he might have received from the premises to the amount of the rent due (*q*).

But if he be sued as assignee for breach of any other covenant, the above plea will not avail him, and his only course seems to be not to enter upon the premises at all (*r*), or to assign it over to some third party (*s*). See, however, the 22 & 23 Vict., c. 35, s. 27, *post*, p. 333.

He will not, however, be liable as assignee for future breaches of covenant when he has expended the amount of the sale of the lease, and all the other assets, in payment of simple contract debts (*t*).

The profits of the land are to be applied, in the first

656; Penfold *v.* Abbot, 32 L. J. Q. B. 67.
(*n*) Rubery *v.* Steevens, 4 B. & Ad. 241; Hornidge *v.* Wilson, 11 Ad. & Ell. 645.
(*o*) Patten *v.* Reid, 6 L. T. N. S. 281 Q. B.
(*p*) Hornidge *v.* Wilson, *supra*.
(*q*) Hopwood *v.* Whaley, 6 C. B. 744.
(*r*) Tremere *v.* Morison, 1 Bing. N.C. 89; Sleap *v.* Newman, 12

C. B. N.S. 116; Wollaston *v.* Hakewill, 3 M. & Gr. 297.
(*s*) Taylor *v.* Shum, 1 B. & P. 21; Pitcher *v.* Tovey, 4 Mod. 71; Wilson *v.* Wigg, 10 East. 313. See *ante*, Covenants which Run with the Land, p. 324.
(*t*) Collins *v.* Crouch, 13 Q. B. 542; and it seems that he need not retain the *profits* of the land in order to provide for a future breach of covenant, unless it be for payment of rent.

place, by the executor to the discharge of the rent. If the profits are insufficient, he must pay the rent out of the assets, and he will not be answerable beyond his assets if he plead as above (*u*).

Where a term is specifically bequeathed, it vests at first in the executor, and the legatee cannot enter until the assent of the executor is given (*v*). The executor cannot waive the term, although it be worth nothing, for he must renounce the executorship *in toto* or not at all (*w*).

Formerly executors could not be charged in trespass for any personal wrong done by the testator, as for cutting down trees, &c.; but now, by the 3 & 4 Will. IV., c. 42, s. 2, they may be sued for such wrongs committed within six months before the death of the testator (*x*).

Personal representatives are now protected from subsequent claims under leases after assignment by the 22 & 23 Vict., c. 35, s. 27, by which it is enacted, that where an executor or administrator, liable as such to the rents, covenants, or agreements contained in any lease or agreement, for a lease granted or assigned to the testator or intestate whose estate is being administered, shall have satisfied all such liabilities under the said lease or agreement for a lease as may have accrued due and been claimed up to the time of the assignment hereafter mentioned, and shall have set apart a sufficient fund to answer any future claim that may be made in respect of any fixed and ascertained sum covenanted

(*u*) *Ante*, p. 332.
(*v*) Doe *d.* Maberly *v.* Maberly, 6 C. & P. 126; Wollaston *v.* Hakewill, *supra*.
(*w*) Hellier *v.* Casbard, 1 Sid. 266, 1 Lev. 127; Ruhery *v.* Stevens, 4 B. & Ad. 244, 1 Wms. Exors. 642.
(*x*) Powell *v.* Rees, 7 A. & E. 426.

or agreed by the lessee to be laid out on the property demised or agreed to be demised, although the period for laying out the same may not have arrived, and shall have assigned the lease, or agreement for a lease, to a purchaser thereof, he shall be at liberty to distribute the residuary personal estate of the deceased to and amongst the parties entitled thereto respectively, without appropriating any part or any further part (as the case may be) of the personal estate of the deceased to meet any future liability under the said lease or agreement for a lease; and the executor or administrator so distributing the residuary estate shall not, after having assigned the said lease or agreement for a lease, and having, where necessary, set apart such sufficient fund as aforesaid, be personally liable in respect of any subsequent claim under the said lease or agreement for a lease; but nothing herein contained shall prejudice the right of the lessor, or those claiming under him, to follow the assets of the deceased into the hands of the person or persons to or amongst whom the said assets may have been distributed.

A similar provision is contained in sect. 28, for the protection of personal representatives liable as such to the rents, covenants, or agreements contained in any conveyance of chief rent, or rent-charge, or agreement for such conveyance.

Leases made before the statute are within the above section (y).

2. BANKRUPTCY.

Bankruptcy. The Bankruptcy Act, 1869, 32 & 33 Vict., c. 71 (z),

(y) Dodson v. Sammell, 1 Drew & Sm. 575, 30 L. J. Ch. 799; Smith v. Smith, 1 Drew & Sm. 384.

(z) The 12 & 13 Vict. c. 106, 24 & 25 Vict. c. 134, 25 & 26 Vict. c. 99 (except s. 4, as to County Court Judges sitting in

after providing that the property of the bankrupt shall become divisible amongst his creditors, and for the appointment of trustee by a general meeting of creditors who are to give directions as to the manner in which the property is to be administered by the trustee (a), enacts, by sect. 22, "that where any portion of such estate (the property of the bankrupt) consists of copyhold or customary property, or any like property, passing by surrender and admittance, or in any similar manner, the trustees shall not be compellable to be admitted to such property, but may deal with the same in the same manner as if such property had been capable of being, and had been, duly surrendered or otherwise conveyed to such uses as the trustee may appoint; and any appointee of the trustee shall be admitted or otherwise invested with the property accordingly."

"Where any portion of the property of the bankrupt consists of things in action, any action, suit, or other proceeding for the recovery of such things, instituted by the trustee, shall be instituted in his official name, as in this Act provided; and such things shall, for the purpose of such action, suit, or other proceeding, be deemed to be assignable in law, and to have been duly assigned to the trustee in his official capacity."

By sect. 23, "When any property of the bankrupt acquired by the trustee under this Act consists of land of any tenure burdened with onerous covenants, of unmarketable shares in companies, of unprofitable contracts, or of any other property that is unsaleable, or not readily saleable, by reason of its binding the

Parliament), and 31 & 32 Vict. c. 104, are repealed except as to past transactions. See 32 & 33   Vict. c. 83, s. 20, and the schedule.
(a) Sects. 14, 20.

possessor thereof to the performance of any onerous act, or to the payment of any sum of money, the trustee, notwithstanding he has endeavoured to sell, or has taken possession of such property, or exercised any act of ownership in relation thereto, may, by writing under his hand, disclaim such property, and upon the execution of such disclaimer the property disclaimed shall, if the same is a contract, be deemed to be determined from the date of the order of adjudication, and if the same is a lease, be deemed to have been surrendered on the same date, and if the same be shares in any company, be deemed to be forfeited from that date, and if any other species of property, it shall revert to the person entitled on the determination of the estate or interest of the bankrupt, but if there shall be no person in existence so entitled, then in no case shall any estate or interest therein remain in the bankrupt. Any person interested in any disclaimed property may apply to the Court, and the Court may, upon such application, order possession of the disclaimed property to be delivered up to him, or make such other order as to the possession thereof as may be just."

"Any person injured by the operation of this section shall be deemed a creditor of the bankrupt, to the extent of such injury, and may accordingly prove the same as a debt under the bankruptcy."

By sect. 24, "The trustee shall not be entitled to disclaim any property in pursuance of this Act in cases where an application in writing has been made to him by any person interested in such property, requiring such trustee to decide whether he will disclaim or not, and the trustee has for a period of not less than twenty-eight days after the receipt of such application, or such further time as may be allowed by the Court, declined or neglected to give notice whether he disclaims the same or not.

If parties choose to conduct their affairs at common law, instead of taking the protection of this statute, they do it at their own risk, and cannot obtain any assistance from the statute, the provisions of which they have elected to disregard. Therefore if a man, whether as an assignee for creditors, or in his own right, takes an assignment of a lease, it becomes his by virtue of that assignment without any further act of acceptance (*b*).

A point of a somewhat similar nature arose in several cases in Chancery, where the distinctions between cases of liquidation in bankruptcy, of composition by arrangement, and of ordinary bankruptcy, were pointed out (*c*).

When a trustee disclaims, he will not be able to enforce a covenant by the landlord to purchase any buildings, fixtures, or improvements at the end of the term (*d*).

By sect. 25 it is enacted, that, subject to the provisions of this Act, the trustee shall have power to do the following things:—

1. To receive and decide upon proof of debts in the prescribed manner, and for such purpose to administer oaths.

(*b*) White *v.* Hunt, L. R. 6 Ex. 32; Williams *v.* Bosanquet, 1 B. & B. 238.
(*c*) Ex parte Veness, *in re* Gwynn, L. R. 10 Eq. 419; Ex parte Todhunter, *in re* Norton, ib. 425; Ex parte Key, *in re* Skinner, ib. 433; Birmingham Gas Light Company, *in re* Adams, L. R. 11 Eq. 204.
(*d*) Kearsey *v.* Carstairs, 2 B. & Ad. 716.

2. To carry on the business of the bankrupt so far as may be necessary for the beneficial winding up of the same.

3. To bring or defend any action, suit, or other legal proceeding relating to the property of the bankrupt.

4. To deal with any property to which the bankrupt is beneficially entitled as tenant in tail, in the same manner as the bankrupt might have dealt with the same; and sects. 56 to 73 (both inclusive) of the Act of the session of the third and fourth years of the reign of King William the Fourth (chap. 74), for "the abolition of fines and recoveries, and for the substitution of more simple modes of assurance," shall extend and apply to proceedings in bankruptcy under this Act, as if those sections were here re-enacted and made applicable in terms to such proceedings.

5. To exercise any powers the capacity to exercise which is vested in him under this Act, and to execute all powers of attorney, deeds, and other instruments, expedient or necessary for the purpose of carrying into effect the provisions of this Act.

6. To sell all the property of the bankrupt (including the goodwill of the business, if any, and the book-debts due, or growing due to the bankrupt), by public auction or private contract; with power, if he thinks fit, to transfer the whole thereof to any person or company, or to sell the same in parcels.

7. To give receipts for any money received by him, which receipt shall effectually discharge the person paying such moneys from all responsibility in respect of the application thereof.

8. To prove, rank, claim, and draw a dividend in the matter of the bankruptcy or sequestration of any debtor of the bankrupt.

By sect. 26, the trustee has power to appoint the bankrupt to superintend the management of the property for the benefit of the creditors.

By sect. 27, the trustee may, with the sanction of the committee of inspection, amongst other things, mortgage or pledge any part of the property of the bankrupt for the purpose of raising money for the payment of his debts.

The trustee in bankruptcy may assign the bankrupt's lease without the landlord's license, notwithstanding the lessee's covenant not to assign without license (*e*); and where the bankrupt had assigned for the benefit of his creditors, yet the forfeiture was void against the assignee in bankruptcy (*f*).

Trust property remains vested in the bankrupt (*g*); but by the 117th section, where the bankrupt is a trustee within the "Trustee Act, 1850" (*h*), the Court may appoint a new trustee.

Where the bankrupt has any beneficial interest, as, for example, in right of his wife, it passes to the trustee in bankruptcy (*i*).

Machinery and fixtures attached to the freehold are part of the freehold during the term, and on the bankruptcy of the tenant do not pass to the trustee (*j*).

(*e*) Doe *d.* Goodbehere *v.* Bevan, 3 M. & S. 353; Doe *d.* Cheere *v.* Smith, 5 Taunt. 795.
(*f*) Doe *d.* Lloyd *v.* Powell, 5 B. & C. 308.
(*g*) 32 & 33 Vict. c. 71, s. 15, pl. 1; Dangerfield *v.* Thomas, 9 A. & E. 292; Houghton *v.* Kœnig, 18 C. B. 235.
(*h*) 13 & 14 Vict. c. 60.

(*i*) Michel *v.* Hughes, 6 Bing. 689; Doe *d.* Shaw *v.* Steward. So also a mere equity of redemption passes; Vandenanker *v.* Desborough, 2 Vern. 96.
(*j*) Boydell *v.* M'Michael, 1 C. M. & R. 177; *Ex parte* Reynall, 2 M. D. & D. 443; Walmsley *v.* Milne, 7 C. B. N.S. 115, 29 L. J. C. P. 97.

By sect. 34, the landlord or other person to whom any rent is due from the bankrupt may at any time, either before or after the commencement of the bankruptcy, distrain upon the goods or effects of the bankrupt for the rent due to him from the bankrupt, with this limitation, that if such distress for rent be levied after the commencement of the bankruptcy, it shall be available only for one year's rent, accrued due prior to the date of the order of adjudication; but the landlord or other person to whom the rent may be due from the bankrupt may prove under the bankruptcy for the overplus due for which the distress may not have been available.

By sect. 35, when any rent or other payment falls due at stated periods, and the order of adjudication is made at any time other than one of such periods, the person entitled to such rent or payment may prove for a proportionate part thereof up to the day of the adjudication, as if such rent or payment grew due from day to day.

A landlord cannot enforce payment in full by the trustee of rent due before the bankruptcy, except by a distress for the arrears not exceeding one year's rent (*k*). He may distrain for all subsequent rent (*l*).

A lease may contain a proviso for re-entry upon the bankruptcy of the lessee, his executors, administrators, or assigns (*m*), or be limited so as to cease upon the bankruptcy of the lessee (*n*), and the landlord may enter accordingly (*o*).

(*k*) Gethin *v*. Wilkes, 2 Dowl. 189.

(*l*) Briggs *v*. Sowry, 8 M. & W. 729; Newton *v*. Scott, 9 M. & W. 431, 10 Id. 471.

(*m*) Roe *d*. Hunter *v*. Galliers, 2 T. R. 133.

(*n*) Doe *d*. Lockwood *v*. Clarke 8 East. 185.

(*o*) Doe *d*. Bridgman *v*. David, 1 C. M. & R. 405.

By the Companies Act, 1862, s. 63 (*p*), "When an order has been made for winding up a company under this Act, no suit, action or other proceeding shall be proceeded with, or commenced against the company, except with the leave of the Court, and subject to such terms as the Court may impose." And by sect. 163, "Where any company is being wound up by the Court, or subject to the supervision of the Court, any attachment, sequestration, distress, or execution put in force against the estate or effects of the Company, after the commencement of the winding up, shall be void to all intents."

Where an execution has been perfected by seizure before the commencement of the winding up, a sale after the commencement is not a "putting in force of the execution within sect. 163 (*q*). But where a landlord, after an order for the winding up of a company, distrained for the rent of the offices due prior to the winding up, it was held that the distress was void (*r*).

3. MARRIAGE.

A change is also effected in the relations of the parties to a lease by the marriage of a female lessor or lessee.

Marriage.

The relations of husband and wife have been in some respect altered by the "Married Women's Property Act, 1870" (*s*).

(*p*) 25 & 26 Vict. c. 89.
(*q*) *Ex parte* Parry, *in re* The Great Ship Co., 33 L. J. Ch. 245.
(*r*) *In re* The Progress Assurance Co., *ex parte* The Liverpool Exchange Co., 39 L. J. Ch. 504, L. R. 9 Eq. 370. See also *In re* The London Cotton Co., 35 L. J. Ch. 425, L. R. 2 Eq. 53 ; *In re* Bastow & Co., 36 L. J. Ch. 899, L. R. 4 Eq. 618 ; *In re* The Exhall Coal Mining Co., 33 L. J. Ch. 595.

(*s*) 33 & 34 Vict. c. 93. See *post*, p. 346.

Of female lessor.

In the case of a female lessor, upon her marriage, her husband takes, during coverture, a freehold interest in her freeholds of inheritance (unless they be settled upon her with his consent at her marriage), and he may dispose of them by deed for their joint-lives, without her concurrence (*t*).

When issue is born, the husband becomes tenant for life by the courtesy of her freeholds and estates tail in possession (*u*).

If there be no issue, then, on the death of the wife, the husband's interest ceases, and he cannot sue for rent accruing due subsequently (*v*).

If, however, the letting were by the husband alone, he could sue, and the tenant would be estopped from denying his title (*w*).

Upon covenants running with the wife's land or reversion, the husband may either sue alone or jointly with his wife, if the breaches are subsequent to the coverture (*x*), except for breaches of covenants for title and further assurance (*y*).

(*t*) Co. Litt. 351 a ; Bac. Abr. tit. Baron and Feme,(C) 1 ; Robertson *v.* Norris, 11 Q. B. 916. He can also make leases for twenty-one years. See the 19 & 20 Vict. c. 120 ; and she can convey her estate by deed acknowledged under the 3 & 4 Will. IV. c. 74, with the husband's concurrence. See Jolly *v.* Handcock, 7 Exch. 820.

(*u*) Co. Litt. 29 a, 30 b ; Doe *d.* Neville *v.* Rivers, 7 T. R. 276, 278.

(*v*) Hill *v.* Saunders, 4 B. & C. 529 ; Howe *v.* Scarrott, 4 H. & N. 723, 28 L. J. Exch. 325.

(*w*) See *per* Martin, B., in Howe *v.* Scarrott, *supra ;* Wallis *v.* Harrison, 5 M. & W. 142 ; North *v.* Wyard, 2 Bulst. 233 ; Harcourt *v.* Wyman, 3 Exch. 824 ; Parry *v.* Hindle, 2 Taunt. 180.

(*x*) Alebury *v.* Walby, 1 Str. 229 ; Dunstan *v.* Berwell, 1 Wils. 224 ; Howell *v.* Maine, 3 Lev. 403 ; Bret *v.* Cumberland, Cro. Jac. 399.

(*y*) Middlemore *v.* Goodall, 1 Roll. Abr. 348.

Arrears of rent, breaches of covenant, &c., before marriage, are *choses in action*, which must be sued for jointly (*z*).

If the husband die without reducing into possession the wife's choses in action, they survive to her (*a*).

See, as to contracts, this subject fully treated of in "Addison on Contracts," 6th edit., 751.

By the 15 & 16 Vict., c. 76, s. 40, counts and claims in actions by husband and wife may be joined, and separate actions consolidated (*b*).

By sect. 141, marriage of the female plaintiff or defendant will not abate an action (*c*).

A female lessor who has made a lease at will does not void the lease by marriage, nor can she avoid it without the consent of her husband (*d*).

The wife's acceptance of rent will confirm leases for years by deed made by her husband, or by herself and husband; and her issue or heir will have the same power to confirm or avoid them (*e*).

In the case of a female lessee, marriage gives to the *Of female lessee.*

(*z*) Hardey *v.* Robinson, 1 Keb. 89; Milner *v.* Milnes, 3 T. R. 631; Caudell *v.* Shaw, 4 T. R. 361. So where the husband becomes bankrupt, the assignees must join; Sherrington *v.* Yates, 12 M. & W. 855.
(*a*) Richards *v.* Richards, 2 B. & Ad. 447; Gaters *v.* Madeley, 6 M. & W. 423; Scarpellini *v.* Atcheson, 7 Q. B. 864.

(*b*) See Stowe *v.* Jackson, 16 C. B. 199; Morris *v.* Moore, 19 C. B. N.S. 359; Hemstead *v.* Phœnix Gas Co., 3 H. & C. 745.
(*c*) Wynne *v.* Wynne, 2 M. & Gr. 8.
(*d*) Bac. Abr. tit. Baron and Feme, (E); tit. Leases, (C).
(*e*) Bac. Abr. tit. Leases, (C).

husband all the wife's chattels not put into settlement (*f*), and he may dispose of them without her concurrence. If he demise for part of a term of years, the rent will go to his executor or administrator, though the wife survive, or if he make a lease to commence after his death. But if the husband does not dispose of a chattel real of his wife, if she survive she shall have it (*g*).

So a part of a term undisposed of survives to the wife (*h*).

Where lands are demised to husband and wife, and husband grants an underlease, he may sue for an injury to the reversion, without joining his wife as a party to the suit (*i*).

A husband cannot assign his wife's reversionary interest in leaseholds, if that interest could not have vested in the wife during coverture (*j*).

A joint-tenancy may exist between a married woman and another, until the husband breaks it by disposing of the wife's moiety; and if he die without disposing of it, the joint-tenancy will continue; and if the wife die, the surviving joint-tenant, and not the husband, shall take the whole (*k*).

A female lessee at will does not avoid the lease by

(*f*) The husband can dispose of a wife's chattels settled on her without his concurrence. Turner's case, 1 Vern. 7; Factor *v.* Semayne, 2 Vern. 270; Bates *v.* Dandy, 2 Atk. 207.

(*g*) Bac. Abr. tit. Baron and Feme, (C) 2. T.; Com. Dig. tit. Baron and Feme, (E) 2.

(*h*) Sym's case, Cro. Eliz. 33.
(*i*) Wallis *v.* Harrison, 5 M. & W. 142.
(*j*) Day *v.* Duberley, 16 Beav. 33, 5 H. L. Cas. 388.
(*k*) Co. Litt. 185 b; Com. Dig. tit. Baron and Feme, (E) 2; Bac. Abr. tit. Baron and Feme, (C) 2.

marriage, and she cannot avoid it subsequently without the consent of her husband (*l*).

The husband is not liable in an action for use and occupation for occupation by his wife before marriage, unless at his special instance and request (*m*).

If the husband and wife be evicted of a term which he has in right of his wife, and if he recover it in his own name, this vests the term in the husband (*n*).

By the 6 Anne, c. 18, s. 35, every husband seised in right of his wife only, who after the determination of the estate or interest shall hold over, shall be adjudged a trespasser, and the persons entitled to the premises may recover in damages the full value of the profits received during the wrongful possession (*o*).

As was stated, *ante*, pp. 341, 342, certain alterations have been introduced into the mode of dealing with the property of married women by the "Married Women's Property Act, 1870" (*p*).

The different species of property affected by that Act are apparently:—

1. Wages and earnings acquired (after the Act) in any employment, occupation, or trade (*q*).
2. Money or property acquired (after the Act) by literary, artistic, or scientific skill (*r*).
3. All investments of the above (*s*).

(*l*) Bac. Abr. tit. Baron and Feme, (E).
(*m*) Richardson *v.* Hall, 1 Br. & B. 50.
(*n*) Bac. Abr. tit. Baron and Feme, (C) 2.
(*o*) See also Caton *v.* Coles, L. R. 1 Eq. 581.
(*p*) 33 & 34 Vict. c. 93.
(*q*) Sect. 1.
(*r*) Ibid.
(*s*) Ibid.

4. Any personal property to which a woman married after the Act becomes entitled during marriage as next of kin to an intestate (*t*).

5. Any sum of money, not exceeding £200, to which a woman married after the Act becomes entitled during marriage under any deed or will.

6. Freehold, copyhold, or customary-hold property, which descends upon any woman married after the Act, as heiress of an intestate, as far as regards the rents and profits thereof.

The sections which seem most material to the present subject are as follows:—

By sect. 1, it is enacted, that the wages and earnings of any married woman acquired or gained by her after the passing of this Act (*u*), in any employment, occupation, or trade, in which she is engaged, or which she carries on separately from her husband, and also any money or property so acquired by her through the exercise of any literary, artistic, or scientific skill, and all investments of such wages, earnings, money, or property, shall be deemed and taken to be property held and settled to her separate use, independent of any husband to whom she may be married, and her receipts alone shall be a good discharge for such wages, earnings, money, and property.

By sect. 7, where any woman married after the passing of this Act shall, during her marriage, become entitled to any personal property as next of kin, or one of the next of kin of an intestate, or to any sum of money not exceeding £200, under any deed or will, such property shall, subject and without prejudice to

(*t*) Sect. 7.   (*u*) 9th of August 1870. See s. 15.

the trusts of any settlement affecting the same, belong to the woman for her separate use, and her receipts alone shall be a good discharge for the same.

By sect. 8, where any freehold, copyhold, or customary-hold property shall descend upon any woman, married after the passing of this Act, as heiress or co-heiress of an intestate, the rents and profits of such property shall, subject and without prejudice to the trusts of any settlement affecting the same, belong to such woman for her separate use, and her receipts alone shall be a good discharge for the same.

By sect. 11, a married woman may maintain an action in her own name for the recovery of any wages, earnings, money, and property by this Act declared to be her separate property, or of any property belonging to her before marriage, and which her husband shall, by writing under his hand, have agreed with her shall belong to her after marriage as her separate property; and she shall have, in her own name, the same remedies, both civil and criminal, against all persons whomsoever, for the protection and security of such wages, earnings, money, and property, and of any chattels or other property purchased or obtained by means thereof for her own use, as if such wages, earnings, money, chattels, and property belonged to her as an unmarried woman; and in an indictment or other proceeding it shall be sufficient to allege such wages, earnings, money, chattels, and property to be her property.

By sect. 12, a husband shall not, by reason of any marriage which shall take place after this Act has come into operation, be liable for the debts of his wife contracted before marriage; but the wife shall be liable to be sued for, and any property belonging to her for her separate use shall be liable to satisfy, such debts as if she had continued unmarried.

4. BY WRITS OF EXECUTION.

By writs of execution.

Lastly, it remains to be considered what is the effect produced upon the relations in which the parties stand to one another by the operation of a writ of *fieri facias* or of *elegit*.

It is the duty of the sheriff upon seizure and sale under a writ of *fieri facias*, to assign the term by deed, and until he does so the term remains in the debtor, who may bring ejectment against the person to whom possession has been given (*v*).

The purchaser is generally left to obtain possession by ejectment, or to recover his rent by distress or action (*w*).

He is liable for the rent, and upon covenants contained in the lease (*x*); but the lessee continues liable notwithstanding the estate is taken from him against his consent (*y*).

An equitable reversionary interest in a term cannot be seized and sold under a *fi. fa.* or *elegit* (*z*).

By the 1 & 2 Vict., c. 110, s. 11, it is enacted, that

(*v*) Doe d. Hughes *v.* Jones, 9 M. & W. 372; Playfair *v.* Musgrove, 14 M. & W. 239.
(*w*) Lloyd *v.* Davies, 2 Ex. 103; Mayor of Poole *v.* Whitt, 15 M. & W. 571.
(*x*) 1 Doug. 184.
(*y*) Auriol *v.* Mills, 4 T. R. 99.
(*z*) Scott *v.* Scholey, 8 East. 467; Metcalfe *v.* Scholey, 2 B. &

P. N. R. 461; Mayor of Poole *v.* Whitt, 15 M. & W. 571. It seems it may be by equity where the creditor has sued out an *elegit* without effect. See Gore *v.* Bowser, 3 Sm. & Giff. 1; Partridge *v.* Foster, 34 Beav. 1; Godfrey *v.* Tucker, 33 L. J. Ch. 559. See, however, Thornton *v.* Finch, 4 Giff. 505 34, L. J. Ch. 466.

it shall be lawful for the sheriff, or other officer to whom any writ of *elegit*, or any precept in pursuance thereof shall be directed, at the suit of any person upon any judgment which, at the time appointed for the commencement of this Act, shall have been recovered, or shall be thereafter recovered, in any action in any of Her Majesty's superior Courts at Westminster, to make and deliver execution unto the party in that behalf suing, of all such lands, tenements, rectories, tithes, rents, and hereditaments, including lands and hereditaments of copyhold or customary tenure, as the person against whom execution is so sued, or any person in trust for him, shall have been seised or possessed of at the time of entering up the said judgment, or at any time afterwards, or over which such person shall, at the time of entering up such judgment, or at any time afterwards, have any disposing power which he might, without the assent of any other person, exercise for his own benefit, in like manner as the sheriff or other officer may now make and deliver execution of one moiety of the lands and tenements of any person against whom a writ of *elegit* is sued out; which lands, tenements, rectories, tithes, rents, and hereditaments, by force and virtue of such execution, shall accordingly be held and enjoyed by the party to whom such execution shall be so made and delivered, subject to such account in the Court out of which such execution shall have been sued out as a tenant by *elegit* is now subject to in a court of equity: provided always, that such party suing out execution, and to whom any copyhold or customary lands shall be so delivered in execution shall be liable, and is hereby required to make, perform, and render to the lord of the manor, or other person entitled, all such and the like payments and services as the person against whom such execution shall be issued would have been bound to make, perform, and render in case such execution had not issued; and that the party so suing out such execution, and to whom any such copyhold or customary lands shall have been so delivered in execution, shall be entitled to hold the same until the amount of such payments, and the value of such services, as well as the amount of the judgment, shall have been levied: provided also, that, as against purchasers, mortgagees, or creditors who shall have become such before the time appointed for the commencement of this Act, such writ of *elegit* shall have no greater or other effect than a writ of *elegit* would have had in case the Act had not passed.

After the execution of an inquisition by the jury, the sheriff returns the finding of the jury, and that he has caused the lands " to be delivered to [the execution creditor], by a reasonable price and extent, to hold, to him and his assigns, according to the nature and tenure thereof, according to the form of the statutes in such case made and provided, until the [debt and damages] in the writ mentioned, together with interest upon the same, as therein mentioned, shall have been levied, as by the said writ is commanded " (*a*).

This return when filed operates as an assignment of the reversion (*b*).

The sheriff may deliver possession where the debtor is himself the occupier (*c*); but the tenants cannot

---

(*a*) Chit. Forms, 342, 11th edit.
(*b*) Lowthall *v.* Tomkins, 2 Eq. Cas. Abr. 380; Taylor *v.* Cole, 3 T. R. 295; Doe *d.* Da Costa *v.* Wharton, 8 T. R. 2.

(*c*) Rogers *v.* Pitcher, 6 Taunt. 206; Chatfield *v.* Parker, 8 B. & C. 543.

be turned out of possession until the expiration of their terms (*d*).

But the tenant by *elegit* may sue or distrain for rent accrued after the return of the writ (*d*), but not before (*e*).

For the law relating generally to writs of *fi. fa.* and *elegit*, see Chit. Arch. Practice of Q. B., vol. i., 634–670.

(*d*) Taylor *v.* Cole, *supra;* Doe d. Da Costa *v.* Wharton, *supra.*
(*e*) Lloyd *v.* Davies, 2 Ex. 103; Ramsbottom *v.* Buckhurst, 2 M. & S. 565; Arnold *v.* Ridge, 13 C. B. 745.
(*f*) Sharp *v.* Key, 8 M. & W. 379.

INDEX.

A.

ABANDONMENT of distress, 206.
ACCEPTANCE of rent by lessor operates as a waiver of breach of covenant to insure, 125.
        waiver of notice to quit, 273.
        waiver of forfeiture, 260, 261.
        evidence of presumed yearly tenancy, 48, 105, 107, 261.
ACCIDENTAL fire.—See FIRE.
ACKNOWLEDGMENT by married women, 26.
ACTION for apportioning rent, 179.
  for non-payment of rent, 180.
  assumpsit, 180, 182.
  covenant, 180.
  use and occupation, 180.
  for wrongful distress.—See DISTRESS.
  for not farming according to good husbandry, 235.
  for non-repair, 236.
  of fences, 237.
  for waste, 237.
  of ejectment, 238.
  for breach of quiet enjoyment, 243.
  for not giving possession, 243.
  for holding over, 275.
  for double value, 284.
  for double rent, 287.
  by tenant for tillages, &c., 294.
  by landlord in trover against out-going tenant, 294.
  for breaches of covenant after assignment over to third party, 324.
ADMINISTRATORS.— See EXECUTORS.
     of convict, leases by, 25.
     leases to, 30.
ADVANCE, rent payable in, 161.

ADVOWSONS, lease of, 36.
AGENTS, distress by, 189.
    notice to quit by or to, 271.
AGREEMENT, distinction between, and leases.—See LEASES.
    for future lease operating as a present lease, 58.
    for present lease operating as agreement for future lease, 61.
    effect of 8 & 9 Vict., c. 106, s. 3, 65.
    evidence of terms of holding, 66.
    enforceable in equity, 67.
AGRICULTURAL fixtures.—See FIXTURES.
ALIENS, leases to, 30.
ALLOWANCES.—See DEDUCTIONS.
ANIMALS, leases of, 35.
    not to be distrained, 192 n. (c), 196.
    when *levant* and *couchant*, 192 n. (c).
    of a stranger ejecting, 192 n. (c).
    feræ naturæ not distrainable, 200.
    beasts of the plough and beasts which gain the land, 201.
    pursuit of beasts escaping, 201, 202.
    impounding of cattle, 211.
ANNUITIES, leases of, 40.
APARTMENTS.—See LODGINGS.
APPORTIONMENT of rent by ecclesiastical corporations, 18.
    by act of parties, or by law, 170.
    where rent will be apportioned, 170.
    where reversion of lessor is severed by alienation, 170.
    in respect of time under the Act of 1870, 176.
    where lessee's interest in part is destroyed, 170.
    where lessee loses interest before his rent is due, 172.
    where lessor dies before rent is due, 179.
    under 11 Geo. II. c. 19, 172.
    4 & 5 Will. IV. c. 22, 173.
    action for apportionment of rent, 179.
    of rent on assignment of part, 328.
    of covenants.—See ASSIGNMENT OF PART, 329.
APPRAISEMENT on distress for rent, 215.
APPURTENANCES, what is included in the word, 86.
ARCHBISHOPS, leases by.—See CORPORATIONS.
ARREARS of rent go to executor, 331.
ASSENT of executors to a bequest, 333.
ASSESSED taxes recoverable in debt against executor, 331.—See DEDUCTIONS.
ASSIGNEES.—See ASSIGNMENT.
ASSIGNEES of bankrupts.—See BANKRUPTCY.

INDEX.

ASSIGNMENT, a lease for the whole term operates as an assignment, 11.
    consequences of, at common law, 321.
    by the 32 Hen. VIII. c. 34, assignee of reversion and of term may sue and be sued on the covenants, 322.
    limitations to the operation of the statute, 323.
    lessee continues liable, notwithstanding assignment, 311, 323, 324.
    implied promise by successive assignees to indemnify original lessee, 324.
    action after assignment over to third party, 324.
    where right of action given to assignee by statute, 324.
    of part of term in whole of lands, 328.
    of whole of term as to part of lands, 328.
    assignee of part of lands only liable for proportional rent, 329.
    assignee liable for the whole, 329.
    apportionment of covenants and conditions at common law, 329.
    by the 22 & 23 Vict. c. 35, s. 3.
ASSIGNS, effect of the word in a covenant, 327.
ASSUMPSIT.—See ACTION.
ATTACHMENT of rent when due, 183.
ATTAINTED persons, leases by, 25.
    leases to, 29.
ATTORNMENT, definition of, 318.
    no longer necessary to complete a grant, 318.
    does not affect possession of lands, 318.
    unless with consent of landlord, 318.
    or to mortgagee after mortgage forfeited, 318.
    or by direction of court, 318.
    tenant not prejudiced by payment of rent before notice, 318.
    except by payment of rent before due, 319.
    effect of 4 & 5 Anne, c. 16, 319.
    no attornment necessary where party comes in by judgment of law, 319.
    attornment of tenant of mortgagee, 319.
    notice by mortgagee to pay rent operates as, 319.
    payment of rent evidence of attornment, 319.
    instrument of attornment not amounting to an agreement, 320.
    where terms of holding are varied, it amounts to an agreement, 320.
    estoppel by attornment, 320.
AUCTIONEER, goods sent to, for sale, not distrainable, 198.
AUTRE VIE, leases by tenant *pur autre vie*, 8.

AUTRE VIE, presumption as to death of, 8.
    production of *cestui que vie*, 9.
AVOIDANCE of lease.—See VOID and VOIDABLE LEASES, CONFIRMATION of LEASES.
AWAY-GOING crop.—See EMBLEMENTS.

B.

BAILIFFS, distress by, 189.
BANKRUPTCY—
    The Bankruptcy Act (1869), 334.
    appointment of trustee, 335.
    admittance of trustee to copyholds, 335.
    actions in name of trustee, 335.
    disclaimer by trustee, 336.
    neglecting to give notice of disclaimer, 336, 337.
    parties not acting under the statute do not take the benefit of it, 337.
    trustee cannot enforce covenant after disclaimer, 337.
    powers of trustee, 337–339.
    trust property remains vested in the bankrupt, 339.
    beneficial interest passes to the trustee, 339.
    fixtures do not pass to the trustee, 339.
    landlord may distrain for one year's rent, 340.
    and prove under bankruptcy for the overplus, 340.
    may prove for proportionate part up to day of adjudication, 340.
    proviso for re-entry, or determination of lease on bankruptcy of tenant, 340.
    winding up under Companies' Act, 341.
BEASTS of the plough, distress of, 201.
BEER, covenant to purchase from lessor, 128.
BISHOPS, leases by, 16.—See CORPORATIONS.
BOTES.—See ESTOVERS.
BREACHES of covenants.—See COVENANTS.
BREWERS, leases by, covenant to deal with lessors for all the beer, 128.
BROKER, should not be appraiser of distress, 216.
    costs of distress, 217.
BUILDINGS, tenants' right to remove, 307–309.
    for public and charitable purposes, leases of, 33.
BUILDING or repairing leases—
    granted by the Crown, 16.
        by municipal corporations, 16.
        by ecclesiastical corporations, 19, 20.

C.

CARRIAGES, whether distrainable, 199.
CATTLE.—See ANIMALS.
    may be demised, 36.

CATTLE, young of cattle belong to lessee, 36.
CESSER of tenancy.—See EFFLUXION OF TIME, CHANGE OF PARTIES,
    FORFEITURE.
    Assignment, 321.
    Holding over, 274.
    Double value, 284.
    Double rent, 287.
CESTUI QUI VIE, production of, 9.
    death of presumed, 8.
CHANGE of parties, 317.
    By Act of Parties.
        How a change may take place, 317.
        by landlord, 317.
        by tenant, 321.
        consequences of assignment, 322.
            at common law, 322.
            by 32 Hen. VIII. c. 34.
        See ASSIGNMENT, ATTORNMENT, COVENANTS RUNNING
            WITH LAND.
    By Act of Law.
        death of lessor, 330.
        death of lessee, 331.
        bankruptcy, 334.
        marriage of female lessor, 342.
        marriage of female lessee, 344.
        writs of execution, 348.
CHANGE of possession.—See UNDER-LEASES.
CHARITABLE uses, trustees for, may take leases, 33.
CHARITABLE purposes, buildings for, 33.
CHATTELS, leases of, 35.
CHURCH, lease in right of.—See CORPORATIONS.
CHURCHWARDENS and overseers, leases by, 20.—See PARISH OFFICER.
COAL mines.—See MINES.
COLLEGE LEASES, rent reserved in, 109, n. (c).
COMMENCEMENT of term, 94.
    must be stated with certainty, 94.
    fixed by reference to contingency, 95.
    lease by deed, term commences from delivery, 95.
    no date stated, 95.
    where date stated, 96.
    old Michaelmas day, 96.
    "to commence from the date," construction of, 96.
    leases for lives and for years, 96.
    to commence *in futuro*, 97.
    lease by parol from day of entering, 97.
    presumed tenancy from year to year, 98.
COMMISSIVE waste.—See WASTE.

COMMITTEES of lunatics.—See LUNATICS.
COMMONS, lease of, 37.
COMPANIES' Act, 1862, 341.
CONDITIONS.—See PROVISOS.
CONFIRMATION of leases.
    by issue in tail, 3.
    what acts amount to, 3.
    by wife, 10.
    by infant, 27, 31.
    by ecclesiastical corporations, 16, 17.
    by municipal corporations, 16.
    by trustee of bankrupt, 335.
CONSENT.—See LICENSE.
    by tenant to landlord continuing distress beyond the five days, 216.
CONSTRUCTION of leases, description of property, 82.
CONVICT, leases by, 25.
CO-PARCENERS.—See LESSORS.
    leases by, 13.
    distress by, 186.
COPYHOLD, leases of, under Settled Estates Act, 8.
    leases *pur autre vie*, presumption as to death of *cestui que vie*, 8, 9.
    no lease for more than one year without license, 14.
    license to demise, 15.
    by special custom, 15.
    under Settled Estates Act, 15.
    not within Act relating to property of parish officers, 21.
CORPOREAL hereditaments in expectancy, lease of, 40, 41.
CORRODIES, lease of, 38.
CORN and growing crops, distress on, 193, 199, 215.
CORN-rent, 110.
CORPORATIONS.—See LESSORS.
    confirmation of leases by, 16, 17.
    successors bound by their leases, 16.
    leases by the crown, 16.
    municipal corporations, 16.
    cannot be made for more than thirty-one years without consent, 16.
    by ecclesiastical and eleemosynary corporations, 16.
    leases must be under seal, 16, 43.
    effect of lease not under seal, 16, n. (*v*).
    leases to, 32.
    leases to or from one member to another, 32.
    to ecclesiastical persons, 32.
    ecclesiastical leases excepted from the operation of the 12 & 13 Vict. c. 26, 18.

CORPORATIONS—apportionment of rent by ecclesiastical corporations, 18.
CORPOREAL hereditaments, leases of, 35.
CORRODIES, lease of, 38.
COSTS of distress, &c., 217.
COUNTERPART of lease.
    by tenant for life under Settled Estates Act, 7.
COUNTY Court.—See SMALL TENEMENTS ACT.
COVENANT.—See ACTION.
COVENANTS, usual covenants in leases by tenant for life under Settled Estates Act, 7.
    definition of, 114.
    must not be illegal, impossible, or prejudicial to the public, 114.
    liability of covenantee under such covenants, 115.
    dependent covenants void where lease is void, 116.
    independent covenants, 116.
    Express covenants, 116.
        may be in form of exception, 116.
        usual express covenants, 116.
        for payment of rent, 117.
            of taxes, 117.
        for repairs 120.
        to repair and to repair after notice, 120.
        by lessor to repair, 121.
        as to main walls, notice to be given by lessee of want of repair, 121.
        subsequent erections, 121.
        liability of lessee for extraordinary damage, 122.
        to keep in repair, 122.
        for unsubstantial damage, 122.
        sufficiency of repairs a question for the jury, 123.
        "habitable repair," 123.
        "external parts," 123.
        conditional upon the landlord putting in repair, 123.
    for good husbandry, 124.—See CULTIVATION.
        custom of the country excluded by express covenant, 124.
    for insurance, 124.—See FIRE.
    not to underlet or assign, 125.
        not a common and usual covenant, 126.
        to lessee and assigns, 126.
            executors and administrators, 126.
    not to carry on certain trades, 127.
    not to trade with particular persons, 128.
            within a particular radius, 128, 129.
    for quiet enjoyment, 130.
        form of covenant, 130.

Covenants, Express, for interruption by person claiming under lessor, 130.
    general or unqualified covenant, 131.
    against acts of a particular person, 131.
   for renewal of leases, 132.
    run with the land, 132.
    creating a perpetuity invalid, 133.
    forfeiture of right of renewal, 133.
    specific performance by Court of Chancery, 133.
    4 Geo. IV. c. 28, s. 6, 134.
    surrender by under-lessees unnecessary, 134.
    8 & 9 Vict. 106., s. 9
Implied covenants, 135.
   covenants in law, 135, 136.
   cease with the estate of lessor, 136.
   run with the land, 136, 140.
   express will control implied, 136-138.
   may be implied from express words, 136.
   implied covenant from recital, 136.
   for payment of rent, 137.
   "yielding and paying," 137.
   for repairs, 137.
    express will control implied, 137.
    liability of tenant to rebuild after fire, and to pay rent, 233.
    no implied covenant that house fit for habitation, 137.
    or that lessor will repair, 138.
    or that tenant may quit on breach, 138.
    or that he may deduct repairs from rent, 138.
   for cultivation, 138, 233.
    custom of the country, 138, 233.
    express will control implied, 138.
   for title, 139.
    quiet enjoyment, 139.
    use of words "demise," "let," or "lease," 139.
    use of words "give" or "grant," 140.
    8 & 9 Vict. c. 106, s. 4, only affects disturbance by person having title, 140.
    agreement for lease in implied covenant, 140.
    express will control implied, 140.
Covenants which run with the land, definition of, 116, 325.
   for payment of rent, 117.
   for repairs, 120, 325, 326.
   for further assurance, 325.
   not to assign without license, 325.
   not to carry on certain trades, 127, 325.
   trading with particular persons, 128.

INDEX. 361

Covenants which run with the land—or in a particular radius, 128.
    for renewal of leases, 132, 325.
    implied covenants, 135, 325.
    for quiet enjoyment, 140, 325.
    to maintain a sea-wall, 325.
    lessee to reside on the premises, 325.
    option to determine, 325.
    cultivation of the land, 325.
    to produce title-deeds, 325.
    to supply water, 325.
    to insure, the sum insured being laid out on the premises, 326.
    doing suit to a mill by grinding corn there, 326.
    to build a new mill, 326.
    repair of fixtures, 326.
    relating to ways and profits appurtenant, 326.
    and provisos which are merely collateral do not run with the land, 142, 327.
    even where assigns are expressly named, 327.
    use of the word "assignees," 327.
    covenants which relate to movables, 328.
    joint covenants with tenants in common, 328.
    breach of negative covenants, 147, n. (*x*).
    breach of covenant against immoral or illegal act, if waived, cannot subsequently recover, 151.
CROPS.—See CORN and GROWING CROPS.
    way-going, 293.
CROWN, leases by, 16.
CULTIVATION.—See COVENANTS, EMBLEMENTS.
    neglect to cultivate no waste, 233.
    sheriff not to carry off certain products of cultivation, 233.
    nor certain other products after notice of existing covenant, 234.
    except after agreement to expend them on the land, 234.
    growing crops sold under execution liable for rent, 235.
    remedies for neglect to cultivate, 235.
    injunction, 239–241.
CURTESY, leases by tenants by the, 9.
    distress by, 187.
    executors of tenant entitled to emblements, 280.
CUSTODY of the law—
    goods in, cannot be distrained, 200.
    nor rescued, 225.
    nor replevied, 226.

CUSTOM.—See COPYHOLD, LORD OF THE MANOR.
    of the country with respect to emblements, 292-294.

D.

DATE, commencement of term from, 96.
DEAN AND CHAPTER, leases by, 16.—See CORPORATIONS.
DEATH of parties to a lease, 330-334.
DE DONIS, statute of, 2.
DEDUCTIONS operate as payment of rent *pro tanto*, 163, 167.
    land-tax, 164.
    income tax, 166.
    sewers' rate, 167.
    poor-rates, 167.
    other rates, 168.
    tithe rent-charge, 169.
DEEDS, demises by deed, 43, 47.
DEFECTS in leases under powers, how cured, 154, 155.
DELIVERY of lease, term commences from, 95.
DEMAND of possession, 274.
    summons in lieu of demand and entry, 280.
    double value, 284.
    double rent, 287.
    of rent, demand to be made before entry, 257.
        requisites of a demand, 258.
        when unnecessary, 258.
DEMESNES, cannot be demised by tenant for life under Settled Estates Act, 6.
DEMISE.—See LEASE.
    who may.—See LESSORS.
    void by reason of part being void, 35.
    effect of word, 56-65.
DENIZENS, leases to, 30.
DEPENDENT and independent covenants, 116.
DESERTION by tenant—
    where premises held at rack-rent, 281.
    justices to view premises twice, 281.
    if rent not paid, to put landlord in possession, 282.
    reviewed by judge going circuit, 282.
    statutes extended to tenements on written or verbal agreement, 282.
    and to cases where no right of re-entry is reserved, 282.
    apply to all demises for any term, at any rent, 282.
    conditions of the statutes to be fulfilled, 283.
    no information on oath required, 283.
    what the justices have to determine on the view, 283.
    what is a desertion, 283.

INDEX. 363

DETERMINATION of lease by effluxion of time, 246.
   by change of parties.—See CHANGE OF PARTIES.
   by forfeiture.—See FORFEITURE.
   by surrender, 248.
   by merger, 252.
   by disclaimer, 262.
   by notice to quit.—See NOTICE TO QUIT.
   option to determine, 107.
   on bankruptcy of tenant, 340.
DILAPIDATIONS.—See REPAIRS, COVENANTS.
DISABILITY to make leases, 23-28.
   to accept leases, 29-32.
DISCLAIMER, forfeiture by, 262.
   must in general be by writing, 262.
   must deny existence of relation of landlord and tenant, 263.
   by tenant from year to year operates as waiver of notice to quit, 262.
   by bringing action of ejectment against landlord, 263.
   by trustee in bankruptcy, 336, 337.
   waiver of disclaimer, 263.
DISTRESS by joint tenant or tenant in common, 13.
   a necessary incident to rent reserved, 111.
   lessor may distrain on lease of herbage, 111.
   sum in gross cannot be distrained for as rent, 112.
   definition of distress, 183.
     rent must be issuing out of real property, 184.
     must be certain, 184.
   Who may distrain, 184.
     relation of landlord and tenant must continue to exist, 184.
     joint-tenants, 185.
     coparceners, 186.
     tenants in common, 186.
     husband and wife, 187.
     tenant *pur autre vie*, 188.
     tenant by *elegit*, 188.
     mortgagee, 188.
     agents, bailiffs, receivers, 189.
     guardians, 190.
     executors and administrators, 190.
     sequestrators, 192.
   What things may be distrained, 192.
     general rule, 192.
     growing crops, hay, straw, &c., 193, 199.
       taken in execution, 194, 200.
   What may not be distrained, 196.
     Things absolutely privileged, 196.

DISTRESS—*What may not be distrained—*
    Things annexed to the freehold, 197.
        delivered to a tenant to be wrought upon, &c., 198.
        which cannot be restored in same plight, 199.
        in actual use, 200.
        animals *feræ naturæ*, 200.
        in custody of law,
        growing crops taken in execution, 194, 200.
        goods of guest at an inn, 201.
    Things conditionally privileged, 201.
        beasts of the plough, 201.
        which improve the land, 201.
        instruments of husbandry, 201.
        of trade, 201.
Where the distress may be made, 201.
    upon the premises, 201.
    fraudulent removals, 201, 202.
    fresh pursuit, 202.
    animals feeding on a common, 203.
When the distress may be made, 204.
    time of day, 204.
    after determination of term, 204.
    limitation of time, 205.
    second distress, 206.
    abandonment and recontinuance of, 206.
How a distress should be made, 207.
    What is a sufficient entering and seizure, 207.
    illegal distress, 207, 208.
    inventory, 208.
    notice of the distress and of appraisement and sale, 209.
    form of the notice, 209.
    effect of want of, or defect in notice, 209.
    tender of rent in arrear, 209.
    tender within five days ground of action for subsequent sale, 210, 224.
    requisites of a good tender, 210.
What is to be done with the distress, 211.
    impounding, 211.
    feeding of animals impounded, 212.
    user of the thing distrained, 213.
    where to be impounded, 213.
        growing crops, 215.
    time between notice of sale, 215.
    appraisement, 215.

INDEX. 365

DISTRESS—*What is to be done with the distress*—sale, 217.
    costs of a distress, 217-219.
    what is to be done with the overplus, 217-219.
    for one year's rent after bankruptcy, 340.
    Tenants' remedies for wrongful distress, 220.
    effect of irregularity, 220.
    not applicable to unlawful distress, 220.
    action of trespass, 220.
        on the case, 220.
        when no rent is due, 221.
        when distress for more than is due, 221.
        for distraining twice for the same rent, 221.
        for excessive distress, 222.
        for distraining thing not the subject of distress, 223.
        for distress after tender, 224.
        for driving distress out of hundred, 224.
        for remaining on premises an unreasonable time, 224.
        for selling before five days, or without notice, 210, 224.
            without appraisement, 224.
            at a low price, 224.
    action for not returning the surplus, 224.
        will not lie for mere omission, 224.
    rescue.—See RESCUE.
    replevin.—See REPLEVIN.
DOOR, outer, not to be broken open in distraining, 207, 208.
DOUBLE RENT, tenant holding over after notice to quit given by him, 287.
    to be sued for in same manner as single rent, 287.
    landlord may distrain or bring action, 287.
    tenancy may be in writing or by parol, 287.
    notice to quit need not be in writing, 287.
    weekly tenants excepted, 287.
    tenant who has given notice and paid double rent may quit at any time, 287.
    waiver by acceptance of single rent, 287.
DOUBLE VALUE, persons holding over after demand and notice in writing, 284.
    recoverable by action of debt in any court of record, 284.
    not by distress, 285, n. (*l*).
    defendant to give special bail, 285.
    must be wilful, 285.
    not where there is a claim of title, 285.
    or where there is a treaty for a further term, 285.

DOUBLE VALUE—new lessee cannot sue, 286.
    action for after recovery of premises by ejectment, 286.
    notice to quit will operate as demand, 286.
    insufficient notice, 286.
    weekly tenant not liable for, 286.
    nor tenant from quarter to quarter, 286.
DOWER, leases by tenant in, 9.
    tenant in, entitled to emblements, 289.
DRUNKENNESS.—See INTOXICATION.
DUPLICATE.—See COUNTERPART.
DURESS, leases by person in state of, 25.
DURATION of term, 98.
    leases determinable upon an uncertain event void as leases for years, 98.
    will operate as leases at will or from year to year, 99.
    of lease by deed where no term mentioned, 100.
    of lease by parol where no term mentioned, 100.
    of lease for years, 100.
    as long as both parties please, 100.
    of lease at will, 101.
    option to determine, 107.

E.

EASEMENTS, lease of, 40, 41, 88.
    included in the word "appurtenances," 86.
    how conveyed, &c., 88.
EASEMENTS in gross, lease of, 40, 88.
ECCLESIASTICAL Commissioners, 19, 20.
ECCLESIASTICAL Corporations.—See CORPORATIONS.
    leases by, 16.
    leases to, 32.
EDUCATIONAL purposes, lease of buildings for, 33.
EFFLUXION of time, 246.
    determination of lease by, 246.
EJECTMENT for non-repair, 238.—See ACTION, HOLDING OVER.
ELECTION to confirm or avoid leases.—See CONFIRMATION OF LEASES.
    by alienee of issue in tail, 3.
    by infant, 27, 31.
    by trustee of bankrupt, 335-337.
    by wife, 10.
ELEGIT, distress by tenant in, 188, 351.
EMBLEMENTS, mortgagor in possession not entitled to, 102, 103.
    Where there is no contract, 288.
    definition of right to, 288.
    where they may be claimed, 288.
    out of what claimed, 291.
    right of entry to take them, 292.

EMBLEMENTS—*Where there is a contract*, 292.
    implied contract from custom of country, 292, 293.
    way-going crops, 293.
    common usage of the country sufficient, 294.
    value of tillages recoverable from landlord, 294.
    or from incoming tenant, 294.
    landlord may bring trover for carrying away corn
     &c., 294.
    contracts and customs with respect to, 295.
ENABLING and disabling statutes, 3, 13.
ENTRY.—See RE-ENTRY.
    right of entry of lessee, 242, 243.
EQUITY, agreement enforceable in, 67.
ESTIMATE.—See VALUATION.
EXPIRATION of term, 246.—See CESSER OF ESTATE, DETERMINATION OF
  TERM.
    landlord entitled to possession, 246.
ESTOPPEL, by one of two tenants in common, 13.
    in recitals.—See RECITALS.
    leases by, 156–158.
    general doctrine of estoppel, 157.
    of landlord, 157.
    of tenant, 158.
    by under-lease, 158.
    by attornment, 320.
ESTOVERS, leases of, 38.
EVICTION.—See QUIET ENJOYMENT.
EXCEPTIONS.—See RESERVATIONS.
EXECUTORS and administrators, leases by, 22.
    lease by one of several, 22.
    lease by executor after assent to legatee's interest, 22.
    infant appointed executor, 23.
    married woman appointed executrix, 23.
      husband's consent necessary to act, 23.
      husband acting without her, 23.
    assent of executor to a bequest, 333.
    entitled to arrears of rent, 337.
    assessed taxes recoverable against, 331.
EXCESSIVE distress, action for, 222.
EXECUTION, writs of.—See WRITS OF EXECUTION.
EXPENSES of distress.—See COSTS.

F.

FACTORS, goods delivered in the way of trade not distrainable, 198.
FARM, what the word includes, 80.
FAIR and market, lease of, 39.
FEE-SIMPLE, leases by tenants in, 2.

FEE-SIMPLE, tenant in, not liable for waste, 228.
FEE-TAIL, leases by tenants in, 2.
    tenant in, not liable for waste, 228.
FELONS, leases by, 25.
    leases to, 29.
FENCES, action for non-repair of, 237.
    waste of.—See WASTE.
FERÆ NATURÆ.—See ANIMALS.
FERRY, lease of, 39.
FIERI FACIAS.—See WRITS OF EXECUTION.
FIRE, liability of tenant at common law, 232.
    tenant for life or years under Statute of Gloucester, 232.
    now no action except on special agreement, 232.
    except by malice or negligence, 232.
    under covenant to repair tenant may have to rebuild and pay rent, 233.
FISHERY, lease of must be by deed, 43.
FIXTURES—
    Where there is no agreement.
        definition of, 289.
        what is a fixture, 299.
        tenants' fixtures, 300.
        trade fixtures, 303.
        what a tenant may remove, 305.
        agricultural fixtures, 307.
        new erections, 308, 309.
        when to be removed, 309.
    Where there is an agreement.
        express agreement overrules general principles, 311.
        and customs, 312.
        contracts for sale of fixtures not within the Statute of Frauds, 313.
        memorandum of sale requires conveyance stamp, 313.
        reversionary interest will pass by writing not under seal, 313.
        not goods and chattels within Statute of Frauds, 313.
        nor an interest in land, 313.
        as between mortgagor and mortgagee, 314.
        valuation of fixtures, 315.
        as between outgoing and incoming tenant, 315.
        do not pass to trustee in bankruptcy, 339.
        schedule of fixtures, 315.
FOOD and water to animals impounded.—See IMPOUNDING.
FORCIBLE entry no longer allowable, 275.
FORFEITURE for treason or felony, 25.
    determination of term by, 256.
    re-entry for.—See RE-ENTRY.

FORFEITURE by disclaimer.—See DISCLAIMER.
   waiver of.—See WAIVER.
FRANCHISES, lease of, 39.
  fairs, 39.
  markets, 39.
  ferries, 39.
  tolls, 39.
FRAUD, plea of, to action for not granting a lease, 150.
FRAUDS.—See STATUTE OF FRAUDS.
FRAUDULENT representation.
   of collateral matter will not avoid the lease, 150.
FRAUDULENT removal to avoid distress, 201, 202.
FURNISHED apartments.—See LODGINGS.
FURNITURE, rent does not issue out of, 41.
  distrained for rent, how kept, 214.
FURTHER assurance, covenant for, runs with the land, 325.

G.

GAME, rights of hunting, shooting, and fishing may be leased, 40.
  exceptions and reservations of, 90.
GIVE, no covenant implied from the word, 140.
GOODS and chattels.—See FURNITURE.
   may be leased, 35.
   fixtures not within Statute of Frauds, 313.
GRANGE, what the word includes, 81.
GRANT, no covenant implied from the word, 140.
  leases of things in, 35.
GROWING CROPS.—See CORN, EMBLEMENTS, HOLDING OVER, DISTRESS.
GUARDIANS OF UNIONS.—See PARISH OFFICERS.
GUARDIANS in socage, leases by, 21.
  by election, leases by, 21.
  confirmation by infant of leases by guardian, 21.
  by nature, leases by, 21.
  may make lease at will, 21.
  testamentary, leases by, 22.
  lease for years by, whether void, 22.
  appointed by Lord Chancellor, leases by, 22.
  appointed for infant executor, 23.

H.

HABENDUM, 93.
  effect of the premises upon, 93, 94.
  effect upon the commencement of the term, 94-96.
HAY.—See CORN.
HAY-BOTE, lease of, 38.
HERBAGE, lease of, reserving rent, 111.
HEREDITAMENTS, what is included in the word, 82.
HOLDING OVER, tenant to give up possession at end of term, 274.
    fixtures, 274
    growing crops, 274.

2 A

HOLDING OVER, damages for, 274.
    under-tenant holding over, tenant still liable, 274.
    entry by landlord, 275.
    without breach of the peace, 275.
    trespass for damages and ejectment, 275.
    action for double value.—See DOUBLE VALUE.
    action or distress for double rent.—See DOUBLE RENT.
HORSES, distress of, 96.
    at livery stables, 199.
HOUSE, what is included in the word, 82.
HOUSE-BOTE, lease of, 38.
HUNTING, shooting, and fishing.—See GAME.
HUSBAND AND WIFE—
    leasing wife's land, 9.
    under Settled Estates Act, 7, 10, 11.
    confirmation of lease by wife, 10.
    leasing wife's chattel interests, 11.
    leases by and to married women.—See MARRIED WOMEN.
    leases by, must be by deed, 43.
    effect of marriage of female lessor or lessee.—See MARRIAGE.
HUSBANDRY.—See CULTIVATION, COVENANTS.

I.

IDIOTS, leases by, 23.
    leases to, 29.
ILLEGAL distress, remedies for, 220, 227.
    See DISTRESS.
ILLEGAL covenants, 114, 115.
IMPLIED authority to distrain, 186.
IMPLIED covenants.—See COVENANTS.
IMPOSSIBLE covenants, 115.
IMPOUNDING of cattle under distress, 211.
INCAPACITY to make leases, 23–28.
    to accept leases, 29–32.
INCORPOREAL hereditaments lease of, 40, 41.
INCOMING TENANT.—See EMBLEMENTS.
INCUMBENTS, leases by, 17.
INDENTURE.—See DEED.
INFANTS, leases by, 27, 28.
    election as to, 27.
    acts necessary to show election, 27.
    confirmation of leases by, 27.
    renewals of leases by, 28.
    leases to, 31.
    election as to, 31.
    renewal as to, 32.
INJUNCTION for waste, 239.
    at common law, 239.
    in chancery, 239.
    in what cases, 240, 244.

INN, distress of goods at, 201.
INSURANCE, covenant for, 124.
    production of the policy, 124.
    money applied in re-building, 124.
    lessees' liability under covenant to repair, 125.
    breach of covenant, 125.
    See FIRE.
INTERESSE TERMINI, 3.
    meaning of, 45, n. (*u*).
INTOXICATION, leases by persons in state of, 24.
INVENTORY on a distress, 208, 209.
IRREGULAR distress.—See ILLEGAL DISTRESS.

J.

JOINT-TENANTS, distress by, 185.
    leases by, 12, 13.
JOINTURE, leases by tenants in, 9.
    emblements, 289.
JUSTICES, proceedings before them.
    for small tenements held over, 275.
    for desertion by tenant, 281.

L.

LADYDAY, old or new style, 159.
LAND, what passes under the word, 80.
    what words will pass the land or soil, 81.
LANDLORD AND TENANT, relation of, 2.
LAND-TAX.—See DEDUCTIONS.
LEASES, who may make.—See LESSORS.
    who may take.—See LESSEES.
    void by reason of part being void, 35.
    by deed, 43, 47.
    by writing not under seal, 44.
    verbal, 44, 47.
    of things lying in grant, 43.
    must be under seal, 43.
    of things lying in livery, 44.
    may commence *in futuro*, 45, 96.
    interesse termini, 45.
    for years at common law only conferred right to profits, 44, 45.
    distinction between leases and agreements, 56.
    effect of the word " demise " in creating a lease, 56.
    agreement for future lease operating as demise, 58.
    effect of the 8 & 9 Vict. c. 106. s. 3, 65, 66.
    void lease used as evidence of the terms of the holding, 66.
    specific performance of terms of void leases, 67.
    distinction between leases and licenses, 68.
    description of parcels in, 80–88.

LEASES, for years or lives may commence from a past or future day, 96.
    may commence at one date in interest and another in time, 97.
    by parol, commencement of, 97.
    duration of term, 98.
    for two years certain, 100.
    tenancy at will, 101.
    right to have a lease granted, 244.
    under powers.—See POWERS.
    for whole term operates as assignment, 11.
LESSEES, who may be, 29.
    lunatics, 29.
    outlaws, &c., 29.
    aliens and denizens, 30.
    married women, 30.
    infants, 31.
    corporations, 32.
    ecclesiastical persons, 32.
    parish officers, 33.
    lessee not taking possession under verbal lease, 48.
    liable after assignment, 321, 323, 324.
    implied promise by successive assignees to indemnify original lessee, 324.
LESSORS, who may be, 2.
    tenants in fee simple, 2.
        in tail, 2.
        for life, 5.
        pur autre vie, 8.
        after possibility of issue extinct, 9.
    tenants by the curtesy, 9.
        in dower or jointure, 9.
        husband leasing wife's land, 9.
        for years, 11.
        from year to year, 12.
        for less than years, 12.
        at will or on sufferance, 12.
    joint-tenants, tenants in common, and coparceners, 12.
    mortgagor and mortgagee, 13.
    lords of the manor and copyholders, 14.
    corporations, 16.
    lessors not giving possession on verbal lease, 48.
LET, effect of word.—See DEMISE.
LICENSE, by lord of the manor to lease.—See COPYHOLD.
    distinction between lease and license, 68.
    to assign, 144.
        when presumed, 145.
        only extends to one act, 146.
        license unreasonably held, 147.
    where lessor permits breach of immoral or illegal covenant, and derives gain from it, he cannot recover, 151.

INDEX.   373

LIFE, leases for—
  to commence from past or future date, 45, 96.
  determination of, 99.
  duration of, 99.
 tenant for—
  leases by, 5.
  under Settled Estates Act, 6.
  liability for waste, 229.
LIVE stock, lease of, 35.
LIVERY, lease of things in, 41.
LODGINGS.—See WEEKLY TENANCY.
  letting of, 41.
  rent issues out of realty, not out of furniture, 41.
  within Statute of Frauds, 46, n. (x).
  yearly tenancy not presumed, 106, 107.
  quarterly, monthly, or weekly tenancy presumed, 107.
  letting room to lodger no breach of covenant not to underlet, 126.
LORD OF THE MANOR.—See LESSORS, COPYHOLDS.
   rights reserved under Settled Estates Act, 8.
   leases *pur autre vie* by, 8.
   presumption as to death of *cestui que vie*.
LUNATICS and idiots, leases by, 24.
  committee of lunatic may make building leases, 24.
    may renew leases, 24.
    may make repairs or improvements, 24.
    may make allowances for repairs, 24.
    other acts of committees, 24.
  tenant in tail, committee of, to apply to Court, 24.
  leases to, 29.
   renewals for benefit of, 29.

M.

MACHINERY and fixtures.—See FIXTURES.
MANOR.—See LORD OF, COPYHOLD.
MANSION-HOUSE, cannot be demised by tenant for life under Settled
 Estates Act, 6.
MARKET, lease of, 39.
MARRIAGE of female lessor, 342.
  of female lessee, 343.
MARRIED women.—See HUSBAND AND WIFE.
  leases by, 26.
  husband's rights to rents and profits of freehold, 26.
  leases to, 31.
  renewal and surrender of leases by, 31.
MASTER AND SERVANT.—See SERVANT.
MERGER.—See SURRENDER.
MESSUAGE, what is included in the word, 82.
MICHAELMAS DAY, 96, 266, 272.
MIDNIGHT, rent not in arrear till, 204.

MINES, exceptions of, in lease, 90.
MINING leases by ecclesiastical corporations, 19, 20.
MIS-DESCRIPTION of property, effect of in construction of leases, 82.
MONTH, meaning of—
    six months' notice to quit, 268.
MONTHLY tenancies.—See LODGINGS, WEEKLY TENANCIES.
"MORE OR LESS," how construed, 86.
MORTGAGOR and mortgagee—
    leases by.—See also LESSORS.
    leases by mortgagor after mortgage, 13.
    by estoppel between parties, 13.
    should join in lease, 14.
    notice from mortgagee, 14.
    to whom rents to be paid until notice, 14.
    mortgagor not tenant to mortgagee by occupation, 50.
    mortgagor not tenant at will except by express agreement, 102, 103.
    claim by mortgagee for rent does not raise presumption of authority of lessor, 164.
    distress by mortgagee, 188.
    injunction against mortgagor or mortgagee, 241.
    tenant of mortgagor after the mortgage must attorn to mortgagee to become tenant to him, 279.
    right to fixtures as between mortgagor and mortgagee, 314.
    mortgage of property subsequent to lease operates as assignment of reversion, 317, 319.
    attornment to mortgagee, 318, 319.
    notice by mortgagee to pay rent operates as attornment, 319.
    right to fixtures as between, 315.
MORTMAIN Acts, 33.
MUNICIPAL corporations.—See CORPORATIONS.
    consent of Lords Commissioners of Treasury to leases by, 16.
    building leases granted by, 16.

N.

NEW or old style, 96, 159, 266, 272.
NON-REPAIR, remedies for.—See ACTION, RE-ENTRY, WASTE.
NOON, notice to quit at noon on right day bad, 265, n. (j).
NOTICE, by mortgagee to tenant of mortgagor, 14.
                operates as an attornment, 319.
    by lessee to landlord of state of repair, 121.
    of distress and of appraisement and sale, 209.
    by tenant of intention to remove agricultural fixtures, 309.
    to tenant holding over of intention to recover possession, 276.
                for double value, 284.
NOTICE to quit—
    two years' notice inconsistent with yearly tenancy, 52.
    usual notice in case of presumed yearly tenancy, 53.
    at end of term not necessary in presumed yearly tenancy, 53.

INDEX. 375

NOTICE to quit—
    not necessary in case of morgtagor in possession, 102, 103, 270.
    landlord cannot distrain after, 185.
    disclaimer operates as waiver of, 263, 273.
    operates as demand of possession in case of tenant holding over, 284.
    claim for double rent after notice to quit by tenant, 287.
1. *As to form* of, 264.
        notice in writing, 264.
        what is a good notice, 264.
        what is a bad notice, 265.
        must not be ambiguous or optional, 265.
        to quit at expiration of term, 265, 266.
        interpretation of notice to quit on Michaelmas Day, &c., 266.
        must extend to all the premises, 266.
        joint-tenant, notice to quit all his part or share, 266.
        notice not stating to whom possession to be given, 266.
        need state the day of quitting, 266.
        at expiration of current year, &c., 267.
        notice by agent, 267.
        must be delivered to the tenant as tenant, 267.
        waiver of objection to notice, 267.
        how proved, 268.
2. *When to be given.*
        half a year's notice, 268.
        special agreement, 268.
        six lunar months, 268.
        tenancy for two or three years at least, 268.
        lease determinable on certain event, 269.
        lodgings, &c., notice corresponding to mode of letting, 269.
        but demand necessary, 270.
        reasonable notice in case of weekly tenancy, 269.
        no notice in case of tenancy at will, 269.
        not in case of stranger, 270.
        or mortgagor in possession, 270, 102, 103.
        tenants of mortgagor before and after the mortgage, 270.
        plaintiff claiming by title paramount, 270.
        disclaimer operates as waiver, 270.
        in time if delivered on day at place of business, 272.
3. *By whom and to whom given.*
        by landlord to immediate tenant, 270.
        by tenant to under-tenant, 270.
        by tenant to immediate landlord, 271.
            or immediate reversioner, 271.
        by agent or receiver, 271.
        by one executor, 271.
        by joint-tenant, 271.
        by tenant in common, 271

NOTICE to quit—
   4. *How served.*
          at the dwelling-house, 272.
          on tenant, or wife, or servant, 272.
          may be sent by post, 272.
          sent to place of business on the last day, 272.
   5. *Waiver of notice.*
          parties may agree to waive, 272.
          tenant holding over after notice, landlord cannot waive and distrain, 273.
          presumed from receipt of rent 273.
          not from demand of rent, 273.
          second notice a waiver of first, 273.
          tenant cannot treat mere indulgence as a waiver, 273 .
          disclaimance operates as waiver, 262, 273.

O.

OCCUPATION evidence of tenancy, 50.
          on terms of void lease, 51.
OFFICE found abolished, 25.
OFFICES, lease of, 39.
OFFICIAL trustee.—See BANKRUPTCY.
OLD or new style, 96, 159, 266, 272.
OPERATIVE words —See HABENDUM.
OPTION to determine, 107.
OUTLAWS, leases by, 25.
   leases to, 29.
OUTER-DOOR not to be broken open to make distress, 207, 208.
OUTGOING and incoming tenants—See EMBLEMENTS, FIXTURES.
OVERPLUS of distress, 217, 219.
          action for not returning, 224.
OVERSEERS of the poor, leases by, 20.
          leases to, 34.

P.

PARCELS demised, 80.
          what passes under certain words, 80–88.
PARISH officers, leases by, 20.
          leases to, 33.
PARLIAMENTARY taxes.—See DEDUCTIONS.
PAROCHIAL taxes.—See DEDUCTIONS.
PARSONS, leases by.—See ECCLESIASTICAL CORPORATIONS.
PART of land.—See ASSIGNMENT OF PART.
PARTIES, change of, 317.
PASTURE, what passes under the word, 81.
PAWNBROKER, goods in pledge with, cannot be distrained, 198.
PAYMENT of rent.—See RENT.
          evidence of yearly tenancy, 48, 51.
          only presumptive, 49.

INDEX. 377

PAYMENT of rent, promise of payment, 49.
    payment must have reference to a year, 51, 107.
    though payable quarterly or weekly, 107.
    tenancy presumed to be on terms of lease, 51.
    commencement of the term in a presumed yearly tenancy, 98.
    on tenant holding over, 246.
    for lodgings.—See LODGINGS.
    express covenant for, 117.
    claim by mortgagee for rent does not raise presumption of authority of lessor, 164.
    apportionment of.—See APPORTIONMENT.
    Time of Payment, 159.
        time of year, 160.
        payable in advance, 161.
        time of day, 161.
        time for demand, 161.
        payment before due, 162.
    Mode of Payment, 162.
        upon the land, 162.
        by post, 162.
        demand for rent ranks higher than specialty debt, 163.
        receipts for rent, stamp, 163.
    Deductions.—See DEDUCTIONS.
        operate as payment of rent *pro tanto*, 163.

PENSIONS, leases of, 40.
PERMISSIVE waste.—See WASTE.
PERSONAL representatives.—See EXECUTORS AND ADMINISTRATORS.
POOR-RATES.—See DEDUCTIONS.
POSSESSION or reversion, leases in under powers, 152.
POSSESSION, right to, by tenant.—See QUIET ENJOYMENT.
    right to a lease, 244.
    where covenant to grant a lease, 244.
    where money expended on faith of agreement, 244.
    right to, by landlord on determination of lease, 274.
POST, payment of rent by, 162.
    notice to quit sent by, 272.
POUND.—See IMPOUNDING, DISTRESS.
POWERS of re-entry.—See RE-ENTRY.
POWERS, leases under, 151.
    construction of powers, 151.
    court will support an appointment under a power, 151.
    doing less or more than the power gives, 152.
    omission to take notice of a power, 152.
    previous charge on estate, 152.
    possession or reversion, 152.
    covenants inserted in lease under a power, 152.
    " usual covenants " a question for the jury, 152.

POWERS, confirmation of invalid leases under powers by acceptance of
    rent, 153, 156.
    execution of leases under powers, 153.
    consent, 153.
    precedent act to be done, 153.
    defects in lease, how cured, 154, 155.
    invalid lease treated as contract in equity, 154.
PREMISES, meaning of the word, 82.—See PARCELS.
PRESUMED yearly tenancy.—See PAYMENT OF RENT, OCCUPATION,
    YEARLY TENANCY.
PRIOR distress.—See SECOND DISTRESS.
PRODUCTION of *cesui qui vie*, 9.
PROGRESSIVE duty abolished, 71.
PROVISOS and conditions, 141.
    effect of, 141.
    definition of, 141.
    intention of the parties, 141.
    covenant and condition running with the land, 142.
    not to assign or underlet, 142.—See COVENANTS.
    breach of condition not to assign, 143.
    license, 144.—See LICENSE.
PROPERTY-TAX.—See DEDUCTIONS.

Q.

QUARTERLY tenancies.—See LODGINGS, WEEKLY TENANCY.
QUIA EMPTORES, Statute of, 2.
QUIET ENJOYMENT, covenants for, 130, 139.—See COVENANTS.
    right to possession and quiet enjoyment, 242.
    agreement to let an agreement to give possession, 243.
    remedies for disturbance, 243.
    damages for breach of covenant, 243.
    injunction for breach, 244.
QUITTING possession.—See HOLDING OVER.

R.

RATES.—See TAXES, COVENANTS, DEDUCTIONS.
REAL or personal covenants, 116, 327.
RECEIPT of rent.—See ACCEPTANCE.
RECEIVERS, distress by, 189.
RECITALS in a lease, 53.
    estoppel by, 53.
    what is necessary to create an estoppel, 56.
    estoppel confined to party having knowledge, 56.
    may amount to implied covenant, 136, 137.
REDDENDUM, 108.—See RENT, PAYMENT OF RENT.
RE-ENTRY, condition of, 7.
    in leases by tenant for life under Settled Estates Act, 7.
    for forfeiture after license, 145, 146.

INDEX. 379

RE-ENTRY, license as to part, or as to one of several lessees, 146, 147.
    powers of re-entry, 147.
    form of power, 147.
    re-entry for breach of a negative covenant, 147, n. (x).
    entry for a mere omission, 149.
    construed according to intention of the parties, 148.
    most strictly against the covenantor, 149.
    election as to entry, and treating lease as void, 149.—See
        VOID, VOIDABLE LEASES.
    entry for breach of covenant to repair, 238.
    re-entry for forfeiture, 256.
    grantees of reversion and their assigns, 257.
    lessor must do act showing intention to enter for a forfeiture, 257.
    onus of proof of forfeiture, 257.
    for non-payment of rent, 257.
    landlord must make a demand for rent, 257.
    requisites of the demand, 258.
    no demand necessary in certain cases, 258.
    waiver of forfeiture, 259.—See WAIVER.
    proviso for, on bankruptcy of tenant, 340.
RELIGIOUS purposes, leases of building for, 33.
REMAINDERMAN.—See REVERSIONER.
    Bound by permitting tenant to lay out money, 6.
REMOVAL of fixtures.—See FIXTURES.
    of goods to avoid distress.—See FRAUDULENT REMOVAL,
        DISTRESS.
RENEWAL OF LEASES by municipal corporations, 16.
    by ecclesiastical corporations, 18.
    covenants for, 132-135.
        run with the land, 132.
        valid without surrender of underleases, 134.
RENT.—See PAYMENT OF RENT, ACCEPTANCE OF RENT.
    acceptance of, by issue in tail, 3.—See CONFIRMATION OF
        LEASES.
    acceptance by wife.—See CONFIRMATION OF LEASES, HUSBAND
        AND WIFE.
    acceptance by remainderman creates yearly tenancy, 106, 107
    reddendum in a lease, 108.
    kinds of rent, rent-services, rent-seck, rent-charge, 108.
    definition of rent, 108.
    out of what rent issues, 108.
    nature of rent, 109.
    must be certain, 109.
    need not be of money, 108, 109.
    reservation of corn as rent, 110.
    must not be part of the thing demised, 111.
    when bad as rent, may be good as a contract, 111-113.
    reserved on future interest, 111.
    reserved on lease of herbage, 111.

RENT, crown may reserve rent on incorporeal hereditament, 111.
    reserved out of two things good as to one, 112.
    must be the consideration for the lease, 112.
    where a mere sum in gross, 112, 113.
    where there is no demise, but an occupation, 113.
    runs with the reversion, 113.
    should not be reserved to a third party, 113.
    express covenant for payment of, 117.
    demand for rent ranks higher than specialty debt, 163.
    charge, 108.
    service, 108.
    seck, 108.
    and annuities, lease of, 40.
REPAIRS.—See COVENANTS, WASTE, FIRE.
    notice to landlord of state of repair, 121.
    action for non-repair, 236.
        of fences, 237.
    re-entry for non-repair, 238.
    ejectment for non-repair, 238.
    specific performance of covenant to repair, 238.
    injunction, 239.
    liability of tenant in case of fire under covenant to repair, 233.
REPLEVIN of goods wrongfully taken under distress, 225.
    time allowed for replevying, 226.
    goods under an execution, 226.
    action for, cannot be joined with other cause, 226.
    what is recoverable by action of, 226, 227.
    no second action for same distress, 226.
    registrar of County Court to re-deliver goods, 227.
    jurisdiction of superior and County Court, 227.
RESCUE, definition of, 225.
    before impounding, 225.
    after abandonment, 225.
    preventing the wrongful user of a distress, 225.
    action by person aggrieved by rescue or pound breach, 225.
RESERVATIONS, exceptions and reservations out of parcels, 89.
    requisites of a good exception, 90.
    what is excepted, 92.
    exception of wood extends to soil, 92.
    cannot be made to a stranger to the estate, 92.
    exception may amount to covenant, 116.
RESTRAINT of trade, covenants in.—See COVENANTS.
REVERSION, Assignee of—
    may sue and be sued on covenants, 322, 323.
    distress incident to reversion, 185.
    assignment of.—See ASSIGNMENT.
    leases in under powers, 152.
REVERSIONER.—See TENANTS IN TAIL.
    how bound by leases of tenant in tail, 3-5.

INDEX.

REVERSIONER, confirmation of leases by tenants for life by, 5, 6.
RIGHT of entry, 45 n. (u).
RUN with the land.—See COVENANTS.

S.

SALE under distress.—See DISTRESS.
SCHEDULE of Stamp Act, 77.—See STAMPS.
    of fixtures, 315.—See FIXTURES.
SCIENTIFIC purposes, lease of buildings for, 33.
SECOND distress, 206.
    notice to quit, 273.
SEIZURE of goods under distress, 207.
SEQUESTRATORS, distress by, 192.
SERVANT, occupation by, does not create tenancy, 50.
SERVICE of notice to quit.—See NOTICE to QUIT.
SETTLED Estates Act, 19 & 20 Vict. c. 120, 4, 6.
    leases under, 6.
    execution of lease under evidence of counterpart, 7.
    estates charged on encumbered, possession in, 8.
    copyholds under, 8.
SET-OFF, of deductions from rent, 163.
SEWERS' RATES.—See DEDUCTIONS.
SHEEP, distress of, 196, 201.—See ANIMALS.
SHERIFF.—See WRITS OF EXECUTION.
    overplus of distress paid into hands of, 217, 219.
SHOOTING, lease of right of, must be by deed, 43.
SMALL Tenements Acts—
    The 1 & 2 *Vict.* c. 74, s. 1, 275.
    tenement not exceeding £20, 275.
    written notice by landlord or agent of intention to recover premises, 276.
    tenant to show cause before justices, 276.
    proof to be adduced by landlord, 276.
    justices to issue warrant and give possession in twenty-one days, 276.
    entry not to be made at certain times and on certain days, 277.
    proviso where person had no right to possession, 277.
    saving of rights of outgoing tenant, 277.
    remedy to valuer under Inclosure Acts, 277.
        to trustees under Charitable Trusts Act, 277.
        to churchwardens and overseers.
    The 19 & 20 *Vict.* c. 108, ss. 50, 52, 278, 279.
    when tenement not exceeding £50, 278.
    plaint in County Court, 278.
    summons to tenant, 278.
    cause to be shown by tenant, 278.
    proof to be adduced by landlord, 278.
    judge to order possession to be given when he thinks fit, 278.
    registrar to issue warrant to give possession, 279.

SMALL Tenements Acts—
    The 19 & 20 Vict. c. 108, ss. 50, 52, 278, 279.
    relation of landlord and tenant must exist, 279.
    County Court no jurisdiction where claim of title, 279.
    except by consent, 279.
    tenant estopped from denying his landlord's title, 279.
    plaintiff may add claim for rent or mesne profits, 279.
    where rent in arrear for half year, landlord may enter plaint in County Court, 280.
    summons in lieu of demand or re-entry, 280.
    action to cease on payment of arrears, &c., 280.
    or tenant to show cause, 280.
    proof to be given by landlord, 280.
    judge to order possession to be given at end of four weeks, 280.
    unless rent and cost paid sooner, 280.
    registrar to issue warrant to give possession, 280.
SOIL.—See LAND.
SOVEREIGN, leases by, must be by deed, 43.
SPECIFIC performance, 224.
SPORTING.—See GAME, SHOOTING.
STAMPS on leases, &c., 68–80.
    on receipt for rent, 163.
    on appraisement, 216.
STATUTE of Frauds, 46.
            leases not in writing only leases at will, 46.
            leases for three years only, 46.
            contracts as to lands void unless agreement or note in writing, 46.
            leases in writing must be by deed, 47.
            effect of non-compliance with, 48.
STRAW.—See CORN, EMBLEMENTS.
STRAWBERRY-BEDS, not removeable by tenant, 308.
STYLE.—See OLD AND NEW STYLE.
SUFFERANCE, tenants on, cannot demise, 12.
            notice to quit, 270.
            removal of fixtures by tenant on.
            mortgagee tenant on, 102, 103, 270.
SUNSET AND SUNRISE, landlord cannot distrain between, 204.
SURRENDER of leases of married women.
            express, 248.
            by law, 248, 250.
            Statute of Frauds, 248.
            who may surrender, 249.
            to whom surrender may be made, 249.
            in what words, 249.
            by operation of law, 250.
            by taking a new lease, 250.
            by other acts, 251.
            by merger, 252.

SURRENDER, effect on under leases, 254.
    operation of merger, 255.
SURVEY AND VALUATION.—See VALUATION.

T.

TAIL, tenants in.
    leases by, 2–5.
    confirmation of leases by issue, 3.
TAXES, covenant for payment of, 117.—See COVENANTS.
    what is a parliamentary tax, 118.
    property-tax, landlord to pay, 120.
TENANCY, meaning of, 1, 2.
TENANCY, implied.—See PRESUMED YEARLY TENANCY, PAYMENT OF
    RENT, ACCEPTANCE OF RENT.
TENANT, power to lease.
    in fee-simple, 2.
    in tail, 2.
    for life, 5.
    pur autre vie, 8.
    after possibility of issue extinct, 9.
    by the curtesy, in dower, or jointure, 9.
    from year to year, 12.
    for years, 11.
    for less than years, 12.
    at will, 12.
    on sufferance, 12.
    joint-tenants, 12.
    in common, 12.
TENANT'S fixtures.—See FIXTURES.
TENDER.—See DISTRESS.
TENEMENT, what is included in the word, 82.
TERMINATION of tenancy.—See DETERMINATION OF LEASE, EFFLUXION
    OF TIME.
    by surrender, 248.
    merger, 252.
    forfeiture, 256.
    by notice to quit, 264.
    disclaimer, 262.
    death, 330.
TERMS of years.—See COMMENCEMENT OF TERM, DURATION OF TERM.
TILLAGES.—See EMBLEMENTS.
TIMBER.—See TREES.
TITHES, lease of, 36.
    leases of, by ecclesiastical persons, 36.
    lease of, must be by deed, 43.
TITLE.—See ESTOPEL.
    covenant for.—See COVENANTS.
TOLLS, lease of, 39.
    market with right of toll, 39.
    without deed, 43.

TRADES, covenants against particular, 127.
  contracts to trade with particular persons, 128.
      within a certain radius, 128.
TRUSTEES of bankrupts, leases by, 23.
      fixtures do not pass to, 339.
    See BANKRUPTCY.
TRUSTEES for charitable uses may take leases, 33.
TREES and timber, reservations of, 90, 92.
      waste as to, 228, 230, 231.
TRESPASS.—See ACTION.
TROVER.—See ACTION.
TURF, right to dig, lease of, without deed, 43.

U.

UNDER-LEASES, change of possession by under-letting, 321.
  original lessee still liable on covenants, 321, 323, 324.
  under-lease should contain express covenant to perform all the covenants of the original lease, 321.
UNDER-LESSEE.—See LODGINGS.
  under-lessees not surrendering on renewal, 134.
  refusing to give up possession, 271.
USAGE.—See CUSTOM.
USE and occupation.—See ACTION.
USUAL covenants, what included in, 126, 127, 152.
UTENSILS of trade, exempt from distress, 201.

V.

VALUATION, as between outgoing and incoming tenant, 315.
  emblements, 294, 296.
  fixtures, 315.
  of distress, 208, 215, 216.
VERBAL disclaimer, 262.
  leases, 44, 47.
VEXATIOUS second distress, 206.
VICARS, leases by.—See ECCLESIASTICAL CORPORATIONS.
VOID AND VOIDABLE LEASES, void as to part void altogether, 3.
      form of clause in lease as to, 150.
      made void by some act of lessor, 150.
      lessee cannot elect to make lease void, 150.
      fraudulent representation does not avoid lease, 150.
VOLUNTARY WASTE.—See WASTE.

W.

WAIVER, distraining for rent after forfeiture, 259.
  receipt of rent operating as a waiver, 260, 261.
  action for rent, 260.

WAIVER, notice to repair a waiver, 260.
    insufficient distress no waiver, 260.
    of continuing breach, 261.
    knowledge of forfeiture by lessor, 261.
    confined to one breach under the 23 & 24 Vict. c. 38, s. 6.
    of double rent, 287.
    of double value, 285.
    of disclaimer.—See DISCLAIMER.
    of notice to quit.—See NOTICE TO QUIT.
WARRANT under Small Tenements Act, 276.
WASTE, leases by tenant for life not to be made without impeachment of, 7.
    definition of, 228.
    voluntary and permissive, 228.
    tenant in fee-simple or tail not liable for, 228.
    estovers and botes, 228.
    by tenant for years or life, 229.
    tenant at will not liable for, 229.
    of the soil, 229.
    of buildings, 230.
    of trees, fences, &c., 230.
    of live-stock, 231.
    impeachment of, 231, 241.
    injunction against tenant without impeachment of waste, 231, 241.
    tenant in common cannot bring trespass for waste against co-tenant, 232.
    may have injunction, 241.
    action for waste, 237.
    by fire.—See FIRE.
    for neglect of cultivation.—See CULTIVATION.
    injunction for waste.—See INJUNCTION.
WAY, lease of right of, 38, 39.
    must be by deed, 43.
    right of appurtenant without deed, 43, 88, 89.
WEEKLY tenancy.—See LODGINGS.
    reasonable time to remove goods, 247.
    reasonable notice to quit, 269.
    no double rent, 287.
WIFE.—See HUSBAND AND WIFE, MARRIAGE.
WILL, lease at will under Statute of Frauds, 46-48.
    how changed into yearly tenancy, 48, 105.
    tenancy at will, 101.
    duration of, 101.
    for years, with proviso to enter at will, 101.
    where constructive yearly tenancy inconsistent with facts, 101.
    agreement for future lease, 101, 105.
    payment of rent presumptive tenancy from year to year, 102, 105.
    mortgagor and mortgagee, 102, 103.
    determination of, 103, 104.

WILL, not entitled to notice to quit, 270.
    not liable for waste, 229.
WINDING-UP under Companies' Act, 1862, 341.
WITHOUT impeachment of waste.—See WASTE.
WRITS of execution, effect on relation of parties to a lease, 348.
        assignment by sheriff on writ of *fieri facias*, 348.
        liability of assignee, 348.
        of lessee, 348.
        equitable reversionary interest cannot be sold, 348.
        provisions of the 1 & 2 Vict. c. 110, s. 11, 348.
        return by sheriff, 350.
        operates as assignment of reversion, 350.
        sheriff may deliver possession where debtor is occupier, 350.
        but tenants cannot be turned out, 351.
        tenant by elegit may distrain, 351.
WRONGFUL distress.—See DISTRESS.

Y.

YEAR, tenant for a, not entitled to notice to quit, 269.
YEARLY tenancy presumed, 48, 105, 107.
    by payment of rent, 49-51.
    by promise to pay, 49.
    or settlement in account, 49.
    on terms of void lease, 51.
    unless inconsistent with yearly tenancy, 52.
    commencement of the term, 98.
    on tenant holding over, 246.
YEARS, tenant for, lease by, 11.
        liability for waste, 229.
        may commence in future, 45, 96.
        duration of, 99.
    tenancy for, certainty of term, 98-100.
YEAR TO YEAR, tenant from, lease by, 12.
        tenancy from, implied.—See YEARLY TENANCY.